This Business of Relief

I0029169

This Business of Relief

Confronting Poverty in a Southern City, 1740–1940

ELNA C. GREEN

The University of Georgia Press • Athens and London

© 2003 by the University of Georgia Press

Athens, Georgia 30602

All rights reserved

Set in Minion by Bookcomp, Inc.

Printed Digitally

Library of Congress Cataloging-in-Publication Data

Green, Elna C.

This business of relief : confronting poverty in a Southern city,
 1740–1940 / Elna C. Green.

　　　p.　cm.

Includes bibliographical references and index.

ISBN 0-8203-2451-5 (alk. paper)

— ISBN 0-8203-2552-X (pbk. : alk. paper)

1. Public welfare—Virginia—Richmond—History.

 2. Charities—Virginia—Richmond—History.

 3. Poverty—Virginia—Richmond—History.

 4. Richmond (Va.)—Social policy.　I. Title.

HV99.R5 G74　2003

362.5'53'09755451—dc21　　　　2003008366

British Library Cataloging-in-Publication Data available

Paperback ISBN-13: 978-0-8203-2552-1

2017 Hardcover Reissue ISBN-13: 978-0-8203-5263-3

DEDICATED TO THE MEMORY OF

Mary Epps

Memory Floyd

Elna Stallings

and

Gilmer Green Sr.

None of them lived to see its completion;

all of them lived through many of the events

detailed herein; each of them shaped it,

by their influences on me.

There can never be another Richmond, for she is old, beautiful, historic, glamorous, languorous, cultured, ignorant, prejudiced, generous. We all know people like that, soft-voiced, self-centered, at the same time naive, interesting, exciting. That's Richmond; contradictory and full of contrasts; gorgeous in its gardens in the spring, hideous and unsanitary in its Negro quarters; delightful in sporadic hospitality; disturbing in self-content and indifference to reality; amazing in constant references to the Living Savior of Men and willingness to let His faithful followers suffer neglect; horrifying in Jeffersonian oratory and disregard of the fundamentals of human welfare and justice.

JUNE PURCELL GUILD, 1934

CONTENTS

ILLUSTRATIONS

FREQUENTLY USED ABBREVIATIONS

AC   Associated Charities

CCC   Civilian Conservation Corps

COS   charity-organization societies

ER   Eleanor Roosevelt

FDR   Franklin D. Roosevelt

FERA   Federal Emergency Relief Administration

GPO   Government Printing Office

IVNA   Instructive Visiting Nurses Association

LoV   Library of Virginia

NARA National Archives Records Administration

VCU   Virginia Commonwealth University

WPA   Works Progress Administration

ACKNOWLEDGMENTS

Producing a scholarly monograph requires a great deal of time, and money. I have been very fortunate to receive funds to support this project from a variety of sources, all of which I am pleased to thank publicly. At a very early stage in the project, a fellowship from the American Council of Learned Societies allowed a semester off from my teaching responsibilities to concentrate on conceptualizing this book. I will always be grateful for the inspiration that semester provided. Several grants from Sweet Briar College and one from Florida State University permitted me to hire data entry assistants, who converted the manuscript admissions registers of the Richmond City Almshouse into usable databases. (I am particularly in debt to Dean George Lenz and former president Barbara Hill, of Sweet Briar College, who came up with an emergency grant to keep the data entry going at a time when the original funds had run out.) Another substantial award from Florida State University allowed me the luxury of hiring graduate research assistants, who ploughed through hundreds of reels of microfilmed newspapers. Thanks to Bryan Adeline, Paul Berk, Stewart Edwards, Jeffery Strickland, and Kevin Witherspoon for their diligence in that task. Special thanks to Jeffery Strickland for translations of the German-language newspaper *Die Virginische Zeitung*. A travel-to-collections grant from the Franklin Roosevelt Library at Hyde Park supported a week's research in those rich presidential papers. Granting research support funds is an act of faith, an indication of trust in the scholar's project and in his or her ability to complete it. I hope that all of these funding agencies will be pleased with the results of their investments.

Numerous individuals have aided and encouraged this project in a variety of ways, and their advice and support have helped to bring this monograph to print. They offered a variety of citations, information, critiques of chapters, and large doses of encouragement. Tony Badger, John Boles, Eileen Boris, Ruth Crocker, Frank Deserino, David Goldfield, James Pickett Jones, Gregg Kimball, Sandra Treadway, Daniel Walkowitz, and James Watkinson all stand out as supporters of this effort. J. Anthony Stallins offered desperately needed assistance on the organization of the quantitative data, with hardly a smirk at some of my more embarrassing mistakes. My colleagues and graduate students at Florida State University have been unstinting in their interest in, and encouragement of, this work. I appreciate so much the community of scholars around me. Finally, I would like to thank my sons, Eli and Noah, for occasionally allowing me to use "their" computer to work on this book.

This Business of Relief

INTRODUCTION

Presenting his plan for a massive public works project to Congress in January 1935, Franklin Delano Roosevelt announced his intention to get the federal government out of "this business of relief."[1] Work, not a dole, would be the basis of the federal programs to deal with the dislocation of the Great Depression. Despite Roosevelt's intentions, and despite the widespread opposition to a government dole, the federal government remained deeply involved in the "relief" business. In fact Roosevelt's policies assured that the federal government would be involved in relief for decades to come, as programs for old-age assistance, aid to dependent children, and general assistance became a permanent part of the federal welfare state.

"Relief" had in fact been the business of government in the United States since before the Revolution. And big business it had been too: For most of American history, local governments had operated vast, sometimes quite expensive, relief programs. By the nineteenth century, state governments had added a second layer of publicly funded relief, usually in the form of asylums to care for various classes of "dependents." The federal government added yet a third layer of relief, through the activities of the Freedmen's Bureau and through its military pension program. Roosevelt's New Deal therefore did not put the federal government in the relief business for the first time, but it did force a dramatic reorganization of the system of relief, which we now generically call welfare.

Not practitioners, not scholars, not even the lay public have really acknowledged the vast scope of welfare provision in American history.[2] In every community, large numbers of people were involved, at some point, in the business of relief: local officials and volunteers who distributed public or private assistance; pharmacists who filled prescriptions for local relief agencies; grocers who filled food orders or redeemed food tickets; merchants who sold shoes, blankets, and clothing to those paying with relief tickets; businesses that sold or transported coal or wood to be delivered either to the poorhouses or to the outdoor poor. So vast was this involvement in poor relief, so important to local economies, and so rich with political possibilities that it is tempting to think of it—even in the nineteenth century—as the "welfare/industrial complex." Even if this label exaggerates the power of the forces involved, the concept nevertheless helps to explain why welfare was, and is, so hard to reform. Too many people—or, more accurately, too many interest groups—derived benefit from the system's status quo. For every reformer with a plan for improvement, there stood a local businessman with an interest in blocking change.

1

The history of relief, or welfare, has had many practitioners in recent decades. Social-welfare history has been, in recent years, a thriving field. "Welfare reform," "workfare," "ending welfare as we know it"—these catchphrases from the 1990s epitomize the tone of the great national discussion in the United States regarding public-welfare policy. The federal social safety net, first established by Roosevelt's New Deal and then augmented by Johnson's Great Society, came under critical scrutiny at the end of the century. Politicians and policy makers have initiated this national debate; historians have been attempting to inform it. In an effort to enrich the debate, scholars have been reexamining the origins and evolution of our current system of public assistance. This literature explains why American social policy has taken the form it has, often by comparing it with other industrial democracies that have developed different systems of social provision. Gender, race, and class issues have been central to this literature.[3]

This new generation of social-welfare history, as rich as it is, has almost wholly ignored the U.S. South. This oversight is important, for the evolution of social-welfare policy in the South has often taken a different trajectory than elsewhere, and the differences can be significant in understanding current public opinion on welfare. Moreover, the South and southerners have played central roles in the 1990s discussions about welfare and public policy. The ideology of states' rights, for so long primarily limited to the South, has received new life outside the region in the 1980s and 1990s as a justification for the dismemberment of the welfare state. The language of welfare reform has often had a southern accent, as policy makers speak of returning power to the states at the expense of the federal government. The South's history of social welfare seems all the more pertinent here.

This project did not start out as a large history of southern social welfare. My initial plan was much smaller—an examination of settlement houses in the South. Settlement houses, a topic explored by historians for decades now, were in many ways the quintessentially progressive institution. Yet their story did not seem to fit well with conditions in the South. Middle-class reformers, so the story goes, used settlement houses as a means of improving the quality of life in turn-of-the-century cities, while simultaneously attempting to speed the process of assimilation for recently arrived immigrants. But the South in this era had fewer "teeming" industrial cities, far less urban squalor, and far fewer foreign-born immigrants. I wondered, then, how settlement houses adapted their purposes for the regionally distinct conditions in the South.

That initial interest, however, soon took me far beyond the settlements themselves and into the larger question of social-welfare policy. Settlements were only a small piece of a much larger story of public and private efforts to aid the poor and the dependent. The focus of the study changed as I sought to understand the evolution of social-welfare policy in the South. I had to broaden the coverage, to include many more institutions, agencies, and movements than just the settlements. I also had to broaden the chronology to understand how social policy had changed over time. With such an enlarged—and ambitious— project, I felt I had to narrow the geographic focus to make the research manageable.

I chose to focus on Richmond, Virginia, for several reasons. First, Richmond had early private charitable associations (such as the Female Humane Association) and a public almshouse dating from 1810, which provided the opportunity to observe change over a longer period of time than would be possible in some other southern cities. Second, as the capital of the Confederacy, Richmond was a hot spot when it came to questions of poverty and its relief during the Civil War. The Richmond Bread Riots, and the careful attention given to indigence by the Confederate government, made Richmond a central flash point in the southern discussion of public assistance. Third, postbellum Richmond was one of the South's most important industrial cities, and it quickly caught up to its northern counterparts in problems of urban underemployment, homelessness, prostitution, and sanitation nightmares. Fourth, Richmond's City Almshouse has an unusually rich set of admissions registers, which run from the 1870s to the 1910s. These data document the cases of thousands of poor people who turned to the city for assistance. And finally, Richmond was a city greatly torn between its "New South" aspirations and its "Old South" traditions, illuminating the regional dilemma of protecting the past while embracing the future. As historian Edward L. Ayers has written, southern cities "even more than the rest of the region, felt the conflicting pull of South and the world, of unique and universal."[4] Richmond, then, offered a rich array of people, events, institutions, and documents for my analysis.

Any local case study confronts the question of typicality. How typical is this one community? Is it truly representative, or is its story unique? Let me say from the outset that I do not claim that Richmond is typically southern. The outline of social-welfare history given here has little parallel for much of the rural South. But I do think that Richmond's story can stand for that of the urban, industrial, commercial South. Further studies of other similar cities will be required to test my arguments, but my reading suggests that cities like Memphis, Birmingham, Atlanta, and Norfolk experienced many of the same evolutions in social policy that I have uncovered for Richmond. The former capital of the Confederacy may have confronted some of these policy questions earlier than did other southern cities, given its earlier industrial, commercial economy. But, as Jane Dailey has recently written, even though the nineteenth-century South remained predominately rural, the trend was clearly toward urbanization. That trend was even stronger in the upper South, and in Virginia more than anywhere else.[5] Where Richmond went, others soon followed, and events in Richmond can thus be seen as predictive of the future of other urban communities in the region.

Local studies also allow the scholar the luxury of delving deeply and extensively into local records, something that becomes prohibitively difficult in more comprehensive studies. It is feasible to survey thoroughly local, state, and federal records, over a two-century stretch, for one community. More important, a case study offers the opportunity to talk about themes larger than the one locality. Not only did cities throughout the region struggle with issues of public welfare, but also cities throughout the country. In a real sense, these were universal questions, and the actions of numerous local governments and local reformers pile up to make a national story. To study a southern city is to investigate the role of the South in influencing national welfare policy; and to study a southern city is to question how deeply national welfare trends permeated regional boundaries.

The case for local studies in social-welfare history has been made most eloquently by Lynn Hollen Lees. Her critique of the transnational trend, although referring to her work on England, applies well here. Comparisons between nations enlighten, Lees argues, but they do not explain all. "The welfare story is as much a local and a national story as an international one, a tale of clients, assumptions, fears, and hopes" played out at the local level. Even when welfare policies were written at the national level, "they were enacted locally, where face-to-face negotiations determined their impact. Therefore, understanding their cultural meaning requires attention to local as well as to national arenas of decision making."[6]

This book therefore seeks to understand national policy by focusing on its workings in the locality. It also seeks to redirect current work on social-welfare history by focusing attention on the southern states. Furthermore, this book seeks to answer these questions: To what degree did southern welfare policies differ from those elsewhere in the United States? Did the experiences of the Civil War and Reconstruction have any lasting impact on the South's social-welfare policy? How did evolving race relations and an emerging urban/industrial class structure affect regional social-welfare policies? And what was the impact of the New Deal on the South's social-welfare institutions and practices?

This book also tests some past assumptions about the South's social-welfare history. Is it true (as John Hope Franklin has argued) that many postbellum social-welfare policies were intended to bolster racial solidarity by providing services such as public education for whites only? Is it true (as Dewey W. Grantham has asserted) that care for the poor in the postbellum South was nearly exclusively private, with the state avoiding both involvement and expenditure? Is it true (as Steven Noll has suggested) that twentieth-century reformers imitated northern institutions and practices so wholeheartedly that the South no longer had distinctively regional social-welfare practices? And is it true (as Elizabeth Wisner once speculated) that the New Deal's money and regulations had more impact in the South than in any other region in the country?[7]

Attention to regional differences can also inform our understanding of national social-welfare policy. This book seeks to challenge one long-standing interpretation of American history. It is regularly asserted that the New Deal, with its funneling of dollars into a prostrate economy and its creation of both jobs and a social safety net, was responsible for changing American views on the proper role of government. Roosevelt's work-relief programs and the proto-welfare state helped to convince millions that the government had an obligation to care for the poor and to protect its citizens from future poverty. Previously, so the story goes, Americans had firmly resisted any government involvement in poor relief and social welfare.

While I don't think this construction is completely false, I do think it is too simple. In the South, large numbers of people had been convinced of the abilities and obligations of government during an earlier crisis. The Civil War, with its massive dislocation and upheaval, provided a similar crisis situation; many southerners turned to government for help then too. When state governments proved inadequate to the task, desperate southerners demanded that their national (Confederate) government step in and provide relief.

That southerners asked for government help, even of the "national" government, is an indication of a previous understanding of poverty, poor relief, and government responsibility. Southerners had in fact relied on government to provide relief for the poor since the founding of the colonies. Local governments had centuries of experience in poor relief before the New Deal. What was new about the New Deal's welfare policies, then, was that the *federal* government acted.

This book also seeks to reinterpret almshouses. The poorhouse, which has disappeared from the American landscape, is an institution that is much misunderstood. Almshouses reflected both the local community's mores regarding poverty and the ideals of the individuals who ran them. In other words, there is no such thing as "the almshouse experience." Some almshouses deserved their reputation for inhumane treatment; some almshouses should rightly be considered public hospitals; some almshouses were really functioning farms. The content of public provision varied from community to community; it also changed over time, as changes in the economy, population, and politics affected social-welfare policy. We should see almshouses as possessing a range of qualities, serving a variety of functions, and serving a number of (sometimes contradictory) agendas.

This story engages other lines of historiographical debate as well. The question of whether public welfare is more efficacious than private charity has been at the heart of many public-policy debates as well as many scholarly discussions. Many Americans consider public welfare an unwelcome intrusion into what they believe was once the sole domain of religious groups and private voluntary associations. Others understand the relationship between public and private charities as a partnership, with government relief programs moving in to supplement efforts when the private sector cannot supply all the needs, such as in the case of the Great Depression. This book counters both of those positions. What most twenty-first-century Americans consider private charity—United Way, city missions, orphanages, homeless shelters, and related private endeavors—were largely nineteenth-century innovations. Such private-sector initiatives were responses to changing conditions that public-welfare programs failed to address quickly enough. In other words, they emerged to fill in the gaps left by inadequate, often antiquated government relief efforts. But the bulk of poor-relief expenditures, then and now, continued to come from public coffers. Public welfare was the foundation; private charity was the supplement.

As will become clear, the relationships between public and private relief efforts are one of the central concerns of this work. The Richmond city almshouse, with its nearly two-hundred-year history, provides a focal point, a unifying theme. But a wide variety of private organizations also have a role in this story. Although the Richmond almshouse was clearly a public welfare agency, it was also powerfully influenced by private charitable efforts in the city. As Theda Skocpol observed, the public and private sectors "have never been simple opposites" in U.S. welfare provision.[8] Both public and private organizations shaped social-welfare policy, and understanding the relationships between these organizations is critical to understanding the evolution of public provision.

Although a great number of endeavors might fall under the rubric of "social welfare" (public education or highway construction, for example), this book is concerned with one central category of social welfare. "Social welfare" is defined here as the public and private efforts to care for the needy and dependent of the community. This is not to suggest that public education and public health are unimportant. But their stories are quite different and should be told in their own context. The focus here is on a specific category of welfare.

Like any work on southern history, this one must be concerned with the question of southern exceptionalism. Was the South's evolving social-welfare policy regionally distinctive? Or was it merely a mirror image of national trends?

This book suggests that the South's social-welfare history was, in its broadest brush strokes, typically national. Local government responsibility, deserving versus undeserving poor, the gendered nature of poverty, the rise of the organized charity movement, the emergence of professional social work, and the emergency arrival of a federal social safety net in the 1930s, these and other trends were experienced by southerners and nonsoutherners alike. However, the devil lies in the details. When one examines the South more closely, the region's social-welfare history does look distinctively different at certain points. Sometimes, the differences seem to be more a matter of degree than of kind. For example, southern states less frequently "auctioned" off paupers to the care of the lowest bidder, when compared to New England, although the practice occurred in both regions.[9] At other times, however, the regional differences seem more absolute. Here, the example of the Freedmen's Bureau, which operated exclusively in the South, seems sufficient to illustrate the point. The chapters that follow will point to both the regional and the national features of public policy. Overall, I see the South's welfare history as following the broadest outlines of national welfare history, from colonial to the twentieth century, but with occasional regional variations that distort the picture in places. I have sometimes used the analogy of a fun-house mirror to describe this: the image remains recognizable, but the features get twisted and contorted in ways that make it something different from the original.

Notes on Terminology

Although "almshouse" and "poorhouse" might in many cases be used as interchangeable terms, the records for Richmond in the nineteenth century show a different pattern. Prior to 1860, the term "poorhouse" was used consistently; beginning around 1860, when the city began construction of a new facility, the records begin using the term "almshouse." And in the early twentieth century, the building was officially renamed the "City Home." I have chosen to use whichever term was in current usage at the time, because the very words seem to connote certain assumptions about poor relief to contemporaries.

The city council of Richmond was originally called the Common Hall, later the Common Council, and finally the City Council. To avoid confusion, I use the label "city council," a term with which most people are more familiar, throughout the text. In citations, I use the official nomenclature of the archives.

CHAPTER ONE

Colonial Origins

The Elizabethan Poor Laws in Virginia

Robert Beverley, planter and gentleman historian, proclaimed Virginia to be the "best poor Man's Country in the World." He wrote in 1705 that the colonists in Virginia "live in so happy a Climate, and have so fertile a Soil, that no body is poor enough to beg, or want Food." Beverley recognized that some people were indeed poor, but only "by Accident or Sickness any Person is disabled from Working, and so is forc't to depend upon the Alms of the Parish." The old and sick "will sometimes ask to be free from Levies and Taxes; but very few do ever ask for the Parish-Alms, or indeed, so much as stand in need of them."[1] Beverley's rosy account, written largely to attract more settlers to colonial Virginia, is starkly contradicted by the numerous and extensive records of assistance given to the poor in the colonial era. Indeed, poor relief was one of the most important functions of local governments in early American history, although it has seldom been accorded such status by historians.

The history of social welfare policy in the South begins with the English settlers of colonial Virginia—Robert Beverley and his neighbors. Although the sources of poverty they confronted were sometimes new—such as the malaria that left large numbers of dependent widows and orphans in its wake—their solutions to poverty drew upon old, familiar English models. Colonial Virginians established a public-welfare system that stood as the anchor of public policy for centuries to come. That system, originating in sixteenth-century English conditions, would prove ill suited for nineteenth-century realities in the urban South.

English Precedents in Colonial Virginia

The English settlers who came to the Virginia colony in the seventeenth century brought with them assumptions about the proper way to order society. They assumed that there would be distinctions between the classes, which were natural, perhaps even divinely ordained. Likewise they continued to hold presumptions about the relationships between the sexes, and the proper ordering of marriage and the family. A hierarchy of human races, or skin colors, also seemed to English settlers to be natural and God given.[2]

These fundamental assumptions guided colonial Virginians in crafting their social-welfare policies. Public welfare came to Virginia in the seventeenth century as an inheritance of the English poor laws.[3] As one historian of the poor laws reminds us, "the provision of welfare is, therefore, not a modern invention, but a long-term practice of groups to buffer members from the full impact of individual or collective disasters."[4] (All English colonies followed these basic principles; later states, North and South, did so as well. The only exception was Louisiana, which drew upon French precedents and had no equivalent to the English poor laws.)[5] At the time the first colonists arrived in Jamestown, "relief of the poor was one of the most pressing questions of the day," as England's population and economy were undergoing tremendous upheaval. The Elizabethans paid such close attention to the poor laws because of rising problems of poverty and crime.[6]

The Elizabethan-era poor laws codified several preexisting principles. First, poor relief was to be a local function. Local governments financed and administered assistance to the poor. (In New England, town councils administered the poor relief; in Virginia, the parish vestry did so.[7]) Local governments were required to aid their own poor, but not the poor from outside the community.[8] Since those receiving aid were members of the local community, they were friends and neighbors. Poor relief thereby had a face-to-face quality, which tended to result in relatively less hostility or suspicion than would be seen in later generations.[9] Second, assistance was to be given in the form that most suited the needs of the individual. Some of the poor might best be served by direct grants, while they continued to live in their own homes; others might require institutionalization; still others might require apprenticeship, or work relief. Colonial communities used a variety of forms of poor relief simultaneously, understanding implicitly that no single model of relief worked for all the poor. Third, the English poor-relief system viewed relief as both a civic and a religious duty, an obligation that members of the community owed one another. As such, the poor received assistance as a right, an entitlement. This assumption also made the transatlantic voyage: one woman in Augusta County indicated that she felt no shame in asking for assistance: "I would be glad to go on the Parish," she told the local overseers.[10] Such applicants were neither stigmatized nor ostracized for receiving public charity.

Virginia settlers followed these English precedents fully, with very little question about their applicability in the New World. The Virginia colonists also followed the English model of blending church and state functions. Early Virginians were accustomed to an established church that collected taxes and undertook some decidedly secular activities. The Anglican Church, as the established church of Virginia, carried out a variety of secular functions, including marking the boundaries of lands, the apprenticing of children, assigning "overseers" of the highways, and caring for the poor, in addition to more clearly religious functions of hiring the ministers and tending to the condition of the chapel. (After disestablishment, responsibility for the more secular functions would be assumed by the state.)[11]

The parish vestry was the unit charged with carrying out these blended church/state functions. Parish vestrymen, laymen chosen for service by their high standing in the community, typically met quarterly, heard requests, and determined needs. After adding up all the approved expenditures, the sum was simply divided equally among the parish's "tithables." This sum, called the poll tax, covered all the parish's expenses, including the minister's salary, costs of maintenance on the church, and poor relief. (By this method, there existed no conception of a separate "poor tax" as such, which existed elsewhere.)[12] Then the vestry collected the amount from each tithable, usually in the form of tobacco.

All this was done with little investigation into the question of the causes of an individual's indigence.[13] Communities had little need for extensive investigations into the backgrounds of relief applicants, since all were residents of the same parish. Family circumstances were known, personalities and "character" well established. Indeed, character as such did not figure in the decision to grant relief. The central question for colonial public welfare instead was residency: did the given individual deserve assistance based on legal residency? In Virginia, residency was established after twelve months.[14] Although the wealthy traveler might, as Robert Beverley reported, find hospitality and open-armed reception by strangers,[15] those who roamed outside their home parish without visible means of support were met with less courtesy. As was the case in England, Virginia parishes regularly "removed" nonresidents in order to discontinue their support. In a few instances, "removal" might even mean return to England, as in the case of William Pemberton in 1684, or Elizabeth Purser in 1725.[16]

The settlement requirement, part of the inherited English poor-relief system,[17] harkened back to a more static era, when individuals were assumed to live their entire lives in the parish in which they were born. In a precapitalist or feudal economy, this assumption may have had more validity. But even as the Elizabethan poor laws were being drafted, that economy was already making its frequently painful transition to a more fluid, more mobile capitalism. Indeed, the Elizabethan statutes were themselves attempting to wrestle with the problems caused by this new mobility. Residency requirements, therefore, were at odds with a system that encouraged workers to move to wherever the jobs were. Workers found themselves caught between the static assumptions of the residency laws and the mobile demands of the emerging capitalist economy. They might move to another location looking for opportunities, but by doing so made themselves ineligible for public support in the new parish should those opportunities prove illusory. Their home parish would also refuse to grant them assistance, so long as they resided elsewhere.

Parish vestries remained on guard against any possible infringements by people pretending to have established legal residency. In 1681, the vestrymen of Petsworth Parish warned residents against entertaining "forreign" "impotent & Sick people" in their homes, for every year there were "Sundry & great Charges brought on this parish" on their account.[18] The vestrymen were much displeased several years later to discover that Thomas Grindy had "entertained Margrit Steward and she bigg with Child so long [a] time that she became an inhabitant of this parish." Both she and her child were now legally eligible for the support of the parish for as long as they decided to remain there, and possibly for the rest of their lives.[19]

The community members held much deeper sympathy for their own residents who were impoverished by illness, infirmity, or age. The public, through the agency of the parish, provided for these dependents in a variety of ways. One common method of "relief" was the granting of exemption from taxation. The elderly and the sick often received this tax relief, granted on an individual basis, after application to the vestry. Richard Ireland, in 1693, "maid his complaint of being much afflictted with sickness" and was granted exemption from all future parish levies. The vestrymen explicitly noted that he was "very Anttiant and past his Labor." Samuel Hope, in 1700, convinced the vestry that his "Low and mean condition" made it impossible for him to provide for his five "Helpless" children and wife. The parish relieved him of his taxes "during the time of His Poverty."[20] In many cases, it seems that such tax relief was all that was required, and those exempted from the levy did not require further assistance.[21]

The vestrymen also gave direct payments, either in cash or in kind, to poor members of the parish. Food, clothing, medical care, and fuel were the most commonly granted items.[22] This "outdoor" relief might rightly be seen as a preventative measure that protected vulnerable neighbors from slipping into true destitution. Able to maintain their own homes, many times still owning property, they often needed short-term help only. Parish relief allowed them to keep their lands and other property during a temporary crisis caused by illness, injury, or bad harvests. Such outdoor relief would thereby prevent long-term poverty by allowing the temporarily poor to weather short-term adversity.[23]

The parish also reimbursed the expenses that individuals incurred caring for their poor neighbors. In 1737, for example, Henrico Parish reimbursed Elizabeth Fussell for keeping John West, an infant, and similarly compensated Thomas Jennet for keeping Elizabeth Pike. Others received assistance for caring for their own family members who could not contribute to the family's income, such as Edmond Allen, who kept his son, "an Ideot."[24] Colonists knew that the parish was obligated to care for the poor. But they also recognized that there could be considerable time to pass before the next session of the vestry or the county court would meet. In the interim, neighbors often took in the sick, orphaned, or destitute and then presented the vestry/court with the bill at the next meeting.[25]

The parish vestry was also responsible for the care of dependent children, most commonly by binding them out as indentured servants. Orphans, half-orphans, "bastards," and the children of the destitute could be bound to a master who assumed the care of the child until the age of majority. The very youngest children usually remained in the care of a local woman, with an annual payment from the parish. Thus Sarah Yeaman received 466 pounds of tobacco for caring for the child of Sarah Carter in 1720. But by the age of four or five, the vestry undertook to bind these children to local landowners. Richard Allen, at the age of four years and four months, was indentured in 1700 until the age of twenty-one; as was James Lewis, a five-year-old.[26] This system was seen as both cost effective and humane: children were raised in family settings and were trained to useful work; the parish did not have to build orphanages or other institutions for their care.

For adults, an early form of work relief was occasionally afforded. Samuel Hope, who had earlier been granted exemption from taxation, was hired by the parish six months later to serve as "clarke." His pay of 317 pounds of tobacco was supplemented by a direct grant of 400 pounds of tobacco. John Mackwilliams, also a previous recipient of poor relief, was paid as sexton in 1681.[27] Richard Ireland, excused from the levy since 1693, was appointed sexton in 1701 and paid 1,000 pounds of tobacco. Two years later, "Widdow" Ireland was appointed sexton, presumably after the death of Richard.[28] In fact, the position of sexton seemed to be a standard form of work relief in this parish.[29]

The vestry occasionally combined two forms of poor relief by paying one poor person to care for another—a cost savings to the parish. Isaac Oliver, who himself received a cash grant from the parish in October 1701, was then paid a small sum of tobacco for "keeping and burying" Elizabeth Stark's child.[30] "Widdow" Hogsden, who served as sexton of Popler Spring Church, was also paid for "keeping Two women one yeare."[31] It was, it should be noted, more common to board the parish poor with wealthier members of the community, who could better afford the burden and were more likely to have houses large enough to accommodate an extra resident.[32]

These major precepts of the Elizabethan poor laws—local control, individualized relief, and residency requirements—were so enmeshed in colonial thinking that Virginians put them into practice without waiting for enabling legislation. Colonial parishes began collecting and distributing poor relief before they had any clear legal authority to do so. Even those who might resist other forms of taxation demonstrated their affinity for the poor tax: one group of Quakers who petitioned for exemption from paying taxes to the established church specifically indicated their willingness to continue paying their share of the parish poor relief.[33]

In addition to these assumptions about the nature of society and poor relief, English settlers in Virginia also brought with them ideas about the nature of humanity and work, which were part of the newly emerging Protestant worldview. The virtue of hard work, the sin of idleness, the desirability of economic independence—these concepts were also essential components of the social ideology of colonial Virginians. These ideas, combined with the tremendous need for labor in the English colonies, resulted in the firmly and widely held belief that all able-bodied persons should work. The idle but able-bodied were subject to numerous incitements to work throughout colonial America, including being whipped, run out of town, put in jail, or bound out as an indentured servant.[34]

Workhouses, institutions originally seen as quite separate from almshouses, served as another incitement to work. "Tramps" and other idle men were frequently threatened with incarceration in the workhouse. Contemporaries presumed that a stint in the workhouse would convince such persons of the desirability of obtaining work outside the institution. In 1710, Henrico County proposed, but apparently did not build, a workhouse for such men.[35] The workhouse, another social-welfare institution familiar from England, was considered (and rejected) in other American colonies during this same period.[36]

Colonial Virginia's poor laws, like their English counterparts, made no special provision for women as such but were deeply gendered nonetheless. The gendered assumptions of society were embedded in the poor-relief system. Intended to care for dependency, poor relief had to care for large numbers of women and their children. In a sense, contemporary notions of female dependency privileged women in the poor-relief system. Healthy adult males, even with legal settlement, would usually be ineligible for assistance since they were understood to be able to provide for themselves. Healthy adult females, however, might still be entitled to aid since their childbearing and child-rearing functions often effectively resulted in their temporary dependency.[37]

These, then, were the assumptions and the precedents under which early poor-relief policies rested. But colonial conditions often required refinements

of and adjustments to the English example. Starting in the earliest years of settlement, Virginians would demonstrate a practical approach to poor relief and
would also manifest considerable imagination in dealing with an old problem
in a new setting.

As early as 1618, the colonial authorities were considering formal means of
caring for the poor of the communities. In that year, the Virginia Company instructed the governor to secure corn and cattle for new settlers by restoring to
cultivation the public lands, which had been allowed to languish. The products
of the public lands would care for the public charges.[38] In 1642, the provincial
assembly passed an act authorizing the church wardens of every parish to relieve "helpless poor persons" from the payment of all taxes except that of the
ministers' salaries.[39] Four years later, under pressure from the authorities in
England, the assembly passed legislation providing for the establishment of a
workhouse at James City (Jamestown). At the same time, Parliament gave the
county courts the authority to apprentice dependent children to "flax houses,"
where they would learn useful skills, but such a facility was apparently never
built.[40]

Institutionalization, in either a poorhouse or a workhouse, was far less common than outdoor relief in Virginia's colonial era. While some communities
established almshouses, most local governments handled their welfare responsibilities without building such facilities. According to David Rothman, almshouses tended to care for those who had no relatives who could take them in;
thus almshouses cared for the exceptional cases. Colonial Virginia fit this pattern, building a few small almshouses but relying mainly on outdoor relief.[41]

Colonial residents of Virginia appeared not to have considered the poor-relief
system too financially burdensome. The costs of poor relief were kept low for
several reasons. First, a large number of people who might otherwise have "gone
on the parish," in the language of the day, were supported instead by their masters. Slaves and indentured servants, a significant portion of colonial Virginia's
population, were supported by their owners or masters (an obligation written
into law). Edmund Morgan has speculated that Virginia's laws against manumission were at least partly intended to prevent slave owners from freeing elderly or decrepit slaves who would then have to be supported by the parish.[42]

Orphans and other dependent children made up another group that often
went "on the parish." Virginia law required church wardens to bind out illegitimate children of single white women, whether free or indentured, to avoid
their becoming a public charge.[43] Other children—"legitimate" but nevertheless dependent—might also be bound out by the county court. The insatiable
demand for labor in the colony meant that "parish children," a source of considerable public expense in England, were more easily apprenticed in Virginia.

Planters did not wait for the parish authorities to come to them to take such children; like William Crimes in 1677, they made the requests themselves.[44] Indeed, planters occasionally found themselves in a bidding war in their attempts to acquire apprenticed children.[45] Under these conditions, relatively few children remained financial burdens on the local government.[46]

Second, the constantly growing population of colonial Virginia was accompanied by a constantly expanding tax base. Even as parishes increased their total expenditures on poor relief, the individual taxpayer's contribution declined over time.[47] In Henrico Parish, the number of "tithables" increased from 1,013 in 1735 to 1,503 in 1755 and rose to 2,106 tithables by 1770. As a result of a larger pool of taxpayers, the amount collected from the individual tithable declined from thirty-three pounds of tobacco in 1735 to eighteen pounds of tobacco by 1770.[48]

Third, local governments were extremely diligent in "removing" those poor who properly belonged to another jurisdiction.[49] Moreover, the local officials were quick to cut off assistance when they determined that an individual no longer needed it. Petsworth Parish terminated support for George Stickel, William Bowels, Sarah Michell, and Sarah Allen in 1711 when their neighbors "represented" to the vestry that these four could in fact "mentayn" themselves.[50] In 1793, residents of Augusta County informed the overseers that Thomas Staunton no longer required assistance, because his previous "inability is removed."[51] For all these reasons, the numbers of poor cared for by the public remained small in Virginia during the colonial period.[52]

There has been no systematic study of colonial poor-relief rates, and given the often sketchy and scattered records, it would be difficult to do so for Virginia. But there are several local studies that provide insight into the size and scope of poor relief in the period. (The differences in methodologies between the various studies do make it difficult to draw direct comparisons between them.) One study of Truro Parish traced both the total estimated white population and the number of relief recipients from 1733 to 1785. It found that, while the white population grew from sixteen hundred to more than fifty-five hundred at one point, and while the number receiving parish relief varied from two to twenty-three in a given year, the percentage of the population receiving aid never reached 1 percent in the entire fifty-two-year period.[53] Similarly, in Christ Church Parish the numbers receiving relief might vary from three to thirteen (between 1660 and 1730), but the percentage of the population who received parish aid remained consistently below .5 percent throughout the period.[54]

Not only were the numbers of poor-relief recipients small, but also the amounts spent on their relief usually represented a small proportion of public expenditures. The level of expenditures varied over time and could reach more substantial heights during an economic crisis. In Bristol Parish, between 1720 and 1730, the vestry devoted approximately 9 percent of its budget to poor relief.[55] In Christ Church Parish, anywhere from 8 to 20 percent of the annual budget was spent on poor relief between 1666 and 1730.[56] In Truro Parish, the amount of the annual budget spent on poor relief varied from less than 1 percent of the whole up to nearly 18 percent of the budget on the eve of the Revolutionary War.[57]

Thus overall, the poor-relief burden remained mostly small, and the numbers of taxpayers carrying that burden were growing. The colonial records are notable for the absence of complaints registered about poor relief. Other complaints surfaced in the records. Residents of Middlesex County, for example, complained more than once about having to pay too high a salary to their minister, but they did not complain about the cost of maintaining their poor.[58] The system, as simple and small as it was, served the needs of the community adequately during years with no crises.

Although far smaller in scope than public charity, private charitable efforts also emerged in the colonial period. Individuals sometimes included in their wills bequests to the parish "for the poor," leaving it up to the vestrymen to distribute it appropriately. In 1680, for example, Robert Lee left ten pounds sterling to the Petsworth Parish of Gloucester County, which the vestrymen then dispensed to seven selected recipients. Similarly, the vestry distributed to five individuals the ten pounds sterling left by Captain John Smith in 1698.[59] In 1674, one James Bennett of Nansemond gave the parish two acres of lands, the rents of which were to be given to the church vestry for the use of the poor.[60] In all three of these examples, the vestrymen, not the donor, decided who received the funds. This particular method of private charity further entwined public and private benevolence and highlights how difficult it is to separate public from private charity in colonial Virginia.

Formal acts of private charity seem to have been limited in the colonial era, at least based on the paper trail they have left behind. One study of seventeenth-century wills in four Virginia counties found only two bequests to the poor out of 229 probate records. A second study, from Middlesex County, found no poor-relief bequests at all.[61] While there undoubtedly must have been informal acts of almsgiving and charity that escaped being recorded anywhere, in the absence of other evidence, we must conclude that formal private charitable activity was far less important than public poor relief.[62]

Organized private charitable groups were also largely insignificant in the colonial era. The first organized private charitable acts in Virginia should properly be credited to the Native Americans who gave the English settlers food when their own supplies ran out in 1607.[63] Organized charitable efforts by the English settlers came much later. Although scholars have sometimes asserted that public charity served to supplement needs when private charity could not cover the burdens,[64] in fact it usually worked the other way around. Private charitable movements usually moved to fill in gaps where public charity failed to keep up with need, such as in the event of a crisis or disaster, or when population growth had outpaced the government's mechanisms for collecting and distributing poor funds. Richmond's first known charitable organization is illustrative. The Amicable Society, founded by "a company of gentlemen" in 1788, was intended to assist "strangers and wayfarers in distress."[65] As such, the Amicable Society filled a gap in the existing public welfare system: those who had not established residency were ineligible for public assistance. They had to rely on private charity, and the Amicable Society filled this particular niche.[66] Eighteenth-century southerners saw only a handful of such private charitable efforts, however, such as the Bethesda orphanage, near Savannah, founded by Methodists in 1738.[67]

Problems with the Colonial Poor Laws

That gaps in the welfare system existed in the colonial period is clear. Medical care was one area where the system had tremendous flaws. Those already "on the parish" could receive medical care gratis; those outside the poor-relief system had to obtain their own medical care. Some poor Virginians, desperate to obtain medical care but unable to pay for it, were driven to indenture themselves as servants in exchange for treatment. In the early eighteenth century, Martha Wakeling and Thomas Barber, both of Prince George County, became servants in order to pay their medical bills. Poor parents sometimes indentured their children for long periods of time in order to pay for their children's health care.[68]

It is also true that some of these gaps in the welfare system were present by design. Colonial poor relief was never intended to care for every single poor person. Some people were purposefully left out. Slaves, for example, were to be supported by their owners, and nonresidents were to be cared for by their home parishes. In other words, it was not the case that the welfare system was incapable of caring for all who needed help. Instead, it is that the colonial welfare system was never designed to do so. Colonial Virginians expected that some people would remain outside the system.

This welfare system, designed for an earlier age, was strained to the breaking point in the late colonial period, as the scope of the problem of poverty appears to have increased in Virginia.[69] In the 1750s and 1760s, several factors were at work. First, younger men began moving to the piedmont frontier, where opportunities to obtain cheap land were greater. That resulted in the "graying" of the Tidewater, that is an increase in the proportion of older adults in the population, a group more likely to become public charges. At the same time, tougher tobacco inspection laws reduced the production on marginal farmlands and pushed more people onto the relief rolls. The mid-1750s also saw a devastating drought, which hurt tobacco planters and subsistence farmers alike. The result of all of this was to increase notably the numbers of people requiring public assistance. Sussex County, for example, saw its poor list grow from one family in thirty in 1742, up to one in seventeen by 1774.[70] Truro Parish saw its poor list peak in the early 1760s as well, although the numbers remained very small.[71]

The General Assembly responded to these new conditions with a change in poor-relief policy. In 1755, the General Assembly authorized, but did not require, the parishes to establish workhouses for the housing of the poor. Local government was still obligated to care for the poor, but could do so in a manner presumed to be less expensive. The assembly also required that anyone resident in the workhouses would wear "upon the shoulder of the right sleeve of his or her uppermost garment . . . a badge, with the name of the parish . . . cut either in blue, red, or green cloth."[72] (Such badges identifying the worthy poor to the public were another feature inherited from the English example.)[73] One can infer from this provision that residents of the workhouse were still free to move about in the community and were not completely physically restricted to the confines of the workhouse. Such a badge would be relatively meaningless within the workhouse, where everyone wore one. But in the community at large, such a badge would mark the individual as a "pauper" and would carry significant meaning to those who saw the marker, and possibly provoke shame in those forced to wear it.

Practically speaking, however, few "paupers" were subjected to this treatment since only a handful of localities resorted to building workhouses.[74] One of these was Petsworth Parish in Gloucester County, which elected to build a workhouse in 1764. The parish vestry book is frustratingly silent on the issue, recording no discussion of the reasons for this major shift in poor-relief policy. Within a year of the order, the workhouse—described only as a twelve-foot-square house—was completed and Mrs. Johannah Mackindree, a recent widow, was hired as "mistress."[75] Who was sent to live there or what work they did went unrecorded.[76] The vestry book never discussed it again. It should be noted that the parish also continued to provide outdoor relief even though it had built a workhouse. Alongside entries for funds for the workhouse stood numerous entries for individuals receiving grants.

Contemporarily to this period of workhouse building came another remarkable change in the fundamental assumptions regarding poor relief. In 1773, Virginia opened a state-funded asylum for the insane. Located in Williamsburg, still the capital for the moment, the Eastern Asylum was intended to treat only the curable insane, not permanently house the incurable. This institution was "unique in British North America," for the government would pay for the maintenance of anyone admitted who was unable to afford its services. The founding of the Eastern Asylum represented a significant leap forward in the state's developing role in poor relief. It set a precedent for state level, rather than local, activity on behalf of one group of dependents.[77]

Although the numbers of people treated in this institution, and the dollars expended on them, remained quite small, the establishment of this institution nevertheless was enormously important for what it said about the contemporary understanding of social-welfare policy. Care for the impoverished remained a local function, yes, but one that was granted to the local jurisdictions by the state. In effect, the state itself held ultimate responsibility for the dependent, and the state could reclaim that responsibility from the local governments when it chose to do so.[78] In this instance, a state-level institution was deemed the most cost-effective method of caring for one particular group of indigents. This precedent, seemingly insignificant at the time, would come to take on much larger meaning in the nineteenth and twentieth centuries.

On the eve of the American Revolution, then, Virginia had a well-established system of public poor relief. Guided by the principles of the English poor laws, local governments cared for their own residents with a variety of measures adapted to the needs of the individual. While some few localities had begun building poorhouses or workhouses in the late colonial period, outdoor relief still remained the standard practice. In addition, one particular group of the poor—the indigent insane—had been granted assistance by the state government. Recognizing that local communities could not each afford to build insane asylums for the handful of people needing services in their individual jurisdictions, the state accepted responsibility for them all.

This eighteenth-century public-welfare system appears to have worked reasonably well under normal conditions. That is, when the economy was steady, and there were no demographic crises, the local relief monies collected by the vestrymen were sufficient to care for the local poor. Nor were the tax burdens considered onerous by those who paid them. But the system had very little flexibility for times of crisis. There were no "rainy day funds" set aside for emergencies, and no provisions for raising additional monies in a crisis. An epidemic, a bad harvest, a sudden influx of unskilled workers, an Indian raid—any such emergency would stretch the system beyond its capacity.[79] On the eve of the American Revolution, many such strains on the system were present, and Virginians more often perceived the poor-relief system as inadequate. Many were as a result eager to dissolve the vestries and replace them with something else.[80]

THE AMERICAN REVOLUTION had several important ramifications for the poor of Virginia, particularly for those in Richmond. First, the disestablishment of the Anglican Church resulted in the removal of the responsibility for caring for the poor from the vestrymen and relocating that responsibility in the state (at the county level). The law of 1785, which became the foundation of poor relief in Virginia until the twentieth century, gave county courts the authority to divide counties into districts and to hold elections for overseers of the poor in each district. The overseers would thereafter hold the powers formerly held by the vestrymen. Where there were poorhouses, the overseers would appoint superintendents of those facilities.[81]

A second product of the Revolution was the state's expanded activity in poor relief, in the form of veterans' pensions. As early as 1775, the Convention of Delegates recognized that a soldier might "be so maimed or disabled as to be rendered incapable of maintaining himself" and should therefore be "supported at the expense of the publick." By 1778, widows of soldiers were also made eligible for half pay for the remainder of their lives. Ultimately, the federal government would take over responsibility for many Revolutionary veterans, and Virginia willingly relinquished its obligation where it could. But as late as the 1850s, there were still veterans and their widows receiving state pensions in Virginia.[82] Although there are no firm numbers on the aggregate amounts expended on veterans' and widows' pensions, the significance of state pensions lies more in policy consideration than in dollar amounts. The "worthy" poor, thereafter, would include a new category: military veterans and their dependents. And for a second time, the state had singled out one particular group of needy individuals for state-level assistance.[83]

Another change produced by the Revolution was the relocation of the capital to Richmond. Concerns about vulnerability in Williamsburg and demands from the backcountry regarding accessibility led to the move, and Richmond was considered "more safe and central than any other town situated on navigable water."[84] The impact on Richmond would prove enormous and would come to affect the poor and poor-relief policies in that town in numerous ways. The next chapter begins the task of tracing Richmond's social-welfare history and watching the evolution of the poor laws in Virginia in the years following the Revolution.

CHAPTER TWO

Poor Relief in Early Richmond

The Poor- and Workhouse

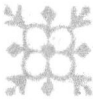

Almost from its very foundation, Richmond was a community ill served by the Elizabethan poor laws. Established as a commercial trading center on the James River, Richmond would, by definition, have a highly mobile population. Many people who came to the town for trade stayed days, weeks, or even months and never established legal residency as required by the poor laws. Sailors, landless laborers, and itinerant preachers, among others, moved in and out of the city without ever becoming citizens. As in other port towns, Richmond's population was always in flux. The old poor laws made a poor fit for a city in motion.

The city "fathers," seeing stability as a key to prosperity, hoped to civilize this frontier town. One of the tools in this effort would be the establishment of a poorhouse, a traditional form of relief that seemed to offer a means to rein in the behavior of the poor in this modern setting. That goal was, at best, only partly met. The poorhouse would never entirely succeed in modifying the behavior of the poor, especially since only a small number of the city's poor ever took up residence there.

Instead, the poorhouse grew to be an important civic fixture in Richmond. It would come to stand as a symbol of the city's "modern" sensibilities, its progressive thinking. The presence of the poorhouse was as much a comfort to the urban middle class as to the poor, standing as brick-and-mortar testimony of the community's civic-mindedness. The middle-class residents could see in the building a reflection of their prosperity and of their generosity. The city's poor saw the building as yet another option in their survival strategies.

Early Richmond

Richmond, a tiny crossroads community at the falls of the James River, had been laid out by William Byrd II in the 1730s and was incorporated as a town by the General Assembly in 1742. Byrd had carefully picked the location, a part of his own vast landholdings in the region: Richmond's situation at the falls of the

James made it a natural center for colonial trade. Tobacco warehouses, a ferry, taverns, and other necessary facilities appeared quickly, although its population remained quite small. The Anglican Church replaced its former "chapel" with a new church building in 1741, to be called St. John's.[1] Richmond was designated the county seat of Henrico in 1752, and a courthouse and jail were constructed. Within a generation, Richmond had become an important center for trade in the James River valley, shipping (in 1765) over twenty thousand hogsheads of tobacco and seventy-five thousand bushels of wheat. On the eve of the Revolution, Richmond consisted of about 250 householders, a quarter of whom were merchants and shopkeepers. Another two-fifths of the employed men were artisans or worked in the town's several taverns.[2]

Trades related to the tobacco and flour industries flourished. The city's location on the rapids gave it the ability to harness waterpower for the use of mills, and an important flour-milling industry developed. Tobacco manufacture and export constituted the second major industry in the town. Coopers and stave makers filled the demand for hogsheads and boxes. The rapidly growing population required housing, meaning a variety of artisans and their apprentices, both black and white, held an important position in the local economy. Symbolic of the importance of commercial enterprises in Richmond, the town soon acquired banks, including a branch of the Bank of the United States, and an insurance company, the Mutual Assurance Society. Also highlighting the significance of commerce in the city, the men elected to serve in Richmond's first city council were all merchants, and merchants continued to dominate the council for decades to come.[3]

As the new state capital, Richmond also became the political center of the state. In addition to the merchants and artisans who already made Richmond home, lawyers, bureaucrats, and politicians relocated to the city. These members of the colonial elite brought with them their slaves, which (by 1786) constituted half of the town's population of eighteen hundred. Others who made their living off the state government included clerks and printers.[4]

The combination of political and commercial opportunities soon attracted other new arrivals. German Jews, concentrated in the mercantile trades, were sufficient in number by 1789 to found their own synagogue, Beth Shalome. Refugees from the revolutions in France and Santo Domingo came in the 1790s, including a number who became French language teachers and dance instructors. The French were followed by immigrants from Scotland, Ireland, Spain, and Portugal. By the opening of the nineteenth century, Richmond's population was remarkably diverse. The population had also more than tripled in the twenty years since the city had been named the state capital, with nearly six thousand residents in 1800 (see table 1 in the appendix). Some of those new residents were free blacks, a growing proportion of the community after the short-lived Manumission Act of 1782, which permitted Virginians to free their slaves without penalty. Many of those freed migrated to towns like Richmond, looking for employment.[5]

This mobility was itself symptomatic of the poor-relief problems that urban centers faced. The contemporary poor-relief system barely sufficed to cover the needs of rural society. That it sufficed at all was often because the rural poor had additional resources to draw upon to supplement their meager poor relief. Extended families and kinship networks were an important resource, more commonly available in a less mobile traditional society. Urban dwellers, by contrast, had to contend with heightened unpredictability in the economy with fewer familial support systems.[6] Large numbers of Richmonders were newly arrived, many without family, kin, or other networks of support.

Although growing rapidly, turn-of-the-century Richmond remained in many ways a rough-and-tumble frontier town. Clearly, Richmond offered opportunities, especially for single men. As a result the sex ratio among whites was greatly skewed: in 1784, there were two men for every one woman.[7] This also created a busy tavern world, with street brawlers, gambling, and prostitution. Town residents perceived a growing crime rate, with an "astonish[ing] . . . amount of blood shed at taverns, around gaming tables, and at the racetrack." The local paper was peppered with stories of gambling, drinking, fighting, and arrests. The warehouse area on the waterfront became especially crowded, and unruly. Slaves, free blacks, and white laborers worked and lived together in the warehouse neighborhoods, enjoying a freedom of association and forms of relationships new to most residents of Richmond.[8]

Poverty was a part of this unruly world, and it seems that the transfer of responsibility for the poor from church vestry to local government had not gone smoothly. In 1785, the city council complained of the vestry's "inattention to the necessities of the poor" when, in fact, the city was supposed to have taken over responsibility for their welfare. The result of this was many "difficulties under which the City labours." Once the council recognized its new role, it began by attempting to gain some idea of the scope of the poverty in the city. The council appointed a committee "to go through the streets" and collect the names of the poor, along with information regarding their sex, age, condition, occupation, length of residence, and last place of residence.[9] In 1792, the committee reported nine people who should be provided for by the city; the list for the following year included eleven names. In both cases, all those listed appear to have been women and children. The city council then began caring for the city's poor in much the same way the vestrymen had previously done—that is, in a variety of means, suited to the needs of the individual. They paid individuals for boarding the poor in their homes, paid the rent of the poor who could otherwise maintain themselves, paid local doctors for medical services for the poor, and made direct cash payments to others.[10]

In addition to the usual tax money, officials employed some imaginative ways of raising additional funds for the support of the poor. As early as 1773, an ordinance permitted the city to capture and kill any swine or goats running free in the town limits, and, if no owner could be identified, the meat was to be given for the use of the poor. Likewise, wood offered for public sale that did not meet city regulations, or any goods offered for sale found to have used false weights or measures, were forfeited to the city and then turned over to the poor.[11]

The increasingly visible poverty, the rapid growth of the population, the preponderance of young single men, the growing number of free blacks, and the failed slave revolt of Gabriel Prosser[12] all created a sense of danger and disorder. White middle-class Richmonders began to complain of the racial mixing at dances and of the vagrants and beggars in the streets.[13] The city council devoted much attention to gaining control over the disorder. To reduce the market for stolen goods, the city required licenses for all peddlers and street hucksters. Gambling, horse racing, and liquor sales were strictly regulated, as were loitering and vagrancy. The city passed ordinances restricting the activities of hired-out slaves. Slaves were forbidden to hire themselves out; masters had to make the arrangements. Slaves had to carry a pass at all times or face public whipping. They were prohibited from playing cards, gambling, or attending horse races. Slaves were prohibited from meeting for religious purposes without a white person present. The authorities tried to limit the contact between free blacks and slaves; unsupervised meetings of the two groups of blacks were outlawed, and free blacks were prohibited from selling alcohol to slaves or teaching them to read. In addition, the General Assembly reversed the Manumission Act of 1782, making it more difficult for owners to free their slaves and requiring those newly emancipated to leave the state.[14]

In 1805, as part of the effort to establish order in Richmond, the city began construction of a poorhouse.[15] Richmond therefore anticipated somewhat the Jacksonian-era "discovery of the asylum" analyzed by David J. Rothman. Other southern communities would soon follow suit.[16] The "poor and work house," as the records of these years frequently called it, was located on the north side of town, just at what was then the city's outer limits. While this might make it difficult for the ill, the aged, or the lame to make their way to such a remote location, this was consistent with a larger urban pattern in the nineteenth century. By locating the facility at the fringe of the city, the overseers were effectively removing the poor from the numerous urban temptations that might be contributing to their destitution. Separated from taverns, gambling dens, and other amusements that might serve to impoverish the vulnerable, the poorhouse was intended to act as a reformatory.[17]

One of the few extant descriptions of the building comes from the insurance policy issued by the Mutual Assurance Society in 1814. A sketch of the building shows a simple, brick, four-story building. The plain facility boasted only one decorative feature, an elaborate cupola, rather at odds with the rest of the building.[18] A later description included a few further details: the building was a "commodious structure" of brick, with room for about ninety persons, and stood on "a healthful and pleasant eminence" on a tract of approximately twenty-eight acres of city property.[19] A decade later, the city would lay out a public burial ground adjacent to the poorhouse, with sections set aside for free people of color and slaves.[20]

The burial ground helped to tie the poorhouse more closely to the city than its remote location might otherwise have allowed. For several decades at least, the Shockoe cemetery would be the main burial ground for the city, and nearly all funerals would take place there.[21] Anyone attending a funeral or visiting a grave of a loved one would see the poorhouse as part of the backdrop of that event. Nearly everyone in town would thereby have irregular contact with the poorhouse. Geographically, the poorhouse stood on the edge of town; symbolically, it stood centrally in civic life.

Just a few years after its opening, the city undertook a systematic study of the facility, under orders from the Hustings Court.[22] The resulting report, in the spring of 1811, included several recommendations for reforms and improvements in the poorhouse. Taken together, those recommendations indicate that the city had built, but not organized, a poorhouse. As the city council noted, "It is much to be regretted that some system has not been earlier adopted."[23]

The first recommendation of the investigating committee was to enclose the grounds, with a "substantial" fence, "at least ten or twelve feet high." Although the report suggested that this was to give the inmates a large "space of ground" for health and exercise, such an enclosure would also restrain the inmates from going about the town, which the local newspaper complained caused "corruption and intoxication."[24]

The report next recommended that some of the smaller, adjoining rooms be combined into larger rooms, one of which would serve as a "female hospital," the other to be used as "a work shop," for "spinning, weaving, &c."[25] To assist the numerous sick women in the "female hospital," the committee was "deeply impressed with the necessity of furnishing a matron." (The city soon decided to pay Mrs. Nathaniel Shepard, wife of the keeper of the poorhouse, as matron of the poorhouse.)[26] To furnish the "work shop," the committee requested the purchase of hemp, flax, cotton, and wool, and "a domestic carding and spinning

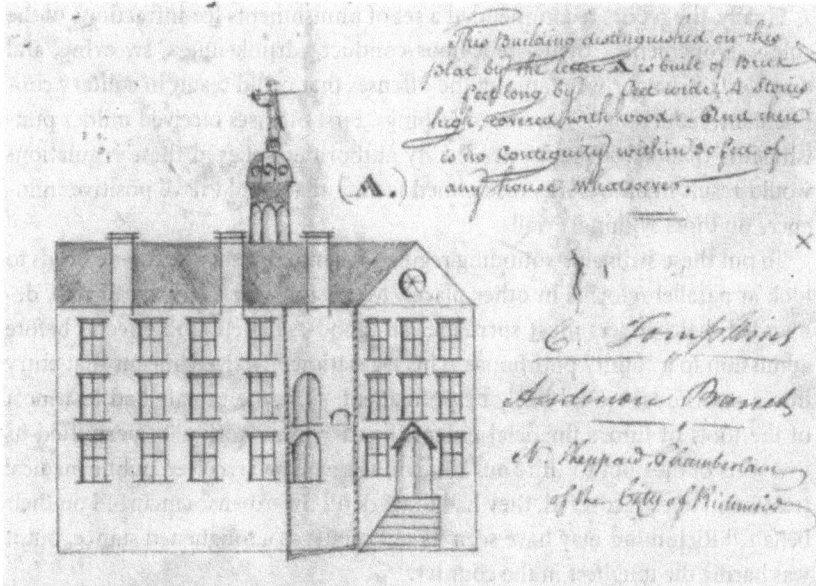

Original Richmond Poorhouse, from Mutual Assurance Society policy, 1814.
Although simple in design, it was one of the largest public buildings in the city at
the time. Note the ornate cupola. Courtesy of the Library of Virginia.

machine." The keeper of the poorhouse was instructed to keep monthly reports
on the "species and quantity manufactured, and how disposed of." At the point
of admission, the keeper was instructed to assign "such employment as he may
think the person best capable of performing . . . most required for the benefit
of the institution."[27]

On the fourth floor, two rooms were to be "appropriated as solitary rooms
of confinement." The windows were to be covered by both iron grates and cov-
erings, which would "prevent those therein confined from amusing themselves
with passing objects, and thereby induce them to exercise their minds of their
former conduct which may eventuate in their reformation." The committee was
also concerned with "the internal government of the poor and work house."
"[T]here should be an uniform system of rules and regulations adopted" that
would be followed by the staff and residents alike. "For the promotion of regular
and industrious habits," a horn or bell at sunrise would signal the start of the
day, at which time the keeper would assign the day's duties to "all who are not
confined by sickness." On Sundays, "those who have established an orderly and
good character" were permitted to attend church services in the city, as long as
they returned in time for dinner.[28]

Finally, the report recommended a set of punishments for infractions of the rules. "Elopements," theft, "rebellious conduct," drunkenness, swearing, and disorderly behavior were among the offenses that could result in solitary confinement, reduction of rations, or lashings. First offenses received milder punishments than subsequent ones.[29] City authorities believed these regulations would result in an orderly, disciplined facility that would have positive influences on those within its walls.

To put these stringent-sounding regulations into some context, one needs to look at parallel reforms in other places. Mississippi, for example, in 1821, demanded that paupers must surrender all "goods, chattels, and effects" before admission to a county poorhouse. This legislation effectively meant that entry into a poorhouse would likely be permanent, since the inmate had lost most of the tools of future financial independence.[30] New York City permitted its overseers of the poor to "hire out" individuals who had received public medical treatment; once recovered, they had to work off the expenses incurred on their behalf.[31] Richmond may have seen its 1811 report as a toughened stance, but it was hardly the toughest in the country.

The 1811 report and other records from the early nineteenth century suggest that Richmonders had some varying, contradictory expectations about their newly built poorhouse. Some, like newspaper editor Thomas Ritchie, saw it as a workhouse on the English model, where harsh treatment and purposefully miserable conditions were to serve as a deterrent to indolence. Ritchie praised the plans to model the poorhouse after the penitentiary and to "furnish the poor, not so much with subsistence itself, as with the materials of work, so far as they are able to work."[32] By contrast, Robert Greenhow, president of the overseers of the poor, recognized that the institution was "known by the name of the 'City Alms and Work-house,' but infinitely more worthy is it of the name of the City Hospital" because of the condition of the majority of its inmates.[33] The report of the investigating committee of 1811 contained both ideas. Initially insisting that they considered "the said building as a work house, or house of correction for the safekeeping, employment and reformation [of] the idle and dissolute," the committee also acknowledged that some portion of the building must be set aside for a "female hospital" because the facility "principally abounds" with sick women.[34]

These contradictory understandings of the purposes and functions of the city poorhouse would continue throughout the rest of the nineteenth century. Part of the explanation for the confusion was that the building in fact carried out multiple functions under one roof. It served as a public hospital, where even nonresidents could get emergency medical care. It served as an asylum for the "virtuous, good and well-meaning" poor, including orphans.[35] It served as a

workhouse, where the idle could be retained "at labour until they by their service make a reasonable remuneration to the institution for expenses incurred
in their support."[36] These mingled functions not only caused public confusion
about the purpose of the institution, but they apparently also caused managerial problems. Overseer Robert Greenhow would have preferred that separate
facilities be built for each function, with "no intercourse to be had, either with
the other."[37]

The poorhouse also served a further purpose. For more than a century, its
presence would be a source of great pride for residents of the city. They took
out-of-town visitors to see it, praised it, and funded it. Richmonders saw in
the poorhouse a visible symbol of their civility; it reminded them of their own
generosity. The city poorhouse became part of the definition of civic life, an
important part of the generational effort to civilize and refine the rough-and-
tumble town of 1800.

In addition to the poorhouse, the growing city began to host other features of
urban life. Residents soon had several newspapers from which to choose. The
semiweekly *Virginia Gazette* had relocated from Williamsburg along with the
state government; or residents could look forward to the partisan newspaper
editorials of Thomas Ritchie's *Enquirer,* established in 1804. Subscribers could
"draw" books from the newly organized Richmond Library. Numerous, sometimes short-lived, schools and academies appeared, offering geography, music,
painting, needlework, and "both living and dead languages." A Lancasterian
school was established in 1816, where the "children of the wealthy were taught
at the most reasonable rates and the children of the poor gratis." The city donated a lot and five thousand dollars toward a building, plus an endowment of
six hundred dollars per year.[38]

Richmond's more prosperous residents began to acquire and display the
trappings of wealth. Merchants with national and international connections
brought a remarkably wide range of goods to town. Persian quilts, English furniture, and Dutch quills could be bought in local shops, as could Jamaican spirits and French silk stockings. Or, they could spend their money on organized
entertainment in the form of the Jockey Club races, held twice a year. And in
1787 the "New Theater on Shockoe Hill," also known as Academy Hall, opened
with a performance of *The Beggar's Opera.*[39]

Religious organizations began to establish themselves in the city, although
few were large enough to begin building churches yet. Religious services were irregular, informal, and might be held in a "mere barn."[40] The Anglicans, who did
have a chapel, conducted services there only three times a year, "to which sometimes as few as half a dozen people came."[41] Quakers established a "meeting" in
1795; Roman Catholics a "mission" in 1796; and Methodists made Richmond

a "station" for circuit riders in 1798. Richmond's Jews opened their small synagogue in 1789, organized with twenty-six families as members. And Baptists, who had organized their biracial church in 1780, erected a frame meetinghouse in 1800.[42]

Voluntary associations, most of which were charitable in nature, soon followed, as Virginians joined in the national movement for associations that came to characterize American public life in the nineteenth century. Quakers organized the short-lived Virginia Abolition Society in Richmond in 1790. The aforementioned Amicable Society was joined in the effort to aid travelers in need by a new organization, Ezrat Orchim, founded by members of Beth Shalome synagogue in 1790. Baptist women formed a mission society in 1813 to support the spreading of the gospel.[43]

One of the earliest and longest-lived of these voluntary associations was the Female Humane Association. Founded in 1805 as a nonsectarian charity of leading Protestant women, the association operated an asylum for white girls. At any given time, the asylum housed fifteen to twenty orphans and half orphans, who received basic education and training in "domestic business" such as needlework, spinning, and knitting.[44] The Female Humane Association was part of a larger network of such benevolences founded in this era: the growing towns of Fredericksburg, Petersburg, and Norfolk also established female-run charities in this decade.[45]

Panic of 1819

By the 1810s, Richmond had developed into a busy commercial center with a vibrant urban life. With a growing population and economy, Richmond experienced a land boom in the mid-1810s that produced wild speculation in real estate. "The Flush Times," as locals later called it, saw frenzied spending on land. "There were not days enough in the week," wrote memoirist Samuel Mordecai, "nor hours enough in the day, for the rival auction sales in real estate" as city lots increased in price "two, three, five, aye ten fold." Speculation affected tobacco prices as well, as tobacco sold for five or six times the rate of the early decade.[46]

As a fledgling commercial, manufacturing community, the city had a fragile economy that teetered through the Embargo years. Then the depression of 1819 hit Richmond particularly hard. Tobacco prices plummeted. The flour-milling industry was devastated, as output and prices both dropped. Land prices, which had been artificially inflated by speculation, dropped precipitously. The tax values of buildings were cut in half in 1819, and cut in half again in 1820.[47] In a particularly local aspect of the panic, an embezzlement scheme by the city treasurer robbed the city of desperately needed funds. The economic situation was so severe that business had not fully recovered by the time of the 1837 panic, which again devastated the city.[48]

The Panic of 1819 produced immense suffering of the city's poor and working class. Independent artisans, especially in the construction trades, and small entrepreneurs were hit the worst.[49] The poorhouse was flooded: where the poorhouse had held 46 residents in June 1818, the number had swelled to 83 by December 1822. The overseers noted, "the House is at present full; very few more can, for want of Room, be admitted." At least 200 more people received city assistance in the form of outdoor relief.[50] Another report published in 1824 claimed that the average number in the poorhouse was "about" 70, with at least another 320 receiving outdoor relief.[51]

Table 2 summarizes the numbers receiving city assistance from 1818 to 1829. These statistics indicate several things about poor relief in these years of economic upheaval. First, the construction of a poorhouse did not eliminate outdoor relief in the city. Outdoor relief remained the most important form of assistance; institutionalization affected only a relatively small number of the poor. However, the outdoor poor received trifling amounts each. It is likely that such people would have had to seek further assistance from friends, relatives, or private charities. Outdoor relief alone would not have carried a family through the depression. Second, white residents received the bulk of city aid, while only a tiny number of free blacks obtained relief.[52] And third, the numbers on relief, and the amounts expended, rose during the middle of the 1820s, reaching a peak of eight thousand dollars in 1823. Similarly, in 1824, the number admitted to the poorhouse reached a high of 102.

Of course, Richmond was not the only city experiencing economic upheaval. Other Virginia cities experienced many of the same problems. In nearby Petersburg, the economic crisis produced a social crisis. Poor-relief expenses tripled or quadrupled the normal level, and the taxpayers demanded relief. The official response was to get tough on the poor. In 1823, the city abolished outdoor relief in Petersburg. The following year, the poorhouse was ordered to be "used as a Work-house."[53]

Richmond's response was similar, as the city attempted to crack down on poverty, disorder, and public expenses. In 1820, Robert Greenhow, president of the overseers of the poor, announced that the city had new plans and policies designed to deal with the crisis. The overseers were ordered to take to the streets, investigating residency, arresting street beggars, and requiring poor parents to send their children to the Lancastrian and "Sundy" schools, or else receive no public relief. Greenhow also hoped to send the city's poor children to the country to work, although he feared that "the court may not sanction their being bound without the limits of the city or the state; we [also] have to encounter the feelings of relations, who may not yield to the proposition, because their children are to be sent to a distant clime, however advantageous it may be demonstrated to be for their welfare." The public was also assured that the overseers were using "every effort to free ourselves by colonization of our black population."[54]

Like their counterparts in Petersburg, the overseers attempted to put the poorhouse residents to work. In March 1821, after their regular, periodic visit to the poorhouse, the overseers noted that they found "nothing to complain of but the Idleness of the male portion of the paupers for whom their ingenuity has been long taxed to find a species of Employ to exercise them in." A second visit in April found that women, "except those that were indisposed" were busy spinning, but the men apparently were, again, doing little work. A third visit in July resulted in the overseers warning the keeper that he must "keep the Paupers that are not absolutely confined to their beds, constantly employed as well within Doors, as in the Yard and Garden."[55]

The growing numbers of poor made increasing financial demands on the city. As figure 1 demonstrates, the decade saw continued heightened welfare expenditures, despite the council's efforts at economy. Greenhow began to make repeated requests to the city council for additional funds. Each year, usually in the winter months, Greenhow wrote pointed and poignant accounts of the sufferings of the city's poor, accompanied by requests for extra appropriations. The predictability of these letters illuminates the pattern: the city council regularly appropriated the minimum amount possible, and then had to appropriate additional sums later.[56] In 1826, the city was unable to meet its expenses and was forced to borrow two thousand dollars by bank loan "to answer the present pressing demands for the support of the poor of the city."[57]

The financial crisis produced a contest between the city council, which "held the purse strings," and the overseers—especially Robert Greenhow—who had the most regular contact with the poor. President of the overseers for more than a decade, Greenhow took his responsibilities seriously and served as a powerful and articulate defender of the poor-relief system. More than anyone else, Greenhow personified the more paternalistic approach to poor relief that the overseers manifested, as opposed to the more fiscal concerns of the city councilmen.[58]

The city council attempted to restrain the growth of expenditures, telling the overseers in 1825 to use the regular appropriations for reshingling the roof. Irritated from the constant demands for more aid, the city council went on the offensive. Convinced that poor-relief costs were too high, while poor-relief policies were too lax, the councilmen came to believe that they could better administer public welfare than could the overseers. The council established a committee to "enquire and report where it will not be advantageous to the City to procure

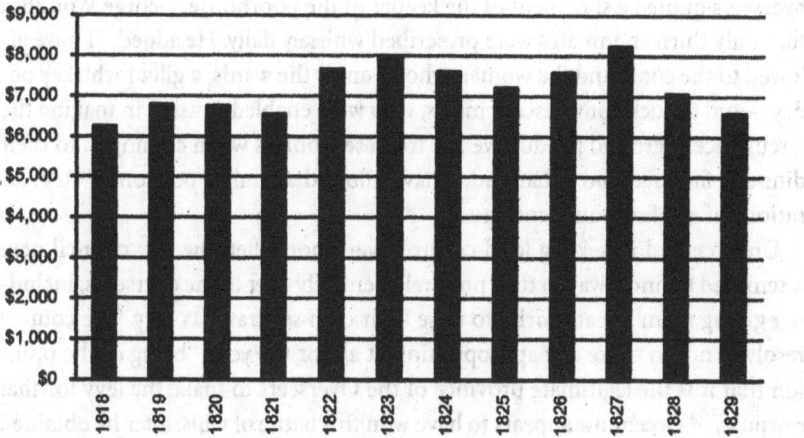

Figure 1. *Total Relief Costs, Richmond, 1818–1829*
Sources: Auditors of Public Accounts, State of Virginia; Annual Reports, Overseers of the Poor, Richmond City, 16 June 1829.

from the Legislature the enactment of a law transforming the control of the Poor to the [city council]."[59] Fortunately for the poor, nothing came of this plan.

Moreover, the council took the battle public. In 1826, the council passed a resolution "that in the opinion of this Hall, the present system pursued for supporting the Poor of the City is defective, is extravagantly expensive, and ought to be changed."[60] The battle lines moved to the local newspapers. The chair of the city's finance committee, Robert Scott, publicly charged that the costs had grown "beyond any precedent known in this country, and . . . should be diminished." Scott suggested that three to four thousand dollars a year could be saved by adding a farm to the poorhouse and requiring the inmates to work there to raise "a sufficient quantity of food for those received into the institution." Scott also complained that the overseers were extravagant in their expenditures. He pointed in particular to the "very large quantity of spirituous liquors furnished for the Paupers . . . [which] appeared not to be one of those articles of necessity which should be furnished at the cost of the City to her poor."[61]

Tired of the charges that had "been a theme . . . for several of the preceding years," the overseers defended their expenditures and their policies in the local paper the following day. Explaining first that the poorhouse was full, and still could not take care of even a fifth of the people who needed assistance, the overseers then turned to the charges of extravagance and mismanagement. They offered testimony by the poorhouse physician, Dr. Thomas Nelson, who insisted that he "frequently had occasion to prescribe spirituous liquors for the paupers . . . because I thought it most beneficial to these patients." Next, the overseers quoted a statement of the keeper of the poorhouse, George Woodfin, that only thirteen inmates were prescribed whiskey daily. He added, "I have allowed to the cook, and the woman who cleanses the wards, a gill of whiskey per day—and to such convalescent males, who were enabled to assist in making the circumjacent ground productive . . . to these laborers when coming in to their dinners, fatigued and exhausted, I have allowed a similar portion."[62] Regular rations of alcohol would continue.

Unsuccessful in seizing legal control over poor relief, the city council next attempted to find a way to turn poor relief entirely over to the overseers, including giving them the authority to raise their own separate tax levy. The council resolved not to make any appropriation at all for the year, "being of the opinion that it is the legitimate province of the Overseers to make the levy for that purpose."[63] Greenhow appears to have won this battle of wills; after he obtained legal counsel from the city attorney, the city council resumed its appropriations and there was no further discussion of a separate tax levy.

This very public debate about the poorhouse offers some insight into the contemporary understandings of poor relief and their evolution since the seventeenth century. The complaints suggested that taxpayers were unhappy with the cost of public relief, but not with the existence of public relief itself. No one was calling for the abolishment of the system, or a privatization of relief. The poorhouse was not in danger of closure. Instead, the taxpayers wanted to find ways to reduce the costs of the system, and suspected that the costs had been artificially inflated by extravagant expenditures and by providing for those who might actually be able to provide for themselves. Putting the idle inmates to work seemed a logical solution to these problems.

While the overseers themselves had often complained about the idleness of the inmates, and their inability to find appropriate work for the men in particular, they nevertheless found it galling that others would criticize them for this. They had, after all, tried various work plans for years, with little effect. The overseers, at least, understood what those without close contact with the institution did not: the poorhouse was in reality "a complete Hospital; not one of [the men] able to render any personal services."[64] It was also a nursery of sorts: at any given time, a large minority of the "inmates" were children.[65] Very few poorhouse residents were physically capable of working.

While taxpayers chafed at the costs of public welfare, the economic depression spurred the creation of new private efforts to alleviate poverty. In 1819, Mrs. Mehetable Dabney petitioned the city council for permission to establish a "society for the promotion of industry." This society would operate a "house of industry" that would offer work relief for poor women. The city council approved and offered an appropriation for its support.[66] This "house of industry" was not a workhouse, in the punitive sense, where the idle able-bodied were incarcerated and compelled to work. Instead, the society would buy supplies such as cloth, yarn, and thread, which poor women would then be given to sew and sell. This would permit them some level of self-sufficiency. As such, the "house of industry" presaged the later women's exchange plan, which became nationally popular later in the century.[67]

Although the council approved the idea of the women's workshop, the city's finances soon convinced the council to withdraw its support. "Whereas the funds of the City require to be economised as much as possible in every branch of its expenditure," stated the council in 1821, "and the allowance heretofore contemplated for the house of Industry being one which can be omitted as well as any other," the council cut off its allowance to the House of Industry and ordered "the ladies who were so good as to undertake and conduct the establishment . . . to close the business of said house."[68]

This little vignette offers some insight into the social structure and power relations in Richmond in 1821 and allows an assessment of the level of tolerance for women's social activism at the time. The ladies clearly felt comfortable organizing this kind of public activity and approaching the city fathers with a request for funding. The councilmen apparently held no objection to the principle, the Female Humane Association and other similar organizations having laid the precedent for this form of local women's activism. But the council's brusque dismissal ("the house of Industry being one which can be omitted as well as any other") and its order to close the facility, rather than merely terminating its financial support, indicate that the men who ran the city felt that they held ultimate veto power over women's voluntary activities. Although middle-class women were growing increasingly active in Richmond's public life, not all its citizens had yet grown to accept these new, and still controversial, roles. Poor relief had been, after all, traditionally an exclusively male activity since it fell within the public sphere. City council flexed its muscles, reminding residents that this was the public arena. Earlier precedents notwithstanding, women's activism in poor relief was not yet fully welcome.[69]

Inside the Poorhouse: Race, Gender, and Alcohol

While taxpayers griped about the high costs of the city's public-welfare system and private citizens grappled with alternative solutions to poor relief, the administrators of the poorhouse had additional problems with which to contend during these years. One of the perceived advantages of institutionalization was closer supervision of the poor.[70] Yet, despite the "tough-love" rules of 1811 for governing the poorhouse, the institution never ran as smoothly as the administrators desired. The unruliness was partly the product of overcrowding and underfunding. It was also partly a chimera, an interpretation clouded by middle-class views of working-class autonomy.

The small size of the poorhouse staff, especially in periods of overcrowding like the 1820s, meant that the institution simply could never be firmly under the control of the administrators. The desire for economy contributed to the small size of the staff; utilizing the labor of the "inmates" for such chores as cleaning and caring for children allowed the overseers to dispense with extra paid laborers. This resulted in a very small supervisory staff at the facility. There was simply inadequate staff to watch the women in the house, the men on the grounds, the sick in the hospital wards, and the children everywhere. Under the circumstances, the residents likely felt considerable autonomy in their daily routines.[71]

Interracial mingling was an example of the perceived disorder in the institution. Although the number of blacks in the poorhouse was always small, as indicated in table 2, their presence nevertheless caused concern. In 1822, for example, there were nine free blacks in the total of eighty-three inmates. Of those nine, eight were "in a state of sore disease," and all were "huddled together in one small room, on the ground floor, leaving actually not space enough for the Physician to administer to them." More were petitioning for admission, but there was no place to put them.[72]

The overseers' solution to this problem was to request funding to build a new, separate building for "coloured paupers." A year later, there had been no action from the city council, "those who hold the purse string of the city." The overseers assumed that the races should be segregated within the facility. But they also assumed that the sexes should be separated too, and they were distressed that they could not do both within the single building they had at their disposal. A few months later, the overseers discussed turning the room "at present used as a prison" into a space for more black inmates.[73]

The city continued to refuse requests for a separate building.[74] In the meantime, the overseers continued to contend with the difficulty of separating the races and the sexes within the confines of a single building. Clearly, there was easy contact between whites and blacks. In 1822, Samuel Bridgewater, "coloured," was responsible for giving a Mrs. Wade, a white woman, strong liquor.[75] Race, then, was one of the sources of the perceived "disorder."

Similarly, alcohol was apparently easily obtained by the inmates and was a constant source of problems in the home. The 1811 regulations specifically mentioned the abuse of alcohol, and one can only presume they did so because there had already been difficulties. *Enquirer* editor Thomas Ritchie's 1811 editorial applauded the plan to build a fence around the facility in part because it would keep the inmates from intoxication. In 1822, "strong liquor" was an element of a Mrs. Wade's attack on the poorhouse keeper.[76] And the 1827 complaints by the city's finance director again drew attention to the use of alcohol in the house.

But contemporaries held mixed views on the use of alcohol. The physicians, as noted previously, regularly dispensed whiskey as medicine. The keeper also viewed a shot after a day's hard labor as acceptable. He likewise rewarded the staff with a "gill" after finishing their duties. While the city council, with its increasingly "bottom line" mentality, complained about the use of alcohol in the poorhouse, those who had the most regular contact with the poor saw little harm in its regular use and, instead, found some positive good in its (limited) distribution. Alcohol would continue to be a source of disorderly conduct in the poorhouse for decades to come.

The Richmond city poorhouse was also a gendered institution, and by that I mean more than just "segregated by sex." Gender shaped the expectations that the poor had of the poorhouse; it also shaped the expectations that the administrators held of the inmates. City officials viewed the female poor quite differently than they did males. While city administrators fretted year after year over the able-bodied men sitting idle in the poorhouse, they seldom complained about idle women. Part of the explanation for this is that the women were actually more often engaged in some kind of labor. As studies in other cities also discovered, it was easier for administrators to find appropriate work for women than for men.[77] Women inmates helped with the laundry, with serving meals, and with tending to the children in the wards. Even women who were there for pregnancy and childbirth could—and did—undertake mending and other small chores. And with no evidence to the contrary, it seems that women did these daily unpaid tasks with little complaint; they too appear to have assumed that it was their duty to do so.[78] Their unpaid labors in these "domestic" duties helped keep the facility functioning, as well as reduced the number of paid staff required to do so. Visitors to the poorhouse would have seen the female "inmates" sweeping, washing, and sewing, and therefore earning their keep to the satisfaction of the city council.

Male inmates, by contrast, could not be asked to hang out the laundry, rock the colicky baby, or darn socks. Men would be expected to do more physically demanding tasks. But given the limited physical capacities of most of the inmates, most men were unable to help with the physical maintenance of the facility. Many of the poorhouse residents were elderly, making it even more difficult to engage in gender specific labors. (Elderly women might still knit; elderly men might not be able to chop firewood.) The men appeared to be idle, while the women appeared to be contributing to the upkeep of the home.

Gender assumptions also might work to the disadvantage of "unruly" women.

Men were generally punished for disobeying the staff by being confined in the "cells." But disruptive women were more severely punished. Women who challenged the authorities were seen as more dangerous, and more brazen, than the men who stood up for themselves. In 1824, when Mrs. Billy Warner was rebuked by the superintendent for staying out longer than he had granted permission, she verbally attacked him. Apparently she scored some points, because she so infuriated him that he beat the elderly woman severely.[79]

Another rebellious, sharp-tongued woman, Mrs. Tomlinson, caused a furor in the poorhouse later that same year. As the overseers reported, "having kept the institution in an almost constant state of disquiet," and having threatened to burn down the building the first chance she got, the board decided to take steps to "allay if possible the impetuosity of her temper . . . she was placed in a fit Situation, and two buckets of fresh drawn water, from an Eminence of 5 feet above, were poured on her head and Body. Severe as the operation was, she had no sooner recovered from the Shock when her inflammatory disposition again evinced itself." Concluding that they could not control Mrs. Tomlinson, the board members resolved to dismiss her from the facility.[80] The rich detail with which this story was recorded—quite rare in these accounts—betrays the level of outrage the administrators felt at being unable to control this woman.

Moreover, the disorder at the poorhouse was not limited to the inmates alone. The staff, often drawn from classes of residents just slightly above the status of the inmates themselves, contributed to the occasional mayhem. In June 1818, for instance, Thomas LeTellier was fired from his position of teacher to the poorhouse children "in consequence of his riotous and highly indecorous conduct for some time past."[81] (LeTellier's family was familiar with the institution, having been occasional residents there.)

Despite their best efforts, then, the city council and the overseers of the poor could not always make the poorhouse function the way they wished. The "inmates" influenced the day-to-day operations of the facility on several levels. The race and gender codes of the era imposed other limitations on the city's ability to demand a certain code of behavior from poor-relief recipients. Other social norms of the period, such as the widespread tolerance of alcohol consumption in the "alcoholic republic," further limited the ability of the poorhouse to impose social controls on its residents.[82] In the early national years, the poorhouse remained as "disorderly" as the city that hosted it.

THE POOR-RELIEF POLICIES of Richmond, born in a colonial setting, had already demonstrated their shortcomings by the 1820s. The establishment of indoor relief early in the century had apparently done little to quell the disorder in the city, and instead had created new managerial problems. Meanwhile, the continuing growth of Richmond and the erratic instability of its economy in the first decades of the nineteenth century had combined to produce more needy residents than ever before. Poor-relief expenses grew, and city authorities could find little solution to the mounting problems. With a financial structure dependent almost entirely upon property taxes, the city had little means to increase its revenue during emergencies such as the Panic of 1819.

Still, in the 1820s, the public continued to understand poverty and poor relief in much the same ways their colonial predecessors had. Poor relief remained a local, publicly funded obligation, and there appeared to be no more stigma attached to public charity than there had been in previous generations. Indeed, the severity of the depression after 1819 made it all the easier to see poverty as a product of economic forces beyond the control of the individual. The poorhouse remained a central civic institution in Richmond. Meanwhile, private charitable efforts began to expand, as middle-class residents (often women) saw numerous needs going unmet by the city.

Beginning in the early 1830s, several important events would profoundly affect poor relief in Richmond. New causes of poverty would appear, and new solutions for it would be offered. Many of the colonial assumptions upon which generations of Virginians had given and received poor relief would evaporate in the decades before the Civil War, as the next chapter details.

CHAPTER THREE

Antebellum Richmond

From Poorhouse to Almshouse

Beginning in the early 1830s, several national, regional, and local trends converged to reconfigure social-welfare policy in Richmond. The integration of the local economy into the developing national market economy, the emergence of powerful evangelical Protestantism, and an accompanying growth of related voluntary associations all worked to influence both poverty and poor relief. Changing gender roles and the articulation of a new mode of maternalist activism, the influence of national reform movements, and a regional reaction against militant abolitionism would likewise influence popular perceptions of poverty and policies toward its amelioration. These trends, combined with explosive population growth and demographic changes, would affect poor relief through the remainder of the antebellum period.

Symbolically, Robert Greenhow stepped down from his longtime position as president of the overseers of the poor in the early 1830s. His successors would demonstrate less concern for the care of the impoverished and more concern for the city budget. This generational shift in attitudes was demonstrated in other ways as well, as the city authorities in charge of public welfare grew more hostile to the poor, more determined to punish the idle, and more convinced that the poor had brought their problems upon themselves. As a result, the city councilmen neglected the maintenance of the poorhouse for years, until, on the eve of the Civil War, they realized the building was beyond repair and would have to be replaced.

By the close of the antebellum period, Richmond's poor-relief system had evolved in line with most other American urban centers. The social philosophies regarding poverty and its relief largely mirrored those predominating in the rest of the country. The city seemed thoroughly modern in its approach to the poor. The sudden outbreak of war, however, would quickly change conditions, and Richmond's social-welfare trajectory would rapidly change as well.

Economic and Demographic Change

By the early 1840s, Richmond's economy had finally rebounded from its earlier setbacks and entered a period of growth, expansion, and prosperity. In the two decades before the Civil War, business and civic leaders in the city felt a heady optimism, despite periodic fluctuations in the economy.[1] The recovery of the city's fortunes was largely produced by several outside factors. The entire state experienced a rebound in the agricultural economy; railroad construction and other internal improvements such as the James River and Kanawha Canal improved trade connections; and the federal tariff afforded considerable protection to the local manufacturing concerns, especially the iron industry.[2]

Richmond's economic growth was concentrated in several key industries: iron manufacturing, tobacco manufacturing, and the continued expansion of the milling industry. The soon-to-be-famous Tredegar Ironworks, along with several other smaller firms, made Richmond the most important "iron city" in the antebellum South.[3] As important as iron was, it was still far outpaced by tobacco manufacturing, which came to be the central industry of the city. In 1850, there were nineteen tobacco factories in Richmond employing fourteen hundred workers; in the following decade, the number of each nearly tripled. The flour-milling industry continued its expansion as well, and by 1860, Richmond was home to the second- and third-largest mills in the country.[4]

Although Richmond was not a single-industry town, it could still be devastated by upheaval in any one of its several major industries. The Panic of 1857, for example, closed the city's tobacco factories and threw thousands of people out of work, with a devastating ripple effect throughout the economy. Antebellum Richmond's maturing manufacturing and commercial sector became fully entangled in the larger national and global markets, and as a result its economy became more vulnerable to the fluctuations in those markets. Because of its manufacturing and commercial sectors, Richmond was more affected by the series of antebellum recessions (1838–43, 1851, 1854, and 1857) than were many other southern cities.[5]

Railroads, canals, and shipping lines connected Richmond to other mercantile and manufacturing cities in the South, but also forged ties far outside the region. Social and cultural connections linked Richmonders to the greater world as well, and late-antebellum residents often lived quite cosmopolitan lives. Merchants frequently traveled to New York and other northern cities on business, often taking family members with them. Back at home, elegant new hotels appeared. Traveling theater groups brought famous actors and opera performances. Richmond's prospering business classes could read the *New York*

Herald, the *Philadelphia Ledger,* and the *Baltimore Sun.* Periodicals such as *Godey's Ladies Book, Scientific American,* and the *Saturday Post* enmeshed local readers in national cultural trends, from women's fashions to educational ideology.[6]

The economic growth of the antebellum years required an expanded labor supply, which manufacturers obtained with some difficulty.[7] The new labor supply to fill this need came from two major sources: slaves hired out by their owners to work in the city, and the sudden appearance of Irish and German immigrants. These new residents, black and white, helped to make Richmond "among the most diverse and prosperous of antebellum American cities."[8]

Richmond tobacco factories hired hundreds of black workers, both slave and free. Immigration supplied the rest of the needed workers for Richmond's expanding manufacturing sector. The James River and Kanawha Canal Company played an important role in recruiting foreign workers, many of whom soon fled the horrific working conditions on the canal project and made their way to Richmond looking for other opportunities.[9] German and Irish immigrants in particular began arriving in the 1840s and 1850s, living in industrial neighborhoods and often residing next to free blacks and slaves.[10]

The Irish in Richmond had numbered fewer than five hundred in 1850 but were more than twenty-two hundred by 1860, an increase of over 400 percent.[11] With relatively few skills and less experience in industrial labor, the Irish immigrants especially moved to the lowest rungs of the job ladder, competing for unskilled positions with free blacks and slaves. They worked as day laborers on the docks, loading and unloading ships, or as unskilled laborers for the city gasworks. In all such jobs, slaves and free blacks worked side by side with immigrants, competing not only for work but also for housing in the city's industrial section.

Competing for the lowest paid jobs in town, disadvantaged by the lack of skills and experience, and with fewer familial or organizational resources than native-born whites, the Irish were the poorest white people in Richmond.[12] They soon began to take up a disproportionate share of public-welfare resources as a result. A small number of immigrants were among the "inmates" of the city poorhouse in the 1850 census (see table 4). But by 1860, the foreign-born population in the poorhouse had reached 50 percent of the total, fifty-seven of whom were Irish.[13] In an episode dripping with historical irony, Richmond's First African Church collected a small donation for the city's Irish poor during the economic depression of 1857.[14]

Germans were the second largest ethnic minority group in antebellum Richmond. Similarly small in number in 1850, Germans constituted nearly 25 percent of the white population by 1860, and one local wondered "whether German or English is the language of the country."[15] Although many Germans were unskilled—such as the laborers imported to work on the massive Kanawha Canal project—many others were artisans, and German immigrants tended to prosper more quickly than the Irish.[16] One study found that, by 1860, 92 percent of all German-born workers in the city qualified as skilled laborers (compared to only 39 percent of all Irish-born workers).[17] Other German immigrants, like William Thalhimer, found their niche as merchants and saloon keepers. One stretch of Broad Street was the home of forty-one German-owned shops in 1850.[18]

Germans created a vibrant ethnic community in the city, complete with two German-language newspapers and dozens of social, religious, and cultural organizations. Social-welfare organizations constituted an important part of that cultural life. The Deutsche Krankengesellschaft (German Society for the Relief of the Sick), founded in 1841,[19] was followed by the Society Shebeth Achim, chartered in 1851 as a mutual-aid society.[20] By 1860, the City Directory listed the following under the heading of "German Societies": the German Beneficial Society, the Schiller Lodge, the Gymnastic Association, the Singing Society, the German Club Eintracht, the Quartette Club, and the Concordia Singing Society.

Native-born whites held mixed opinions about the new influx of foreigners. Some saw immigrants as the solution to the city's labor problems, and applauded their arrival. Samuel Mordecai, for one, believed that the Germans at least were "a valuable acquisition to our city, in many useful trades."[21] Some local residents argued that white labor would be far preferable to blacks, and would be less expensive as well. Others reacted with fear, worried that immigrants would not share their views on slavery and white supremacy. They watched nervously as immigrants lived, worked, drank, and gambled with blacks, and began to air publicly their fears about the riverfront neighborhoods where "large numbers of strangers from all quarters of the world . . . settled together with our extensive negro population."[22] Although some scholars have argued that Richmond's immigrants shared the racial views of natives, owned slaves occasionally, and for those reasons were never a threat to the racial order,[23] contemporaries were not as certain. Especially after the European revolutions of 1848, which brought "radical" refugees into the city, natives observed the activities of the working-class neighborhoods suspiciously.[24]

The German and Irish immigration brought religious diversity, in addition to fears of radicalism and worries about racial solidarity, to a city whose native-born leadership was increasingly drawn to evangelicalism. Irish Catholics founded St. Peter's Roman Catholic Church in 1834. German Jews were sufficient in number by 1840 to establish a second synagogue in the city, Beth Ahabah. And German Catholics formed St. Mary's congregation in 1849.[25] So visible was this ethnic community building that the *Richmond Penny Post* warned that the city was being overrun by "German infidels."[26]

These economic and demographic changes laid a foundation for new perceptions of poverty, with complex—sometimes contradictory—results. On the one hand, the unpredictable industrial economy, with its periodic booms and busts, made it easy upon occasion for observers to see poverty as the product of forces beyond the control of the individual. During one such economic downturn, a local editorial recognized, "There are many causes operating hardly upon the poor at this season. The price of provisions is enormously high, so that the necessaries of life can scarcely be procured even by the laborer who is in employment. The pressure in the money market is so great that many employers have been compelled to suspend operations until money gets easier, so that many who are willing and able to labor cannot find employment. At this season, too, there is necessarily, a suspension of some of the trades, which cannot go on during the cold weather."[27] A recognition of the workings of the business cycle might produce understanding, even sympathy, for its victims.

On the other hand, while the colonial distinctions between the "deserving" and the "undeserving" poor still stood, there were now emerging new understandings of which people fit into which category. Ethnic biases began to influence the assumptions that native-born Richmonders held about the poor, as locals noted the prominence of immigrants in the poorhouse.[28] The residency requirement for public assistance, an inheritance from the English poor laws, still stood as law, but the deluge of immigrants made locals wish it did not. When an economic downturn put factory hands out of work, taxpayers grew more resistant to supporting these "outsiders," regardless of whether they had established legal settlement or not.

The rapid growth of the city also meant that the previously face-to-face relationships were disappearing. No longer was it possible to know every family in town. Increasingly, taxpayers felt that their money went for the support of strangers. One contemporary wrote in 1854, with some exaggeration, "I meet every day hundred[s] of new faces."[29] It became much easier to assume that the stranger was "undeserving," since one had no personal knowledge to the contrary. When Samuel Mordecai noted that the poorhouse was "overflowing, chiefly with foreign paupers," he was also tacitly acknowledging that he, a longtime resident of the city, would have known almost none of the "inmates."[30]

Contemporary social thought about the nature of poverty was also undergoing change. National thinking on welfare adapted to embrace the emerging liberalism associated with market capitalism. Antebellum Americans came to see the collective efforts of individuals, unfettered by artificial restraints on the free market, as the foundation of success, prosperity, and liberty. This version of liberal ideology was more hostile to public relief than to private charity, for the taxes used to pay for public welfare functioned as just the kind of governmental intrusion into the free market that nineteenth-century liberalism abhorred. Poor relief, especially outdoor relief, allowed some people to survive without working, a perilous precedent to set.[31] The same local editorialist, quoted earlier, who recognized that the capitalist business cycle threw able-bodied men out of work, called for increased private charitable relief. He did not mention public welfare.[32]

In the free states, nineteenth-century liberalism fed the growth of "free soil" and "free labor" ideals. In slave states like Virginia, liberalism stood uncomfortably alongside the proslavery ideal. Mercantile interests, such as those that dominated Richmond, had to straddle two competing ideologies, advocating both probusiness and proslavery policies. Southerners remained snared in this ideological trap until released by the Civil War (although emancipation certainly did not result in an instantaneous adoption of the free-labor ideal). In the meantime, liberalism offered antebellum southerners ammunition for an attack on public welfare.[33]

Moreover, the expansion of the American frontier, thanks to the acquisitiveness of the Jeffersonian and Jacksonian generations, offered what appeared to be boundless economic opportunities for all. Unlike overcrowded Europe, the United States had no Malthusian crisis; in fact, just the opposite situation prevailed, as vast new tracts of lands were opened up and waited for laborers to develop them. Those who failed to prosper under such circumstances must not have been trying very hard, thought their contemporaries. Indigence began to look positively un-American.[34]

Evangelicalism and Voluntary Associations

Even more clearly, the evangelical turn in American religion also affected charitable practices in the antebellum period. A nationwide religious impulse, the emergence of evangelical Protestantism, profoundly changed American civic life, although its impact was quite complicated.[35] On the one hand, it encouraged charitable activities that might serve as tools for reaching out to save souls. Evangelicals would for this reason establish a great variety of missions, orphanages, and the like. On the other hand, evangelicalism's emphasis on personal moral responsibility led to a further demonizing of the "unworthy" poor. Evangelicals saw poverty as the product of a moral defect in the individual and stressed individual morality as the key to overcoming poverty. Thomas Cooper's widely read lectures on political economy, published in 1828, neatly summarized this evangelical ideology: rather than relief, the poor needed habits of temperance, thrift, and self-denial.[36] In much the same spirit, a southern evangelical editorialist wrote that poverty was the result of "dissolute habits, intemperate living, idleness, and vice."[37] Reforming those immoral habits would eliminate poverty, whereas poor relief only acted as a temporary ameliorative.

Restraint from the use of alcohol was the most important form of self-denial the poor needed to learn. In case after case, alcoholism appeared in poor families and seemed to middle-class observers to be a cause of poverty. As one temperance advocate put it in 1856, if the temperance movement succeeded, then "shall wickedness in a great measure cease, our alms-houses, jail and penitentiaries will stand as empty, silent, monuments of the degradation and misery which Intemperance produced."[38] The crusade against alcohol then took on the trappings of a charitable movement, a means of ending poverty and suffering. But at the same time, temperance advocates condemned even more strongly than before those who resisted their message of personal morality and succumbed to "vice."

Evangelicals also saw charity as a means of diminishing the tensions between the classes. Most visible in cities like Richmond, the "feelings of envy, jealousy, and even hostility" toward the rich might be assuaged by the generous distribution of private charity. In an age of growing class distinctions, charity might prevent class antagonisms, or even revolution.[39] But it had to be private charity, which would bind the poor to the rich; public charity could only bind the poor to the state, not the wealthy. Evangelical charity might also serve as a counter to the radicalism being imported by foreign immigrants. Although it would be inaccurate to suggest that evangelicalism was a direct response to immigration, since many other factors contributed to the emergence of the movement, it would be accurate to see immigrants as providing a particular focus for evangelical efforts.

Evangelical religion also provided a framework from which women might engage in organized charitable activities, which would come to have enormous impact on social-welfare practices. Evangelical women's organizations, grounded in a maternalist ideology, focused in particular on the needs of poor women and their children.[40] Southern women embraced this new public role with nearly as much fervor as their northern counterparts, eager to utilize their skills and resources in activities that would improve their local communities. The opportunities for such organized activities were most numerous in urban settings, and women's benevolent associations flowered throughout the region during these years.[41] And, unlike in cities such as Charleston, women's organizations in Richmond remained vigorously active throughout the remainder of the antebellum period.[42]

Although staid Episcopal Richmond had largely resisted the evangelical impulse at the opening of the century,[43] by the 1830s Richmond had become an evangelical city, with a plethora of new charities and voluntary associations.[44] Like evangelicals throughout the region and the country, Richmonders engaged in a brand of reform that focused on personal morality: domestic missions, Bible societies, and temperance unions all worked to convert the individual sinner to a personal salvation that would then improve the quality of the convert's life.[45] Beginning in the 1830s, evangelicals hired city missionaries to evangelize among the poor. The Richmond City Mission Society supported two such missionaries, while the City Mission Sewing Circle of the First Baptist Church supported a third.[46] By 1860, Richmond housed a local chapter of the Young Men's Christian Association, the American Tract Society, the Bible Society of Virginia, the Young Men's Aid Society (Methodist Episcopal), and dozens of other organizations.[47] Temperance groups were among the most popular forms of voluntary associations in the city. As early as 1834, more than one thousand residents of the city had announced their support of temperance in some fashion. By the 1840s, there were multiple organizations from which the convert might choose, the Sons of Temperance and the Washingtonians among them.[48] In 1860, the city directory listed six different divisions of the Sons of Temperance.[49]

While some benevolent organizations attempted to help the poor by moral reform, other associations addressed poverty by direct assistance. Churches regularly dispensed aid to their own needy members. As Suzanne Lebsock has noted, church membership could serve as a form of antebellum social insurance. In exchange for years of membership and service, an elderly or sick congregant could turn to the church in time of need.[50] Church-based organizations also offered charity to those outside their own membership by contributing to the various nonsectarian associations in the city, such as the Dorcas Society, which provided clothing to poor children.[51]

Still other evangelical efforts were intended to prevent poverty through self-help. These mutual-aid societies took various forms but generally worked by pooling resources that were then given to members in time of need. Aid might be in the form of unemployment benefits, medical coverage, or burial benefits. Mutual-aid societies often formed within churches and served as an endogamous charity, binding a community together through mutual assistance. Mutual-aid societies also reflected the racial, ethnic, and sectarian divisions of the city, as people came together to help those most like themselves.

Richmond's first, and largest, black church established such a self-help mechanism within a few years of its founding. The First African Baptist Church, created in 1841 by splitting off from the previously biracial First Baptist Church, established a Poor Saints Fund in 1848. Church trustees collected donations, visited needy households, and attended to "all applications of aid." The Poor Saints Fund distributed over two hundred dollars a year to assist the "needy [and] helpless from disease or old age" of their own church. (In 1856, the Poor Saints committee asked the deacons for permission to distribute charity to those outside the church membership, but the deacons refused the request.)[52] Other similar organizations for African Americans are harder to document because of their desire for secrecy. Members feared they would be arrested for illegally congregating. Suspicious whites believed these secret societies to be widespread, and also believed that they were less charitable in nature than subversive.[53]

Charitable activity in black churches did in fact offer an occasional direct challenge to slavery. Members of the First African Baptist, pooling their resources, helped individual slaves to purchase their freedom. The practice was not widespread and was usually directed toward ministers and their families, but it nevertheless helped to unravel slavery in the urban setting. Free blacks also appealed to black churches for money to emigrate to Africa. Black churches also provided funds for the temporary relief of those waiting in Norfolk to board ship, and then raised further funds to build churches and schools in Liberia.[54] Such activities gave charity a uniquely political meaning to the black community of Richmond.

Slaves found mutual-aid activities especially critical, as they would likely find themselves denied public relief no matter how dire their need. Since the poor-relief system presumed that owners cared for their slaves, the city simply routinely denied slaves any public assistance.[55] But Richmond's slaves, many of whom were hired out and had absentee owners, might not have access to their owners' benevolence. They were largely responsible for themselves, permitted to find their own jobs and their own housing.[56] This highly desired autonomy, however, also meant caring for themselves in time of sickness or other problems. Unable to turn to the city for help, then, urban slaves filled an important gap in the social-welfare system through mutual aid.

Sectarian competition played some role in this mania for voluntary organizations.[57] Catholics were fearful of losing members to the militant evangelical Protestants. Protestants were suspicious of Catholic "secrecy" and were openly aggressive. Richmond's Jews were inclined to be very cautious in their public actions, lest they incite latent anti-Semitism.[58] Moreover, the antebellum public officials seemed little inclined to use their poorhouse as a means of conversion, so the sectarian impetus required that each religious group would need to sponsor its own private asylums.[59] The Ladies Hebrew Association was founded in 1849 as a mutual-benefit society. It was soon followed by a men's group called Shebeth Achim in 1851, and the Hebrew Beneficial Society in 1852, both of which rendered assistance to members in case of death or illness.[60] Catholics in the city had begun operating an orphan asylum in the early 1840s under the charge of the Sisters of Charity.[61] During the 1850s, Richmond's Catholics also formed the Young Catholic's Friends Society, St. Vincent's Catholic Beneficial Society, and the Hibernian Society.[62] This sectarian competition would grow even more pronounced in the postbellum years, when sectarian foundling homes will compete for abandoned babies who can then be adopted into the "proper" faith.

While most of these voluntary associations intended to serve a small group of people, one organization, the Union Benevolent Society, saw the entire city as its "mission."[63] Founded in 1836 as an ecumenical women's effort, the UBS has been termed by one historian as the "most ambitious" of these new evangelical organizations. The Union Benevolent Society divided the city into twenty districts and assigned two "visitors" to each. The visitors canvassed their districts to collect information that would "ascertain the habits and circumstances of the poor, the causes of their poverty, to devise means for the improvement of their situation, [and] to suggest plans of calling into existence their own endeavors to improve their condition." Their initial canvass uncovered 111 poor families, with many "worthy females who were suffering extreme want from their inability to procure employment."[64]

The proposed solution of the UBS was to open a "Depository of Work" for poor women, reviving the idea of the "House of Industry" from an earlier generation. The Depository intended originally to provide work for one hundred women, but the inability of the organization to raise sufficient funds required the operation be scaled down to thirty women.[65] In addition to the depository, the UBS conducted sewing classes for young girls and distributed clothing, blankets, fuel, and money to the poor in the city.[66] A Gentlemen's Benevolent Society organized to support the women's group, assigning visitors for each district. Male visitors were instructed clearly that their role was auxiliary to the female visitors: they were to visit "either alone, or with a Lady Visitor, or making such visits as she may suggest, and reporting to her, all cases which in your opinion require and render proper her assistance; but in no case will you give directions for the supplying any want."[67] The women of the UBS wanted male assistance but insisted on retaining full control over the operation.

The UBS continued to operate throughout the remainder of the antebellum period and came to represent in the public mind organized women's activity in the city. The "ladies of the Union Benevolent" and the "ladies of the city" almost came to be interchangeable terms. The strength of this organization may explain why Richmond never developed a branch of the Association for the Improvement of the Condition of the Poor. A growing national organization in the 1840s and 1850s, the AICP established branches in Norfolk and Petersburg, but not Richmond.[68] Its activities, nearly identical to those of the Union Benevolent, were effectively preempted by the UBS in Richmond.

The antebellum years, then, saw the development of numerous, sometimes overlapping, charitable organizations. Both clergy and laity might be engaged in multiple philanthropic efforts. One local minister confessed to his brother that he had "so much business to transact for various boards, societies, etc." that he had "scarcely any opportunity for the prosecution of those branches of knowledge which a minister should be well versed in."[69] The multiplicity of organizations also meant that at least some of the poor had several places to which they could turn in times of need. Those with a church affiliation had the most options; those without any church membership or other mutual-aid association might have only the city's municipal charity on which to rely.

Moreover, poor women and their children had more numerous organizations working on their behalf than did men. This was due partly to the continuing public perception that women and children nearly always fell into the category of "deserving" poor. Dependent upon a male breadwinner and rendered "helpless" without one, women and children had been seen as the most deserving of the deserving poor since the colonial era. But the larger number of charitable endeavors directed at women and children during the antebellum era was also the product of the rise of evangelical women's organizational activism, which was grounded in maternalism and which concentrated most efforts toward women and children. The evangelical and maternalist ideologies also promoted the expansion of older private associations. The Female Humane Association, founded in 1805, expanded its orphanage for girls substantially during the antebellum period, responding to the new energy of, and respect for, women's public activism.[70]

Thus the effect of both evangelicalism and changing gender roles on the direction of poor relief was profound. To a lesser degree, social welfare in Richmond was also affected by the rise of militant abolitionism and the region's increasingly defensive posture toward slavery. William Lloyd Garrison's abolitionist newspaper, *The Liberator*, begun in 1831, is often credited as the starting point for the more militant version of abolitionism. In response, white southerners rallied in defense of the peculiar institution and began crafting an interpretation of slavery that emphasized its positive benefits.[71] Poverty and poor relief appeared in the rhetoric of both the militant abolitionists and the aggressive proslavery ideologues.

In the northern states, the movements for temperance, abolitionism, and women's rights were connected at many points. Abolitionists attempted to promote their cause as a form of Christian charity, adopting the language of "benevolence" and "reform" for their movement. One abolitionist organization even renamed its publication the *Philanthropist.*[72] The similar ideologies that supported these movements, the common actions they undertook, and the overlapping memberships of the various organizations linked these efforts. Those links did not escape southern observers: one writer in *DeBow's Review* called such people "the abolitionist-woman's-rights-spiritual-rapper-negro-server-reformer[s]."[73]

Southern apologists responded with a critique of northern "free society" that concentrated on the poverty of whites in northern cities. Richmond's "J.H." wrote that "the amount of positive beggary and want, and of consequent crime and misery, which meets you everywhere in the Northern cities, would be absolutely revolting, if it did not excite the profoundest sympathy and commiseration." "J.H." contrasted these "consequences of the radical vice of 'Free Society' " with "the happy and prosperous 'laboring population' of the South. Paupers, indeed, we have among us . . . but these in the main are the really old and infirm, the disabled and diseased. . . . So long as the system of slavery is maintained in its integrity, there can be no paupers in the land."[74]

As Barbara Bellows has written, as long as the evangelical movements focused on personal morality, southerners could feel comfortable in this nation-wide religious phenomenon.[75] Once abolitionism seemed to "taint" evangelical reforms, many southerners began to distance themselves from previously popular movements, such as temperance, in order not to associate with ones unacceptable in the South, such as abolitionism and women's rights. The colonization movement suffered similar stigma after the rise of abolitionism. The effort to colonize free blacks in Liberia served many purposes, of course, some of which might not be categorized as admirable. But many of the proponents of colonization considered it an act of benevolence, a moral duty to an oppressed and suffering class of people. Others saw it as a Christian mission, a means of spreading Christianity to the "heathens" of Africa. But in the changed political climate of the 1830s, colonization began to look like a covert version of abolitionism, and its supporters drifted away from the movement. The southern colonization movement went into decline.[76]

Most other charitable activities escaped the "taint" of northern radicalism and continued to thrive in the antebellum years. Many of these so-called "private" charities also received substantial public support, creating an interconnected public/private sphere of poor relief. The city provided funding to several private groups, such as the three-hundred-dollar annual contribution to the Female Humane Association, and similar support for the Male Orphan Society. The Male Orphan Asylum entered into an agreement with the city to take from the poorhouse several white male children, too young to be bound out, and the city would contribute to their upkeep.[77] The city also subsidized Sunday schools. Beginning in 1824, the school commissioners in Richmond appropriated sums for every Sunday school pupil.[78] Similarly, the UBS applied for, and received, annual subsidies from the city. The city provided support in the form of tax relief for several private charitable organizations, including the Sisters of Charity orphan asylum.[79]

City subsidies to private charities, a practice common throughout the country, continued to blur the line between public and private welfare in the antebellum period. Although antebellum Americans articulated a distinction between public and private charities, in contrast to their colonial predecessors, the distinction was often honored in the breach. Private organizations depended on public funds for their operations; the city council relied on private citizens to act as "friendly visitors" who made investigations and referrals for the worthy poor. Despite the contemporary celebration of private charity over public welfare, the two in fact remained heavily entangled.

In sum, the wide-ranging, often overlapping charitable and voluntary associations in Richmond served multiple purposes. They helped to reinforce ties of ethnicity, race, and religion. They provided opportunities for sociability and religious expression. They allowed non-elites the chance to operate in a very public space. And, for some at least, they afforded the prospects of chipping away at the restrictions of race and gender in a slave-based patriarchal society.

Public Welfare

These private charitable organizations, as numerous as they grew to be, never displaced the public-welfare system. As Barbara Bellows has noted, at no time in the nineteenth century was there a "golden age of benevolence" in which the generosity of neighbors and private charities cared for all the needy.[80] Nor, as Peter Mandler has argued, did the forms in which that charity was offered ever entirely match the precise needs of the poor.[81] Bible tracts, while possibly welcomed by the recipients, might not meet the immediate needs of the family that day. Instead, Richmond's public-relief efforts continued to grow even as the private charities multiplied. The city officials who ran the public-welfare programs were, naturally, influenced by the contemporary ideas regarding poverty and its relief. Themselves members of the evangelical middle classes, welfare officials absorbed and implemented the ideologies of their peers, and those ideas began to affect the distribution of public relief.

Take, for example, the officials' understanding of the causes of pauperism. At times, the city authorities seemed to understand that inflation pushed the economically marginal into poverty. The overseers of the poor understood that their own ability to trim costs sometimes rested on the "diminished price of bacon, fish, and foodstuffs generally." They understood that their own increased expenses were explained by "the increased charge of subsistence," or "an advance of from twenty to thirty per cent in the price of bacon, fish and meal." Yet, at the same time, the prevailing evangelical emphasis on personal morality and personal responsibility for poverty could overpower the economic explanations of the causes of need. "It is well known to the City Council," read the minutes in 1842, "that the most fruitful sources of pauperism, and ultimate causes of crime . . . have their origin in those departures from the code of morality which are mainly visited by only the censure of public opinion a penalty which, all experience proves, is too feeble to suppress or cure."[82]

The language used by city officials in the 1850s indicated that their feelings toward the poor had hardened considerably in these years. No longer did the "reform" of the poor seem possible. "There are doubtless exceptions," said Joseph Anderson, owner of the Tredegar Ironworks, but "return to a life of sobriety, industry and honesty is believed to be a rare case with such." Anderson was convinced that idle and drunken parents sent their children out to beg and steal to support them in their vice. "[L]et their children be taken from them and placed in [asylums] before they are ruined by the evil influences surrounding them at home."[83]

These hardened feelings toward the poor resulted in an unwillingness to spend on their behalf, as detailed in figure 2. In 1839, Richmond's total budget was $85,000. Of that, $5,000 went for poor relief, and another $2,000 for public schools—considered charity schools in this period—and the orphan asylum.[84] Combined, these poor-relief expenses constituted 8.2 percent of the total budget in 1839. By 1860, however, the figure had dropped to 2.9 percent of the budget. (Total expenditures were $501,296.13. Of that figure, $9,697.28 was for the city's poor, and $4,958.13 was for public schools.)[85]

Even with this reduced commitment, the taxpaying public was unhappy, because overall tax rates were on the rise. The city's expenses continued to grow, as the city took on new functions, such as waterworks. In the wake of a 30 percent across the board tax hike in 1855, local taxpayers held a public protest, led by attorney James Lyons.[86] Although taxpayers did not necessarily blame public welfare alone for the rise in tax rates, residents looked for any way to reduce the tax burden, including cutting poor relief.

Resistance to public support for immigrants also found expression in the overseers' reports. "An evil of considerable magnitude has increased and we fear will continue to increase," wrote the overseers in 1852, "so long as the large number of white labourers are employed on the public works in the vicinity in Richmond. Many of them are foreigners who have not acquired a permanent or legal residence in the County where they are employed, or elsewhere in the State.

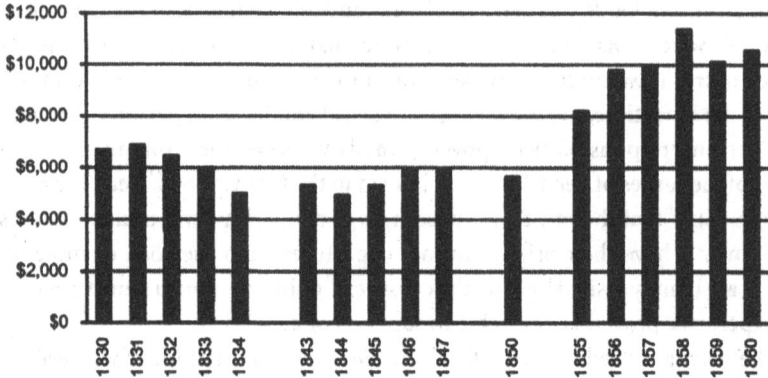

Figure 2. *Total Relief Costs, Richmond, 1830–1860*
Sources: Auditors of Public Accounts, State of Virginia; Annual Reports, Overseers of the Poor, Richmond City (broken series).

Sickness overtakes them, and their improvidence compels them to seek shelter in some charitable Institution." Desperate not to incur recurring expenses for such "foreigners," the overseers were willing "to pay their passage to their native Country," as they did for four such individuals in 1858.[87]

So, city officials reflected the concerns and biases of their peers. Notably, where the previous generation had witnessed considerable conflict between the city council and the overseers of the poor, no such conflicts appear in the records by the late 1830s. These two groups of middle-class leaders had reached a consensus on social policy, a consensus heavily influenced by the factors discussed previously. Table 3 summarizes the statistics on the growth of the city's relief program from 1830 to 1860. These numbers suggest several ways in which the attitudes toward public charity were changing in the antebellum period.

Beginning in 1833, the city dramatically cut its outdoor relief. The numbers receiving assistance in their homes dwindled down to single digits, and the amounts expended were cut to nearly nothing. At the same time, the numbers institutionalized in the poorhouse steadily climbed. This placed Richmond firmly in the contemporary national trend toward retrenchment in outdoor relief. A few cities abolished outdoor relief altogether, such as Philadelphia in 1827 and Chicago in 1848.[88] Richmond did not abandon outdoor relief completely, but certainly reversed its previous reliance on outdoor relief in favor of institutionalization.

Although for most antebellum years there are merely statistical compilations, there are extant two detailed reports that list all poorhouse residents by name.

One is for the year 1836–37, the other for the year 1850–51.[89] In addition, the federal census for 1850 and 1860 provides some data on the current residents of the poorhouse. These sources contain different sets of data and therefore cannot be compared at all points, but collectively they nevertheless permit a more detailed scrutiny into the characteristics of the indoor poor (see table 4 for a compilation of the demographic data).

The most consistent statistic in the four documents was race: in each of the sources, whites were the overwhelming majority of poorhouse inmates. More-over, whites were increasing their demographic dominance as time passed: in the 1830s figures, blacks were 21 percent of the whole, but by the 1860 census, they were only 12 percent of the whole poorhouse population. This is the product of the convergence of two factors. Throughout the period, slaves were mostly excluded from the poorhouse and were dependent upon their owners for assistance. This would mean that African Americans would be underrepresented in the poorhouse. At the same time, after 1830, the black population in Richmond was declining as a percentage of the whole. The white population was increasing far more rapidly in the decades after 1830 and was increasing its numbers in the poorhouse as well (see table 1).

Race also played a role in the age of the inmates: in none of the three sets of documents were there black children present in the poorhouse. White children appear relatively frequently, either by virtue of birth in the facility or by accompanying their mothers. But black inmates were almost always elderly: the average age of the fifteen blacks in the 1860 census was sixty-one, while the average age of whites was thirty-seven.

The sex ratio was more volatile than the racial figures. Men were 56 percent of the total in 1836–37; down to 48 percent of the total in 1850–51; and back up to 57 percent of the total in 1860. This fluctuation may be seen as evidence of the gendered nature of poverty. The sources of women's dependency and poverty were relatively constant: pregnancy, childbirth, and widowhood were typical events in women's life cycles and did not respond directly to the business cycle. Although men certainly found themselves in the poorhouse as a result of illness and age, men's dependency and poverty were often the product of economic conditions as well. More men than women may have been thrown out of work during the recessions of the 1830s and the late 1850s.

The 1836–37 report listed a total of 183 people admitted to the poorhouse that year, including two identified as slaves. Table 4 details the reasons given for their institutionalization. Not surprisingly, fully a quarter of the inmates were ill, another tenth of the admissions had injuries, eight were admitted for old age, seven were "dependents" because of conditions such as insanity, and ten were "intemperate." Although this particular document did not ask for a report of how many were considered "able to work," clearly very few would have had the ability to work at anything resembling physical labor.

In the 1850–51 report, the question of whether the inmates were able to work was addressed explicitly. Of the 236 admitted during the year, 155 were listed as "unable to work." The explanations given for their inability to work echoed those of the 1836–37 report: illness, injury, dependency, age, and intemperance.[90] Those able to work did so for an average of sixty-five days each, doing a variety of unskilled tasks. Women were mostly assigned to wash (nineteen women), to assist in nursing (fifteen women), or to sew (eight women). Men were most commonly required to work on the streets (seventeen men) or in the garden or the graveyards (ten men). A handful of men worked at other odd jobs, like painting, driving the poorhouse "cart," or assisting the cook.

Age did not exempt residents from work: John Birchell, listed as old and infirm, nevertheless spent a total of thirty days painting and whitewashing; Martha Bullefent, described as old and delicate, spent fourteen days sewing. Pregnancy did not automatically excuse women from work either: Sally Dougherty assisted the nurse for eighty-six days, despite her pregnancy and delivery. Indeed, the only group that appeared to be automatically exempt from work at the poorhouse were children. No children were credited with any days at work. (Several older boys were instead apprenticed outside the poorhouse. William Pitts, a white boy "about" twelve years old, and James Suttle, a white boy "about" thirteen, were both "delivered" to E. W. Robinson to learn carpentry.)

How the poor of Richmond viewed the poorhouse or poor relief remains difficult to ascertain. They have left behind no firsthand accounts to record their impressions, and historians are compelled instead to read between the lines of behavior for clues. The evidence in these reports is decidedly mixed. On the one hand, in both compiled reports, several inmates were listed as having run away from the facility. The 1836–37 listing included nine runaways out of the total of 183; the 1850–51 returns showed twenty-one runaways out of 236 admissions. The actions of these thirty "inmates" might be read to mean that they found the conditions in the poorhouse undesirable enough to vote with their feet. Of those thirty runaways, however, ten returned to the facility within the year, making it more difficult to interpret their actions.

Nearly all those who absconded were white (only one black out of the thirty), and most were male (only eleven women of the thirty). This could be evidence that white males found the facility the most repressive, or that white males felt they had the most options outside the facility. Poor blacks (who were mostly elderly, as noted earlier) and poor women (many of whom had young children with them) may have felt they had fewer resources at their disposal, and stayed in the poorhouse when admitted. Richmond at this time had no "old folks homes," no "maternity homes," and few orphanages. Blacks and women relied heavily on the city poorhouse to provide those services in times of need.

Other patterns of behavior provoke doubts that the poor lived in dread of the poorhouse, for they turned to it over and over in times of need. In the 1836–37 roster, at least seven people availed themselves of the city's charity more than once; in the 1850–51 listing, thirty-one residents returned to the facility within the year. Moreover, six people show up on *both* lists, utilizing public charity over at least a fifteen-year period. At least *some* city residents then did not exhibit a fear of the institution, but rather sought out its benefits time and again.

Nor was the poorhouse somehow the equivalent of the penitentiary, with compulsory confinement. The poor were not detained there against their will. With a couple of exceptions, they arrived at the poorhouse voluntarily. (The exceptions were children, who had little say in their own affairs, and those who were ill or otherwise incapacitated and were brought to the poorhouse by the "sick wagon." One might see them as "involuntarily" confined, although as soon as they regained consciousness or clarity they could leave the facility if they chose.) If they could convince the overseers that they held settlement or other rights, they could not be refused admittance in most instances. And they were generally free to leave at their own discretion as well, again with a couple of exceptions. (Doctors were supposed to discharge those who were present for sickness or childbirth. All inmates were supposed to check out formally, presumably so that the superintendent could inspect them before departure, to make certain they were taking with them only their own belongings. Those who "absconded in the night" chose not to submit to this inspection.)

Furthermore, no matter how harsh the regime might be, the poor could often find imaginative ways to put the institutions to work for them. Even if "forbiddingly deterrent," the poorhouse might serve as a refuge from a violent husband. Children could be cared for temporarily, allowing their mothers to take "live-in" domestic jobs.[91] In other cities the poor were found to have sold or pawned goods given them by poor-relief officials. Local officials were outraged at the abuse; the poor perceived this as putting the goods to their most practical use. Although records have not surfaced that document the use of this strategy in Richmond, it would not be surprising to find that local residents exercised this kind of creativity with their limited resources.[92]

How the overseers determined just which of the many poor residents of Richmond should be institutionalized and which should receive relief in their homes remains a mystery. There are no records extant that discuss the criteria by which these privileged few were chosen. Accounts for 1853 and 1855 list seven recipients of outdoor relief each, with short notations about their condition.[93] These provide only hints about the characteristics of the outdoor poor. The most obvious fact is that all those receiving outdoor relief were white. Although small numbers of both slaves and free blacks show up in records of the poorhouse, only whites were included in the outdoor poor.[94] Three individuals appear in both lists: Mr. Tyree, who was paralyzed and bedridden; Mrs. Holland, a widow with "a large family"; and Miss Blount, old and infirm. The remaining names bore similar notations: "old and infirm," "a case of sickness," and so on. There is very little here that appears to distinguish these individuals from those who were institutionalized. But the respectful titles recorded in the returns—"Miss" Blount, "Mr." Tyree, and the like—are dissimilar from other records. For reasons that are not detailed in the official reports, these individuals had earned a level of respect from poor-relief officials in Richmond, and that respect allowed them to stay in their homes while receiving city aid. By means that have escaped documentation, these individuals had demonstrated either a degree of deference or a level of respectability that earned them outdoor relief. Beyond these scant details, the outdoor poor remain a historical mystery.

The 1850s: Hostility and Neglect

By the 1850s, it appeared that the city wished to turn over responsibility for outdoor relief nearly entirely to the private sector. The annual requests of the Union Benevolent Society for city funding were always approved, and the level of support given increased over time. By January 1858, the appropriation was up to $1,000.[95] The city's own direct support for the outdoor poor for that fiscal year amounted to only $140 (see table 2).

Similarly, the council responded enthusiastically to a plan for a privately run soup house, to which the city would have only to give minimum contributions. "An unnamed individual" approached the overseers in 1843 with the proposal: the overseers would provide seed money to buy equipment and rent the building; the anonymous philanthropist did the rest. He solicited donations, including meat from local butchers, and then distributed the soup. During the winter of 1843, up to two hundred people a day, "mostly widows and orphans," received rations of soup. The overseers spent only seventy dollars on this soup house and "believe[d] that no part of their expenditure was of greater service." They then contacted the Gentlemen's Benevolent Society about continuing the program, and possibly expanding it to more than one soup house, with continued city funding.[96]

In one sense, the dramatic cuts in outdoor relief were at least partly a product of creative accounting. The figures for outdoor relief reflected only the numbers of people who received monthly stipends from the city. But simultaneously, the city continued to make annual appropriations for fuel for the poor, and those appropriations were not included in the reports on outdoor relief. For example, in January 1855, the council appropriated $300 to the Union Benevolent Society for the use of the poor. But the city reported that year that it spent only $132.56 on the outdoor poor (see table 2). Similarly, the city gave $1,500 for the use of the outdoor poor in July 1849,[97] while reporting that it supported only twelve outdoor poor at a cost of $53.95 for the year. In other words, the city may have cut down on the number of people it directly maintained in their own homes on a regular basis, but it still supported hundreds more of the outdoor on an irregular basis by subsidizing private charitable efforts. Nineteenth-century Richmonders practiced a form of privatization of public relief, which shifted some (but not all) responsibility to the private sector while providing public funds for the effort.

By relinquishing the outdoor poor to the private sector as much as possible, the city could then concentrate its resources on the indoor poor. Thanks in part to the concerted effort to cut back on outdoor relief, the numbers in the poorhouse grew steadily. The result was overcrowding. The building, "designed originally to accommodate from seventy to seventy-five," had by 1847 reached a daily attendance of more than a hundred. In desperation, the city moved "all the black paupers and a portion of the white ones" to the city's smallpox hospital. "Should the City require it for its original purpose," that is, if there were to be an outbreak of contagious disease, "much suffering among the paupers would be the consequence."[98]

Despite much contradictory evidence on the subject, contemporaries continued to believe that institutionalization was a more cost-efficient method of poor relief than outdoor relief. Institutionalization also offered more opportunities to supervise the activities of the relief recipient and facilitated efforts to compel the poor to work. With even more determination than in the 1820s, city relief officials sought ways to make the poorhouse inmates work. Despite assurances from the overseers that "[t]he paupers themselves perform most of the labour necessarily connected with the management of the Institution," the city council looked for new venues for their efforts. In 1839, the council directed the overseers to "enquire into the expediency of cultivating the silk mulberry on the grounds owned by the city with a view to introduce into the Poor-house a Cocoonery for the production of raw silk by the labour of the inmates." Three years later, the council discussed plans for purchasing "junk" for making oakum, or materials for manufacturing willow baskets that the inmates could then sell. Other ideas were to put the paupers to work sweeping streets, hauling manure, or collecting trash and ashes.[99]

Although the city had hoped that inmate labor would be sufficient to cultivate a large garden on the poorhouse grounds to produce vegetables for the inmates' own use, instead the keeper of the house ended up doing most of the labor, using his own horse, plus some limited work done by "the superannuated paupers." The next year, the same situation prevailed: since none of the paupers was able to plough, "we were compelled to hire a man a few months for that purpose."[100]

Most such plans to put the poor to work were doomed to failure, even for the small number of inmates capable of doing some labor. Basket making, spinning, silk production, and the like required the development of skills, and the vast majority of able-bodied inmates stayed on in the poorhouse for very short periods, too short to learn a new skill. Those who stayed longer periods of time were the extremely elderly and infirm, who would not be productive laborers either.[101]

During the 1850s, the city council returned to the idea of a workhouse, that perennial panacea of public welfare. The council had discussed a workhouse during the previous decade, declaring "we think [it] would do more to rid the City of pauperism generally, than any other means or mode that we can devise." The city approached the state legislature, asking for a revision of the city charter to provide the legal authority to establish a workhouse. That done, the council then appointed a committee to begin plans for building such a facility. By 1842, they had begun referring to the poorhouse as the "Poor house, Work house, and House of Correction," although no new buildings had yet been erected. But the planning for the workhouse dragged on slowly, and some members of the council appeared to be purposefully slowing down the process. A decade later, there had still been no real action, and the public demands for a workhouse grew more insistent. The ladies of the Union Benevolent Society "and a large number of citizens" asked the council in 1852 to take "this subject into immediate consideration."[102]

Yet another committee was appointed in 1855 to consider the establishment of a workhouse. This committee, chaired by Joseph R. Anderson, reported that the inmates of the poorhouse "are for the most part vagrants. Many of them are able to work but no adequate provision has been made to secure the proper performance of labor." The city jail was also filled with "large numbers of worthless vagrants supported in idleness at public expense, thus offering a premium to vagrancy." The committee recommended that the council apply to the state legislature for authority to convert the jail into a jail and workhouse. The male convicts would be taken daily from the jail to work on the city streets, or other jobs. The female convicts would be "kept at hard labor in doors." By removing all the "idle vagrants," the poorhouse could then be "elevated into a House of Refuge for the unfortunate but virtuous poor of your City, who are now deterred from seeking refuge within its walls by the notoriously degraded character of its inmates." The council approved an appropriation for building a workhouse as part of the city jail, not at the poorhouse.[103]

The workhouse's association with the jail rather than the poorhouse was deliberate. The workhouse was seen as a place of punishment, not a "House of Industry." The plans for the workhouse explicitly rejected the establishment of workshops or the use of the "prisoners" on "mechanical pursuits." The committee clearly stated that allowing skilled labor "as a punishment would be less salutory than the Common labor as hereinbefore proposed."[104] The workhouse, under the control of the city police, rarely appeared in subsequent records of the overseers of the poor.

Attaching the workhouse to the city jail rather than to the poorhouse also permitted Richmond to escape the problems that plagued other cities like Charleston. Charleston's city council permitted its workhouse, in addition to housing the "idle poor," to be used to incarcerate those convicted of crimes and sentenced to hard labor. In July 1849, this situation erupted in violence, as slaves who had been sentenced to terms in the workhouse staged an uprising, attacked several whites, and escaped the facility.[105]

Richmond must not be considered unique in this late-antebellum "crackdown" on the poor. Social-welfare thought throughout the country mirrored that of the city. Indeed, city leaders seemed fully versed in current national trends. Middle-class urban southerners like those in Richmond had access to a wide variety of literature that disseminated contemporary welfare thought. As Edward L. Ayers has described in his work on penal reform, southern urban leaders were among "the most cosmopolitan elements of their society." As such, they "shared many of the values and concerns of the outside world."[106] Many such southerners, both men and women, had personal contacts in northern reform circles. Membership in national organizations such as the Washingtonians and the Sons of Temperance helped to fashion links between the local and the national reformers.[107] The presence of local branches of the Association for the Improvement of the Condition of the Poor, in Norfolk and Petersburg, demonstrated formal institutional ties between southern and northern reformers.

Local reformers occasionally had even more direct opportunities to observe northern models of social welfare. In 1859, Charles Dimmock of the Virginia Public Guard visited New York and took a tour of a boys' orphanage. He came away impressed with the quality of the facility.[108] John Hartwell Cocke attended the World Temperance Convention in 1852 (although he came away less than impressed with the "strong-minded women" he found there.)[109] Local reformers did not hesitate to ask "outsiders" for advice on current reform questions.[110] Other southern-based reformers, such as South Carolina's Francis Lieber, spread the word about current thinking on contemporary issues. Lieber translated Tocqueville's book on prisons and agitated for the establishment of a penitentiary in his adopted state.[111] And still other southerners enthusiastically disseminated northern literature on behalf of their chosen causes.[112]

Southerners also gained familiarity with northern trends in social welfare when northern reformers actively courted them. The crusader Dorothea Dix, for example, spent much time in southern states during the 1850s, spreading her ideas about penal reform and treatment of the insane. Because Dix traveled widely, published frequently, and was warmly received in the South, she acted as a one-woman conduit of northern social-welfare thought. The impact of her activities in the region is immeasurable.[113]

Thus national trends in social welfare penetrated the South in many ways, and southern policies reflected the impact. Changing attitudes toward poverty and poor relief after 1830 were embedded in the efforts to eliminate outdoor relief and build a workhouse. These sterner attitudes also countenanced an official disinterest in the poorhouse. The city council began to neglect the facility, only loosely supervising its maintenance and operations. Repairs were authorized only when conditions grew severe, and were done on the cheap. Like urban officials throughout the country, who concluded that poorhouses had failed to reduce relief expenses as promised, Richmond's city council largely abandoned the facility and allowed it to deteriorate.[114]

Moreover, official stinginess might further reduce the applications for admission to the poorhouse. If the conditions were miserable enough, it might serve to discourage all but the truly desperate from seeking such public relief. Allowing the building to grow overcrowded, understaffed, and unappealing effectively stigmatized the poorhouse and anyone who entered it. As Michael Katz has argued, "Poorhouses, which shut the old and sick away from their friends and relatives, were supposed to deter the working class from asking for poor relief."[115]

While the city council practiced not-so-benign neglect, the overseers of the poor began growing concerned about the condition of the poorhouse. As early as the 1840s, the overseers complained that the building was "in a very dilapidated state" and needed extensive repairs. Even worse, it appeared, were the recently built "huts for the accommodation of the blacks, which are situated in rear of the main building." They were "in wretched order" and probably beyond repair. The council approved the recommendations for the repairs, but again limited appropriations to the smallest figures possible.[116]

By 1859, the combination of overcrowding and studied neglect of the poorhouse had produced predictable results: the building was in shambles. A group of city council members who visited in June were horrified at what they saw.

"Except the whitewashing of the interior walls, which had been lately done, there is no indication that any repairs or painting had been put upon the building for many years. They found the kitchen smoking badly, and the whole house dirty and filthy to the last degree. Nor is the furniture in the house in any better condition than the house itself. The sleeping accommodations of the inmates are a disgrace to the city . . . the blankets and coverlids too dirty for a respectable dog kennel."[117]

The investigating committee, chaired by attorney Peachy R. Grattan, concluded that "the poorhouse and the mode in which its inmates are provided for, are not to be longer tolerated." Moreover, the committee, although themselves members of the city council, recognized that the council itself was largely to blame for the problems. "The Committee are under a consciousness that the Council are directly chargeable with a large share of the censure which is properly incurred by the existence of such a state of things, [and] feel no disposition to cast upon others the blame of that which the Council should have prevented."[118]

Some members of the city council resented the accusations and tried to strike the remarks from the record. But the council on the whole was prodded to action and began laying plans for a new building. After surveying the city, the planning committee, again chaired by Grattan, concluded that the present site of the poorhouse was the best one to be had: it had convenient accessibility, a good water supply, and extensive city-owned property. But the old structure would have to be razed first, and that would mean moving the current residents out until a new facility could be completed.[119] Construction of the new building was interrupted by the outbreak of the Civil War. The unfurnished, nearly completed facility would be used during the war for other purposes, including as a military hospital. Not until 1866 would the city's poor be moved into the new building, which was now being referred to in official documents as the "almshouse," rather than the "poorhouse."[120]

The changing nomenclature went unexplained in any records, but the timing and the context suggest some interpretive possibilities. Building the new facility was partly civic boosterism: the old building had come to be seen as a disgrace to the city's desired image as a prosperous commercial center. But civic boosterism in the 1850s South often carried regional meaning as well. At a time when sectional rhetoric was growing increasingly heated, southerners like George Fitzhugh regularly condemned the North for its treatment of its wage laborers. The presence of a dilapidated public poorhouse could only make such criticisms appear hypocritical. Southern cities such as Richmond and Charleston had to take better care of their own poor in order to demonstrate the region's

Richmond Almshouse, at the end of the Civil War. The city had leased the newly constructed building to the Confederate government during the war. Courtesy of the Valentine Richmond History Center.

argued superiority. (Similarly, Charlestonians had recently replaced their own poorhouse because its dilapidated condition harmed the city's self-proclaimed "reputation for benevolence and charity.")[121]

The term "almshouse" also connoted a softened, more benevolent approach to the poor. Richmond's white working class, which had shown itself to be restive on several occasions in the 1850s,[122] might be partially mollified by the gesture of a modern, spacious facility that appeared to offer more dignity and respect than had the old ramshackle building. Universal white male suffrage, instituted in 1851, had given Richmond's artisan class new prominence in civic life. An almshouse with modern conveniences might help to cement the loyalties of these new, still untested voters. And while building a new almshouse would be expensive, it would be far less expensive than expanding outdoor relief.

Also during the antebellum period, the state government enlarged its own role in public-welfare provision. In 1838, after nearly a decade of agitation by private citizens, the state legislature established an asylum for the deaf, dumb, and blind in Staunton. The demands for such an institution had been heard since at least 1825, when Governor James Pleasants recommended that the General Assembly follow the lead of Kentucky and Connecticut in the education of the deaf and mute. When the legislature hesitated, a group of private citizens in Staunton took the initiative to start its own asylum. Granted incorporation

in 1833, the directors of the Deaf and Dumb Asylum of Virginia quickly realized that the endeavor was beyond the means of the private sector. The trustees
approached the legislature for funding. With the support of important leading citizens, such as Governor David Campbell, the proposal was presented as
a form of public welfare. "These two classes of the poor," the deaf and blind,
"who are entirely excluded from all participation in the benefits of the liberal
provision made for the education of the poor generally," could be turned into
productive citizens with specialized training. In 1838, the legislature appropriated twenty thousand dollars for the construction of the school, and an annual
appropriation of ten thousand dollars for its operation. [123]

As was the case in its earlier asylum for the insane, Virginia was one of the first
southern states to establish a state-funded institution for the deaf and blind. In
both instances, the state demonstrated its willingness to enter into the realm of
public welfare by carving out a particular niche for its activities. Focusing on a
single, relatively small group of dependents to whom local governments would
find it difficult to attend, the commonwealth saw its public-welfare role as limited. But clearly, it did not see these activities as inappropriate, even in this age of
laissez-faire philosophies of government. The state's support for these asylums
was an admittedly small portion of the government's annual expenditures. In
the fiscal year 1850–51, for example, the state's appropriations to the various
asylums together represented approximately 4 percent of the year's expenses. [124]

This dramatic expansion in both public and private welfare provision during
the late antebellum years meant that the urban poor had far more opportunities
for some form of assistance than before. This, in combination with self-help
mechanisms such as mutual-aid organizations and the informal networks of
family and friends, meant that Richmond's poorest residents had a variety of
resources from which to choose. Individuals with determination and imagination might combine multiple resources or alternate them according to changing
needs. One family might simultaneously draw upon the city's outdoor relief for
wood, a church charity for food, a neighbor for clothing, the poorhouse for the
temporary shelter of a dependent child, and a mutual-aid society for medicine
for an ailing family member. The following year might find the same family with
different needs, met by a different combination of resources. As one scholar has
noted, "duplication of services," which will come to be seen as a tremendous
social-welfare problem at the end of the nineteenth century, was a way of life
for the poor, "as charitable donations from multiple sources mingled with other
resources in the homes and on the dinner tables of the poor." [125]

All of this was dependent, of course, upon convincing the custodians of these
sources of assistance that the family was indeed both needy and worthy. In the
absence of accurate, comprehensive, and updated records, the local gatekeepers

of social welfare often had little documentary evidence to guide them in their evaluations of applicants. Unlike previous generations (who were more likely to have direct personal knowledge of members of the community) or subsequent generations (who would come to have more extensive records at their disposal), antebellum overseers, district visitors, ministers, and lady benevolents were confronted by large numbers of applicants about whom they knew very little. With little ability to investigate individual cases, the distributors of public relief and private charity in Richmond had to rely largely on the applicants' own testimony. The ability to demonstrate deference, to appear sincere, and to evoke sympathy could carry an applicant a long way in the absence of evidence to the contrary. Ellen Ross has suggested that these negotiations over charity "called for special, carefully orchestrated performances on the part of the working-class recipients."[126] Indeed, one historian has described these exercises as the "theater of charity," so important was the ability to act persuasively.[127] Given these circumstances, the poor might have a stronger position in these negotiations than would be possible otherwise. The middle-class distributors of assistance still held the more powerful position, but the poor held some advantages too.[128]

And finally, it is worth remembering that the poor applicant could always turn down the offer of assistance if the terms seemed too harsh. Poor relief was not mandatory, and if the family in question chose not to agree to the terms, there was little the city officials or charity workers could do. The applicants themselves made the ultimate decision whether institutionalization, for example, was acceptable to them. Turning down admission to the poorhouse did not necessarily preclude getting assistance from other means. The poor had options and exercised them at all turns.

WHILE STILL GROUNDED in the English poor laws, Virginia's system of poor relief had changed considerably in its first two hundred years. Originally a purely local and entirely public function, by 1860 the welfare system had grown more complex. An array of private benevolent and mutual-aid organizations had emerged to care for small, selected groups of dependents. Usually religious in orientation, these private voluntary associations generally provided assistance to members of their own groups. One organization, the Union Benevolent Society, had established a citywide charity, complete with a formal system of district visitors.

Public welfare had shifted its emphasis, away from the previously preferred "outdoor relief" and toward a new concentration on institutionalization. The city had also begun construction of a new almshouse, with increased capacity to handle the larger number of needy residents of this generation. Ironically, just as the building was completed, emancipation meant that the numbers of people eligible for public relief more than doubled, and the new building was immediately rendered inadequate. In addition, the state government had accepted responsibility for two particular groups of dependents: the insane and those made dependent by blindness or other physical impairment.

The public and private welfare activities were intertwined in many places. The city government granted regular subsidies and/or tax breaks to a number of private organizations. Private organizations agreed to care for some dependents who might rightly be public charges (such as orphans). And individuals, both clergy and laypeople alike, were often engaged in public and private welfare efforts simultaneously, further blurring the distinction between them.

This more complex welfare system, still in its infancy in the 1850s, would ultimately break down under the stresses of the Civil War. Unable to meet the needs of its citizens caused by this calamity, the welfare system that emerged after the war would look quite different from its predecessor. New elements, including the first appearance of the federal government, and increased state-level involvement, would redefine the system of poor relief, as the following chapters explain.

CHAPTER FOUR

The Civil War

Redefining the "Worthy" Poor

The 1850s had witnessed a hardening of public opinion in Richmond regarding the poor. Concerns about high taxes, worries about immigrants and their adherence to the slave system, and the evangelical emphasis on personal moral responsibility had combined to produce less sympathy for the poor than in previous generations. The Civil War would dramatically change these public perceptions about poverty and its relief. In a period where nearly everyone seemed impoverished, poverty no longer seemed a product of bad character, dissipated habits, or "inferior" ethnic cultures. For a brief time at least, public opinion embraced increased governmental activity in charity. Richmonders, like other southerners, demanded more and more public provision from local, state, and Confederate governments. And for a brief time, the antebellum trend toward eliminating outdoor relief was also reversed. As Walter Trattner has noted, "direct public aid, on a grand scale, became available once again."[1]

But by the end of Reconstruction, that brief acceptance of a broadened social-welfare state had largely evaporated among white southerners. The Confederate government's poor-relief efforts had been so limited as to constitute near neglect. Southerners came to see their national government's efforts at social welfare as a disillusioning failure. Racism and Reconstruction politics had helped to stigmatize federal welfare in the minds of southern whites, at least. State-level welfare, conversely, did manage to retain much of its approval, because it focused its attention so closely on Confederate veterans and their families. After Reconstruction, the state government would fund medical programs, soldiers' pensions, soldiers' homes, and numerous programs for the dependents of Confederate soldiers (such as orphanages and widows' pensions). White Virginians widely praised these efforts and supported large expenditures on their behalf while crafting an ideology that linked public welfare to Confederate patriotism. In dramatic fashion, the Civil War and Reconstruction reshaped the ideological underpinnings of poor relief in the urban South. This chapter details the rapid changes in public opinion about poor relief that could occur during a crisis.

Options, unthinkable in other years, suddenly became viable. Just as suddenly, they disappeared.

The Wartime Crisis

Although Confederate sympathizers claimed that "the people were unfalteringly with the revolution in all its phases,"[2] scholars have come to understand that the poverty and suffering produced by the Civil War played an important role in the declining enthusiasm for the war effort among the South's nonelite classes.[3] As one soldier, asking for a furlough to go home and plant corn, put it, "I cannot serve my Country with any heart when my poor wife & children are starving at home."[4] The causes of this massive impoverishment were many: the breakdown of transportation lines, which kept food and other critical supplies from their destinations; the conscription of men who were the sole breadwinners for their families; the impressment of food for the armies, without due consideration of civilian needs; and the disastrous inflation produced both by shortages and by government policies of printing more and more paper currency. As Paul D. Escott has written, the extent of the suffering was staggering.[5]

Because urban residents grew less of their food, southern cities felt the impact of shortages first. Beginning with New Orleans in August 1861, dozens of cities throughout the Confederacy witnessed bread riots, usually led by women demanding food at reduced prices. Newspaper editorials, which might have been expected to issue blanket condemnations of such lawlessness, were surprisingly circumspect and occasionally even hinted at approval of the actions of soldiers' wives, at least when they were directed at suspected speculators.[6] Not surprisingly, urban dwellers were among the first to call for government to regulate the market. In Virginia, Charles Button, editor of the *Lynchburg Virginian*, was one of the most insistent advocates of government intervention into the marketplace.[7]

While the impact may have been felt in urban areas more immediately, rural families could not escape the economic crisis. One soldier's wife reported, with surprise, that she and her rural neighbors had had to buy bread, and she feared that there might soon be none to buy at any price.[8] Dr. W. H. Syme of Lewisburg, whose four oldest sons were all in the Confederate armies, lost his two slaves to the enemy and was "rendered quite helpless and dependent."[9] Judith Marr, a widow with three sons in the army, had only one slave for labor; the slave had been impressed by the Confederacy, and she wrote in March 1864 that she would have little choice but to abandon her crop in the field.[10] A desperate Elizabeth Marshall, an eighty-three-year-old widow, wrote the governor begging for the release of her grandson from the army. She offered "to pay to the Government $500 dollars and all of any grain that I have to spair."[11]

In the face of overwhelming destitution, southerners turned to government at all levels for assistance. Long accustomed to systems of poor relief administered by local governments, many southerners naturally looked there first for assistance. Local authorities not only increased the amounts expended on traditional forms of poor relief but also experimented with entirely new forms of relief. Municipal governments in Charlottesville and Lynchburg, for example, began to pay the rents of the impoverished in their communities.[12] Richmond's city council hired an agent to scour the countryside to find food supplies.[13]

Many southerners also asked their state governments for help, often writing poignant letters to state officials explaining their circumstances. One Georgia woman, apparently not knowing how else to express her request, wrote her governor to ask for a personal loan. Another woman, pleading for help from the governor of Alabama, promised to pay back whatever assistance she got.[14] In Virginia, a group of widows from Clarksville wrote to Governor Letcher, "[W]e had thought it hard to do without sugar, coffee, salt and other things but now the stuff of life is being fast taken from us. . . . famine in all its horrors must soon be upon us if the Government comes not to our rescue."[15] In case the state should think that local poor relief would cover the crisis, W. A. Little explained to the governor that Stafford County had "had no session of the county court for two years past—no overseers of the poor, no provision for the families of soldiers or persons in destitute condition. The Justices of the Peace take no action."[16] Indeed local overseers of the poor had numerous challenges to confront, including the conscription act. The overseers in Botetourt County wrote the governor to request exemption from the draft for the superintendent of their almshouse: he "is frequently called upon as a member of the reserves, in case of Raids &c &c, which frequently occur at a time when his services are absolutely necessary for ploughing & other work, which interruptions make the institution a heavy tax upon the County, besides rendering it incapable of providing for its helpless inmates."[17]

The states responded to these demands for assistance with a variety of methods. Some allowed soldiers' families tax exemptions. Some adopted a state-level tax-in-kind and distributed the proceeds to the poor.[18] Some granted direct relief, such as Georgia, which appropriated more than sixteen million dollars to assist the families of soldiers, with additional sums for other civilians. Georgia also tried to intervene in the market by limiting production of cotton (to stimulate production of food) and by limiting the distillation of alcohol (to increase the grain supply).[19] One scholar has observed that states were more willing early in the conflict to provide monetary relief to soldiers' families, but as the Confederate currency collapsed, states increasingly turned to in-kind relief.[20]

Virginians joined this regional chorus demanding state intervention in the economy. Public meetings in the central Virginia counties of Amherst, Buckingham, and Nelson called on the legislature to ban tobacco production altogether, arguing that this was the only solution to the problem of widespread speculation in that commodity.[21] In the fall of 1863, Virginians lobbied the state legislature to set prices on all "necessities." Despite tremendous public support, the legislature rejected the plan.

Virginia's General Assembly continued to view the local governments as the rightful place for poor relief but enlarged the powers of the localities to deal with the crisis. In 1863, the local governments were authorized to borrow sums up to ten thousand dollars for each one thousand white inhabitants, with the money to be used on the behalf of the poor. The assembly took additional action directed specifically at the families of soldiers: each county court was empowered to appoint an impressment agent, whose function was to acquire supplies from speculators. Paying the same prices as the set rates of the Confederate government, these impressed goods could then be used for the benefit of the poor. The state also suspended the collection of state taxes, which provided some relief to taxpayers.[22]

Bracing for the coming winter, the state assembly passed legislation in October 1863 that required railroad companies to transport all fuel shipments immediately to the state's urban centers. The legislators also tried to limit the distillation of alcohol, hoping to release more grain for food consumption. Governor William "Extra Billy" Smith ordered a state-subsidized railroad to bring food to the capital; his supplies of rice went on the market at fifty cents per pound, compared to the going rate of three dollars. His actions, though competing directly with private enterprise, were widely praised.[23]

By early 1864, Virginia's General Assembly entered the realm of poor relief more directly. In February, the legislature made its first actual appropriation for the care of the needy, in the amount of one million dollars, designated specifically for the families of soldiers who resided in counties controlled by the Federal army. This was intended to fill a gap in the existing system: in counties where the local government had ceased to function, and where the families of rebel soldiers were unlikely to get relief from the Federal armies, the state felt compelled to step in.[24] This action made a great deal of political sense: such families could hardly be expected to retain their loyalty to the cause if the government simply abandoned them to the enemy.

Although this action did represent a fundamental shift in state policy, it was nevertheless a shift that drew upon and enlarged antebellum precedents. The state was assuming responsibility for a group of dependents for whom the usual local systems of relief were insufficient. Just as the state had earlier provided support for the indigent insane and for the blind and deaf, now the state afforded aid to those whom the war emergency had pushed beyond the reach of the county courts.

Finally, southerners showed little hesitation to ask the national (Confederate) government for aid when necessary. As early as 1862, newspapers were demanding that the Confederate government take action against inflation. The *Richmond Examiner* asked for legislation to halt inflation-producing speculation. Others called for price regulations and other interventions into the economy. Numerous Confederates demanded that the national government supplement local charitable efforts by providing rations to the poor, especially the families of soldiers.[25]

Although the Confederate government never launched a massive poor-relief program of any kind, it did take several smaller actions intended to ease suffering and discontent. In Richmond, the Confederate administration attempted to hire as many local poor women as possible as seamstresses, making uniforms. One local elite woman, passing "through a certain quarter of our city where government work was given out to the indigent," saw "hundreds of poor women in waiting for the coarse sewing from which they earned the pittance that saved them from hunger."[26] Beginning in 1862, the Davis administration allowed limited numbers of exceptions to the draft in order to avoid starvation in particularly hard-hit regions. In the conscription act of 1863, the Confederacy gave broader powers to local officials to exempt individuals from the draft when destitution might result.[27] General John G. Winder, in charge of administering martial law in the Confederate capital after March 1862, attempted to use his authority to set prices of foodstuffs and other necessities. His shortlived experiment failed, however, when the War Department reprimanded him for overstepping his authority. Martial law did not include the power to fix prices.[28]

The Confederate tax-in-kind, often criticized by southern farmers because it singled them out for extra contributions to the war effort, also provided a means of supplementing supplies for poor relief. At the end of 1863, the Confederate government permitted local authorities to buy foodstuffs from the quartermaster, if they certified that the food was to be distributed to the poor. This largesse from the tax-in-kind was sold at the government's set rates, which were far lower than the going market prices.[29] When these efforts seemed inadequate to meet the need, some Confederate officers dipped into their own supplies to aid desperate civilians. Brigadier General Thomas Rosser, witnessing tremendous deprivations in Spotsylvania County, ordered his commissary "to issue a few days rations to them," noting that, "unless something can be done to alleviate their sufferings by the Army I can't see how they will live."[30]

The Confederate government expanded its efforts at poor relief in 1864, when it further modified the conscription laws. Planters who wished to gain exemptions for their overseers were required to supply the government with one hundred pounds of bacon and one hundred pounds of beef for every slave they owned. These and other supplies had to be sold either to the government or to soldiers' families at set—low—prices. Local relief agents could also purchase these foodstuffs from the Confederate government at costs far below the inflated market prices. Although this was not exactly the same thing as assuming full responsibility for feeding the poor, it nevertheless enlarged the Confederate government's role in poor relief. In August 1864, the Confederate government granted all civilian employees the right to purchase foodstuffs from the commissary, and Congress debated extending the privilege to all citizens. (A bill to this effect, which would have fully nationalized prices for food, was defeated.)[31]

Collectively, these actions by local, state, and Confederate governments "sent the Confederacy toward the brink of becoming a welfare state."[32] In Paul D. Escott's words, "By 1864, both the Richmond administration and the states had left narrow ideas of limited government far behind."[33] The general public had also come to share this thinking, as southerners demonstrated little adherence to a rigid localism when it came to poor relief during the war. In a sense, government aid was government aid, and they cared little whether it was the municipal, state, or national level.[34] At the same time, however, as Escott has noted, these policies could do nothing to fix the underlying economic and demographic problems that had produced the poverty and dislocation: they could not increase production, solve the labor shortage, or restore broken transportation networks. Moreover, when faced with a choice of feeding the armies or feeding the poor, the Confederate government felt that it had little option but to put the military's needs first. In February 1864, the Congress gave its commissary agents the right to impress up to half of any family's yearly supply of meat, an action clearly counterproductive for poor relief.[35]

The combined efforts of all levels of government remained insufficient to meet the great needs. The record of the Confederate government in particular remained shabby and contributed to the declining morale of the South's white population. War-produced poverty led to mass desertion from the armies, bread riots, and widespread theft as the southern masses registered their discontent with the inadequacies of government relief efforts.[36]

Richmond and Civil War Poverty

The Civil War would have affected the city of Richmond under any circumstances, but as the capital of the Confederacy, the impact on Richmond was more pronounced than it would have been otherwise. Initially, local residents hoped that the war might prove an economic windfall for the city. Local businessmen received government contracts, business and industry expanded, property values increased, and new jobs opened up. One contemporary observer believed that the poor were the greatest beneficiaries of these changes, since "such employment . . . secured to them a plentiful support."[37]

But the wartime changes soon overwhelmed the city's resources. Legislators, bureaucrats, military officials—and their families—converged on Richmond, beginning the growth of population that would soon cause enormous social disarray. Other newcomers included prisoners, wounded soldiers, war refugees, prostitutes, and workers in war industries. In four years' time, the population more than doubled, and "strange faces greeted the citizens at every turn."[38] Housing was in critically short supply, or as Mary Chesnut put it, "Richmond was crowded to suffocation—hardly standing room left."[39] In the first two years of the conflict, rents quadrupled in the city.[40] One local quipped that houses "seemed of india-rubber capacity, from the numbers frequently packed in them."[41]

The city's difficulties were compounded by the proximity of the battle lines. When the battlefront came perilously close to Richmond, transportation was disrupted, making it difficult for the city to obtain food, medicine, and other supplies. Prices soared. Those living on fixed incomes suffered grievously from the inflation. An employee in the Confederate Ordnance office in Richmond wrote the governor asking for a higher paying appointment, which "would relieve the painful embarrassment which crushes me."[42] Sallie Putnam, whose memoir of life in the Confederate capital was published just after the war, made frequent mention of the "homeless and destitute crowded into our city for safety and support,"[43] as war refugees poured into the city, compounding the food shortages.

Residents of all races and classes were affected, but the poor and working classes, with fewer savings and extra resources, suffered the most from the economic displacement that occurred in the early stages of the war.[44] Winter months, always the hardest on the poor, could produce heart-rending stories. One local paper reported on the case of a soldier's wife, "left at home with a family of children, the youngest at the breast, without a particle of coal, and without money to get any, nor even enough to buy milk for her babe, she being in too weak a condition to nurse her offspring from the maternal fount."[45] The following winter, another story demonstrated great sympathy for the condition of the poor: "A lad of some ten years old was among the criminals at the Mayor's Court yesterday, for larceny. He was pale and emaciated, clad in rags, and his answers to questions proved clearly that he was an idiot. His feet were bare and nearly frozen from a long walk through the snow."[46]

Even in the first year of the war, many residents of the city were driven to desperation, and crime became a serious problem. The city increased the size of the police force, raised the height of the walls around the jail to prevent escapes, and resumed use of the chain gang "to ease the pressure on Richmond's bulging jail." After the Confederate government imposed martial law on the city in 1862, General Winder added an armed soldier to accompany each of the civilian patrolmen of the night watch.[47]

Remarkably, many wealthier citizens of Richmond found ways to ignore the signs of the massive suffering that surrounded them. Sallie Putnam believed that the wealthy suffered more than the poor. "It is noticeable in connection with the scarcity of food and the high prices, that the class usually know[n] as the poor, was not the class which experienced the most serious inconvenience, and was reduced to the most dreadful misery." Putnam believed, "They were provided by the Common Council of the city with such staple articles of food as could be obtained, and in quantity sufficient to secure them from suffering. They had small quantities furnished to them rations of corn-meal, sorghum syrup, and small quantities of bacon and flour. Starvation to them was not imminent, and the pauper class were indeed in more comfortable circumstances than persons who lived on salaries, or depended upon a moderate income for support."[48] Writing in his diary just two weeks before the Bread Riot (discussed later), J. B. Jones claimed, "Not a beggar is yet to be seen in this city of 100,000 inhabitants!"[49]

The city's political leaders held a more realistic view and took real actions to relieve the suffering. Their responses to the crisis reflected both their antebellum understanding of poverty and the wartime pressures for patriotic duty. Traditional forms of poor relief would therefore be enlarged, but with notable changes in policy due to the emergency circumstances. One of the most important changes involved the as-yet-unfinished almshouse. When the city fathers had planned the new almshouse in the late 1850s, they could not have foreseen the timing of the upcoming crisis. They could not have predicted that, at a time when the city needed the larger almshouse more than ever, it would not be available. During construction, which involved razing the old facility and rebuilding on the same site, the resident paupers had been moved to temporary quarters rented by the city. This change alone had caused considerable confusion, since few people were aware of the new location. Indeed, many seemed to assume that there was no facility provided at all, and they believed that the poor were being allowed to roam the streets and beg.[50]

The temporary facility proved clearly inadequate. Located on a "hill directly east of the City Hospital," only one of the buildings had sufficient heat. This was allotted to the women. Male paupers had to sleep in a barn, where "only an inch weatherboarding protects the inmates from the outer air. Lathing and plastering there is none. A pauper's heels might freeze off whilst he was toasting his toes."[51] In the meantime, the new but unfinished almshouse had been rented to the Confederate government for use as a hospital.[52] Given the great needs of the city, many people were unhappy with this decision. As early as 1861, there were public calls for its return to the city, to be used for its original purpose.[53] The city council asked repeatedly that the building be returned to its control,[54] but the Confederate officials instead offered to increase its rental payments. Despite the municipality's great need, the city council continued to rent out the building as a hospital, and then later as temporary quarters for the cadets of the Virginia Military Institute. These arrangements served two purposes: they allowed the city to collect substantial rent revenue, which increased each year of the war, and they served as a patriotic contribution to the war effort. The only losers in all of this were the ill-housed paupers.

Under these circumstances, the city had little option but to rely on ever-increasing outdoor relief, reversing the antebellum trend toward institutionalization. During the first year of the conflict, the city council appropriated over sixty thousand dollars for welfare expenses. This figure included thirty thousand dollars for the almshouse, over thirteen thousand dollars for the outdoor poor, and fifteen thousand dollars for the support of the families of volunteers.[55] Although this was an increase over prewar levels, it still constituted only 7 percent of the city's expenditures. The city also provided other relief for the poor: during the summer of 1861, the city offered free water to the families of volunteers who were unable to pay their water bills. The city also paid for prescription medicines for the families of soldiers.[56]

The second year of the war saw inflation worsen, and conditions in the city deteriorated. One Confederate bureaucrat calculated that his salary of three thousand dollars "will go about as far as $700 would in 1860."[57] The city council appropriated five thousand dollars to obtain firewood for the poor and authorized the city gas works to sell coke to the poor at fifteen cents a bushel. The city also sold salt for five cents per pound, when the commodity was selling for up to ninety cents on the open market. In an attempt to prevent speculation in foodstuffs, the council prohibited anyone from selling goods in the market other than the producer or his agent.[58] These and other interventions into the economy did little to halt the spiraling cost of living. J. B. Jones, a clerk in the Confederate War Department, complained that "[n]o salaries can board families now; and soon the expense of boarding will exceed the incomes of unmarried men."[59] Confederate agents were impressing food supplies destined for Richmond, and by the winter of 1862–63, famine was a real possibility. One soldier, writing home to his wife, joked, "They say that the price of looking at foods in Richmond is five dollars."[60] Others could not joke about the situation: "There was an ominous scantiness of supply in the market this morning," noted J. B. Jones.[61]

The mounting frustrations erupted into violence on 2 April 1863 in the Richmond Bread Riot. A group of white women held a meeting the night of 1 April, at the Belvidere Hill Baptist Church, in the Oregon Hill neighborhood.[62] There they laid plans for the next day: they would meet with the governor to demand food, and if it was not forthcoming, they would take it by force. The city's poor understood that they had a right to relief, and planned to exercise that right. Taking axes and hatchets with them, the women rallied at the statue of George Washington on Capitol Square early on the morning of the second and then went in search of the governor. After a brief and unsatisfactory meeting, they marched silently to Main Street, brandishing their weapons, seizing carts and wagons, and began entering stores and taking food. As word spread, their numbers grew, until several hundreds were at work seizing food, clothing, shoes, and other goods.[63]

It appears that the leaders of the group lost control of the situation shortly after the riot began. What had been planned as a traditional food riot—including the use of the ubiquitous slogan "Bread or Blood"—quickly evolved into widespread and random looting, as observers and bystanders began joining the fray. The mayor, Joseph Mayo, read the riot act; the governor called out the Public Guard; and Jefferson Davis personally appealed to the crowd to disperse. The event was over by noon.[64]

The city fathers, many of whom were themselves part of the mercantile community, were outraged at the urban disorder and responded with "stern repression."[65] Several dozen women and a lesser number of men were arrested (although many of the charges were ultimately dropped). Mayor Joe Mayo argued that no sympathy should be afforded those who broke the law, for there was plenty of public-relief money available. "There is no reason why there should have been any suffering among the poor of this city," claimed Mayo. "More [relief] money has been appropriated than has been applied for."[66]

The local press, which had earlier shown some degree of sympathy for food rioters in other cities, now backed Mayo's assessment of the local situation. A week after the riot, the Examiner claimed, "The City Council has certainly done its duty well in the matter of providing for the poor—not only well, but generously."[67] The *Sentinel* concurred: "Thus there has been no neglect, at any time, to provide for the needs of the suffering poor, nor has there been any necessity for undue excitement on the subject of supplies. . . . There is no danger of suffering among the deserving poor, if they will quietly attend to their business and give no heed to the councils of mischievous agitators."[68]

Moreover, the city's leaders did their best to depict the rioters as prostitutes, Yankees, and Irish immigrants. The *Richmond Examiner* described them as "a handful of prostitutes, professional thieves, Irish and Yankee hags, gallows-birds from all lands but our own."[69] Resident Sallie Putnam believed the rioters were a "heterogeneous crowd of Dutch, Irish, and free negroes."[70] This interpretation was widely accepted, possibly because it was picked up and reproduced in an engraving in *Leslie's Illustrated News.*[71]

But while the city authorities attempted to control the imagery of the event, they also recognized that the bread riot was symptomatic of real desperation, and responded with real and immediate relief for the city's poor. Following the model of New Orleans, the city established two free markets, where the "deserving" poor could obtain free supplies once a week. "Deserving" in this instance specifically meant anyone who had not participated in the bread riot. The city appropriated an initial twenty thousand dollars for the market's operation and followed it up later that same summer with an additional fifty thousand dollars.[72] These and other efforts on the behalf of the poor appeared to reduce the level of popular dissatisfaction enough that no further food riots occurred in the city.[73]

The situation nevertheless remained precarious and residents continued to whisper their fears of famine. One local newspaper began advocating that its readers leave the city and refuge to the countryside.[74] Although there were no more riots, discontent with privations and inadequate relief would be expressed in a variety of other ways. Strikes, seldom seen in antebellum Richmond, were increasingly common in the last half of the war. Just months after the Bread Riot, clerks in the Richmond post office went on strike for higher wages, claiming that their salaries of seven hundred or eight hundred dollars were "equivalent to less than $100 in ordinary times."[75] Gravediggers in Shockoe cemetery struck for higher wages in 1864.[76] Crime rates continued to rise, further evidence of desperation in the city. One local paper, commenting on the nightly thefts of food that police seemed unable to halt, warned residents to "Look Out for Your Meat House." In an act of supreme irony, thieves burglarized the home of General Winder, who directed martial law in the city.[77]

As war refugees from other parts of the state flooded into Richmond, they became automatically defined as "deserving." In calling for charitable contributions on their behalf, the *Examiner* noted that "the demands upon the

Bread rioters, from *Leslie's Illustrated News*, 23 May 1863. Although the women are shown taking only food, some while holding small children, the depiction was nevertheless unsympathetic.

generosity of the people of Richmond have been frequent since the war, but we are satisfied that an appeal in behalf of these suffering exiles will not be made in vain."[78] There was no question that the refugees should be aided; no one suggested that they had to establish legal settlement by a year's residence before they were eligible for public assistance.

Those outside the city limits were still supposed to be ineligible for city assistance. Concerned that the residents of the suburbs would take up scarce supplies, the city's leaders encouraged Henrico County to increase its poor relief. One local editor suggested that the county court establish a free market, as Richmond had done. Private efforts, such as those of the churches on Union Hill, could not handle the burdens alone. Henrico, said the paper, should act at once.[79]

But charitable relief, whether public or private, still could not attack the problems at their roots. Public demands that the government do something to halt the inflation and increase the supplies of necessary goods grew more insistent. In September 1863, Richmond's citizens, well placed to lobby the state legislature, held a mass meeting, "one of the largest meetings that has assembled in this city for years," to instruct their representatives to vote for a bill then under consideration that would regulate prices. The enormously controversial measure would have set prices for all necessities, a dramatic regulation of the free market. The resolutions adopted at this public event suggest how far popular thought had evolved under the pressures of war. "[A]s free men," they announced, "we abhor and detest the idea that the rich must take care of the poor, because we know that without labor and production the man with his money could not exist, from the fact that he consumes all and produces nothing." Moreover, a dependence on the rich "would tend to degrade rather than elevate the human race."[80] Instead, these "free men" preferred independence, with the state intervening to regulate the economy.[81]

Such a solution—government regulation—appealed far more to consumers than to producers and merchants. Most of the city's elites opposed this measure, with only one newspaper breaking ranks and supporting the legislation to regulate prices. The Sentinel pleaded on behalf of the poor: "How long will this state of things continue, no one knows, unless the Legislature will come to the rescue, and pass a stringent law to reduce prices."[82] The city council, in an attempt to orchestrate public opposition to the bill, held a referendum on the issue. The vote was 292 in favor, 867 opposed. As William Blair has carefully explained, the vote substantially misrepresented public opinion, since so few people could participate. Nonresident soldiers, refugees, and noncitizens of all kinds were ineligible to vote in the local referendum. A statewide ballot, with all eligible voters included, would likely have had a quite different outcome.[83] The legislature, without asking for such a statewide referendum, defeated the bill.

The inflationary pressures continued unabated, and the levels of poverty increased. By 1864, the city's expenditures for the poor had swollen to a nearly unimaginable four hundred thousand dollars (in inflated currency).[84] Some of these funds went to the city's free market, which furnished nearly one thousand families with supplies, including flour, candles, wood, and coal, each month.[85] Although the municipal government had modified its definition of the worthy poor—families of soldiers were now automatically included in that category— and increased its expenditures on their behalf, officials were not willing to increase the city's bonded debt to do so. Instead, they continued to take out short-term loans from local banks to buy supplies. Desperate to finds ways to cut other expenditures or find new sources of revenue, the city council sold its railroad stock and was even considering tripling the tax rate.[86]

In another attempt to cut costs by reducing "opportunism," the council turned over responsibility for distributing tickets for the free market to the city policemen. On the assumption that each officer would "be well acquainted" with those in his district, the police were instructed to give tickets to those who were city residents only. Furthermore, they were not to allow tickets for men who earned more than seven dollars a day, or to government employees who received more than twenty-eight hundred dollars per year.[87] Although unstated, it was nevertheless assumed that police officers were less likely to be generous with the relief tickets than the usual "lady visitors."

Private charitable efforts continued to multiply as well. In November 1864, the Richmond Soup Association formed, under the presidency of Rev. Charles Minnegerode, to open a soup house for the poor. The association raised money and donations in kind, secured a room in the Metropolitan Hall, and worked in conjunction with the ladies of the Union Benevolent Society. The UBS was responsible for canvassing the city and distributing tickets to the deserving poor, who still had to pay twenty-five cents for each ticket.[88] Another organization, the Relief Committee of Richmond, formed under the presidency of William P. Munford. The Relief Committee collected food, money, and clothing and was aided by the merchants Martin and Cardoza, who used their store as a collection site for donations.[89] The YMCA continued its relief efforts throughout the war, including operating one of the numerous hospitals in Richmond.[90] New groups appeared in the suburbs, such as the Sidney Relief Society, which served Oregon Hill, Sidney, and Screamersville, outside the city limits.[91]

Private charities suffered from their inability to raise funds by donation, especially in the last year of the war. The Female Orphan Asylum, for example, had to resort to a door-to-door solicitation campaign in 1864 and 1865 in an attempt to raise money to offset the costs of inflation. In the door-to-door campaign of March 1865, some cynical Richmonders "donated" nearly worthless Confederate currency and soon-to-be-worthless Confederate bonds.[92]

Despite the enormous efforts of many individuals, and the large expenditures of the city, conditions in the city nonetheless grew grim in the final year of the war. One resident wrote, "The wolf is at the door here. We dread starvation far more than we do Grant or Sherman."[93] Declining morale was evident even to such "true believers" as Sallie Putnam, who finally acknowledged, "Like individuals, governments have their summer friends; and though we are proud to know that these exceptions in the Confederacy were exceedingly rare, still we are forced to admit, and mourn that we are compelled to admit, they did indeed exist."[94]

Crime—that is, thefts of food and supplies—grew commonplace. Shoplifting was reported to be an "epidemick," and a local paper believed ladies of the "better sort" were participants.[95] "Every night robberies of poultry, salt meats, and even of cows and hogs are occurring," wrote one resident.[96] Burglars broke into the storeroom of the Female Orphan Asylum, taking more than one thousand dollars' worth of provisions, leaving "the little orphans . . . without enough left to break their fast upon."[97] In some places, reports surfaced that the thieves were wearing Confederate uniforms.[98]

In these darkest months of the war, many observers linked poor relief with the survival of the Confederacy. William Munford, who was involved in multiple charitable efforts in the city, wrote, "The coming winter will present the most serious crisis in the fate of the Confederacy, and its capital. Let the farmers second the liberality displayed by the citizens of Richmond, and there will be no danger of starving our city into subjection."[99] Charity, then, became a weapon in the war for southern independence. It became a standard trope to link poverty with service to the Confederacy. One relief worker, asking for further donations from the public, reminded them, "Some of these are persons reared in ease and even affluence, but now (and some in their old age) are reduced to this condition by their adherence to their native State in this her hour of trial. Many are the families of our brave defenders, and but for whom we would soon be in a like state of privation."[100] By the last months of the war, public discussions about the poor and poor relief seldom questioned whether the needy were "worthy" or "deserving." Likewise, the rhetoric about the able-bodied but idle, common before the war, disappeared from the discussion. Instead, Richmonders were reminded to remember the poor, for "[i]t is due to our soldiers that we provide for their families."[101]

The two concepts—"the poor" and "the families of soldiers"—had become virtually interchangeable in public discourse. Nearly every charitable effort emphasized its role in assisting the families of soldiers. New organizations specifically targeting soldiers and their families continued to spring up. The Baptist General Association of Virginia established a school for the children of deceased and disabled soldiers. "Already several hundred orphan children have been entered at school, while efforts are being made to reach thousands, who but for such an enterprise might grow up in ignorance and vice."[102] Aside from the quickly dwindling available resources, there seemed to be no limit to the public and private commitments to the families of Confederate soldiers. The principal of the "Humanity Hall Academy," described as "an accomplished scholar and teacher . . . a patriot also," offered an educational program for disabled veterans, in conjunction with the Confederate War Department. He offered free instruction, and, to those "accustomed to conduct themselves with propriety," he also offered free rooms in his own home. They would be able to draw rations from the Confederacy. "Such, therefore, as are willing to live in soldier style, waiting upon themselves," could attend "an excellent school" free of charge.[103] Public and private assistance to Confederate soldiers and their families came near to defining welfare policy in the last year of the war, setting a precedent that would be far more important in later decades.

Yet soldiers themselves were among those disillusioned by the inadequacies of the government's response to wartime poverty. War Department clerk J. B. Jones recorded in his diary a letter from a soldier complaining to the secretary of war that "his mother is in danger of starving—as she failed to get flour in Richmond, at $100 per barrel. He says if the government has no remedy for this, he and his comrades will throw down their arms and fly to some other country with their families, where a subsistence may be obtained."[104]

By the end of the war, some observers also complained that the rich did not support private charitable efforts adequately either. J. B. Jones noted that "only five ladies had responded to the call to knit socks for the soldiers," issued by the minister of the Monumental Church, which Jones pointedly referred to in his diary as "a *rich* congregation."[105] It undoubtedly produced even more class resentment when still-wealthy residents threw lavish parties, dances, and balls and had plentiful supplies of food shipped in to them from their outlying plantations.[106]

THE CIVIL WAR PRODUCED major shifts in popular views of poverty, poor relief, and the role of the state. Richmond continued its efforts to restrict aid to residents only, in keeping with the long-standing precedents stemming from the settlement laws, but abandoned the year's residency requirements in order to include war refugees in the public distributions. Little ink was spilled on the issue of the "idle but able-bodied" during the war years, as the city seemed less interested in the old issue of distinguishing between the deserving and the undeserving poor. Instead, the trend was to enlarge the category of "deserving" poor to include anyone who had been impoverished by the wartime conditions, especially those who had family members in the military. Although immigrants, namely the Irish, were still occasionally singled out for public disapproval, notably during the Bread Riot, the war emergency largely deflected attention away from foreign immigrants as unsuitable recipients of public welfare.

Practical considerations had also forced Richmond to return to the principle of outdoor relief. Recognizing that it was physically impossible to institutionalize the thousands of needy residents in the city, Richmond's leaders accepted the inevitable. The city provided greatly expanded outdoor relief, and no one complained of the change of principle (though they might complain about the small amounts of assistance they received).

The war had also promoted a shift in public understanding of the role of the state in the economy. The state, meaning government authority at any level, had been recast as a tool of the people in their struggle against speculators. Any government action that might curb inflation, provide relief for the impoverished, or improve the standard of living of the masses had come to be seen as desirable. And it did not seem to matter much which level of government took action, as long as one of them did.

The war had pushed the private sector into a decidedly secondary position. No one rejected private charitable efforts altogether, of course, and private charity continued to be an important function. But the public came to see private charities as more ameliorative, while only legislation could actually stem inflation, halt speculation, or set prices. Where, before the war, the middle classes especially seemed to favor private relief as far superior to the public dole, by war's end, the state appeared more powerful and more effective than decentralized, dispersed private efforts. Much like the depression of the 1930s, the Civil War demonstrated in vivid terms the inability of local relief and private charity to deal with a massive economic crisis.

Some of these changes in welfare policy would come to be reversed during Reconstruction, as seen in the following chapter. But one would have much longer lasting effects: the association of charity with Confederate patriotism would shape Virginia's public and private welfare policies well into the twentieth century.

CHAPTER FIVE

Reconstruction

The Contest over Poor Relief

The Civil War had caused many southerners to see for the first time the shortcomings of the system of relief countenanced by the poor laws. Although periodic economic depressions during the antebellum period had already demonstrated the flaws of the system, it took the war to provoke demands for state- and national-level assistance to the poor. State and Confederate governments offered a variety of direct and indirect relief to the impoverished, but in quantities insufficient to meet the needs. The result was disillusionment with those governments, which worked to undermine popular support for the war.

At the end of the war, the collapse of local and state governments left a void that the Union army and then the Freedmen's Bureau stepped in to fill temporarily. Given the crisis, these federal agencies had little choice but to include a massive, centralized relief program in their efforts to stabilize the South. Initially welcomed by desperate southern communities, this vast federal welfare program might have served as the basis of an entirely new public-welfare policy and might have finally offered the opportunity to abolish the old poor laws. That opportunity would be lost, however, due to the politics of race and Reconstruction. The poor laws would survive Reconstruction largely intact, despite their clear inadequacies. And new reasons to defend their continued existence emerged, as their alternative seemed to be a federal role that the South's leadership feared and rejected.

Reconstruction and the Freedmen's Bureau

The end of the Civil War found Virginia in chaos. The state had seen twenty-six major battles and hundreds of other smaller skirmishes, each of which had left destroyed fields, burned homes, and missing breadwinners in their wake.[1] In April 1865, thousands of whites were homeless, while tens of thousands of freedmen huddled in makeshift camps and on abandoned farms. No other southern state required as many emergency supplies and rations as did Virginia.[2]

Many such displaced persons, black and white, headed to Richmond in search of jobs, scattered relatives, and housing. What they found instead was a city in shambles. During the hurried evacuation of the city on 3 April, departing Confederate troops had set fire to warehouses, railroad trestles, and the major bridge connection over the James River in a misguided and ultimately disastrous attempt to prevent supplies from falling into the hands of the invading army. The fire spread, leveling large portions of the city, including dozens of businesses in the downtown district. Citizens, soldiers, and refugees alike joined the mobs looting stores.[3]

Eighty percent of the city's food supplies had been destroyed by the fire, and starvation was a real threat.[4] Supplying food, clothing, and shelter for the thousands of needy became the first priority for the arriving Union army. During the first week of Union occupation, the army supplied enough emergency rations to feed the entire city.[5] Then, with military efficiency, the army established a civilian relief commission to run its ration program. The commission divided the city into thirty districts and appointed two or three prominent men in each district to certify the needy. William Munford, already experienced in this form of organized relief, headed the commission. By the end of April, the civilian commission was distributing thirteen thousand army rations a day to both blacks and whites.[6]

Northern private charitable organizations rushed in to supply aid to the city as well. The American Union Commission reported that from mid-April to mid-August 1865, it had distributed in Richmond eighty thousand pounds of flour, daily soup rations for six hundred to eight hundred people, as well as garden seeds and agricultural implements.[7] The American Missionary Association (AMA) assisted an average of one hundred people a day in Richmond during the winter of 1866–67. Applicants were provided with small quantities of food and fuel and then sent to the offices of the Freedmen's Bureau if they needed further aid.[8]

The Freedmen's Bureau, "the nation's first federal welfare agency," had been established by Congress in March 1865, with wide latitude for its activities.[9] But, as W. E. B. Du Bois recognized, the bureau was given few tools to carry out its "stupendous" assignments: as an emergency operation, it had little time for careful advance planning; it was given no initial funding, but rather was to depend upon the "chance accumulations" of wartime; and it had to rely upon a "rough military machine for administrating delicate social reform."[10] Its commissioner, General Oliver Otis Howard, saw the bureau's poor-relief function as one of its lesser roles and believed that it would be discontinued "speedily." Moreover, Howard intended that the bureau would not take over poor relief entirely, but rather would work in conjunction with private charities and existing local agencies.[11] In Richmond, as in communities throughout the South, local authorities would demonstrate that they viewed the situation quite differently.

The Freedmen's Bureau in Virginia was under the command of Colonel Orlando Brown, a former army assistant quartermaster. Brown was selected for the position primarily because he had previous experience as the military's superintendent of Negro Affairs in Norfolk. He was already acquainted with the distribution of relief aid, as well as the establishment of schools for blacks. In addition, Brown was experienced in working with the AMA, which soon operated as an unofficial adjunct of the Freedmen's Bureau.[12]

In the initial weeks after the end of the war, southern whites seldom complained that the federal government (through the army) provided rations to both blacks and whites. Although whites often found it distasteful to offer a loyalty oath as a condition of receiving rations, true hunger made the federal largesse acceptable. The Freedmen's Bureau followed this precedent, and its services—including rations—were offered regardless of race. Whites, in fact, received the majority of rations in many locales and were the principal beneficiaries of federal charity in some districts.[13] As a Richmond newspaper put it, "If the Bureau would extend its benefits always to whites as well as blacks our people would be willing to help support it."[14]

This initial tolerance of the Freedmen's Bureau quickly dissipated. As the region's local governments reorganized themselves, and as people went about the business of planting and rebuilding, white southerners began to see the Freedmen's Bureau as an interference with their goals for the postbellum South. The bureau's role in writing labor contracts endeared it to few southern planters; its vast program of schools for blacks threatened landowners' access to black labor; and its defense of black civil rights in the courts added further layers of hostility from the white South.[15] Southern whites, like Georgia's Gertrude Clanton Thomas, believed that bureau agents "aided as much as was possible in sowing broadcast the seed of dissention between the former master and slave and caused what might have continued to be a kind interest to become in many cases a bitter enmity."[16] Soon, in the words of W. E. B. Du Bois, "nothing [was] more convenient than to heap on the Freedmen's Bureau all the evils of that evil day, and damn it utterly for every mistake and blunder that was made."[17]

As early as the summer of 1865, then, the leadership of the white South had defined the Freedmen's Bureau as the enemy. Poor relief would be one of the areas of heated contest between the two. The struggle centered largely over the question of which government should care for which groups of the poor. White local authorities throughout the region insisted that the bureau take the full responsibility for the freedmen, offering several arguments in defense of this position. First, many white officials claimed that they were financially unable to care for the large numbers of freedmen suddenly requiring aid. W. K. Kean of Madison County reminded the bureau that the county's appropriations for the year had been made months before the end of the war and emancipation, and therefore had included no money for relief of indigent freedmen.[18] Ben Leavell of Spotsylvania County reported that he did "not think the County is in a condition to be levied at this time."[19] Former Confederate official Robert Kean believed, "The community is wholly unable . . . to take up the burden of a vast pauper system."[20]

Other local authorities claimed that their poorhouses were already full, and they could admit no one else, whether black or white. C. A. Holcomb, clerk of Campbell County, advised the bureau, "We cannot provide for the care and support of any more paupers at this time, as our rooms are filled to their full capacity."[21] Orange County likewise reported that its "[p]oorhouse is already filled to its utmost capacity by destitute poor whites."[22] Bureau agents recognized that this argument was largely disingenuous, that expanded facilities would be possible if the counties were willing to erect them. "The colored people get but little support from the County Poor Houses; they are filled with whites and an applicant is turned off with the remark that 'they have no room,'" wrote a bureau operative in Lynchburg. But, "the fact is quite clear to my mind that they do not intend to increase the Poor levy to include the colored People or to increase the capacity of their Poor Houses."[23] Journalist Whitelaw Reid, for one, was skeptical that whites in most parts of Virginia really needed assistance (although he had no doubts that African Americans did).[24]

Some local officials took a more combative stance, suggesting that it was unjust to require the local governments to support the freedmen under the current conditions. "In consequence of coloured persons not having been taxed, the board [of overseers] cannot assist any at present," wrote John Clift of King George County. "The board propose when they [freedmen] are taxed as white persons to provide for them as they do for white persons."[25] Finally, some localities attempted to hide behind the settlement laws to avoid supporting the freedmen. G. F. Harrison of Goochland County wrote, "My opinion is that those negroes who left the County to seek their fortunes elsewhere, and upon failure, or disappointment of their calculations, were returned upon us, have no claim for provision here."[26]

City officials resorted to all of these arguments in Richmond's struggle with the Freedmen's Bureau. This contest began in earnest in November 1865, when the bureau asked the city council to take over responsibility for the two hundred pauper freedmen "belonging to your city." The council refused, claiming that the freedmen instead had come from all parts of the state and therefore were the responsibility of their home counties. Although no such concern for legal technicalities had prevented the support of white refugees during the war, the city continued to deny assistance to freedmen on this basis for three more years.[27]

The city authorities also complained that the federal government granted the freedmen privileges and protections that whites did not receive. "The United States authorities have taken the coloured population under their protection," wrote T. P. August, chair of the city council's committee on the relief of the poor.

> Until very lately the state courts and justices were not allowed to try any offense in which they were the actors. . . . They are moreover, if we are correctly informed, exempted from all the burthens of government which other people have to bear. They pay no taxes; we presume they cannot be required to perform any other public duty; and by express orders they are exempted from the restraint of laws to which the white population are subjected. Thus exempted from the common burthes [sic] and from our control, we do not think that they are entitled or we are bound to take upon ourselves the burthen of their support.[28]

White local officials made it clear that they would do little to care for black indigents. Planters, who in antebellum years had been required to care for their own indigent slaves, now took advantage of the opportunity to relieve themselves of this burden. Numerous planters declared that they would no longer care for their dependent former slaves and began attempts to remove old and infirm freedmen from their property. In December 1865, the Freedmen's Bureau intervened and ordered that all former owners were required to continue to care for their indigent former slaves until such time as the local overseers of the poor were ready to care for them.[29] With such obstructionism, the bureau agent in Richmond worried what would happen to the freedmen once federal rations were ended. "From present indications there will be considerable destitution in this city during the forthcoming winter, should the Bureau cease its operations on Jan. 1 [1869] as contemplated. . . . Whenever we can force the civil authorities to make suitable provision for the colored population the Bureau can be successfully withdrawn, but how far we can compel them to assume this responsibility I am unable to determine."[30]

Hostile whites throughout the South scrutinized every action of the bureau and exulted in every opportunity to discredit its activities.[31] Whites in Richmond suggested that black poverty was in fact being caused by the bureau's actions. "Any one who wants to know the straits to which these unhappy victims of misguided philanthropy are reduced, may form a conception of their misery during the cold weather by going out about twilight on the Williamsburg turnpike and see them bringing in scraps of wood, and bags of brush."[32] The *Daily Dispatch* reported smugly: "A negro woman was found dead yesterday . . . and from the facts presented there can be no doubt that she died of starvation. This is a comment upon the Freedmen's Bureau which it is perfectly unnecessary to enlarge upon. We may say, however, that no such cases were known while the American citizens of African descent were in a state of servitude."[33]

Local whites asserted that the bureau's relief activities would promote idleness by allowing freed people to live without working. Commenting on the bureau's soup house, the *Dispatch* contended, "A surprising number of strong, hearty men are found among these petitioners for charity—most of them, we regret to say, lazy, saucy fellows, who wouldn't accept work if they had it, but prefer to lounge about the city, shivering with cold and subsisting upon the bounty of the United States. Bad habits these, which they are forming. Remember, boys, the Bureau won't last forever."[34]

Moreover, local residents feared that the availability of government relief acted as a magnet, drawing in the hungry and homeless from other areas. "It will hardly be credited that the small allowance granted by the Freedmen's Bureau draws colored people from places far in the country. They travel eight or ten miles to wait for hours, or a whole day, for that which will not probably supply their wants for as long as twenty-four hours. This evil prolongs itself, and the gifts of the Bureau promote poverty and starvation."[35]

For its part, the bureau contended that southern governments must learn to assume responsibility for the freedmen. Just as the bureau believed it must teach the freedmen the value of work, the bureau also believed it must teach southern governmental authorities what their duties and responsibilities were in a free-labor economy. Commissioner O. O. Howard himself realized how difficult that would be, as long as the bureau was present and continued to supply rations to the black population. This was one of the reasons Howard wished to curtail relief efforts as quickly as possible.[36]

Southern relief officials also battled the bureau over which white poor were entitled to relief. Local white elites wished to punish known Unionists by denying them aid; bureau agents resisted supporting former rebels. The Freedmen's Bureau, at the end of the summer of 1865, ceased distributing rations to all whites and instead began providing them only to whites who had been loyal to the Union.[37] Meanwhile, local authorities openly discriminated in the distribution of relief: the local bureau agent in Greene County noted on a monthly list of destitute whites that "All these Persons are entirely destitute, having during the War lost all their property, are helpless and have at this time no means of making a support, nor have the Civil Authorities made any Provision for them."[38] Another bureau agent reported that one W. H. Woodward needed support, for he "is a refugee and can not obtain work from his neighbors for that reason."[39] Assistant superintendent Henry Ayres noted the resistance of local whites in his district: "The better or *higher* class of whites are all opposed to rations being issued to this poor class, that is especially to those who have been *diserters* [*sic*] and Refugees from the late rebel cause."[40] Monthly reports from the local Richmond agent, which listed the names and ages of those receiving bureau rations, noted that these were "destitute and suffering white citizens who do not receive relief from the civil authorities [in] Richmond City."[41]

O. O. Howard's hopes aside, the Freedmen's Bureau functioned as a vast social-welfare agency in the South and continued to do so until it was shut down by Congress. The relief effort was enormous, as the monthly accounts demonstrated. In the month of October 1865, the bureau issued 230,180 rations to freedmen in Virginia.[42] During the winter of 1865–66, fuel and clothing expenses for the Virginia freedmen alone cost $23,868.29.[43] By the time the bureau ceased to function, it had spent over $3,000,000 just on food and clothing.[44] As John Hope Franklin has observed, the relief efforts of the Freedmen's Bureau ought "to be ranked with the great efforts of recent depressions and wars."[45]

Bureau agents became de facto social-welfare workers. (Historians have yet to pay full attention to the impact that experiences in the bureau, missionary relief associations, and the Sanitary Commission had on the creation of social work as a field.)[46] As such, an analysis of the welfare activities of the bureau affords an opportunity to examine closely the welfare ideals of midcentury America and the interaction of national trends with regional realities. Freedmen's Bureau agents, most of whom came from outside the South, reflected the assumptions of their peers regarding poverty and poor relief. Their experiences in distributing relief in the South would also teach them many of the lessons that other welfare workers learned in the nineteenth century.

Despite the unusually catastrophic economic circumstances, the bureau expressed a constant fear that relief aid would serve to pauperize the recipients. Colonel Orlando Brown, assistant superintendent in charge of Virginia, instructed his subordinates: "Your attention is particularly called to the improvidence of the Freedmen. You will instruct them that . . . neither laws or proclamations can make them really free until by frugality and economy they place themselves in a Situation where their dependence on government of charity, for support, shall cease."[47] In a tone that reflected the paternalistic approach of the larger welfare community, Brown contended that blacks must "feel the spur of necessity, if it be needed to make them self-reliant, industrious and provident."[48] Bureau agents remained alert to the possibility that the "undeserving" would receive rations. This concern with the "undeserving" poor went all the way to the top of the bureau: General Howard himself issued rules that able-bodied freedmen were to be encouraged "and if necessary compelled" to support themselves rather than receive bureau assistance.[49]

Bureau agents, like most middle-class Americans of their day, believed in the intrinsic value of work, and they believed that teaching the freedmen the value of work was one of their most fundamental roles.[50] The bureau expected the freedmen to take paid work at any price and were confounded by the freed people's reluctance to take certain jobs. "It is reported here on good authority," wrote one staffer, "that some of the Freemen of City Point who are out of employment have refused offers of work at $8 per month and Board. I am instructed to inform you that such a course must find no continuance from the Bureau, but that on the contrary should you find such instances you will at once shut them off from rations and any assistance whatever of fuel, quarters, or anything of the kind. Such cases must be made an example of for the benifit [sic] of the others."[51] Northern observers, even those essentially sympathetic to the plight of the freedmen, supported the bureau's efforts to teach the work ethic. The journalist and radical Republican Whitelaw Reid put it bluntly: "[D]o not gather them in colonies at military posts, and feed them on Government rations; but throw them in the water and have them learn to swim by finding the necessity of swimming."[52] If a former abolitionist like Reid could take such an unbending position, one can imagine the lack of sympathy and generosity that might come from other quarters.

Despite the explanatory evidence often at their fingertips, most bureau agents could not comprehend why many freedmen refused to move from their homes in search of better paying jobs. The assistant superintendent in Yorktown, for example, noted, "Men, women and children are here who could if removed to other places find employment and be provided with comfortable homes, but seem to prefer to live here in almost starvation. Every effort has been put forth to urge upon the Freedmen the benefits which would accrue to them, by a removal, but to a great extent without avail." Then, as if in answer to his own question, the agent continued: "Many however have now small plots of ground under cultivation and it is hoped when their crops are gathered that greater success will attend efforts [at] their removal."[53] Months later, the same agent reported the continued resistance of the freedmen of "all efforts which tends to their removal to other points where regular labor could be obtained for them. Wedded to the land on which they were placed by the Government, they do not wish to change homes, but remain here doing an occasional job instead of providing themselves with comfortable homes in other neighborhoods."[54]

Although frustrated by their lack of cooperation, some bureau officials at least could appreciate some of the reasons for the freed people's "cat-like attachment to places."[55] General S. C. Armstrong was one who understood that there were "many very worthy widowed women who have large families who, poorly off as they are here, can do no better elsewhere, who have no assurance of getting employment away from here, [and] have not the means (besides transportation) of moving and setting up new homes in other parts."[56] The gendered nature of poverty—so visible for whites since the seventeenth century—now became a fact of life for freedwomen as well.

Like charity workers throughout the country, Freedmen's Bureau agents were concerned about the role of alcohol in producing poverty. The bureau directed its agents to work to establish temperance organizations among the freedmen and constantly preached the adverse economic impact of drinking. Benjamin Cook, a local bureau agent in Richmond, reported that "the Temperance movement amongst the Freedmen of this Division is being carried on with the utmost vigor. I have succeeded thus far in perfecting arrangements to establish permanent and uniformed societies. . . . I believe that an organization of this kind in which they can make an imposing display by turning out in processions in full regalia of the order is much more preferable to any other organization that can be instituted. . . . Vigorous appeals will be made by the Societies to induce the Colored men to . . . take the whole of their hard earned wages to the homes of their families."[57] The next year, Cook reported that his temperance work "is gaining ground, several meetings have been held during the month with favorable results. This work I shall encourage knowing full well how important it is that the freedmen at this time should economize by leaving off their intemperate habits."[58]

Freedmen's Bureau officials also learned how to run charitable institutions, including hospitals and almshouses. In Richmond, the Chimborazo Hospital, which was being used to house homeless whites and blacks, was converted into a temporary almshouse—operated by the bureau—for the freedmen. It was soon being referred to in official correspondence as the "Chimborazo Hospital and Almshouse."[59] Administrators of this institution soon learned what the Richmond overseers already knew: controlling the activities of the "inmates" was a challenge. Without a fence to keep the residents in the compound at Chimborazo, it was quite difficult to control them. In November 1865, the president of a local railroad line wrote to the bureau to complain that the inmates at Chimborazo were "supplying themselves with fuel by tearing up the track . . . and burning the cross ties."[60] Later that winter, the freedmen at Chimborazo were reported to be cutting down telegraph poles, presumably for the same purpose.[61]

Like welfare agencies elsewhere, the bureau was concerned with keeping expenses as low as possible. Agents studied their own statistical data to detect places where cuts might be made. When one state official realized that the monthly rations in Petersburg were the highest in the state, he ordered the local bureau agents to reduce "the number of rations issued to the lowest possible figures. No greater harm can be done the Freedmen than supporting those who should support themselves."[62] The state official did not question whether there might be valid reasons for higher expenses in Petersburg; he assumed that "higher" equaled "inexcusable."

The lessons learned by bureau officials included the fact of the gendered nature of poverty.[63] "Women and girls have not generally remunerative employment," wrote one official. "At this season, and in the fall they can sometimes get field work at low wages. But there is constantly a large amount of uncalled for female help."[64] The Richmond agent empathetically explained why women remained "uncalled for": "I will also bring to your notice another class of unfortunates, these are freedwomen whose husbands have either died or deserted, leaving behind them several small children; these poor mothers with their helpless and dependent family of little ones are totally debared [sic] from obtaining employment because of their encumbrance, eke out a miserable existence, notwithstanding their industry and willingness to work there can be no question raised involving the perseverance or self denial of many of these women in behalf of their helpless children, such is the true condition of the indigent freedpeople in Richmond at this time."[65] The situation in Alexandria was identical: there were no able-bodied unemployed "except in some cases of women with children whom no one seems disposed to employ on account of the encumbrances."[66]

The Freedmen's Bureau also learned that welfare work could require considerable involvement in the lives of the poor. One Elizabeth Norris asked the bureau to compel her husband to support her. She explained that her husband had deserted her and was living with another woman in another county, under an assumed name. She wanted the bureau to force her husband to support her and her children.[67] Norris thus pushed the bureau to assume even more of the functions of antebellum local governments, which had frequently compelled spouses and other family members to provide for their own indigents.

Bureau agents learned as well the importance of the practice of "removal." As local governments had done since the seventeenth century, the bureau spent considerable sums of money and great quantities of administrative time arranging transportation of the poor, both black and white, to relieve the government of the burden of their care. The bureau negotiated with the railroads to find the "most favorable terms" by which it could "gather the scattered families together in order that as few as possible of the helpless be left a burden on the govt. or on private charity."[68] In October 1865, one bureau agent reported on the dozens of freedmen he was transporting, in each instance noting that the action would "relieve the Govt of their support."[69]

Observing the welfare activities of the short-lived Freedmen's Bureau in Richmond provides an opportunity to consider simultaneously national and regional attitudes toward poverty and poor relief in this era. Despite the white South's vocal and bitter complaints about the bureau, it is striking how similar the South's views on poor relief were to those of the North. The South did not complain that the bureau used the categories of "deserving" and "undeserving" to decide who received relief, although southerners disagreed with the bureau's definitions of just who fit into which category. Likewise, both North and South were in agreement that all who could work, should work. Both the vanquished and the victorious feared that indiscriminate relief would pauperize the recipients and produce a permanently dependent class. Local whites could even upon occasion offer praise to the bureau for its efforts to see that no relief was granted to those who did not really require it.[70] Union officials and former Confederates alike continued to believe in the principle of local relief, and both wished to return poor relief to the control of local authorities as soon as possible.

The experience of the Freedmen's Bureau in Richmond suggests that the South's prevailing views on poor relief were in fact in keeping with national ideology. The only real point of difference was over race, and the politics of Reconstruction only served to inflame that difference.

Reconstruction and Local Relief

The Freedmen's Bureau was without doubt the single most important relief agency in Richmond from its arrival in the city in June 1865 through the termination of its relief activities in January 1869. But local efforts, both public and private, continued to expand alongside the bureau's relief activities. Local leaders assumed that, despite the dominating presence of the bureau, provision for the poor should return to its prewar modus operandi. All agreed that public relief, both indoor and outdoor, should work in cooperation with private charity.

The almshouse returned to its central position in the city's welfare program. The newly constructed facility, now relinquished by the departing cadets of the Virginia Military Institute, reopened for the care of the city's white poor. For the black poor, the city would soon convert its former smallpox hospital, called Howard's Grove, into an almshouse for African Americans.[71]

Management of the city almshouses, first under W. S. Phillips and then under Charles P. Bigger, produced frequent complaints by the inmates, who had the temporary advantage of being able to turn to the military authorities with their grievances. One such incident took place in the winter of 1865–66. Mrs.

E. M. Jeter wrote to General Terry, charging Superintendent Phillips with several counts of abuse. Mrs. Jeter claimed that Phillips ordered several of the female inmates to work in the washhouse in the severe weather, with "no shoes, nor stockings, and some were without anything except a single garment (a chemise)." Jeter also charged that the superintendent made sick and pregnant women do heavy lifting and that he made "base propositions to the females under his care; and while some reject, others submit, through fear, to his wishes." Unfortunately for Mrs. Jeter, the military turned the case over to the civil authorities for investigation. The city council, predictably, found the charges "to be entirely without foundation." Then, in retaliation, the local police arrested Jeter and three of the corroborating witnesses on charges of keeping a house of ill fame. [72]

By January 1867, the almshouse was under the management of Charles Bigger, a former Confederate officer. [73] The *Daily Dispatch* applauded his handiwork: "The institution is governed in the same way as a military barracks, and the rules are carried out to the letter." [74] Not everyone agreed with this assessment. Patrick Fay, a Union veteran and inmate of the white almshouse, complained to bureau chief Orlando Brown about his mistreatment at the hands of Superintendent Bigger. Once again, the bureau turned the case over to the city council; once again the council backed the local official, concluding that Bigger was justified in his "rigid" enforcement of the rules. The council also dismissed the charge that Bigger was prejudiced against Fay, accepting the defense that "the Superintendent never knew that Fay had been a soldier in the Federal Army until after he had left the institution." [75] The federal authorities, reviewing the case, appeared not to have accepted the explanation and removed Bigger from his position. [76]

These two incidents were just the first signs that not all would return to the status quo antebellum. While the control over the institution was being contested, the numbers of residents in the almshouses continued to grow during Reconstruction far beyond the prewar levels. The white almshouse continued to house "all nationalities." According to the *Dispatch*, the facility held "representatives of all of the nations of the Old World and nearly all of the States of this country." [77] Clearly the newspaper exaggerated a little here, since the article also reported that the total number of whites in the almshouse at the time was only 106. But, hyperbole aside, the point remains that the almshouse now cared for greatly increased numbers of people, including foreign immigrants and recent domestic migrants. The city's black almshouse housed another 111 people, separate from the hundreds of African Americans in the federally run almshouse at Chimborazo.

In addition to the two almshouses, the city continued its enlarged outdoor relief efforts. The city distributed wood free to applicants who brought with them a "certificate of his or her minister or physician, or the certificate of some well known and reliable citizen, that the party applying for fuel is unable to purchase it."[78]

The presence of the Freedmen's Bureau (through the end of 1868) further complicated the local relief program. The animosities of the war continued and made the working relationship between the city and federal authorities contentious. The city council and the Freedmen's Bureau wrangled for months over how to coordinate their efforts in poor relief.[79] The council finally appropriated one thousand dollars to a special committee authorized to work with the bureau, but then the committee apparently refused to spend the funds. When the bureau formally complained about the lack of cooperation, the chairman of the special committee replied, "Satisfactory reasons were given for the non-action of the standing committee on the subject." Another councilman, Mr. Taylor, "thought it a hard case that the Freedmen's Bureau, with all the wealth of the Federal Government to back it, should come here and ask of an impoverished people an appropriation to support the poor."[80] Bitterness over Confederate defeat played a role in the stinginess of the local government's provision of social welfare.

The city's financial condition also contributed to its hardening position on poor relief. The city council attempted to cut costs wherever possible; it also renewed its earlier attempts to make the facilities as undesirable as possible. In December 1870, the city's committee on the relief of the poor ruled that all inmates must wear uniforms provided by the institution. Any personal clothing they brought with them would be labeled and stored until they were discharged.[81] (Although the regimentation of uniform clothing was intended to instill discipline and order in the institution, while making it a less desirable place to go, it may very well have had another product: inmate solidarity. Standardized uniforms would have obliterated the differences between people distinguishable by their clothing.)

Just as the public sector struggled to deal with poor relief in a changed political environment, private charities struggled to survive in a changed economic environment. Private charities continued to multiply in the postbellum period, although in the straitened financial conditions of the times, they had difficulty collecting sufficient funds. In January 1866, a meeting was held to form the Richmond Relief Association. "We regretted to see so few in attendance," noted the local press. The organizers discussed raising funds by solicitation throughout the country. A Mr. Witter objected, saying he did not believe in begging aid from the North. William Munford, chairing the meeting, retorted that he did not believe they should refuse aid from any quarter, since so few local people had either money or provisions to give.[82] A week later, the new group asked the military authorities for continued assistance in distributing medicine to the poor.[83]

The Richmond Relief Association, chaired by James A. Scott (with William Munford acting as one of the directors), set out to systematize relief efforts in the city. The members divided the city into twenty-four districts and assigned male visitors to each. A second such association formed several weeks later, for the Church Hill and Union Hill districts of town, and it too assigned visitors to canvass the neighborhoods. "The reports of its visitors are the result of personal inspection and inquiry. . . . in this way imposition is frequently detected."[84]

With funds so limited and needs so great, concerns about "imposition" grew. The *Dispatch* believed that the city, "like all others, is infested with a set of professional paupers, who flock, like vampires at the smell of blood, to suck every eleemosynary institution as soon as its doors are opened." The newspaper warned, "There are sufferers, and they are too many, and the means of the more favored classes are too limited to justify any careless measures which may result in wasting gifts upon imposters."[85] Concerns about "imposition" by the able-bodied, which had largely disappeared during the war years, now returned more vigorously than before.

Local philanthropists scrambled to meet emergency cases and to coordinate the efforts of the mushrooming—and often competing—private charitable efforts. A handful of individuals emerged from the chaos, such as the aforementioned William Munford, who would become involved in multiple charitable efforts during these years, and would later spend much of their lives involved in welfare activities in the city. One such new face in the crowd was Dr. William W. Parker. A former Confederate artillery officer, Parker had gained his first experience in charity work in the 1840s, when he served as a visitor for the Gentlemen's Benevolent Society.[86] Now he stepped up to become a leader in civic work and was involved in a wide array of activities.[87] Parker announced in May 1866 that he had been contacted by several people who wished to adopt orphans of deceased Confederate soldiers.[88] In October 1867, Parker proposed a plan to help the many sick residents who could not afford food and medicines. He announced in the press that he was setting up a box in the YMCA building where local doctors could drop in the names of those who they knew needed assistance. Then volunteers could pick out names and assist those who had been screened by the physicians. This scheme would be especially useful to "ladies who desire to do good, but the pathway is not always open. Timidity restrains many."[89]

Parker in fact acted as something of a self-appointed director of private charitable efforts in the first years after the war, using the local newspaper as his informal organizing system. Parker would collect donations, order supplies such as wood, decide how much it would sell for, and announce in the paper its availability for the poor.[90] Parker regularly used the columns of the *Daily Dispatch* to make public acknowledgments of the donations of private individuals to his efforts.[91] Indeed, Parker came to be viewed as *the* distributor of private relief in the city, and many people assumed, incorrectly, that he was also in charge of public charities as well.[92]

In addition to organizations providing direct relief, private groups also created new asylums to care for dependents, particularly dependent children. The Male Orphan Asylum and the Female Humane Association Asylum, both with antebellum origins, continued their operations, while new institutions appeared. In 1868, the city's Catholic community incorporated the St. Joseph's Academy and Orphan Asylum. Almost simultaneously, St. Mark's Episcopal Church opened a Free School in its chapel.[93]

The numerous private charitable efforts continued to rely upon Confederate sympathies for support. In an appeal for support of orphans, for example, former governor Henry Wise reminded his listeners that some of these orphans were the children of Confederate soldiers. "Our Southern community must be really as barbarous as it is represented to be by those paragons of civilization, Wendell Phillips and Sumner, if it did not promptly, cordially, and effectually answer such appeals," he said.[94] Similarly, a newspaper editorial by "Loyal" appealed to Confederate sympathies in supplying aid to the poor: "Remember your homes were defended in time of trouble by them that have sacrificed their lives upon the battle-field, and now you are enjoying that home, while the widows and orphans are forgotten."[95]

Despite the continuous appeals to Confederate patriotism, private charitable groups in Richmond had difficulty raising funds, and some turned to the city for support. Following the antebellum precedent of city subsidies for private charities, the city council gave the Richmond Relief Association one thousand dollars in February 1866.[96] The council continued to support the private orphan asylums as well, with the Female Humane Association, St. Joseph's Orphan Asylum, and St. Patrick's Orphan School each receiving annual grants of one thousand dollars.[97] "After much discussion," the council also agreed to grant five hundred dollars to the Friends' Colored Orphan Asylum.[98]

So many private charities appealed to the city for aid that it began to cause problems, stretching the city's finances past the limit. In January 1869, the city council was unable to make its usual appropriation to the Male Orphan Asylum, which the board of directors warned threatened the institution's survival.[99] The editor of the *Dispatch* criticized the council for having "no well defined system in making charitable appropriations. A member moves to appropriate a sum of money to some charitable institution or object, and it is carried. This is several times repeated early in the winter. Later, when equally deserving societies or objects are presented, aid is refused because the city has already expended quite as much as the condition of its treasury will permit." The *Dispatch* offered a reform plan: "Would it not be better at once to appoint a committee on public charities, to whom all applications shall be referred, and who shall be required to report at any early day the aggregate sum which should be thus expended, and the amount to each charity."[100] The *Dispatch* thereby anticipated by several decades the emergence of boards of public welfare, born of the need to coordinate the numerous, often competing, charities.

Despite the combined efforts of the Freedmen's Bureau, the city, and the private charities, the numbers of ill-fed and ill-clothed in Richmond remained enormous. Though many agencies were involved, most criticism was directed at the city government for not doing enough to take care of its poor. Bureau agent Benjamin Cook wrote his superior that even the widows and orphans of Confederate soldiers were left to suffer at the hands of the municipal authorities.[101] Although one might dismiss the criticism as coming from a biased source, local voices added weight to the charges. The *Daily Dispatch* charged that "the Common Council, limited as are its means, should do something more in the way of providing for those in want and distress."[102]

Significantly, critics of the city's efforts did not ask for the state government or the federal government to step in and fill the unmet needs. The willingness of southern whites to embrace an enlarged state-welfare apparatus disappeared during Reconstruction as quickly as it had emerged in the Civil War. Instead, Richmonders now demanded more relief from the city government, supplemented as necessary by private charities. The remarkable expansion of private charitable organizations was, in a very concrete form, a repudiation of the federal government's relief efforts.

That burden suddenly grew greater when the Freedmen's Bureau closed its operations in the city on 1 January 1869. Although city officials had criticized the bureau, antagonized its agents, and refused to cooperate with its programs for more than three years, they now came to realize that the city would have to take over a significant portion of the bureau's relief activities after its demise. After consulting with the bureau, the city council concluded it would have to provide food for at least two thousand people a day, at a cost of approximately one hundred dollars per day, at least during the remainder of the winter. This was in addition to the regular expenses of the almshouses, then housing between 160 and 260 people each day, and the city's usual outdoor-relief supplies of fuel, medicine, and food.[103]

Ironically, the city found itself operating the very same soup house it had so frequently criticized when under the bureau's auspices.[104] To manage the soup house, the city council appointed Captain Charles Bigger, the former superintendent of the almshouse who had recently been removed from his post by the federal authorities. One imagines that placing Bigger in charge of the bureau's soup house felt like vindication to the local officials. Bigger's reputation for strict discipline and record of hostility toward Unionists may also explain the reduction in the numbers of rations the soup house supplied. (At the end of the first month of operation, Bigger reported that he had spent $1,604 on the soup house, averaging 1,367 rations per day, or $51.76 per day.[105] This represented a considerably smaller program than the city had previously estimated.) By 1870, after the federal authorities had left the city, Bigger had been returned to the office of the superintendent of the almshouses, where he resumed his "most efficient" management.[106]

The city's public and private relief efforts, often intertwined, reserved the majority of their resources for whites. Only a tiny number of private charities served the freedmen, such as the Friends Orphan Asylum. Public relief, including the soup house and the almshouse, was available to blacks but was disproportionately distributed. Whites received more public aid, despite the relatively greater needs of the black community. Under these circumstances, black self-help efforts expanded to fill in the gaps. Mutual-aid associations such as the Baptist Helping Society, the Colored Friendly Aid Society, and the Freedmen's Benefit Society allowed working-class blacks to pool their meager resources into larger funds, many of which were then deposited in the Freedmen's Bank of Richmond.[107] Offering sickness and burial benefits, mutual-aid societies functioned as self-insurance schemes. But they also afforded poor relief to members who found themselves temporarily out of work and in need.

ALTHOUGH THE "FREEDMEN'S Bureau had shown that the federal government could provide for the welfare of people on a broad scale when poverty and hardship could (or would) not be treated locally,"[108] the politics of Reconstruction worked to limit the possibility that the bureau would serve as the foundation of a permanent federal welfare system after the Civil War. The contest between local and federal officials over who cared for which poor finally produced this settlement: the city authorities would provide for (pro-Confederate) whites, and the bureau would provide for blacks. This compromise had three very important consequences. First, it reinforced the antebellum preference for segregation of welfare services, particularly regarding institutional forms of relief. This antebellum precedent now gained the sanction of the federal government for its continuation. Second, the association of federal welfare provision with African Americans would serve to stigmatize federal welfare activism in the eyes of southern whites. Given that the federal government was still the hated enemy in many quarters and was still seen as the recent conqueror of the South, federal welfare for the freedmen during Reconstruction gave many unrecon-structed southerners yet another reason to despise the federal government. The white South would continue to oppose federal activities in the area of public welfare for another century. (And southern political opposition would prove to be a powerful force for limiting the scope of the federal welfare state during the New Deal, as will be seen in chapter 9.)

Third, after the withdrawal of the Freedmen's Bureau, southern blacks would find themselves left largely to their own devices. The city's public welfare would be extended to African Americans on a begrudging, segregated basis. White pri-vate charities would regularly exclude blacks from their programs. Self-help and mutual-aid activities would be propelled to the forefront in black communities faced with local white hostility and the absence of federal support.

The Civil War and Reconstruction years can be seen as an opportunity lost in the history of southern social welfare. With the clear evidence of the shortcom-ings of local welfare, with the war-induced popular acceptance of the enlarged role of the state in poor relief, and with the federal government's willingness to experiment with a massive, centralized relief program during Reconstruction, the time could have been ripe to abolish the antiquated poor laws and craft a new system in their stead. That opportunity was lost because of the politics of race and Reconstruction. It would take another massive economic upheaval, in a changed political climate, before the opportunity returned.

CHAPTER SIX

The New South, Part I

Scientific Charity and

Confederate Commemoration

In 1905, the head of Washington state's Associated Charities visited Richmond as part of a southern tour of welfare agencies. Expecting to find a city of "ancient landmarks," Charles Weller was surprised—and pleased—to find instead "a nucleus of noble-spirited, modern-minded social service."[1] Early-twentieth-century Richmond was in fact both a city of ancient landmarks, where the commemoration of the Lost Cause dominated public life, and a "modern-minded" New South city where professional social work flourished in a busy industrial community.

This was the product of successive waves of social-welfare thinking that washed over the South in the decades following Reconstruction, leaving in their wake a complex, sometimes contradictory legacy. Southerners would embrace these successive trends in national social-welfare ideology—first "charity organization" and then "progressivism"—but would meld those national trends together with regional concerns about race and the Lost Cause. The result would be a social-welfare policy that paralleled, but did not duplicate, national norms. Richmond, simultaneously modern minded and locked in the past, stood at the center of it all.

From Reconstruction to Depression

After a slow start, post-Reconstruction Virginia finally began its economic recovery. Richmond, with its more diversified economy, seemed to bounce back even faster than most southern cities. The antebellum economic triumvirate of tobacco, flour, and iron production remained centrally important to Richmond's economy, but these economic cornerstones were soon joined by new enterprises. Cotton mills, wood products, and chemical industries helped to create in Richmond the kind of New South economy that Henry Grady had advocated.[2]

That economic recovery was temporarily derailed by the Panic of 1873. The depression of the 1870s hurt the South even more than the rest of the country. Between 1872 and 1877, the price of cotton fell by nearly 50 percent. Tobacco, rice, and sugar prices also fell ominously. The effects rippled through the entire economy, plunging farmers into debt, manufacturers into bankruptcy, and workers into unemployment.[3]

Richmond felt the impact of the Panic of 1873 deeply. Banks closed, including the symbolically and financially important Freedmen's Savings Bank, which swept away $166,000 in hard-earned savings.[4] (In addition to individual savings accounts, the Freedmen's Bank held the collective funds of numerous social-welfare organizations of Richmond's African Americans, such as mutual-aid associations, churches, and labor unions.)[5] Railroads went into receivership, and even the venerable Tredegar Ironworks shut its doors. Massive layoffs were the result.[6] The mayor saw his city's streets filled with "able-bodied paupers, vagrants, and tramps . . . the product of the dullness of business."[7] Local observers looked to "the coming winter with gravest apprehensions." An anonymous editorialist, styling himself "One of the People," wrote, "I cannot say how many fathers and brothers have now been thrown out of employment, nor how many are yet to be dismissed."[8]

Few Virginians had the kind of resources to permit them to survive months of unemployment, especially so soon after the war and Reconstruction. But the poor and working class of Virginia confronted a political regime that preferred to pay off its old war debts rather than provide expanded social-welfare services. Even though the state legislature had been willing to cross over the psychological barrier to the "welfare state" just a decade earlier, by the 1870s the political climate had changed. During this economic crisis, Virginia's political leadership responded with slashed state budgets, making especially deep cuts in social services, to service the state's debt.[9] The Conservative regime diverted over $250,0000 from the school fund in 1877 alone, forcing 127 schools to close their doors.[10] As illustrated in table 5, the state budget was cut repeatedly during the 1870s, with expenditures on asylums (then the primary category of state welfare expense) suffering along with other state functions.

In this context, Richmond's poor had little option but to rely on local public relief and private charities. To their credit, Richmond's public authorities took this crisis seriously. In an emergency meeting of the mayor and the city council, the leaders planned a two-pronged response to the depression: expanded outdoor relief and a substantial public works project. For the first part, the council's committee on the relief of the poor estimated it would need to provide rations for some five thousand people. For the second part, mayor Anthony Keiley argued that the vast pool of unemployed workers, numbering in the thousands, could be used to build a reservoir and other public projects that the city had been contemplating. The city would benefit by getting the work done more cheaply than it might later, during a period of fuller employment; the workers would get the benefit of wages, even if lower than in other periods. The council agreed to the plan and voted to issue bonds to raise the funds.[11] Notably, nowhere in this discussion did the council question whether using a public works project as unemployment relief was a proper area of government activity. The same generation that had created new forms of public relief during the Civil War drew easily on that precedent now.

Meanwhile, the numbers of "inmates" in the city's almshouses began to creep up, as did the numbers receiving outdoor aid from the city (see tables 9 and 10). So many people asked for lodging in the city's jails that the chief of police began plans to convert part of the old city market into a homeless shelter.[12] The demands on the city's relief programs grew so great that the council felt compelled to explain to the public that the "department of out-door poor" "does not pretend to give, in any instance, entire relief, but only partial or temporary assistance. . . . At this time the only ration allowed is corn-meal, which is furnished as follows: for adults, one pound per day; for children, eight ounces per day—issued Thursdays to whites, and to colored on Fridays. Fuel is issued in extreme cold weather only, as follows: Heads of families being allowed one-half of a cord of wood per month, distributed every two weeks."[13]

In the first year of the depression, the city's outdoor relief included 8,989 rations issued to whites and 9,350 rations issued to blacks. By 1875, the rations had risen to 19,719 for whites and 17,323 for blacks. More than two thousand people had sought shelter in the city jail during the latter year.[14] At the height of the depression, the local press estimated that "probably five thousand men, white and black, are totally unemployed, and are without credit or resources and almost without hope." The editorialist sympathized: "the sufferings of the poor in Richmond must be terrible indeed."[15]

Even though the city had provided hundreds with institutionalized care and thousands with rations, this was clearly insufficient to meet the level of need. Meanwhile the state government had made manifest its overriding interest in budget cutting rather than increased public relief. White southerners of the 1870s would hardly turn to the federal government for assistance, given that the despised Freedmen's Bureau had only just withdrawn from the region. Instead, the Panic of 1873 helped to stimulate the creation of even more voluntary associations, on top of those still in place from the war and Reconstruction years. Two organizations, the Richmond Relief Committee and the City Mission, would attempt to establish a system of private charity that would encompass the entire city; other charitable efforts would form on behalf of smaller constituencies.

In December 1873, the Richmond Relief Committee formed to provide food to the city's poor through a ration-ticket system. The committee consisted of one layman from each religious denomination, together with the chairmen of the city council's committee on the relief of the poor and of the council's committee on finance. Visiting committees were assigned to each district of the city to distribute the ration tickets. The committee solicited contributions from the public, in cash or in kind, pledging to distribute them to the worthy poor.[16]

Although a private organization, the Relief Committee wished to work in cooperation with the public authorities, as evidenced by including public officials in its leadership. Nor was the Relief Committee hostile to the concept of public relief. It even urged the city council to increase its public works programs, since there was "every reason to believe that the number of the unemployed in this city will be largely increased during the present winter."[17] The city reciprocated in this desire to cooperate with the private sector, offering the Relief Committee an appropriation of one thousand dollars later that month in addition to its own relief expenditures.[18]

The second citywide charity, called the City Mission, was formed in 1877 by middle-class churchwomen of the city. An interdenominational women's effort, the City Mission began with a soup house at Fourteenth and Franklin Streets. The mission also established a districting system, a long familiar arrangement where "friendly visitors" arranged for clothing, fuel, and rations for the poor in their districts.[19] By the 1880s, the City Mission had added a sewing school to its activities, with sixty-five "scholars" under the direction of eight "teachers." Although still primarily funded by private contributions, the mission had also secured a small subsidy from the city council and had a paid "matron" directing its daily operations.[20] The city also began giving the City Mission annual supplies of coal to distribute to the impoverished.[21]

In most of these details, the Relief Committee and the City Mission followed the typical antebellum patterns of private benevolence, which more often stressed cooperation and connections between private and public efforts, rather than hostility between the two. The Relief Committee and the City Mission saw themselves as private auxiliaries to public welfare and would continue to operate as such for many years. The two charities would serve as the foundation of the city's Associated Charities in the early twentieth century (discussed later), although the ideologies supporting the Associated Charities would be decidedly different from those of the Relief Committee and the City Mission.

The depression of the 1870s also spurred private groups of citizens to organize new mutual-aid societies and new charitable institutions. The Knights of Honor formed in 1876, announcing that it offered members "mutual assistance and advancement in every day pursuits and pecuniary aid and attention during sickness . . . and a death benefit of $2,000 being guaranteed."[22] In 1885, the

Independent Brotherhood was chartered to provide for the sick, bury the dead, lighten the burdens of the poor, promote industry and economy, and provide for widows and orphans of its members.[23] Announcements for numerous such associations filled the columns of the local papers.

Continued exclusion from white benevolent associations and private charities forced African Americans to organize new private organizations of their own. For black Richmonders, mutual-aid associations took on even more importance than they had in the antebellum years. These mutual-assistance efforts, important for the survival of individuals, were also important for the black community as a whole. African American leaders saw these self-help organizations as important statements about the "worthiness" of the race. Black benefactors of private organizations used their donations to demonstrate their own successes, while simultaneously helping to lift the black "masses" out of poverty. African American leaders realized that whites seldom distinguished between different classes of blacks, but rather tended to view them as an undifferentiated group. As Linda Gordon has observed, whites viewed the whole race as the poorest and least educated among them. To work on behalf of the black poor, then, was effectively to work on behalf of all blacks. Social-welfare work within the black community carried a connotation of civil rights activism not present for whites.[24]

By the early 1870s, there were more than four hundred mutual-assistance societies in the city.[25] Indeed, so many societies formed that one effort directly critiqued the proliferation of activities. An organization to build a "Colored Home for the Sick and Indigent" formed in the summer of 1873, under the leadership of Rev. James H. Holmes. The new association argued that a single such institution would be more cost efficient than the current system, in which dozens of independent mutual-aid societies cared for their members separately. By consolidating those efforts, the expenses would be reduced.[26]

In addition to mutual-assistance organizations, the period saw the appearance of new private welfare institutions segregated by race. One such institution was the "Magdalene Home" to rehabilitate prostitutes, established in 1872, under direction of Dr. W. W. Parker and Judge Robert Old. Its name changed to the Spring Street Home in 1874, and its focus shifted to white unmarried mothers rather than prostitutes.[27] Another example was the Friends' (Quakers') Orphan Asylum, which opened in 1869, the first such facility in the city to serve black children. The new asylum applied for and received a small city subsidy. The city had begun subsidizing private charities with small annual appropriations during the antebellum period and extended this policy now to the private black-run organization. The Friends' Asylum agreed to take five children per year from the city almshouse in return for the appropriation.[28]

These and other charitable organizations in the city had to compete for a limited amount of philanthropic donations. They also competed for subsidies from the city. As the number of agencies grew, so did the numbers requesting municipal support. By 1886, the city was contributing sums to fifteen private charities.[29] The annual competitions for the largesse of the city council could be intense. The local paper reported on the "large number of ladies and gentlemen" present at the meeting of the finance committee of the city council, "the greater part of them representing the public charitable institutions. The meeting was given over to the hearing of the requests from the charitable institutions for appropriations for the year." Further requests were heard the following week.[30]

Rather than reducing the incentive to organize, the end of the depression and the subsequent economic boom of the 1880s seemed to stimulate further the desire of Richmonders to create mutual-aid and charitable organizations. A host of new institutions dotted the city map, many of them more specialized than in previous generations: the Baptist Home for Aged Women was founded in 1881; the Richmond Home for Ladies opened in 1883; the Jewish community organized the Hebrew Home for the Aged and Infirm in 1888; the Little Sisters of the Poor operated a home for the elderly, which in 1885 had thirty-two men and thirty-three women in residence.[31]

Nearly every week, the local newspapers carried an announcement of some fundraiser for one group or another: "pound parties," "tag days," "tableaux." Private charities, even those run by women, could be aggressive in their pursuit of funds: " 'Let no man escape' was the motto of the women, who stood in the streets all day. No one got away. The committee members held the corners, camped in front of the banks, besieged the post-office, guarded the emporiums into which men are likely most to wander, made the passengers on street cars surrender, and saw that the denizens of the public buildings came across."[32] During the Christmas season especially, there were almost daily events raising money, often with sentimental stories centered on poor children. Every winter, the papers were filled with pleas for contributions to the groups aiding the suffering poor:

> The snow has brought great suffering to the poor of Richmond. The destitute regard snow with fear, almost amounting to horror. It makes them even more helpless than before. Fagots may be picked up and little fires kindled; feet may be kept dry, with the ground dry beneath and the sun shining overhead, no matter if the temperature be low. But old shoes, such as the poor have, count for little in the slush on the streets at present, and odds and ends of fuel are buried beneath the cruel, though beautiful, snow.[33]

During summer, there were extra solicitations for the "ice mission," the incarnation of the City Mission during the summer months:

The demands upon the ice mission this intensely hot weather are very numerous and in the name of the ladies in charge of this work of mercy the *Dispatch* appeals to its friends—the entire public—to give to this worthy cause and to be both prompt and liberal in their responses. Those of our poor people who have to suffer so many privations should not be allowed when sick to lack for the comfort that a lump of ice affords them.[34]

Charity Organization—a Search for Order

This was the setting, then, for several innovations in charitable practices in late-nineteenth-century Richmond. To straighten out the jumble of overlapping charities and to overcome the problems of competitive fundraising, the benevolent community initiated several new approaches to funding private charities.[35] Some organizations, worried about the unpredictability of the public's generosity, turned to investment and the creation of endowments, rather than constant solicitations. Other philanthropic groups joined the "charity organization" movement, which promised to solve the difficulties of the private sector through scientific methods.

During the 1870s, the Female Humane Association, by then the oldest continuously operating charity in the city, had significantly altered its approach to finances. Rather than depend upon the unpredictable public and the tight-fisted city council for subsidies, the Female Humane Association began to invest its assets, mostly in railroad stocks and municipal bonds, and then used the interest accrued to fund its activities. Although bequests, donations, and annual dues would still be important to the organization, by the 1880s the profits of its investments became the foundation of its finances.[36] This "modern" approach to financing indicates that some private charities had learned important lessons from the political and economic crises of recent decades.

Another modern approach to charity in the 1880s was the "charity organization" movement. Originating in England in the 1870s, the effort to organize charities spread quickly to larger cities in the United States.[37] Organizing charity meant several things at once. Charity-organization societies (COS) proposed to register the names of all who requested assistance, thoroughly investigate the circumstances of their need, send the "deserving" to the appropriate private or public facility, and provide advice to the deserving on how best to improve their condition. The "undeserving" would be blacklisted, and all potential donors would be warned not to help them. Organizing charity also meant reducing the financial burdens of both public and private relief agencies by preventing "imposition" and duplication of services. In theory, charity-organization societies did not hand out relief themselves, but rather served as a clearinghouse of information for other private organizations; in practice, most COS locals did at times resort to direct relief.[38]

Charity organizing reflected its origins in the Protestant middle class; it emphasized moral responsibility, the work ethic, and evangelical—albeit nonsectarian—duty.[39] Charity organizing also made much grander claims than previous private organizations; by its scientific methods, charity organizing would not only reduce the expenses involved in caring for the poor, but also it would ultimately eliminate poverty altogether, by first studying and then eliminating the causes of poverty. Charity organization would also eliminate the opportunities for fraud and "imposition," which advocates claimed permeated the disorderly private charitable sector. As one proponent wrote, "It seems fair to say that the charity organization movement came as a protest to the grave abuses of charitable relief then obtaining."[40]

Charity organizing was also marked by its increasing animosity toward public relief. Public charity, COS advocates insisted, "pauperized" its recipients, while private charity tended to build character in both the poor and the wealthy. "Relying upon the municipality to do those things which may be accomplished through persistent individual effort," wrote one enthusiast, "tends to become chronic, weakens character, and might easily be carried so far as to cause serious social evils." The worthy poor, self-respecting and deserving of assistance, would by definition be reluctant to accept public charity.[41] At the end of the century, charity organizers would marshal their forces and launch a powerful offensive against public welfare.[42]

Public welfare did have its defenders. Stanton Coit, an early leader in the settlement-house movement, argued that the charity organizers had misdirected their efforts. Charity organization, he suggested, should be "a distinctive municipal function. Who but the city can prevent the dispensing of free bread, and can limit the relief of each agency to a given district so that there shall be no waste or overlapping? Who but the city," Coit continued, "can gather, week by week, full and accurate statistics of the condition of the unemployed? . . . Who but the city can compel every agency to follow careful methods to avoid fraud?"[43] Public welfare, strengthened by charity-organization methods, seemed to Coit to offer the best hope for adequate poor relief.

Other supporters of public welfare pointed out the fact that, despite years of efforts by private charities to end public assistance, state agencies remained "by far the most important. The State assists more widows, orphans, defectives, prisoners, aged persons and sick than all church and private persons combined."[44] A survey of fifteen major cities found that more than two-thirds of all relief came from public funds. The director of the survey noted that public welfare continued "on a scale so colossal, in fact, that even the enormous efforts of the private societies seem dwarfed by comparison."[45]

Southern cities experienced the same conditions as other American cities, with overlapping, multiple charitable activities. During an ice storm in Atlanta, for example, critics of the disorderly relief effort contended, "in many cases people in great need had gone unhelped, while in many others, applicants had received ten times as much food, fuel, or clothing as they had really required, and had sold the surplus, using the money for whiskey or morphine."[46] Southern urban residents also grew concerned about "imposition" and fraud in almsgiving. Newspaper accounts, such as this one from Richmond, helped to reinforce these concerns:

An old gray-haired, six-feet-high, beer-bloated fraud is at large in the city, going around passing himself off for a deaf mute. He was discovered in a bar-room yesterday glibly talking politics and abusing the character of the mountain whiskey therein. When a gentleman present called attention to the fact that he had given the man ten cents in charity on account of his being a mute, the old fraud drew a knife and threatened to dissect the informer who had been rash enough to expose his petty game.[47]

Directly addressing these concerns, national representatives of the charity-organization movement traveled the region during the 1880s and 1890s, proselytizing in southern cities for the principles of "scientific charity." The largest southern cities, such as New Orleans and Richmond, were among the first to establish COS chapters.[48] Although southerners tended still to be suspicious of "outsiders" and "foreign" ideas, charity organization rarely met resistance on those grounds. Charity-organization principles meshed fully with the views of the region's elites on racial and economic issues. Unlike more radical poverty analysts in postbellum America, charity organizers did not critique capitalism. Southern elites, under the spell of the New South Creed, could feel confident that the charity organizers would not attempt to regulate business, support labor, or in any way interfere with their pursuit of industrial development of the region. As one early observer noted, the charity-organizing societies seldom attacked the social causes of poverty, but rather blamed the individual "mendicants" themselves for their problems,[49] an approach compatible with the New South Creed.

Nor did the South's political and economic leadership have to worry that the charity-organization movement might challenge the region's post-Reconstruction racial settlement. Charity-organizing societies accepted racial segregation without question, often excluding blacks from their services entirely.[50]

One national COS advocate tried to explain away the problem: "At the south as at the north the colored race is not a begging race. They seldom apply to strangers for alms except in case of death in the family. 'To bury us is the only time we begs,' said a philosophic colored woman recently. Willingness to work at odd jobs is a habit among the colored people which makes them comparatively independent of alms."[51] Another contemporary advocate of charity organization clarified, "This does not mean that nothing was done for negro cases. In but few places, however, were they found to apply to the local charity organization society, and those who did usually needed hospital treatment."[52] In Charleston, the local COS concurred: "Black applicants were not numerous."[53]

Unwelcome in many COS offices, blacks sometimes responded by creating their own organizations. In Charleston, African Americans formed the Colored Relief Society in 1897.[54] In Memphis, the Colored Federated Charities, with its own board of directors, operated as an auxiliary to the local white associated charities.[55] In other cities, African Americans continued to rely on their own self-help and mutual-aid associations instead.

Since southern elites saw nothing in charity organizing that threatened white supremacy, the New South Creed, or unrestrained capitalism, they allowed the movement to proceed. Southern businessmen often gave the movement their full support, since it preached the values of hard work, self-discipline, and sobriety. One of the central convictions of charity organizers was that work should be the condition for relief, and southern charity-organization societies followed fully the northern models of modern relief, including the use of work tests. In Charleston, New Orleans, and other southern cities, the local COS set up a wood yard, where applicants for relief, no matter what their trade or background, were required to labor. A man who refused to cut wood would receive no assistance.[56]

Although charity organization had powerful supporters, the movement also had its southern opponents, many of whom came from long experience in religious charitable relief efforts. Ministers were frequently prominent among the local opposition to charity organization.[57] These critics rejected the rational, scientific method of the COS, preferring instead the personal contact between donor and recipient that benefited both.[58]

Southern women active in benevolent organizations often found that the scientific philanthropy preached by the COS did not mesh with their own charitable culture. Women's charitable activities, sometimes in organizations many decades old, had established patterns of personal association between women. Charitable "visiting" had become a women's ritual in the nineteenth century, passed from mother to daughter.[59] Women's charitable visiting was distinctly different from the "friendly visiting" of the COS, which was designed to uncover evidence of need and worth and report back on the conditions found in the homes of applicants. The contrast between the two styles of benevolence was clear to Richmond writer Ellen Glasgow. After an unrewarding winter working as a district visitor for the City Mission (which had, by then, become a COS stronghold in Richmond), the future novelist began volunteering at the Sheltering Arms Hospital instead. Glasgow appreciated the absence of "winding of red tape" at the Sheltering Arms, "[a] private charity which well merited its romantic name," and felt that "one could reach these people, and I came very close to their personal lives."[60] Much like other middle-class and elite women trained in women's charity, Glasgow found the methods of scientific philanthropy to be distasteful.

Still others resisted the scientific charity method because of their contrary understanding of the causes of poverty. Where the COS emphasized the failings of the individuals and investigated their "cases" to determine the exact problem—alcoholism, feeblemindedness, immorality, and so on—other observers were not as certain that the individuals were always responsible for their poverty. During periods of economic instability especially, the causes of poverty seemed rooted elsewhere. The ladies of the City Mission, who themselves had to buy supplies on the open market, understood that "fuel being much higher and vegetables double the cost of last winter, it is hardly necessary to add that the poor have the prospect of a hard season without any material aid."[61] Conversely, when the economy was improved, the mission could see that it had "not had quite so many applicants for help, owing to the large amount of work on hand for all who were able and willing to take it."[62] During the boom of the early 1880s, one Richmond newspaper reasoned clearly that "the great army of tramps that infested the country three or four years ago has dwindled to almost nothing" because of the "greater demand for labor in this part of the country."[63]

Thus many people had reasons to reject the scientific philanthropy of the COS movement, and its practitioners complained that the public did not fully support the "method of modern charity."[64] As late as 1922, the local office complained that "the idea seems to be prevalent in Richmond that any widow is entitled to fuel, no matter what her financial standing may be."[65] Even worse to the COS was the fact that some of its own members continued to give alms "indiscriminately" rather than practice the "better method of friendly visiting."[66] Charity organizers recognized that the public's apparent lack of support for their movement required continued educational efforts to teach "the whole community . . . the principles of relief-giving."[67]

These forces of resistance slowed, but did not halt, the progress of the charity-organization movement in Richmond. The first organization faltered and sputtered out of existence, only to have the cause renewed with more vigor just a few years later.[68] In 1905, under the guidance of Rev. Robert Strange of St. Paul's

Church, the citywide private charitable organizations met and formally reorganized as the Associated Charities. The agreement signed divided labors between the major organizations: the Relief Association would act as the fundraising arm of the AC; the City Mission would distribute the relief; and the Baptist Council would "turn over all constructive charitable work, and also their Homeless Department" to the Associated Charities.[69]

Support for the new effort, as indicated by the membership of the board of managers of the organization, came from the city's established civic leadership.[70] Businessmen such as John Stewart Bryan (owner of the *Richmond Times*, and railroad entrepreneur); doctors and clergymen such as Dr. Ennion G. Williams, Thomas Semmes, W. J. Young, and A. B. Sharpe; and women's civic leadership including Mrs. C. E. Bolling and Mrs. Norman V. Randolph worked on behalf of the new organization.

The charter of the Richmond AC stated succinctly the purposes of charity organization:

a. To promote efficient cooperation between municipal authorities, the public and private charities, the churches and the benevolent individuals of the city, and to prevent injurious giving and overlapping of relief caused by independent action.
b. To obtain from the proper charities and charitable individuals suitable and adequate relief in cases of actual need and in all possible cases to make employment the basis of relief.
c. To supplement material aid by friendly visiting, which shall gradually build up habits of industry, saving and self-control among the less fortunate, thus organizing a body of volunteer workers.
d. To promote the welfare of the really needy, by the exposure of imposture and fraud, and to enlarge and make more general the constructive work of true charity.[71]

The Associated Charities hired as its first general secretary Rev. James Buchanan, who was currently the city missionary of the Baptist Council. Buchanan's first assignment was to compile a central card index of all applicants for charity in the city, amounting to fourteen hundred white families. Next the city was divided into twenty-nine districts, and visitors assigned to each. The volunteer visitors were all women.[72] Finally, the city had to be educated about the purpose and functions of the organization. A 1906 pamphlet published by the organization explained to the public how to use the services of the AC:

When a beggar approaches you on the street, give him one of our printed cards and send him to the Central Office at 1408 East Franklin Street.

If a case of distress or need is brought to your attention, either send the name and address of the person to 1408 East Franklin Street or call 4850 by telephone. The case will be immediately investigated, the necessities met, and a full report mailed you at once.

In the case of a beggar who has no home, give a card to the Homeless Department of the Associated Charities of Richmond, where he can have a meal, shelter, and opportunity for work.

Where you are helping a family and wish information as to what is being done for them by others, ask for information and a full report will be mailed to you.[73]

The volunteer visitors were made responsible for the care of those in their districts approved for assistance by the AC. The visitors were also to keep up to date the files on each case, held by the central office, in order to "observe the progress of the case under treatment." This system, used by charity organizations throughout the country, became the basis for casework as practiced by social workers. The Richmond Associated Charities, like its fellow charity organizations, stressed that its work was "constructive charity," which helped individuals adjust themselves to the current conditions of society and the economy. The Associated Charities insisted that poverty was the product of the individual's failings to meet the requirements of modern life, or "lack of adjustment to [the] economic environment." "Our people must be taught to perform the work for which there is a demand in the age in which we live," the AC declared.[74]

The charity-organization principles were especially appealing to businessmen and other local elites. Not surprisingly, Richmond's city council embraced the "methods of scientific charity" very early. The committee on the relief of the poor announced in 1881 that it had made arrangements with the City Mission to establish a central relief office at the First Market Hall, "with the view of promoting systematic and discriminating charity by—

1st discouraging street begging
2nd securing employment for the poor
3rd preventing imposition by thoroughly investigating every case reported.
We earnestly ask our fellow citizens to cooperate with us in our efforts to secure a judicious and systematic distribution of our local charities—
1st by refusing to give anything to a beggar
2nd by sending all such applicants to the central office
3rd by sending contributions . . . to the rooms of the city mission.[75]

Henceforth, charity-organizing principles would be one of the foundations of public policy in Richmond. Although charity organizers disapproved of public relief, and especially public outdoor relief, by spreading their "gospel" of scientific charity to the public sector, charity organizers effectively gained indirect control over the practices of public welfare. Moreover, the Associated Charities gained direct control over some portions of public welfare: beginning in 1910,

THE ASSOCIATED CHARITIES OF RICHMOND

FORM OF BEQUEST

I give and bequeath to the Associated Charities of Richmond,

the sum of . . . . .Dollars.

Associated Charities illustration, "The Modern Method," from Associated Charities, *A Year of Service*, 1920–21 pamphlet. Organized charity is represented as superior to almsgiving in this illustration. Courtesy of the Library of Virginia.

the city council appropriated funds to the AC to use for furnishing coal to poor families. The Associated Charities could thereby apply its methods directly to some public provision.[76]

The city saw benefits to working with the AC. The superintendent of the outdoor poor, who "has no time to investigate the merits of the applications to him for relief and is often imposed upon,"[77] could rely on the investigations of the Associated Charities instead. The city got the benefit of "casework" without having to hire its own caseworkers. Having accepted the value of casework, the city used the caseworkers of the Associated Charities as a means of reducing its own expenditures. The lines between public and private charity again blurred in the process of cooperation.

Charity-organization principles spread to other organizations, which then helped to disseminate them even further.[78] The Virginia Conference on Charities and Corrections, a private organization of leaders in welfare organizations, was heavily influenced by the charity-organizing school of thought. From the first year of its existence, the Virginia Conference was not only dedicated to educating "the public mind to a proper conception of the needs of the delinquent, dependent, and defective classes," but it was also devoted to creating "organization in charitable and correctional efforts."[79]

The Richmond School of Social Work (discussed in chapter 7) would also serve as a vehicle for further establishing charity-organization principles. (Throughout the United States, the first schools of social work were organized by COS activists, with the goal of training a new generation of workers who would be firmly grounded in charity-organizing principles.)[80] Charity organizers were among the forces behind organizing a school of social work in Richmond, and they served as some of the original faculty of the new school, such as Loomis Logan of the Associated Charities.[81] The majority of students at the School of Social Work did their field work at the Associated Charities, under the supervision of the case manager of the AC, where their training in casework reinforced their grounding in charity-organization thinking.[82]

By the 1910s, charity organization had come to dominate social-welfare thinking in Richmond. Most public and private welfare agencies had either adopted the philosophies directly or had hired workers trained in those precepts and thereby adopted COS thinking indirectly. The Salvation Army, for example, came to practice casework and work tests. Families were carefully investigated before Christmas baskets were distributed.[83] Both the Hebrew Aid Society and the Bureau of Catholic Charities eventually joined this mainstream of social-welfare thinking, despite its origins in evangelical Protestantism. Through the formal training of social workers, a new generation of workers, both religious and secular, was being prepared to take up the work of scientific charity.

The Lost Cause and Social-Welfare Policy

The COS movement was a national (and international) phenomenon that pro-foundly shaped southern welfare policy. By contrast, the "Lost Cause" com-memorative movement was indigenous to the South but had equally significant impact on the region's welfare programs. The Lost Cause movement would re-sult in widespread support for pensions and other assistance to Confederate veterans, and as such might be seen as a regional parallel to the growing fed-eral support for Civil War veterans. The U.S. government began providing for invalid Union veterans, widows, and orphans even before the Civil War had ended. The first of several federally funded homes for disabled Union veter-ans opened in 1867.[84] By 1893, the greatly expanded veterans' pension program constituted nearly one-third of the federal government's annual expenditures.[85] And by 1910, approximately 28 percent of all men age sixty-five or older were receiving federal veterans' benefits.[86]

A small number of southerners, both white and black, received veterans' ben-efits from the federal government for their contributions to the Union war ef-fort. (By war's end, some 5,700 African American men from Virginia had en-listed in the Union army.)[87] More than 2,400 black women received pensions for being the widow or the mother of a soldier from the U.S. Colored Troops regiments from Virginia.[88] The federal government operated a soldiers' home for Union veterans at Kecoughtan, Virginia.[89] The special census of 1890 listed 169 Union veterans and 25 veterans' widows living in Richmond, although it did not specify how many of them were then receiving pensions.[90] Interestingly, 29 Union veterans were listed in the state penitentiary and 3 were listed in the city jail, but none were listed in the city almshouse. This could be the result of continued discrimination against Union veterans by the city authorities, as seen in chapter 5. Or it could be that veterans received sufficient pension funds to keep them out of the almshouse. The extant records do not clarify the issue. But the majority of southerners, as Confederate veterans, were ineligible for this extensive federal welfare program.

Southern veterans themselves were divided in their opinions as to whether they wanted federal pensions. Although some supported federal relief, oth-ers refused aid from the still-hated enemy, insisting that "a Federal pension is worse than Confederate poverty."[91] Southern opposition to federal pensions contributed to the failure of Congress to include Confederate veterans in the program. Instead, southern states funded their own veterans' benefits pro-grams, beginning first with limited programs for artificial limbs, and expanding later to large pension programs.[92]

Sociologist Theda Skocpol has argued that the South's Confederate pension programs were "the response of the southern states to the precedent of Union Civil War pensions."[93] This is only narrowly true. It is more accurate to see both Union and Confederate pension programs as the natural response to earlier military pension precedents. Americans had grown quite accustomed to providing pensions for veterans, which had a long history. Again drawing on English precedent, American colonies had established pensions for needy veterans of the Imperial and Indian wars in the seventeenth century. Each military conflict afterward produced another round of pension legislation, by the states and by Congress. The generation that crafted pension programs for veterans of the Civil War had living examples of military pensioners all around them, as Congress continued to pay veterans and widows from the Mexican War (and even a handful from the Revolution).[94] Arguably, southern states would likely have instituted some kind of pension plan for needy veterans even without the example set by the Union states.

Skocpol accurately highlights the comparative generosity of federal/Union-state pension programs. Union states and the federal government implemented pensions earlier, included a broader range of recipients in their coverage, and funded them at higher levels. In 1905, for example, Skocpol found that fewer than 20 percent of living Confederate veterans were receiving pensions, compared to more than 80 percent of living Union veterans. By 1910, 5 percent of surviving Union veterans were living in soldiers' homes, while only 1 percent of surviving Confederate veterans did. In addition, Union veterans might draw pensions from both the federal government and their individual state government. In Massachusetts, that meant a state pension averaging $125 per year, on top of the average federal pension of $190.[95] Confederate veterans had fewer options.

These contributions to the maintenance of Confederate veterans remained relatively small through the 1870s and 1880s. In Georgia, for example, the state's pension program represented approximately 2 percent of total expenditures for the years 1886–89.[96] Virginia's program of Confederate pensions also received 2 percent of the state's expenditures in 1885 (see table 6). But the rise of the Lost Cause movement of the 1890s helped to change the connotations of Confederate commemoration and had powerful influence on these state welfare programs. Southern states expanded their pension programs to include more veterans, and then their widows. States added veterans' homes and homes for Confederate women to their budgets as well.[97]

The "cult of the Lost Cause" celebrated the Old South by honoring its defenders. Beginning modestly in the 1860s with Confederate memorial associations dedicated to caring for the graves of Confederate soldiers, the memorializing movement later blossomed into an emotional defense of the war effort, slavery, the Confederacy, and the superiority of southern civilization. In song, poem, and statue, the Lost Cause movement defined the Confederate cause as worthy and the Confederate soldier as noble. By the end of the century, the Lost Cause had come to permeate southern civic life, especially in Richmond, the former Confederate capital.[98]

The cult of the Lost Cause served multiple purposes, as many historians have recognized. The Lost Cause offered a public role for southern white women, many of whom distanced themselves from contemporary reform movements and northern-inspired feminism but desired a realm of public activity nevertheless. The Lost Cause movement allowed some people to reject, or at least critique, the changes of the New South; it allowed others to combine the two, as enterprising New South capitalists made money selling Confederate memorabilia and monuments.[99] But the Lost Cause also allowed southern states to create extensive and expensive social-welfare programs, without appearing to do so. Indeed, these public-welfare programs were so well disguised by Lost Cause rhetoric that social-welfare historians have largely overlooked their presence. Confederate pensions and programs have often been examined by historians of the Lost Cause, but only rarely by historians of social welfare.

In 1882, the Virginia general assembly had authorized payment of "commutations" to veterans who had been injured, but for whom the purchase of a prosthetic device would be of no use. Five years later, the commutation was made payable to the widow or child of the veteran if he had died before receiving his payment.[100] This served as the foundation for a pension program (see figures 3, 4, and 5). Beginning in 1888, the state legislature passed a series of acts establishing, expanding, and refining a Confederate pension program. Pensions were granted to soldiers, sailors, and marines disabled in action, as well as to the widows of those killed in action. The level of disability determined the level of payment, with annual payments (in 1888) ranging from fifteen dollars for partial disability to sixty dollars for those who had lost multiple functions. The state assembly voted an annual appropriation of sixty-five thousand dollars for this program, to come from the general fund. No new source of revenue was initiated to supply the increased expenditures.[101]

For the next four decades, the state government would continue to expand the pension program. In 1900, legislation substantially broadened eligibility by covering disabilities that had occurred after the war and by covering widows whose husbands had died after the war. In 1908, veterans received burial benefits. In 1918, veterans' widows were permitted to retain their benefits even if they subsequently remarried.[102] Although termed "pensions," these programs were also clearly "relief" for the indigent. Recipients had to pass a "means test" before qualifying for the state's support, leaving no doubt that this was a welfare

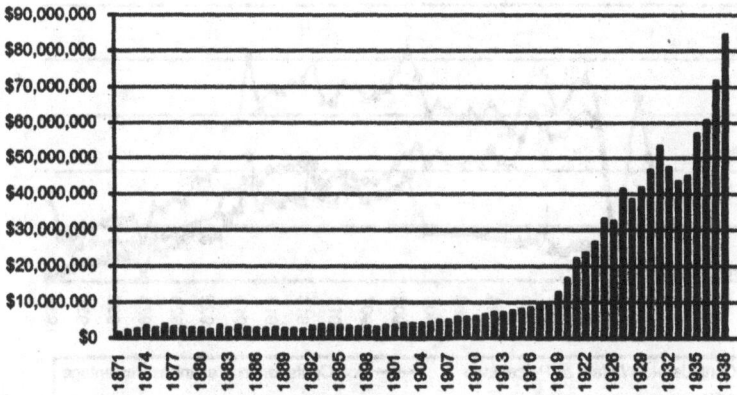

Figure 3. *Virginia's Annual Budget, 1871–1938*
Source: Annual reports, Auditor of Public Accounts, State of Va., various years.

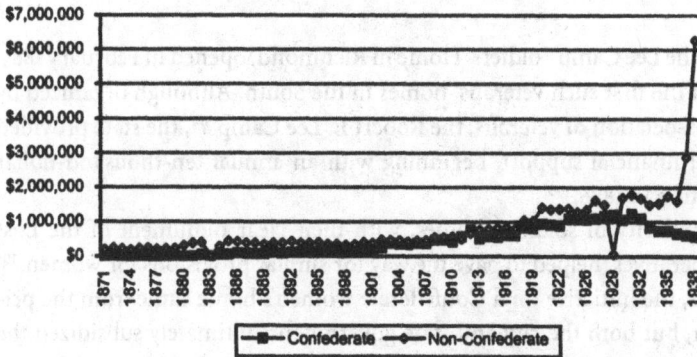

Figure 4. *Virginia's Expenditures on Confederate and Non-Confederate Welfare, 1871–1938*
Source: Annual reports, Auditor of Public Accounts, State of Virginia.

program. No matter how meritorious a veteran's war record might be, he would not receive a pension if he could not show need.

Further state support for Confederate veterans took the form of asylums, usually termed "old soldiers' homes." Some of these veterans' homes had originated as privately funded efforts, with the states and/or cities offering subsidies; many of these private homes were ultimately taken over by state governments entirely.[103] Supporters of the Confederate veterans' homes tried to distinguish them from charity, insisting instead that they were a fulfillment of the states' obligation to compensate their defenders. They were to be seen as a "payment due for services rendered, not an outright gift," and certainly not as a poor-

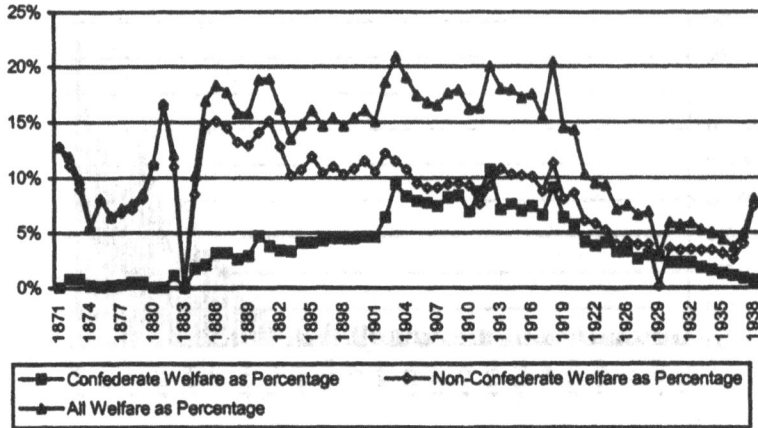

Figure 5. *Welfare as a Percentage of State Expenditures, 1871–1938*
Source: Annual reports, Auditor of Public Accounts, State of Virginia.

house.[104] The Lee Camp Soldiers' Home in Richmond, opened in February 1885, was one of the first such veterans' homes in the South. Although organized by a private association of veterans, the Robert E. Lee Camp #1, the state provided substantial financial support, beginning with an annual ten-thousand-dollar appropriation in 1886.[105]

The popularity of soldiers' homes, with their clear fulfillment of the Lost Cause imperatives, helped to pave the way for similar provisions for women.[106] In Virginia, the initiative for a Confederate women's home came from the private sector, but both the city and state governments ultimately subsidized the institution. Incorporated in 1898 as the Home for Needy Confederate Women, the facility opened in a residential neighborhood in Richmond in 1900. The governing board consisted of prominent local women, with the wife of Confederate general George Pickett serving as honorary president. The home actively courted the United Daughters of the Confederacy and Sons of Confederate Veterans chapters throughout the South for donations, but also depended on state and local funds for its operations.[107]

Confederate organizations such as the United Confederate Veterans conducted very effective lobbying, relentlessly pressuring state legislatures to increase the scope of Confederate welfare programs. The pages of the monthly magazine, the *Confederate Veteran*, were filled with information useful to those who wished to argue the case of the region's heroes. One of the most effective tools was the compilation of comparative data, which put pressure on individual states to keep up with other states. Table 7 reproduces compiled data from

Confederate Soldiers' Home, Richmond, undated photograph. This was one of several buildings on the grounds of R. E. Lee Camp Confederate Soldiers' Home. Courtesy of the Valentine Richmond History Center.

an issue of the *Confederate Veteran* from 1915, demonstrating the impact of such comparative data.

Thanks in part to interest-group lobbying, the expenditures on Confederate veterans grew to be much more significant portions of the southern states' budgets after the turn of the century. In Georgia, where earlier veterans' welfare expenses amounted to 2 percent of the budget, the state spent an average of 15 percent of its annual budget on veterans during the 1890s. The following decade, it rose to average 19 percent of the annual budget. The highest level was reached in 1911 and 1912, when just over 22 percent of the state's appropriations went to veterans.[108]

Virginia's Confederate welfare programs were equally expensive. As shown by table 6, the state's expenditures on Confederate veterans and their widows grew from 2 percent of the state budget in 1885 up to a high of 11 percent of the budget in 1912. After the latter date, the Confederate welfare expenditures declined as a percentage of the whole, but the amount of the appropriations continued to climb until the early 1930s. (The declining percentage of the budget devoted to Confederate welfare after the peak year of 1912 did not represent a declining commitment to Confederate veterans or to the Lost Cause. Nor did the decreasing absolute figures expended after 1932 represent any change of heart regarding the past. Rather, the declining expenditures on Confederate welfare were a reflection of a demographic reality: fewer Confederate veterans and widows remained alive to collect their pensions.)

The expansive, and expensive, Confederate relief programs built upon earlier precedents of providing for indigent veterans and their dependents, and in several ways conformed to older models of veterans' relief. In most cases indigence had to be proven, by affidavits from doctors confirming the inability to labor. Honorable military service also had to be documented, usually with statements of former officers testifying to service and discharge.[109] But Confederate relief programs included a significant departure from past practices: veterans had to demonstrate their continued adherence to the Lost Cause. While honorable service conferred "worthy" or "deserving" status on a veteran and his family, he also had to have lived an honorable Confederate postwar life.

Lost Cause promoters had crafted an image of the Confederate soldier as a noble, self-sacrificing, honorable man. A "true" Confederate would uphold high moral character and honorable habits, reflecting only the best qualities the South had to offer. Insane men, drunkards, or others who had fallen into "dissipation" were regularly excluded from soldiers' homes.[110] Since local boards evaluated pension applications, a veteran's local "reputation for loyalty to the Lost Cause" could—and did—become a factor in the decision to fund a pension.[111]

The Confederate welfare programs also offered southern states the opportunity to provide for poor whites without having to open state coffers to poor blacks. By making honorable Confederate service the criteria for eligibility, southern states could automatically exclude the vast majority of their black citizens without having to resort to subterfuge, fraud, or violence. The Confederate welfare state thereby facilitated the transfer of tax money from blacks to whites, without appearing to do so.

Ironically, Virginia did offer Confederate support to a handful of African Americans, the "faithful among the faithless,"[112] but it was an irony that made sense given the Lost Cause imperatives behind it. In 1872, the state program of artificial limbs was extended to African Americans who had lost limbs "as soldiers or employees during the late war."[113] And in 1924, Virginia granted "servants'" pensions, allowing annual payments of twenty-five dollars to blacks who had accompanied a soldier in service or who had worked on behalf of the Cause in such capacities as cooks, hostlers, or teamsters.[114] Only a small number of men were eligible; in 1925, a total of 254 black men qualified, compared to more than 5,000 white men who received pensions. (In Richmond, only 10 African American men received these pensions that year.)[115] Indeed, the small cost of the program was one of its justifications. For very little money, "servants' " pensions allowed southern whites to celebrate the loyalty of the South's slaves, further illustrating the precepts of the Lost Cause.

The Lost Cause provided justification for substantial state expenditures on social-welfare provision in the South. The depression of the 1890s increased the levels of need and put pressure on states to expand further their Confederate support programs. Veterans' organizations, such as the Sons of Confederate Veterans and the United Daughters of the Confederacy, made constant demands on state legislatures to increase the level of pensions, and their growing clout at the turn of the century made such lobbying very effective.[116] Southern states firmly refused to fund new initiatives in response to the economic depression but allowed their Confederate pension programs to serve the same function. Southern states could thereby collectively provide millions of dollars in relief benefits, camouflaged as veterans' "entitlements."

Finally, the vast expansion of the Confederate welfare programs in Virginia coincided with the state's disfranchisement movement. A secret ballot law, which disfranchised large numbers of illiterates both black and white, laid the groundwork. With a substantially reduced electoral opposition, Democrats then proceeded to rewrite the state constitution to eliminate permanently large numbers of voters, again both blacks and whites. "Promulgated" rather than sent to the voters for ratification, the new constitution specifically included an escape clause for veterans and their sons.[117]

The post-1902 political regime offered poor and marginal whites reduced opportunities to challenge the hegemony of the conservative Democratic Party. (Virginia came to have the smallest percentage of its potential electorate enfranchised of any state in the South, prompting V. O. Key to observe, "By contrast, Mississippi is a hotbed of democracy.")[118] Post-1902 Virginia would have fewer political challengers like the Readjusters, Republicans, or Populists. Confederate veterans and their families, the recipients of both welfare benefits and automatic voting rights, would likely be among the most loyal Democratic voters from the non-elite classes. The combination of pensions and votes served to tie these families to the state, the Lost Cause, and the Democratic Party simultaneously.

Confederate pensions represented another important evolution in the development of the modern welfare state. Building upon the precedent set by state-funded asylums for the insane, the blind, and the deaf, and by state-funded pensions for veterans of earlier wars, Virginia now included another broad class of poor people among its designated dependents. The state agreed to maintain veterans and their widows, defined as worthy by their service to the Lost Cause, for the rest of their lives. But unlike the previous categories of dependents receiving state support, this group was potentially enormous in size. Considering that an estimated 150,000 Virginians survived their service in the Confederate military, the state was making a tremendous commitment of its resources. The Confederate welfare programs absorbed an increasing percentage of the state's total welfare provision; by the 1910s, Confederate welfare rivaled insane asylums as the most expensive item in the state's welfare budget (see tables 8 and 9). Although not as generous as federal pensions, the state's support for its Confederate veterans nevertheless represented a huge financial commitment. Confederate welfare came to be one of the central concerns of state government, placing Civil War veterans above the state's educational needs and other welfare obligations.

Defined as a pension for service, rather than as relief for the needy, Confederate welfare was welfare without stigma. Even though the applicants were clearly means tested, and often morals tested as well, no stigma attached to these programs. Although the recipients hardly lived in luxury, neither did they live in dire poverty, therefore they were kept off the local relief rolls and out of the local poorhouses. Confederate pensions stood in stark contrast to the miserly, demeaning provision made for "paupers" in the late-nineteenth- and early-twentieth-century South. Confederate welfare celebrated one group of poor residents, raising them to a level of honored pensioners, while abandoning large numbers of other poor citizens to the poorhouse.

DESPITE THEIR DISPARATE origins and contradictory ideologies, the movements for charity organization and Confederate commemoration had tremendous impact on late-nineteenth-century welfare policies in the South. Charity organizers articulated very clearly their dislike of public welfare and their desire to improve private efforts sufficiently to eliminate public welfare eventually. In the interim, COS advocates wished to elevate private charitable efforts to a primary position in the relative hierarchy between public and private efforts.

A national—even international—movement, scientific charity was embraced by many southerners who recognized that this "outside" movement offered no threat to southern institutions. Charity organization claimed to be rational and scientific, but it nevertheless accepted racial segregation and/or exclusion by its members. While critiquing duplication and overlapping charities, the COS accepted the necessary duplication required by a Jim Crow system.

Confederate pensions and other forms of support grew out of the Lost Cause commemorative effort, rather than from a social-welfare background. As such, the ideology supporting Confederate pensions and homes endorsed the Confederate state rather than the welfare state. Southern states created vast social-welfare bureaucracies and made tremendous commitment of their resources in those Confederate welfare programs. Because these programs were stimulated by the cult of the Lost Cause, southern states could thereby create protowelfare states without having to craft a prowelfare state ideology.

These two movements remained largely unconcerned with one another. Charity organizers in the South never criticized Confederate welfare programs, even when they took the much-hated form of "outdoor relief," because they were cloaked in the nearly sacrosanct packaging of the Lost Cause. Moreover, charity organizers expressed no hostility to Confederate pensions because they were defined as "entitlements" rather than as "relief." Confederate pensions had been earned by service and could not be considered a state dole. Likewise, nothing in the ideological support system of the Confederate welfare programs was intrinsically hostile to charity organizing.

Both charity organizing and Confederate welfare took quick root in the South and were firmly established institutions by the turn of the century. The progressive movement, as a slightly later arrival on the scene, would therefore have to contend with these two powerful trends in social-welfare policy, as analyzed in the following chapter.

CHAPTER SEVEN

The New South, Part II

Progressivism and the Welfare State

through the 1920s

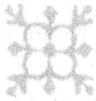

Nannie J. Minor, one of the founders of a visiting nurses program in Richmond, explained succinctly the process that created a "progressive." While providing free nursing care to the poor in their homes, Minor discovered a range of problems much broader than just medical ones:

> [H]ow can the nurse see the poor, frail, overworked, undernourished child—a ready prey to tuberculosis—without a feeling of resentment against the too lax laws which permit the growing child to work ten hours in the close [*sic*] factory; or the puny infant, doomed to an early death, or frail life, because the mother has had to work ten hours or longer every day, almost to the day of its birth, at starvation wages to keep body and soul together—or the baby made ill by impure milk—without longing to do what she can to remedy the evil. And these are just a few of the needs with which she is confronted.[1]

Minor was transformed from "lady benevolent" to "progressive activist" by her experiences as a visiting nurse, an evolution duplicated many times over by others of her generation.

Working as a visiting nurse and living at the Nurses' Settlement house, Nannie Minor stood at the center of progressive reform in Richmond. This "social awakening," as contemporaries often termed it, rewrote social policy in the early-twentieth-century United States by investing the state with the power and the responsibility to protect individuals from the abuses of the economic order. Social-welfare policy would come to be a fundamental tool in the progressives' defense of "the people" against "the interests."

Opposition to progressive social policy came from the political and economic interest groups that benefited from the old order, unsurprisingly. But social-welfare progressives would also have to jockey for public support against the charity organizers and the Confederate welfare advocates, both of whom held positions of formidable strength. Both the COS and the Lost Cause advocates jealously guarded their "turf" against incursions from competitors for the limited resources made available by the public and the state.

The Progressive era, then, witnessed a contest between these streams of social-welfare policy in the South. By the 1920s, the frictions between these factions had worn away many of the roughest edges of the ideological conflicts between them. Several decades of social-welfare activism had produced a greatly enlarged public-welfare sector, including substantial participation at the state level. The period also produced a greatly invigorated private-welfare sector, with a shining new weapon in its arsenal: professional casework. On the eve of the Great Depression, Richmond possessed a modern, professional, highly complex social-welfare system that had done much to improve living conditions in the city.

Social-Welfare Progressivism

Progressivism grew out of the conditions plaguing urban centers in the last decades of the nineteenth century, conditions that were both deepened and highlighted by the great depression of the 1890s.[2] Where the depression of the 1870s had led indirectly to the emergence of the charity-organization movement, the depression of the 1890s stimulated indirectly the emergence of a self-conscious progressive movement. Organizations, activities, and publications (some of which were already decades old) suddenly became recognizable as national trends. Widely dispersed temperance clubs, civic leagues, maternity homes, mothers' clubs, reformatory associations, and city missions—which had all previously seemed local and disparate—came into focus as part of a nationwide effort to reform urban America. The national media played a critical role in the creation of a sense of a progressive movement.[3]

Reformers with these many divergent interests coalesced into a loosely bound movement united under the vague label of "progressivism." Incensed by a variety of serious problems in contemporary America, progressives resolved to study and then solve the numerous conflicts troubling American society. Industrial and urban conditions stood at the center of progressive thought: poor sanitation, dangerous workplaces, child labor, homelessness, unemployment, immigration, and a host of other urban problems were the targets of progressive reformers. Some reformers concentrated on political reforms, hoping to re-democratize a country that seemed to have been taken over by corporate interests. Other progressives focused on regulating big business, for much the same reason.[4]

One branch of the progressive movement concentrated on social-welfare issues. Inspired variously by the social gospel, by ideals of social justice, by radical critiques of the political economy, or by class-driven "maternalism," progressives attempted to reform and improve older forms of relief, such as almshouses; they also created entirely new forms of assistance, such as settlement houses, mothers' pensions, and visiting nurses. Social-welfare progressivism insisted that each poor or dependent person had individual needs; no one-size-fits-all solutions would work. Unlike Jacksonian-era social reformers, who had created an entire generation of institutions following essentially the same model of therapeutic routine, progressives desired flexibility in tailoring solutions to individual problems.[5]

Led by prominent figures such as Jane Addams, Lillian Wald, and Grace and Edith Abbott, social-welfare progressives implicitly rejected much contemporary social thinking on poverty, including social Darwinism and charity organization. They argued instead for an environmental approach to poverty: by changing the environment in which people lived, most especially the environment in which children grew up, poverty could be eliminated at its source. Changing that environment—providing playgrounds, street lighting, workplace safety, day-care centers, pure food and milk, and dozens of other reforms—would require an activist government, since many of these changes could be instituted only by legislation. Progressive reformers came to articulate the need for some kind of a welfare state and began taking steps to create it.[6]

Social-welfare progressivism shared many characteristics typical of the larger progressive movement. Like progressives in other endeavors, social-welfare workers "professionalized," as schools of social work and national associations for social workers helped to define professional standards.[7] Like progressives in other fields, social-welfare progressives found themselves moving from volunteerism to politics, from residence in a settlement house to lobbying the state house. Likewise, social-welfare progressives found the problem of race to be insurmountable, and they tried instead to avoid entanglement with race whenever possible.[8] National welfare journals, such as *Charities Review* (founded in 1891) and *Charities* (founded in 1897), helped to give shape and cohesiveness to what soon became a national welfare community. (Those national periodicals worked hard to spread their views about social welfare throughout the South, sending representatives to cities like Richmond to obtain new subscribers in the local welfare community.)[9]

That national welfare community was torn, however, by competing theories about poor relief. Charity organizing, with its emphasis on casework, enforcing the work ethic, reducing expenditures, and preventing "imposture," operated from a position of considerable strength. By the early twentieth century, the COS approach had come to be firmly institutionalized not only in "associated charities" but also in financial federations such as the community chests, and in schools of social work. Charity organizing had become solidly established as the dominant school of thought in social welfare.

While sharing some characteristics, social-welfare progressivism was nonetheless often at odds with the COS philosophy. Both groups of welfare activists could appreciate the utility of casework, and both agreed that the growing distance between the poor and the rich endangered the future of the republic.[10] But the two sets of welfare workers held very different understandings of the political economy. Charity organizers remained fundamentally hostile to public welfare and saw the perfection of private charity as one method of ending public welfare. Social-welfare progressives, by contrast, came to advocate a wide expansion of public welfare. Abandoning old precepts like laissez-faire, social-welfare progressives hoped to harness the power of the state to work on behalf of the impoverished. Social-welfare progressives did not reject private charity in principle, but rather argued that private charity had proven itself inadequate to the task in an age of industrial capitalism. In the face of giant corporate combinations, social-welfare progressives contended that only the state had the necessary resources to combat poverty. Although many progressives were themselves deeply enmeshed in private reform organizations, most came to see the need for the state to take primacy over private efforts.[11]

Southern Progressivism

Although the late-nineteenth-century South remained more rural and agricultural than the northeast, progressivism nevertheless found eager advocates in the region. There were fertile fields for the work. The rapid industrial development of the postemancipation South had produced enormous wealth for some and great urban difficulties for others. Child labor—the very foundation of the regional textile industry—took a high human toll. Other urban and industrial problems, such as squalid housing, unemployment, sanitation, child care, and recreational opportunities, also stirred concerned southerners to action.[12] Like their northern counterparts, southern progressives were largely urban, middle class, and white, though the generalization should not be drawn so firmly as to ignore the substantial efforts of black progressives.[13]

One should also not overstate the liberalism of southerners. Progressives were likely a minority in the region, even in urban centers. The South was instead in the vanguard of opposition to progressive reforms such as child labor, and especially woman suffrage.[14] Carter Glass's *Lynchburg News*, commenting on protective labor legislation, wrote: "What the *News* contends for is the simple, inalienable right of the laboring man to dispose of his own time upon the best terms he can get without the intervention of restrictive labor legislation.

The working classes do not need legislative wet nurses."[15] Such sentiments were widespread, offering progressives in the South entrenched obstacles.

Moreover, progressive reformers in the region sometimes found that the very people they hoped to help also resisted their efforts. Working-class parents who were dependent upon the wages of their children resented and obstructed child labor laws and compulsory schooling. Opposition to taxation prevented the establishment of public-health units in some counties; religious proscriptions, by groups like the Primitive Baptists, halted the growth of public-health programs in others.[16]

Despite these powerful sources of conservatism, southern progressivism generated a substantial coterie of social-welfare reformers determined to remake the region's system of public and private benevolence. With little initial coordination, local activists in places like Memphis, New Orleans, and Atlanta created maternity homes, orphanages, and day nurseries. Even smaller communities felt the pull of social reform, as local groups organized settlement houses, visiting nurses, and antituberculosis clubs.[17] Many of these southern welfare reformers consciously copied the model of northern urban reformers and embraced the national norms of social-welfare thinking.

The emerging standards of professionally trained social work became part of the South's social-welfare consciousness as well in the Progressive era. Schools of social work were established in several urban centers, including Rice University (1916), the University of North Carolina (1920), and Tulane University (1925). The first school to train African American social workers was established at Atlanta University in 1920. Both public and private welfare agencies in the region quickly accepted the concept of professional social work and hired trained workers whenever their budgets allowed. Southern membership in the National Conference of Social Work grew from 141 in 1908 to 677 in 1928, the latter figure representing 10 percent of the total membership.[18]

While much of this southern progressivism seemed identical to national norms, there were some areas of progressive welfare activism that were more regionally specific, based on conditions more endemic to the South. Public-health crusades to eliminate hookworm, pellagra, and malaria, for example, were mostly concentrated in the South. Focusing heavily on conditions in the rural South, public-health campaigns drew critical resources from northern philanthropy: the Rockefeller monies treated just under seven hundred thousand southerners in eleven states on the eve of the First World War.[19]

Social-welfare progressives in the South devoted most of their attentions to urban centers, where poverty appeared concentrated and where problems like homelessness and periodic unemployment were most visible. For many rural southerners, there simply was no such thing as public welfare, as no county boards existed in many places. State legislatures authorized, but did not mandate, county almshouses, so many areas remained without them. Rural counties often had few private charities either, since the populations were scattered and insufficient to create the necessary organizations to offer private assistance.[20] Just as welfare itself was concentrated in urban centers, so was welfare progressivism.

Progressive Social Welfare in Virginia

Virginia's twentieth-century political leadership has been famously—even infamously—conservative, and historians have frequently stressed how essentially conservative its progressives were as well.[21] A close examination of the social-welfare faction of Virginia's progressives, however, suggests that the characterization has been drawn too rigidly. The term "progressives" covers a wide range of people, with a similarly wide range of views. Even at the height of the progressive movement, Virginia's political leadership may indeed have been several degrees less progressive than in other states, but Virginia's social-welfare community was far more progressive than its political leadership. Concentrated in the city of Richmond, those welfare workers could often be found at the forefront of the region's progressive organizations. Social-welfare progressives in the city took seriously "the social burden of the state" and attempted to enlarge the state's capacities to solve social problems.[22]

Virginia's progressive governors—Andrew Montague (1902–6),[23] Claude A. Swanson (1906–10),[24] and William Hodges Mann (1910–14)—pushed the state legislature to adopt an ambitious progressive-reform agenda, including ending corporate contributions to political campaigns, compulsory school attendance, establishing reform schools, increasing the numbers of and funding for asylums, penal reform, increasing school funding, and road construction. Under this pressure, the state government enlarged its welfare obligation by establishing new asylums for special classes of dependents. A state asylum for the epileptic and the so-called "feebleminded" was approved by the state legislature in 1910.[25] Called the "Colony" by locals, the state hospital at Lynchburg later became nationally known for its practice of "eugenic" involuntary sterilizations of the feebleminded.[26] But for the Progressive era, at least, the Colony put Virginia in the forefront of modern thinking about both mental disability and state responsibility.

The state's expanded welfare program included a new policy of partially subsidizing private charitable asylums. In 1910, for example, the legislature appropriated twenty-five hundred dollars to the Negro Reformatory Association.[27] This initial subsidy eventually turned into complete state ownership, as the state determined to take over the operation of the various reformatories rather than continue to subsidize private institutions over which the state had insufficient control. By 1920, when the state had taken over control of the private facilities, the state budget for reformatories had risen to nearly two hundred thousand dollars a year (see table 5).[28]

Social-welfare progressivism influenced state governments to create boards of charities, in an effort to impose some order on the swelling welfare sector.[29] The Virginia legislature created its State Board of Charities and Corrections in 1908, after several years of lobbying by the private COS-influenced group called the Virginia Conference on Charities and Corrections. Initially, the legislature gave the State Board of Charities and Corrections very limited supervisory powers. It investigated all public and private institutions, collected data, published its findings, and made nonbinding recommendations for improvements. Under the direction of Dr. J. T. Mastin, one of the board's most important contributions to social-welfare policy was to embed emerging ideals of professional social work at the state level.[30]

Another progressive innovation in Virginia was mothers' aid. In 1918, the state legislature passed legislation allowing—but not requiring—local governments to pay monthly allowances to "worthy" widowed mothers. The mothers' aid, or mothers' pension, movement was a national phenomenon in the Progressive era, but one that gained only limited support in southern states. Mothers' pensions were designed to allow women with young children to remain home with them, rather than having to go out to work to support them, sometimes breaking up the family to do so. In Virginia, only two localities took advantage of the enabling legislation, the city of Richmond and Wise County. In Richmond, "the determined and stubborn advocacy" of white clubwomen was responsible for its funding. They successfully lobbied the city council to appropriate three thousand dollars to initiate the program.[31] At the time of a survey of Richmond's social agencies in 1923, the city's mothers' aid program remained pitifully small. The 1923 survey, conducted by the American Association for Organizing Family Social Work, recommended that the city welfare department double the annual appropriation, which would still "be a most conservative advance considering the needs."[32]

The state did not appropriate any funds for the mothers' aid program— the local governments were to provide the funding—and so this particular reform did not add any burden to the state's welfare budget. Other progressive programs were responsible for pushing state expenditures on welfare activities higher. Table 5 shows the state's budgets for welfare activities rising significantly during the 1910s and 1920s. New "asylums" and reformatories account for most of the increase in non-Confederate welfare expenditures. As discussed in chapter 5, the state made a substantial commitment to public welfare, which came in the form of Confederate pensions and subsidies to Confederate homes. When these Confederate welfare appropriations are added in, the state's budget for public welfare looks greatly expanded indeed, hovering between 15 percent and 21 percent of the state's expenditures for most of the first two decades of the twentieth century (see table 8).

It should be noted that the state's areas of commitment remained clearly delineated. The progressive movement may have pushed the state to accept larger responsibility for public welfare, but it did not change one central presumption that had guided state policies since the Revolution. Only special classes of dependents received state-level assistance, and, with the exception of Confederate pensioners, those dependents all received institutional care. The state had essentially added new categories of dependents to its obligation; it had not changed the fundamental assumptions regarding state responsibilities. The poor laws, with their mandate of local responsibility for poor relief, remained effectively intact.

It should also be noted that the state legislature's enthusiasm for progressive reforms during the 1910s waned during the 1920s. During the latter decade, Harry Byrd's "machine" tightened its control over both the state government and the Democratic Party, establishing in Virginia "the most thorough control by an oligarchy" of any southern state.[33] Byrd dominated the "organization," a group of young, conservative politicians once described as "clean-shaven and wearing trim conservative suits, epitomiz[ing] the age of Coolidge, the efficient businessman, and optimistic prosperity."[34] Byrd's economic philosophy increasingly became official policy: low taxes, limited public services, minimal interference with corporate profits.[35] Byrd's "pay-as-you-go" system rejected the reliance on long-term indebtedness and paid for highway construction and other governmental activities by regular forms of annual revenue, such as gasoline taxes. Byrd's policies made the state government fiscally sound, but at the expense of state services. As political scientist V. O. Key put it, the organization did hold a sense of social responsibility, "so long as it does not cost much."[36] The "fetish for economy in government" developed under Byrd resulted in lower expenditures for public services,[37] and both Confederate and non-Confederate welfare dropped to less than 10 percent of the state's expenses during the 1920s. There would be little innovation in social welfare at the state level thereafter.

Progressive Social Welfare in Richmond

Arguably, Richmond's advanced social-welfare activism was the response to the presence of greater need than in other communities. Some of the data on the city were indeed abysmal. In the first decade of the twentieth century, Richmond had a mortality rate higher than all but three other major American cities. In 1905, population density in the city was twenty-two people per acre, making it the most congested city in the South.[38] The city's water supply had become contaminated; Shockoe Creek, which sliced through the middle of town, was "loaded . . . by the contents of several public sewers and the refuse from many slaughter houses emptying into it."[39] Richmond's black population lived in even worse conditions than whites. As late as 1929, over one-third of black households still had no running water in the kitchen, having to pump water in the yard instead; over 70 percent had no bathtub; and over 70 percent had only outside toilets.[40]

The "New South" economy of early-twentieth-century Richmond, a rapidly growing and industrializing city, had produced this urban squalor. The economy had also produced a larger, better educated, and more prosperous middle class than in many smaller southern communities. Middle-class women were a particularly important constituency for the emergence of social-welfare progressivism: they had more leisure time and financial resources to devote to reform causes, and they had a strong tradition of benevolence upon which to draw. Richmond's clubwomen stood behind (and financed) numerous progressive reform efforts, such as the YWCA and the Instructive Visiting Nurses Association.[41]

Some of the earliest stirrings of progressivism in Richmond began even before the depression of the 1890s. A local chapter of the Woman's Christian Temperance Union formed in the city in 1882; a local YWCA opened in 1887; and in 1890, leading citizens of Richmond were among those forming the Prison Association of Virginia, an organization that advocated the creation of juvenile courts.[42] By 1908, the PAV and other children's advocates had convinced one local judge to hold separate, more informal, hearings for juveniles. Rev. James Buchanan, a former settlement-house worker and director of the Associated Charities, acted as the probation officer for Judge John Crutchfield's juvenile court.[43]

Juvenile courts bore many of the hallmarks of progressive philosophy: they attempted to change the environments in which children were raised; they used an expanded state authority on behalf of social reform; and they came ultimately to use professional social workers as part of the individualized approach to poverty.[44] Settlement houses, those "spearheads of reform," shared these characteristics.[45] Religious organizations opened two settlement houses in Richmond in the first decade of the twentieth century. The Methodist Institute, under the direction of George Wiley, opened in 1900; Baptists organized Neighborhood House in 1904 and appointed James Buchanan to run it. Both men saw themselves as city missionaries.[46] By the early 1920s, there were two more settlements serving white neighborhoods (the Nurses' Settlement on Cary Street, and the Neighborhood House).[47] Although settlements in southern cities usually served a native-born population, Richmond's Neighborhood House, sponsored by the Council of Jewish Women, had a large immigrant population in its clientele. As in northeastern settlements, Neighborhood House "has the job of making good American citizens out of these small youngsters" whose foreign-born parents "cannot speak a word of English."[48]

Like the majority of welfare programs in the Progressive-era South, the settlement houses in Richmond were racially segregated institutions. The color line was firmly drawn in private charities. In 1920, for example, the federal census reported that all five of the residents of the Faith Rescue Home were white, all seventeen of the children in the Virginia Home for Infants were white, all thirty of the boys in the Male Orphan Asylum were white, and all ten of the infants in the Foundling Hospital were white.[49] The Children's Home Society practiced "default" segregation: explaining why the society did little to place black orphans, the director claimed that he "couldn't find prosperous colored families that were not already provided with children."[50] The Associated Charities also limited its services to whites. In 1921, the AC worked out an agreement with the "Colored Community House" to furnish "such financial relief as our treasury will permit." For six thousand to eight thousand dollars a year, the Associated Charities could be assured that casework was being practiced by the black settlement house, without having to do the casework itself.[51]

Public-welfare facilities were also either segregated or racially exclusive. The city operated two Tuberculosis Dispensaries, established in 1907 and 1908, so that the races could be treated separately. The city almshouse was fully segregated, with two entirely separate buildings, despite the fact that this resulted in increasing the expenses involved. The city recognized that operating expenses were increased "because of the necessity of conducting two distinct plants, one for white and the other for colored patients, with the result that officers, nurses, heating plants, kitchens and other facilities are necessarily duplicated."[52] But the city continued to view segregation as a necessity.

Although this might be considered a southern pattern in social provision, in fact progressives in the nation as a whole accepted (sometimes enthusiastically) racial segregation in social welfare. Progressive social-welfare thought in the early decades of the century stressed the positive value of segregating the races and the sexes in facilities such as almshouses. One contemporary survey of almshouses, used nationwide as a textbook for training social workers, concluded, "There are four lines of segregation generally laid down as fundamental: by sex, by color, by health, and by mental and moral character."[53] Richmond's city almshouse was frequently praised for its modern, progressive methods, with its ability to segregate inmates by race considered a sign of progressive thinking.[54]

In response to African Americans' exclusion from white private charities, the middle-class black community leaders created their own, parallel, institutions. Blacks established several institutions for children, including Holy Innocents Foundling Asylum, run by the St. Joseph's Society for Colored Missions, founded in 1895. The Colored Day Nursery and Home, sponsored by the Christ Mission Workers, opened in 1907. The Richmond Neighborhood Association, under the longtime presidency of Ora B. Stokes, supported both a Day Nursery on Charity Street and a Home for Girls on Clay Street by 1920.[55] The Negro Reformatory Association of Virginia, founded in 1897, built a privately run reformatory as a means to release black children from the jails. The Reformatory Association included prominent white leaders on its board of directors and attempted to cultivate a cooperative relationship with white reformers.[56]

There were clearly limits to the interracial cooperation, limits that came from both sides of the color line. The Salvation Army's attempt to establish a "colored" corps in Richmond failed. After ten years of "trying to make soldiers among the colored people," the Salvation Army withdrew from the effort in 1926, noting that "the pastors of the colored churches . . . have been very opposed to us."[57] Local black leadership desired assistance and support from whites but resented efforts like the Salvation Army, which appeared to push aside established black leaders.

While largely conforming to national and regional norms of progressivism, African American welfare institutions nevertheless facilitated an additional agenda. These black-provided social-welfare services "represented not dramatic protest but everyday forms of resistance to oppression and demoralization." Black middle-class reformers preached "respectability" as a form of racial uplift; and respectability implied adherence to a set of middle-class values that whites would understand and respect. "Racial uplift" was a broad concept of economic, political, and social reforms led by a black middle class attempting to establish its leadership role in the black community.[58]

Although the black middle class successfully built a private social-welfare structure, it never displaced the extensive network of mutual-aid societies upon which working-class blacks had long relied. In a 1929 survey of 750 black families in Richmond, 481 had insurance of some kind, 444 contributed to "lodges" or mutual-aid associations, and 467 contributed regularly to their churches.[59] Moreover, mutual-aid associations became a lifelong association for many working-class blacks. William Johnson, a former slave who moved to Richmond after emancipation and began working as a laborer in the construction trade,

immediately joined several mutual-aid associations. By the time he was inter-
viewed in the 1930s, he had been a member of Odd Fellows for fifty-seven years
and a member of the Good Samaritans for sixty-four years.[60] Such evidence
suggests that working-class blacks may have valued these self-help mechanisms
over the social-welfare "services" provided them by the middle class.

By the early twentieth century, mutual-aid associations had begun to be involved in other, more commercial endeavors. The Saint Luke Emporium and
the Saint Luke Penny Savings Bank are the best known of these institutions,
thanks to recent historical attention,[61] but others existed as well, such as the
Southern Aid Society.[62] By expanding the commercial aspects of mutual aid,
a new generation of working-class blacks in Richmond could rise to the ranks
of entrepreneurs, occasionally garnering substantial wealth. Mutual aid might
thereby be a route to more than just the more impoverished "respectability"
being touted by the middle class.

In addition to racial concerns, ethnic and sectarian issues shaped social welfare in the city. Despite declining ratios of foreign immigrants in Richmond in
the postbellum decades (see table 1B), immigrants continued to move to the
city, bringing with them interest in ethnic, national, and sectarian charitable
endeavors. Several Catholic organizations, for example, combined efforts into
an Irish Relief Society to aid during the Irish famine in 1880.[63] Germans in Richmond also felt drawn to support their "fellow countrymen" during and after the
First World War. They formed a local branch of the Central Relief Committee
and raised twenty-five hundred dollars for the needy in Germany and Austria
in 1923.[64]

The local German-language newspaper, *Virginische Zeitung*, gave prominent
coverage to charitable activities in the German community, as when Henry
Marks left bequests to Beth Ahaba, the Oakwood Hebrew Association, the
Hebrew Orphanage of Atlanta, the Little Sisters of the Poor, and the Masonic
Home. The remarkably detailed articles describing the amount and nature of
bequests to charitable organizations undoubtedly helped to further such benevolence within the German community.[65]

The Jewish community in Richmond, although relatively small, was divided
by linguistic and cultural differences that influenced the local private charitable efforts. The German and Portuguese Jews, long established in the city, had
well-developed benevolent programs. The Ladies Hebrew Benevolent Association, which began as a mutual-assistance association, had evolved into a larger
charitable endeavor. In 1887, the association began making contributions to the
City Mission and the Male Orphan Asylum. By the early twentieth century,
it had evolved further into a Jewish version of the Associated Charities.[66] (So

powerful was the influence of the charity-organizing ideal that, even though the AC's origins lay in the Protestant evangelical tradition, both Jewish and Catholic charities adopted its precepts during the Progressive era.)[67]

Russian immigrants, more recent arrivals in the city, organized separately from the Germans of longer tenure. A local committee, chaired by Mr. M. Millhiser, assembled to aid Jewish refugees from Russia. The members raised money, established an employment committee to help immigrants find jobs, and contacted "Israelites in the different cities of the State for the purpose of organizing committees for collection of funds."[68] Neighborhood House, the settlement house "in the heart of the Jewish ghetto," was founded in 1912 by the Council of Jewish Women to serve as a community center for the children of recent immigrants. Russian Jews organized the Hebrew Sick Aid Society in 1921, a self-help group separate from the German society.[69]

Private social-welfare activism permitted ethnic, racial, or religious groups to confirm their cultural differences while simultaneously promoting their acceptability to the dominant culture. Jewish charities, for instance, helped to bind together the small community through mutual assistance; through their charities, middle-class Jews also demonstrated to the predominately Christian culture the similarity of their middle-class values. Not surprisingly, Jewish women in Richmond participated in the annual Confederate memorial day activities, decorating the graves of Jews who had given their lives for the Confederacy.[70] Fealty to the Lost Cause gave the minority an identification with the majority; common commemoration might engender more respect for the city's tiny Jewish enclave. For religious and ethnic minorities, organized charity further served as group protection against prejudice. Catholic leaders, for example, were keenly aware that neglecting the Catholic poor "would be charged against them as a failed civic responsibility and would exacerbate anti-Catholic and nativist sentiments" already present in American culture.[71]

The racial and ethnic patterns of private charity were effectively reinforced by public-welfare policy. The city council's annual appropriations to multiple sectarian orphanages, and to multiple ethnic old age homes, served to buttress ethnic solidarity and religious affiliation. Likewise, the Associated Charities reinforced ethnic and sectarian ties by sorting applicants by religious affiliation and then effectively binding the individual to the church charity. Both public and private charities, then, worked to encourage the ethnic and religious divisions in Richmond.[72]

The Progressive era also witnessed a new level of social activism by middle-class women, which brought many Richmond women into close contact with the poor and working class. Ellen Glasgow's memoir betrays the culture shock that daughters of privilege could experience upon their first exposure to the world of the poor:

[A]t seventeen . . . I joined the City Mission, and became the youngest "visitor" in its membership. Though my health was frail, my mental energy was inexhaustible, and I was eager to test life on every side and in every situation. The squalor I saw horrified me, and in the majority of cases, I felt that I was dealing with inanimate matter. Certainly there was not any blessedness in the spiritless whining with which these particular paupers gave up the struggle, and leaned back upon God.[73]

While shocking, such experiences could also be inspiring, and a generation of women like Glasgow organized to relieve the sufferings of the poor and reform the shortcomings of the modern city. Drawing upon an ideology of "maternalism," they gave special attention to the needs of women and children. The Woman's Christian Association, under the leadership of Mrs. J. H. Capers, operated a free kindergarten, mothers' meetings, girls' clubs, and a sewing school for girls. In 1900, the association announced plans for a manual-training class "for the boys who infest the streets in that locality."[74] Churchwomen were behind the establishment of the Infants Home, under direction of Miss Pollard, "a competent nurse, as well as a kind friend." In 1900, the home cared for thirty-two children.[75] In 1923, the Salvation Army opened the Evangeline Booth Home and Hospital, as the focus of its women's branch. The Booth Home operated under much the same principles as the Florence Crittenden Homes: keep mothers and babies together whenever possible, teach domestic skills, and work toward Christian conversion.[76]

One of the most important of these women's progressive organizations was the Instructive Visiting Nurses Association. Modeled after Lillian Wald's Henry Street Settlement in New York, the IVNA began as a visiting nurses program but soon expanded to include a settlement house called the Nurses' Settlement. With its emphasis on trained nursing and trained social workers, the IVNA was an important catalyst in the creation of both public-health work and professional social work in the city. IVNA nurses were instrumental in forming the Richmond School of Social Work.[77]

Incorporated in April 1917, with Dr. J. J. Sherer as president, the Richmond School of Social Work answered a perceived need in the city for trained workers who were from the South. Widely claimed as the "oldest school of social work in the South,"[78] the Richmond School of Social Work argued that bringing trained workers to the South "from the Eastern schools" did not solve the region's problems, for those workers, "however capable or well trained . . . [were] inevitably handicapped at the start by ignorance of local conditions and local ways of doing things. Neither has the sending of Southern students to the Eastern schools solved the problem. The expense is great and not many have, in fact, availed themselves of the opportunity."[79] The first students to enroll in the new school were in fact all from southern states.[80]

The school's arguments about southern social workers seems to be an accurate assessment of contemporary views. When local agencies hired social workers, they actively sought southerners for the positions. In 1924, Louise McMaster of the Associated Charities wrote to the American Association of Social Workers, hoping to identify a southern woman for a position as district secretary: "we want if possible to have a southerner for the job."[81] In 1927, the State Board of Charities hired several new social-work staffers in the Children's Bureau. All four women, Mabel Nussman, Catherine Wilcox, Mary Hardy, and Mary M. Moore, were specifically identified as native southerners in the board's minutes, as if to reassure the members that the two workers who had had experience and training outside the region could nevertheless be trusted to understand regional conditions.[82]

Henry Hibbs was director/dean of the School of Social Work from 1917 to 1940. The original faculty were all acquired from local social work agencies, including Dr. Ennion Williams of the city health department, Nannie J. Minor of the IVNA, and Loomis Logan of the Associated Charities.[83] The program initially was quite small; in the first five years, it produced only twenty graduates in social work.[84] Despite the small scale, the school gained much approval. As early as 1923, the American Association for Organizing Family Social Work could conclude that the Richmond School of Social Work "is furnishing thoroughgoing training both in class and field work, and that its status as a full-fledged school has been definitely established. As the only definitely professional school of social work in the South its location in Richmond is very much to the credit of the city."[85]

Although the Richmond School of Social Work offered a course on urban blacks beginning in 1918, no blacks were permitted to study at the school.[86] The report on "negro welfare" in Richmond prepared by the Council of Social Agencies in 1929 drew attention to the great need for trained social workers for black organizations. "The social and relief programs of Negro churches, lodges, and the Council of Colored Women could without doubt be made much more effective if the negroes themselves had a better understanding of their social problems and knew something about the principles of community organization and case work." The report recommended that the Council of Social Agencies, the Richmond School of Social Work, and the Virginia Union University cooperate to create a training program for black social workers.[87]

The Richmond School of Social Work had the hearty support of the Associated Charities, and the two organizations had a close and cooperative working relationship. The Associated Charities continued its efforts to organize private charitable activities, to prevent duplication of services, and to eliminate "imposture." Acting as a clearinghouse for information on the poor, the AC kept files on all applicants for relief. Trained caseworkers, like Loomis Logan in the early 1920s, supervised the casework. District visitors found jobs for the unemployed, arranged medical treatment for the ill, and provided a range of other services. In most cases, the visitors sent approved applicants to another agency for assistance: in 1923, for example, 190 families were referred to the IVNA, 16 were sent to the Juvenile and Domestic Relations Court for nonsupport, 5 families were sent to the Catholic Charities, and 26 applicants were sent to the City Home. Direct relief was discouraged but remained part of the program of the Associated Charities: 1,233 families received groceries from the AC that same year.[88]

The charity-organizing movement remained critical of public-welfare institutions, like almshouses, for their failure to hire professional caseworkers, who would be more rigorous than city officials in investigating the applicants for relief. One contemporary advocate argued that "what is needed most . . . is the application of organized charities principles to almshouse management. . . . If this were done, the almshouse could be made a source of great help to the aged poor by locating relatives who may be financially able to care for the applicant or inmate, and by placing the responsibility where it belongs."[89] In a similar vein, the Richmond AC reported in 1921 that it had forty-nine cases that could not be made entirely independent, so "we put the burden of their support on relatives and friends, so that they are now no drain on the general public."[90] (How the AC enforced such familial support went unstated.)

Convinced that privately sponsored casework was superior to public welfare, the Associated Charities began to push for an enlarged role in public relief in Richmond. The AC had been receiving small appropriations from the city council for several years and had been distributing a portion of the city's outdoor relief. (In 1921, for example, the AC distributed wood, coal, milk, shoes, and clothing for the city, at an estimated value of just over sixty-one hundred dollars.)[91] The AC would have liked to take over the city's outdoor relief entirely. As articulated by an investigator for the American Association for Organizing Charity, it "would be preferable to have this work handled entirely by the Associated Charities. . . . it would be able to produce much better results than are now being produced through the office of the superintendent of the City Home."[92]

Tensions between the city charity authorities and the AC began to surface in the early 1920s. The Associated Charities often operated as if welfare were its exclusive domain: the language of annual reports suggested that the city's public welfare served to supplement the work of the AC rather than vice versa. The Associated Charities tried to take "custody" over poor relief and viewed the role of other organizations as supplemental help to "our families."[93] The AC frequently criticized the city's public-welfare system, such as its small appropriation for Mothers' Aid. The three thousand dollars the city expended in 1921 was "utterly inadequate to care for the many widows in the city who should receive it," and the AC was forced in response to spend "hundreds of dollars each month in allowances."[94]

Although the city did not air any opinions on this conflict with the private charity, it responded by backing away from its previously cooperative relationship with the Associated Charities. In 1922, when the AC complained that the city's financial contributions to the AC did not equal the value of the work it did for the city and asked for an increased appropriation, the city instead established its own casework bureau. The Social Service Bureau, under the city's Department of Public Welfare, was charged with examining all applications for city welfare, both indoor and outdoor relief, and operated independently of the AC. The city arranged for students from the School of Social Work and Public Health to be caseworkers. This move effectively duplicated the work of the AC and directly challenged the charity organization for control over family casework in the city. Moreover, the city set a new policy of adhering only to its own evaluations and recommendations, not those of the Associated Charities; but the city asked the AC to abide by the assessments of the city's agents. In addition, the city took back responsibility for distributing food and fuel, excluding the Associated Charities from the process.[95] As a result, "for a time the relationship between the public organization and the private agency remained strained."[96]

Financial problems had forced the temporary closing of the Associated Charities in the fall of 1923. After securing sufficient funds to reopen, the AC helped to organize the Richmond Community Fund in 1924.[97] Another national trend in private charities, community chests combined their annual fundraising drives into one single campaign. The Community Fund ended what had become "the almost daily appeals for money" from Richmond's multiple private charities. Organized by Dr. Rolvix Harlan, a sociology professor at the University of Richmond; Louise McMaster, director of the Associated Charities; Judge John L. Ingram; and others, the Community Fund was strongly supported by the city's business leaders. Frequent targets of charitable solicitations, prominent merchants like William Schwarzschild and William Thalhimer gave the movement their endorsement and served as fundraisers.[98]

The Community Fund attempted to impose some control over the rapidly multiplying charitable organizations. Admission to membership in the fund committed the organizations to careful scrutiny of their budgets, their function, and their operations. Those who agreed to abide by the fund's guidelines could receive funding from the annual community campaign. Others found themselves excluded, such as the Women's Christian Temperance Union, whose budget seemed to be largely given over to other organizations.[99] This was the kind of overlap and confusion that the Community Fund hoped to untangle. Other organizations were excluded from membership when they appeared to offer too much duplication to previously existing services. For example, when the Committee on Inter-Racial Cooperation applied for membership in 1927, the Community Fund insisted that they first had to meet with the leadership of the Richmond Urban League to coordinate their activities.[100]

The Richmond Community Fund assured the citizenry that it had introduced "sound business methods into the field of philanthropy" through "the study of agency budgets, the requirement of monthly reports, the systematic collection and disbursement of funds, and the organization of a single city-wide financial campaign."[101] Despite the promise of increased revenues and reliable income, some agencies that were members of the Community Fund continued to request funding from the city.[102]

Progressivism and Public Welfare in Richmond

The public-welfare system of Richmond also evolved during the Progressive era, partly in response to the rise of so many private charitable organizations. Consistent with other progressive trends, public welfare became more specialized (institutions multiplied, then specialized); public welfare became more professional (public agencies hired trained social workers); and public welfare became more generous, or at least less stingy. Symbolically, the Richmond city almshouse was renamed the "City Home" in 1905,[103] a reflection of the softened attitudes toward the poor stimulated by progressive thinking.

One of the most obvious effects of progressive reforms on public welfare was the declining role of the city almshouse in caring for children. Although there was a national movement underway to remove children from poorhouses,[104] Richmond authorities never took action in this regard and continued to permit children to enter the city almshouse either with their mothers or alone (see table 16). Instead, the declining number of children in the almshouse was the product of the rise of new alternatives. By the early twentieth century, Richmond housed numerous orphanages, foundling homes, and maternity homes.[105] Also, working mothers had several day nurseries available. Although the number of spaces available was clearly inadequate to meet the needs, nevertheless many children who would previously have ended up in orphanages or the city almshouse were instead in day care.[106] As a result, fewer children were present in the almshouse. This is reflected in the rising age of the almshouse population: while the average age of almshouse residents in 1860 had been forty years old, by 1907 the average age had reached fifty.[107]

The children who continued to appear on the almshouse admissions rolls were usually there with their mothers. By the twentieth century, far fewer babies were abandoned on the front porch of the almshouse.[108] The superintendent no longer needed to operate so extensive an adoption system as before, although the almshouse continued to place children in adoptive homes occasionally (see table 19). The arrangement of adoptions became a more formal system in the early twentieth century, and private agencies began to specialize in this function.[109] The Children's Home Society in particular, established in 1900, operated a vast adoption agency. Children still arrived at the City Home as temporary residents, as families used the facility as a de facto public boarding home for children, but few were abandoned entirely as in the past.

Another change in the functioning of the city almshouse involved the removal of the medical department. In 1914, the city home's hospital was physically removed to the facilities at the Medical College of Virginia and was named the Virginia Hospital.[110] Contemporaries contended that the "respectable" poor avoided public hospitals that were part of an almshouse. As a social worker in Baltimore wrote, "There is a natural prejudice in the city against going to a hospital very closely associated with the poorhouse, especially among people who are not very clear in their own minds as to whether they are one and the same thing."[111] The City Home continued to offer medical care to its residents and continued to have a full-time nursing staff and regular physicians' visits. Those who needed hospitalization, such as for surgery or childbirth, were now sent to the Medical College of Virginia. This separation of the hospital from the "home," a national urban trend in which Richmond participated, further narrowed the functions of the almshouse, making the institution more specialized than before.[112]

The direction of this specialization was illuminated when, in 1922, the City Home hired its first full-time social worker. Hiring a caseworker to screen applicants for city relief demonstrated just how deeply public welfare had been influenced by the precepts of charity organization. The City Home caseworker operated under many of the same assumptions as the Associated Charities: private welfare agencies, wherever possible, should carry the burden of "constructive charity," leaving the public sector the smallest possible role in welfare. For example, Bess Carter, a "colored" girl who was pregnant, applied to the City Home, but the social worker learned that her mother-in-law was willing to take her in. She arranged for medical care through the IVNA instead of the city.

Male Orphan Asylum, one of Richmond's oldest private charities, ca. 1910. The asylum, like most such institutions, was segregated during this era. Some of the boys in this photo are holding baseball bats and gloves and posing in baseball stances. Courtesy of the Library of Virginia.

Another case was a deserted infant named Lavinia Moody. The social worker managed to trace her mother and convinced the mother's parents to take in the two. Another pregnant woman, Victoria Horsley, was transferred to the privately run Spring Street Home once the social worker convinced the father of the child to support her.[113]

By such methods, a significant number of poor and dependents in Richmond who otherwise would have received assistance from the city could be placed with private-welfare agencies. But this was accompanied by an increase, rather than a decrease, in city expenditures on welfare, as shown in table 10 (see also figures 6 and 7). This apparent contradiction is explained by three things. First, the population growth in Richmond put constant upward pressure on city welfare expenditures. Second, the city continued to subsidize ever-increasing numbers of private welfare organizations on top of its own expenditures for the poor. By 1926, the city was contributing funds to twenty-seven private charities.[114] Third, the improvements in the city's own welfare activities added to its costs. Funding mothers' aid, hiring professional staff, and modernizing the physical

Belle Bryan Day Nursery, ca. 1919. Although segregated, this nursery accepted the children of immigrants. Courtesy of the Valentine Richmond History Center.

plant of the city home in order to raise the standards of care all contributed to higher public-welfare expenses.

With the presence of so many specialized institutions to care for large numbers of poor and dependents, and with the long-standing low reputation of almshouses in general, it was not surprising that progressives often called for the end of almshouses altogether.[115] Virginia's county almshouses attracted strong criticism. The state board of charities concluded that the county almshouse "is not a success because of its isolation, its limited facilities, [and] its cost of maintenance."[116] Year after year, the state board of charities complained of the conditions of the county almshouses. "In the majority of cases, the county almshouses are in worse condition than the county jails. Some of the cases are deplorable. As a rule, the almshouses are located in out-of-the-way sections of the county, the buildings are in bad repair, the house furnishings are inadequate, the inmates poorly attended, and the superintendent discontented with his lot."[117] Arthur James, later the director of the state's department of welfare, explained that the "problem of the poorhouse was largely due to the fact that many of them were located in isolated parts of counties where land was cheap and where there were fewer respectable neighbors to object to the poorhouse population as a vicious and sordid influence."[118]

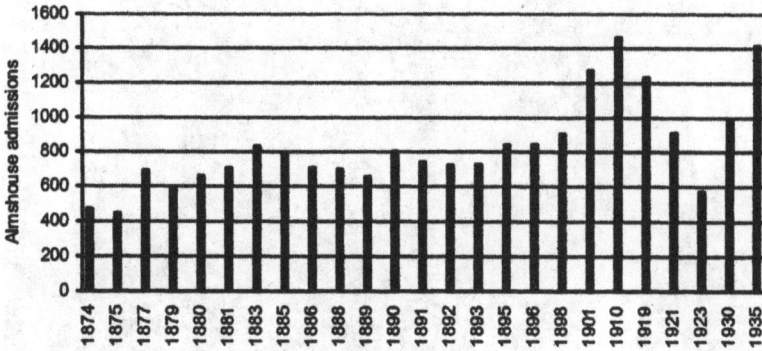

Figure 6. *Richmond City Indoor Relief, 1874–1935*
Source: Annual reports, supt. of almshouse/public welfare, broken series.

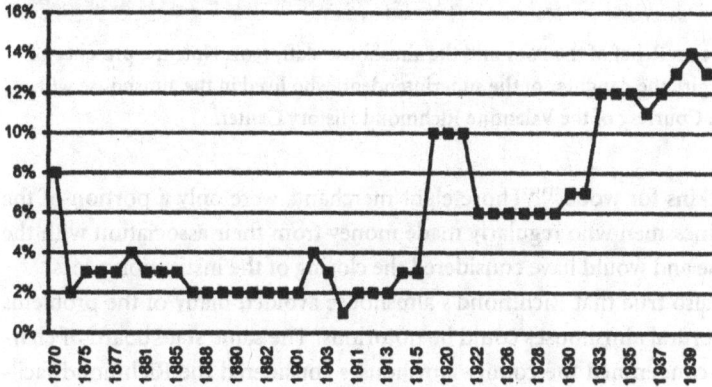

Figure 7. *Richmond Welfare Expenditures as a Percentage of City Budget, 1870–1940*
Sources: Combined from annual reports, city mayor; annual reports, city comptroller.

Although many people worked for their closing, there were many reasons for the continuation of almshouses, particularly in a large community like Richmond. Economy of scale was one reason; the city could buy goods and services for the almshouse in bulk and save money. But also the business community saw the almshouse as a lucrative source of revenue. Furnishing supplies to the almshouse could be an important source of income for numerous local businesses. For services for one quarter in 1893, for example, the almshouse signed contracts with A. Fachel for beef and lamb, L. C. Younger for rice and molasses, J. S. Moore for coffee, sugar, vinegar, salt, lard, and bacon, R. Garcia for soap, J. R. Goode for shoes, Alvey Brothers for hay and feed, C. H. Pase for coal, and

Committee on Relief of the Poor and the almshouse staff, 1902. Note the presence of the young girl, the daughter of the superintendent, who lived in the almshouse with her family. Courtesy of the Valentine Richmond History Center.

B. T. Watkins for wood.[119] Those eight merchants were only a portion of the local businessmen who regularly made money from their association with the almshouse and would have considered the closing of the institution a loss.

It was also true that Richmond's almshouse avoided many of the problems for which rural almshouses could be notorious. The same state board of charities that condemned the county almshouses considered the Richmond facility "more generously provided for by the city than any of its [other] institutions. . . . The place is so clean as to deserve to be called spotless. The officials in charge are not only competent, but kindly, and there is much to commend."[120]

So the Richmond City Home survived the movement to close almshouses. The social-work community in Virginia did succeed in convincing the state legislature to close many of the county almshouses, by consolidating several smaller almshouses into one "district" home. As early as 1910, the State Board of Charities and Corrections was suggesting that counties combine their efforts. Each county would continue to contribute to its support, but their individual expenditures were thereby reduced.[121] The state legislature approved, but did not mandate, consolidations in 1918. The state board of charities then had to convince local governments to cooperate, a process that took decades to complete.[122]

The trend toward consolidation of the county almshouses did little to reduce local public-welfare expenses. Annual public-welfare expenditures continued to climb in the Progressive era, both absolutely and per capita. Social-welfare progressivism, whether public or private, was expensive.

BY THE END OF the 1920s, social-welfare policy in the South had been reconfigured by the influences of the charity-organization movement, the cult of the Lost Cause, and progressivism. Collectively, these movements worked to enlarge both public and private welfare provision. Individually, the three movements contained some elements that contradicted one another. The Lost Cause advocates and most progressives supported an enlarged, activist state as a means to their respective ends. Charity organizers were hostile to public welfare and therefore were less enthusiastic about the expanding welfare state.

Notably, contemporaries did reach some consensus about the position of almshouses in the progressive protowelfare state in the South. Welfare activists of all political stripes seemed to concur that almshouses were flawed institutions that required either dramatic improvement or outright abolition. Many of the earlier functions of almshouses had been replaced by other institutions, such as maternity homes and adoption agencies, leaving the almshouses with a narrower range of activities. Contemporaries saw these newer institutions as more desirable, more modern, more "progressive" than almshouses, which had, after all, been around for centuries. In the Progressive era, more than ever, the almshouse seemed to be the place of last resort. Only after all other options, both public and private, had been exhausted did individuals turn to the almshouse.

This represented a significant shift in perception, which had taken decades to produce. From the founding of the colonies to the early national period, the almshouse had been the primary source of relief. Indeed in many localities, the almshouse would have been the only option for assistance. But by the early twentieth century, the almshouse had become only one of a wide range of public and private services available to the needy. Moreover, the almshouse had come to be seen as the least desirable form of assistance available. As the state board of public welfare put it in 1925, "The Board feels that there is little excuse for an almshouse."[123] The stage was set, then, for the eventual demise of the institution, which would come as a by-product of New Deal welfare programs.

The reforms of the Progressive era helped to push the South closer to the national norms of social-welfare policy. As leading southern progressive Alexander McKelway argued, "Broadly speaking, all our problems are American problems. There is no peculiarly southern problem of poverty, illiteracy or crime; our problems of the city, of rural life and child welfare are the same throughout the nation."[124] By the 1920s, southern states had much the same kinds of public and private institutions as found elsewhere in the country, and the trends in the region mirrored those of the nation: schools of social work produced trained caseworkers who were quickly hired by local welfare agencies; almshouses were closing; budgets were rising; state and local bureaucracies were expanding.

Although Virginia had a well-earned reputation for conservatism, Richmond's social-work community was often on the forefront of southern welfare practice in the Progressive era. Local welfare practitioners, both public and private, maintained strong ties to the national welfare community by attending conferences, subscribing to journals, and participating in professional organizations.[125] Many local activists emerged as regional, and occasionally even national, figures in social-welfare circles.[126]

These social-welfare progressives came to embrace the activist state. Although many social-welfare progressives came from backgrounds in voluntary associations and remained supporters of the ideals of voluntary activism, they nevertheless eventually articulated a rationale for an activist government. Only government had the resources necessary to attack the widespread and entrenched sources of poverty. Social-welfare progressives came to see the state as an essential tool in their efforts to ameliorate suffering and end poverty. These progressive ideas would take on new meaning when confronted with the national economic crisis that followed the stock market crash of 1929.

CHAPTER EIGHT

On the Margins

The Lives of the Poor

In much of the preceding pages, the poor of Richmond have remained off stage, obscured from view largely because of the nature of the records upon which historians traditionally rely. Much of what we know about poverty and poor relief in the past comes from the middle classes and elites of the day, who left us voluminous reports, editorials, letters, and diaries. We know a great deal about what they thought of the poor and poor relief. The recipients of poor relief themselves, often barely literate, seldom left first-hand accounts for historians to read. Consequently we only rarely hear the poor give their opinions about social-welfare provision.

Their actions have often had to speak for them instead, and for a generation now, historians have been learning how to "read" their actions. During the Civil War, the poor and working class in Richmond spoke indirectly about their unmet needs, by the Bread Riot, and by thefts of food and money. Reconstruction offered an additional opportunity for the poor to surface more directly in the public records: the presence of the federal troops in the city gave them the chance to register their complaints about the quality of care offered in the city almshouse, telling us, in the process, some of their expectations about poor relief. After Reconstruction, that opportunity disappeared along with the troops.

Leaving behind the chronological approach for the moment, this chapter proposes to concentrate on the poor themselves, in an attempt to uncover their perspectives on the varieties of assistance offered them in the late nineteenth and early twentieth centuries. Careful reading of the documents produced by the distributors of poor relief can provide some bits of evidence about the world of the poor in Richmond. By filtering out the documentary bias inherent in records of the city council, the overseers of the poor, and the local newspapers, we can glean some insights into the conditions under which people sought assistance. Another rich source is available as well to uncover patterns of behavior that can provide suggestions about the way the poor viewed the city's social welfare provision.[1] After Reconstruction ended, the city almshouse began keeping an admissions register, which detailed basic vital statistics such as age, sex, and race but also included additional data such as religion, educational levels, and medical conditions. A clerk recorded the admissions data in oversized leather-bound ledger books, creating a rich source of information on a group of people who seldom received such systematic attention. The admissions registers, which often contained more information on a given individual than did the census reports, have been converted to a massive database, which serves as one major source for the following analysis.[2]

These rich demographic sources, previously unused for this type of analysis, provide the basis for a composite picture of almshouse residents. With the supplemental help of newspaper accounts, official reports, and unpublished minutes, it is possible to peek into the city almshouse and gain some sense of the contours of daily life therein. Table 11 summarizes the totals of each admission register; this chapter attempts to gain an understanding of the experiences of some twenty thousand people. It will attempt to assess how the poor used the City Home, and will consider in detail the question of whether the poor lived in dread of ending up in the almshouse. Finally, the chapter undertakes a case study of one highly visible almshouse family and the sad resolution of their difficulties.

Daily Life in the City Home

Like the population of Richmond as a whole, the resident population in the city almshouse began to change in the late nineteenth century. Table 12 summarizes the nativity of the inmates, illustrating the nature of the demographic changes. The significant presence of immigrants, which began on the eve of the Civil War, continued, but with some new and notable features. Immigrants listed in the late-nineteenth- and early-twentieth-century volumes came from a much wider range of places than before. Reflecting trends in the nation as a whole, Richmond saw an influx of eastern Europeans, while the numbers of Irish-born immigrants declined both relatively and absolutely. Much like the Irish before them, the eastern European immigrants often arrived with very little financial resources, and they entered a community that offered them only limited access to private charity. As a result, the numbers of immigrants from Russia in the almshouse quickly caught up to that of the Irish-born.

Simultaneously, the number of inmates born in Richmond began to decline at the turn of the century. During the 1870s, native Richmonders had constituted approximately one-fourth of the residents of the almshouse. By the 1910s, native-born Richmonders were less than 7 percent of the whole. These two trends—the increasing number of foreign-born and the declining number of city-born—would have undoubtedly had much impact on the social relations in the almshouse. During the 1870s, with local residents still a substantial proportion of the inmates, the almshouse likely felt much like a cohesive community. An individual probably already knew many other inmates and probably knew many members of the staff as well. The interpersonal relationships may have played a role in facilitating escapes from the facility (as discussed later). The familiarity between staff and residents no doubt also contributed to the difficulty in maintaining discipline in the facility.

By the 1910s, however, the local "culture" of the almshouse would have been much diluted. The overwhelming body of residents came from elsewhere in Virginia. They were mostly rural migrants to the city, looking for work, and their arrival in the almshouse signified their lack of success in the city. However, many of those rural migrants would have found the facilities in the almshouse to be higher standard than their usual lifestyle. Like other urban facilities that served rural migrants, the almshouse would have had large numbers of residents who had little previous contact with running water, gas lighting, or indoor plumbing.[3] Given a better quality of diet, access to medical care, and modern facilities, this group of residents would have less reason to "abscond in the night" and would have contributed to the less uproarious setting in the latter years of this study.[4]

By the late nineteenth century, the city had grown out to reach the previously remote almshouse. Less isolated than before, the almshouse residents found it easier to have visitors than had prior generations. Novelist Ellen Glasgow recalled visiting the almshouse as a young child, when her nursemaid went to visit friends there. "All I remember is that I was petted by old women in drab clothes, and that I was allowed to play with several children under big spreading trees, while my mammy gossiped with these old women on the steps of the porch. When my mother heard of it, she forbade Mammy to take me there again."[5]

Such accessibility permitted residents of Richmond's City Home a level of social contact denied most almshouse residents elsewhere. As the State Board of Charities and Corrections observed in 1909, "One of the general and unfortunate facts about the almshouses is that they are situated so far from the community that they are seldom visited. Among the largest items of the traveling expense of this board is 'team hire to almshouse' from the nearest railroad station. This means that those in charge of county almshouses have been without the stimulus of the active community interest."[6] It also meant that the residents would have had few contacts with the outside world. Those who had family, even within the county, would have few visits because of the difficulties of transportation. By contrast, Richmond's facility was so accessible that administrators found it necessary to try to limit the constant flow of people. "Visitors to the inmates are only admitted on Wednesdays and Sundays from 9 A.M. to 12 M., and from 2 to 6 P.M."[7]

Moreover, Richmond's City Home sponsored social events, religious services, and entertainment that rural almshouses would not have had. Although antebellum administrators had seemed relatively uninterested in religious proselytizing, in the post-Reconstruction years the almshouse instituted more regular religious services. Initially, services were held regularly on Sunday afternoons.[8] By the 1880s, the superintendent was required to supply each room of the almshouse with a Bible.[9] At the end of the century, nonmandatory religious services were held several times a week, with ministers from the different denominations serving in rotation.[10]

There were occasional musical programs by local amateurs, as by "a company of Richmond ladies and gentlemen" who gave "a delightful entertainment" in the chapel. "The programme consisted of song, recitations, and sentimental music."[11] Superintendent George B. Davis also brought "Iardella's Band" and "Stein's Orchestra" to the almshouse for a Christmas entertainment.[12] More attentive to such concerns than his predecessors, superintendent Davis reported in 1903, "I conceived the idea of a 'Sunshine Room,' and prominent citizens contributed to a fund which enabled me to purchase a new upright piano, artificial flowers and a beautiful book-case. The 'Sunshine Room' is now a permanent fixture in the building for the good cheer of the aged and poor unfortunates who rarely ever go out of the building."[13] For those inmates more physically mobile, good behavior warranted a pass to go into the city for the day, offering further diversions.[14]

Despite these very conscious efforts to provide entertainment and cheer, the city almshouse could still be a bleak place. The superintendent himself, required to live on the premises with the inmates, no doubt spoke for many residents when he described the dark setting in 1907: "I am constantly in the midst of the sorrows and woes of the sick and dying, and I am endeavoring to assuage their grief and to relieve those who are suffering from stinging poverty in our City. Our building is surrounded by cemeteries, which add to the gloom. I find it requires all my nerve force to keep in good spirits and to comply with the duties and responsibilities of my office."[15] If a healthy, independent, adult male such as Davis found the atmosphere debilitating, one can only imagine how less well situated "paupers" felt.

One of the cemeteries to which Davis referred was the "potter's field," where many of the inmates of the almshouse would end up. Some of the residents themselves were employed making the dozens—sometimes hundreds—of coffins every year, although the psychological impact of such an assignment was never recognized by the authorities.[16] Death was indeed an everyday part of life at the almshouse, as tabulated in table 13. In the black almshouse, the mortality rates were so high that death was almost literally a daily event.

The higher rates of mortality, along with more crowded conditions and poorer physical facilities, made the almshouse for African Americans a much more dismal place. The city council seemed willfully neglectful of the black almshouse, at least through the end of the nineteenth century. Serious problems with the physical plant surfaced in the 1880s, when stagnant water in a ravine near the "colored almshouse" was reported to be causing a "nuisance."[17] After an investigation, the city engineer advised the council that it was not merely stagnant water but rather was refuse from sewers that was creating the nuisance, and that the best way to abate it would be to move the almshouse away from the place. He offered a resolution in the council to sell the property and build an entirely new facility elsewhere. The committee on the relief of the poor concurred: an immediate change of site was necessary.[18] The city council, however, took no action.

Three years later, the committee on the relief of the poor raised the issue again. The committee submitted plans to the city council for a new almshouse for blacks, to be built in the rear of the white almshouse, at an estimated cost of $46,787.30.[19] The subsequent debates in the council centered on race and money. Although Mr. Gunst supported building a new facility, he "could not favor the placing of the colored paupers in such close proximity with the whites." The council finally adopted a plan to build a new building accommodating three hundred people, to be erected in back of the current white almshouse. The suggested price tag was cut in half, with the city authorizing only $20,000 for the project.[20]

The project moved at a glacier's pace, as the city council continued to drag its heels. In 1906, for example, the council rejected all bids on the construction and then waited months before advertising again.[21] This conscious neglect of the black "paupers" would continue for another decade, while conditions in the building continued to deteriorate. The superintendent reported that the sewerage at the "colored" almshouse was so bad as to endanger the health of the inmates therein confined, as well as the health of the residents of the adjacent property. The city engineer was, again, ordered to look into the matter.[22] Pools of untreated sewage could not have helped the already high mortality rates in the black almshouse. Not until 1908 would the replacement building be completed.

While the move to a new building would have improved the health and the comfort of those therein, it would not have removed entirely the gloom of the place, since both buildings continued to be surrounded by cemeteries. Whether the pall of the cemeteries and the ubiquity of death contributed to alcohol abuse in the facility cannot be determined, but it was clear that alcohol was a problem that continued to plague the facility much as it had a century before. The overseers gave the superintendent the authority to remove residents who were drunk, or deny admission to anyone who appeared to be drunk. Henry Joyce fell victim to this policy and complained that he had been denied readmission to the almshouse because he arrived after "having taken several drinks."[23] William Atkisson, a former inmate, was also refused readmission because he had "several times been provided with clothes and would leave, return drunk, with clothes in bad condition."[24] William Catlett was dismissed in 1898 for being drunk and bringing more alcohol into the almshouse.[25] Administrators waged a continuous battle against alcohol abuse.

Just as in previous decades, alcohol abuse by the almshouse staff, too, continued to vex the city authorities. The committee on the poor heard charges at least twice that one of the resident physicians was intoxicated while on duty.[26] In another case, Thomas Culloden, an inmate of the white almshouse, charged that one of the employees, R. J. Brooke, had "cursed, abused, and hit him, without provocation." He also claimed that Brooke was often drunk at work and was "violent, overbearing, and harsh" with the inmates. The city council committee that heard the charges decided that Brooke had indeed been guilty of conduct unbecoming an officer of the institution; they then shipped Culloden, the complainant, off to Baltimore.[27] In 1889, the superintendent had to discharge the almshouse cook, "on account of drunkenness."[28] In 1897, the committee investigated charges that R. A. Hughes, the steward of the almshouse, had been "very drunk." Hughes kept his position but was required to send the committee a written apology in order to do so.[29]

Such cases as surfaced in the records were undoubtedly just a portion of the problem, as others were likely resolved on site without involving the city council. Tired of dealing with the problem, the committee considered cutting off the use of alcohol in the facility entirely. The staff physician, Dr. Trevilian, replied that it could be done, but that he did not recommend it, "as he believed in the use of whiskey for medicinal purposes."[30] The alcohol continued to flow.[31]

Familiarity between the staff and the residents continued to be a problem as well. "Fraternization" was facilitated because most of the staff were in fact required to live in the almshouse.[32] Administrators recognized the potential complications that too much fraternization might bring, and they officially warned the staff not to engage in "any kind of familiarity with the inmates." Even "conversation . . . other than such as may be indispensably necessary in the discharge of their duties" might lead to problems and was forbidden.[33] The daily routine, however, made it nearly impossible to abide by such strictures.

Although resident at the facility, staff members appeared to consider their "off hours" to be their own. This meant that no one considered himself to be "at work" at night. In response to the complaints and the problems accruing, in 1891, the city council ordered the superintendent to begin keeping staff on duty at all hours of the night.[34] Prior to this, it seems that the inmates were quite literally running the asylum—at night, anyway. The nighttime absence of staff, and the familiarity of staff and residents, both aided the inmates in their efforts to resist some of the more severe controls of the institution. During the nineteenth century in particular, the residents of the almshouse were in frequent struggle against the strictures on their behavior, and the records are filled with punishments meted out to unruly inmates. R. L. Bohannon and Clifton Edwards, both white men, were placed in a cell for three days for "refusing to obey the orders of the officers." Thomas O'Brien was similarly punished for being absent "without leave."[35] Others went "without leave" planning not to return. Table 14 demonstrates that small numbers of residents—mostly white, mostly male—"eloped" from the facility. With more economic opportunities on the outside, and with fewer encumbrances such as young children to care for, some white males found the almshouse unacceptably restrictive and "absconded in the night."

Thus the City Home, considered by state officials to be a model facility in many ways, offered Richmond's poor citizens plenty of opportunities to resist the institution's most rigid rules. The inmates effectively had a great deal of autonomy, as the almshouse relied heavily on their efforts to keep the facility running on a daily basis. This was not the full extent of it, however, as the poor of Richmond worked to shape the almshouse's services to suit their needs. For some women, the almshouse could be used as a temporary boarding home for their children. Late-nineteenth- and early-twentieth-century Richmond still offered working-class women very limited child-care facilities. Desperate women sometimes turned to the almshouse to board their children long term, with plans to retrieve them when conditions made it possible. One such mother, who had left her three boys at the almshouse, came to claim them when she learned the superintendent was about to move them to the Male Orphan Asylum. She "objected to such disposition being made of them" and removed them from the almshouse instead.[36] That the mother knew in advance of the plans to move her children further suggests that there remained continued communication between her and the facility. She probably learned of the plan during a visit with her sons. City officials had apparently accepted that she, and other women, would leave their children in the care of the almshouse and would be permitted to visit them.

Poor women looked at private orphanages in much the same way. W. W. Parker of the Male Orphan Asylum explained: "One of the troubles we encounter, as a Board of Managers, results from the conduct of some of their mothers, who voluntarily commit their boys to our care. We take a boy at five, six, or seven years of age, and when he gets to be ten or eleven, the mother applies to take him out, saying that she can now take care of him. It is often true that she wants the boy, by going into a factory, only half educated and trained, to 'take care' of her."[37] (Families continued to use this "boarding" strategy until at least the 1930s.)[38] While Parker had little sympathy for such women, it is clear that they intended to use the city's public and private welfare services how they saw fit. The city almshouse and the private orphanages became part of the family's strategy for survival in hard times.

Other poor Richmonders attempted, sometimes successfully, to turn their work within the almshouse into paid jobs. One Elisha Bethel, an inmate in the white almshouse, had been "appointed" by the superintendent to help issue rations to the outdoor poor. Recognizing the value of the work he did, Bethel requested that he be paid for his labor. The committee on poor relief initially tabled his request without comment, but later agreed and he was transferred to the payroll.[39] Several months later, James Allen, another inmate who worked as a cook in the black almshouse, also requested compensation. The committee tabled his request; it is unclear whether he ever received the paid appointment he wanted.[40] Thomas Addison, a sixty-five-year-old cooper, was more successful; he was made a cook in the white almshouse in 1897. George M. Bush, a thirty-four-year-old barber, and Pat Costello, a thirty-four-year-old cigar maker, were both appointed as paid "nurses" in the white almshouse.[41] Numerous other inmates turned their admissions into paid positions, demonstrating another way in which the poor put the almshouse to their own uses.

The Dread of the Poorhouse

All contemporary commentators seemed to agree that the poor feared and dreaded the poorhouse. Estelle Stewart believed that Americans were brought up with "a reverence for God, the hope of heaven, and the fear of the poorhouse."[42] Even more certainly, whites were convinced that blacks feared the poorhouse. According to the local newspaper, "In fact, anything which smacks of charity—the ambulance, physicians of the poor, free dispensaries, or what not—galls them to the quick and they avoid such blessings as if they carried pestilence. When a darky goes to the 'po'-house' you can set him down as lost to hope and socially dead."[43]

The convictions of contemporaries aside, the question of whether the poor actually "dreaded" the poorhouse remains mostly untested by historians. Considerable evidence suggests that in fact the poor held no great horror of the institution and that authorities were compelled to make almshouses as undesirable as possible to deflect the numerous willing entrants. Banning children from almshouses, a national trend in postbellum America, was designed partly as a deterrent to their parents. The threat of separation from their children would prevent some parents from seeking such aid.[44] Moreover, married elderly couples would have been discouraged from applying for entry to the almshouse because they would be separated from one another. The wards were rigidly segregated by race and by sex, with no accommodations provided for "an old couple who desired to spend their remaining days together."[45] Although progressive reformers elsewhere provided accommodations for couples, especially when laying out new almshouse facilities, Richmond did not.[46]

In other words, many of the poor and working class had very practical reasons for wishing to avoid the almshouse, reasons that did not necessarily stem from any "stigma" associated with public relief. At the same time, many poor and working-class people did not live in fear and dread of the almshouse, but rather embraced its services without hesitation. The evidence for this contention comes more from their recorded actions than from their recorded words. First, entries in the admissions registers record the speed with which newcomers sought out and entered the almshouse. In some cases, applicants appeared at the almshouse door within a few hours of arriving in the city. This suggests that mobile laborers and other such transients looked at almshouses as places where newcomers could get shelter until they found work and a place to live. These institutions may very well have been seen as an informal network of shelters for transients. People on the move, looking for work, learned that they could gain temporary shelter in the local almshouse.

Others who went directly to the almshouse upon arrival had in fact come to Richmond for that express purpose, especially unmarried mothers who came to bear their children in privacy (see the discussion later in this chapter). It is not clear just how people learned of the almshouse and its services. But it does appear that at least some of the admissions were people who had come to Richmond expressly for the purpose of entering the almshouse. They reported that they had been in the city "a few hours," "one hour," "today." They arrived in town, got directions or transportation to the almshouse, and immediately made their way there. Rather than being a place to avoid, the almshouse was a magnet for some.

Second, recidivism rates suggest that for many people who already knew the institution, the almshouse remained a desirable option. If the poorhouse was actually so dreadful, one would imagine that reentry would be even more avoided. Yet many people entered the almshouse again and again, as shown in table 15. Some recidivists came to see the almshouse as a place of refuge because of their early childhood experiences. William Foster, abandoned by his mother at the age of nine, entered the almshouse in 1882 as an orphan. Discharged eight years later, Foster returned immediately to the almshouse. During the course of the next decade, he turned to the almshouse frequently in times of crisis.[47]

Even runaways from the facility cannot be seen as unqualified evidence of a dread of the poorhouse, for too many of the runaways returned later on their own accord. Some returned even after having run away more than once: James Atkinson, a white male, ran away two out of the fifteen times he entered the almshouse. Others returned after having been expelled from the institution, sometimes more than once. James Roach, for example, was a white male who was kicked out of the facility three times out of the twenty-five times he was admitted.[48]

The fact that the Richmond City Home contained a fully functioning public hospital also served to counteract the fear that many of the poor might hold. Poor residents could and did receive quality care from the resident medical staff, which included trained nurses by the twentieth century.[49] With very few options for medical care in the city, particularly in the nineteenth century, the poor and working class more likely looked at the City Home with a sense of relief rather than dread. The hospital function appeared to carry no stigma; the local press never denigrated the facilities or those who used them. For those who used its medical facilities, it appeared to be just a normal service. The press used matter-of-fact tones in such coverage: "Richard Scott (colored), employed at Pace & Sizer's tobacco-factory, got one of his arms caught in a revolving drum yesterday afternoon, and had it so badly injured that it had to be amputated, which was done after he was removed to the almshouse in the ambulance."[50] Receiving charity medical services was such a common experience for poor families, and one in which the services were usually high quality, that few would have perceived it to entail a stigma.

Finally, in Richmond at least, children were still permitted in the City Home until 1956 (see table 16).[51] This powerful barrier utilized by other communities did not exist for the poor and working class of Richmond. Entering the almshouse could offer some families the opportunity to remain intact under very adverse circumstances. Some of the poor may have preferred the almshouse to other forms of charity because they were often able to keep their children with them. Poor women often had to work the system carefully in order to obtain assistance while not losing control over their children. Mrs. Elizabeth Cramer of Schoolfield wrote the governor in 1931, trying to avoid the Family Service Society. "I have asked the Family Service Society so often to help me with a few groceries, and a little fuel, enough just so we can have one room and have a place of our own but they refuse me each time and try to have my boy taken from me and to have me put in an asylum for the insane. . . . Miss Stuart Blanton of the

Family Service had me commited [*sic*] to the asylum once when I asked her for aid and I am horribly afraid of them and this is why I want your assistance to prevent them from doing this again."[52]

Indeed, Richmond's city almshouse was a far more congenial place than most such facilities. As a large urban institution, Richmond's City Home avoided many of the problems that plagued other almshouses. Rural almshouses, usually operated as poor farms, were especially notorious. The farmers who ran the poor farms were often themselves barely literate. In a study of American almshouses in 1925, an investigator noted, "one of the chief difficulties encountered in making this study has been the almost universal illiteracy of almshouse superintendents."[53] Rural almshouses seldom had the luxury of being able to segregate the ill from the healthy, the sane from the insane, or the criminal from the innocent. Conditions in some rural almshouses could indeed be inhumane.[54]

Such descriptions did not reflect life in the Richmond City Home, and it does not appear that local residents in general lived in fear of ending up there. For some groups, however, the prospect of the poorhouse held more stigma than it did for others. For blacks in Richmond, the almshouse represented visible poverty that reflected poorly on the whole race. Large numbers of African Americans admitted to the almshouse would draw attention to the inability of the black community to care for itself, something about which local black leaders had expressed concern.[55] The black middle class in particular worried that poverty, criminality, and immorality among the black working class worked to tarnish the respectability of all African Americans in the eyes of whites.[56] While the black poor may not have lived in constant dread of the poorhouse, the black community as a whole may have, because of what messages it could signal to white racists.

Similarly, men may have dreaded the almshouse more than women, despite their larger numbers in the facility. Late-nineteenth- and early-twentieth-century Americans held a heavily gendered view of charity, which stemmed from the contemporary understanding of gender roles. Part of the definition of "masculinity" in the period was economic: men were breadwinners. Women and children were lumped together with others as "dependents," while adult males were expected to be independent.[57] Contemporaries frequently suggested that poor relief "unmanned" its recipients. One Georgian argued that "true men" should never be forced into the poorhouse. Some qualified veterans, for example, refused to accept pensions, for they were connected to charity and therefore dependency. As historian R. B. Rosenburg observed, such ex-Confederates perceived this as an assault on their manhood.[58] Dependency would be quite demoralizing to most formerly independent men, and the almshouse would thereby constitute a considerable loss of status.

The entire process of applying for poor relief, whether from public or private sources, would have been made even more humiliating for men because women were nearly always the caseworkers. By the twentieth century, women had come to dominate the newly emerging field of social work, and they became the gate-keepers for many sources of poor relief.[59] Inverting the traditional gendered power relationships, poor men had to apply to women for assistance. While poor women sometimes registered their frustrations with female caseworkers, men frequently expressed their resentment in having to deal with "clerks" who seemed not to afford them the respect they deserved.[60] Erskine Caldwell's fictional relief family, the Douthits, lived these tensions: the husband, Spence, tried to find ways to extract assistance from the women caseworkers without appearing to lose his place as the head of the troubled family; the wife, Maud, worried that the young caseworkers were more attractive than she.[61]

For women, however, dependency was part of the normal course of their lives, and the almshouse by itself did not signal any loss of power or status. Women commonly moved from dependency upon their fathers to dependency upon their husbands. Very few women of these generations would ever be fully economically independent, nor was this a goal toward which women commonly strove. Dependency, then, posed less shame for women than for men, since the former expected to be at least partly dependent on others during much of their lives.

Instead, for women, daily life in the City Home resembled very much their normal routine. Female inmates did much typical domestic work—cleaning, cooking, sewing, and laundry. They also spent much time caring for the children in the almshouse, both their own and the children of others. Table 16 shows the continuing presence of children in the City Home, some of whom were born there, some of whom were abandoned there, and many of whom were there with their mothers. Still more children were sent to the almshouse as wards of the court: since the state provided no facilities for "mentally deficient" children under age ten, those children were cared for in the City Home. Judges of police court sometimes committed young "delinquents" to the City Home rather than sending them to jails. The City Home maintained an informal school for these children, using the inmates themselves for their care and instruction. It was effectively a public charity school, "entirely independent of the city school system," but "the limited physical facilities and limited teaching staff do not provide an educational program in any way approaching the city school standards."[62]

The presence of these children meant that the City Home was not only a place of death and disease, but also a place where children were at play on the grounds. Children's laughter was heard in the halls, helping to offset the institutional feel of the facility. For women who entered the almshouse with their children, whose daily routine revolved around domestic chores and child care, the City Home was more homelike than it was for men. I do not want to overstate the case; I am not suggesting that these were happy, wholesome family units. Many women were there fully intending to give birth and then abandon their babies. Others were there because of abortions, domestic violence, alcoholism, and other unhappy domestic situations. But the domestic routine of the place would have been familiar, and the presence of children served to make the almshouse even more domestic.

Additionally, poor women frequently used the almshouse as a maternity home, providing yet another reason for them to look more favorably on the institution than some others might. Although city leaders never envisioned it as a public maternity home, the city almshouse became one nevertheless. As the charity hospital of Richmond, the city almshouse had little choice but to serve numerous maternity cases.[63] It is not possible to calculate the exact number of births that took place at the almshouse, for there are occasional lapses in the records. It is, however, possible to see a clear outline of the trends of almshouse births. As table 17 shows, from 1874 to 1914, 1,519 births were recorded in the Richmond almshouse, for an average of 38 per year over the forty-year period. Of those, 329 were white, 1,106 were black, and 84 had no race recorded. More babies were born in the city almshouse than in any other single facility in the city, including the private maternity homes.[64] Clearly the almshouse was an important part of the maternity medical care of the city during the period, and for black women, the almshouse may have been the central maternity facility for an entire generation.

The women who gave birth in the Richmond almshouse came from a wide range of experiences. The compiled demographic information on them allows us to draw a general profile of these women. And since the admissions registers were segregated by race, race becomes a focus of the analysis (see table 18). From 1885 to 1907, 224 black women and 80 white women were recorded as entering the almshouse for maternity.[65] The black women were, on average, twenty-two years old; the white women averaged twenty-four years of age. Women of both races were most often from Virginia, were Protestants, were literate, and were unmarried. But beyond those broad generalizations, there are some distinctions worth noting.

Perhaps most notably, African American women giving birth at the city almshouse were more often local residents, and more often from Virginia, than were white women. Only 9 percent of the black mothers came from outside of Virginia, while 20 percent of white women did. This suggests that whites more often went to distant cities to bear their illegitimate children in secrecy. Black mothers were from the local community and would return to the area, taking their newborns with them. (Contemporaries recognized that women frequently went to distant cities to hide illegitimacy, although they did not appear to see a racial distinction in this pattern.)[66]

White women, by contrast, seemed to use the almshouse as a means to hide their pregnancies. In volume D of the almshouse registers, of the forty white women who acknowledged being unmarried, twenty-four had arrived in Richmond since becoming pregnant. Several listed that they had been in the city only a few days. And five of those twenty-four arrived in the city on the same day they delivered their babies.

Perhaps surprisingly, there was only one immigrant in the entire group of women listed for pregnancy. Of the 776 white women and their children entered in the almshouse admissions registers between 1887 and 1907, only 30 were foreign-born, and only 1 of those was admitted for pregnancy. It would seem that immigrant women found other community resources to deal with unwanted pregnancies. Only 2.6 percent of the 306 maternity cases were Catholic, which is consistent with the Catholic population at large. (The 1890 census listed Virginia's Catholic population as 2.2 percent of the whole.) Despite a substantial Jewish minority in the city, there were no Jews listed in the entire group of maternity cases.

The real surprise in the religion category was the large number of black women reporting that they had no religious affiliation at all. Forty-six of the 224 African American women, compared to only 1 white woman, admitted having no religious affiliation. Although many meanings could be attached to this statistic, one way of reading this is to see economic vulnerability being ameliorated by church membership. Churches tried to take care of their own, both by direct relief and by self-help organizations such as mutual assurance associations. In the economically precarious world of Richmond's blacks, membership in a church could be an important resource during hard times. Those without such resources might need to rely upon the city almshouse for maternity care.

Another significant difference between white and black women in the almshouse was marital status. Eighty-six percent of the black mothers-to-be were unmarried, compared to 48 percent of the whites. Of course, one should be skeptical of a self-reported marital status. Although the almshouse did not have a policy of turning away the unmarried, the social stigma attached was still such that many of these white women may have claimed to be married or widowed upon entry. But even if we take the figures at face value, they indicate that three-fourths of the almshouse mothers-to-be had no male breadwinner. So this then is the profile of mothers who chose to deliver their babies in the almshouse: unmarried women in their early twenties, who worked in domestic occupations of various sorts, and who were generally literate, native-born, and Protestant. Now we should turn to the question of why they chose the almshouse rather than another facility to deliver their babies. A privately run maternity home (the Spring Street Home) had opened in Richmond in 1872, and several others would follow. By 1900, there were usually three or four maternity homes operating in the city.[67] Yet more women delivered babies at the city almshouse than at the private maternity homes, despite the prevailing belief that the poor abhorred public charity and preferred private benevolence to the "pauperizing" influence of the public dole. So how can we explain this?

One explanation is cost: extremely poor women could not afford the entry fee for some of these private homes. In 1910, for example, the Spring Street Home charged thirty-five dollars for admission.[68] As a result, the clientele for these homes tended to be the more-secure members of the working class, and some members of the middle class.[69] Segregation policies help to account for some of the women giving birth in the almshouse: before 1910 none of the private maternity homes in the city accepted black women. In 1910, a separate home for black women opened on Second Street. But until that date, the almshouse was the only maternity facility in the city that accepted black women.

Sectarianism might be another part of the explanation. The earliest, and longest lived, institution in the city was a Catholic-run Magdalen Home. Since the Catholic population in the city remained small, many women may have felt uncomfortable with that option and preferred the public institution instead. (It is also possible that the reputation of the Magdalen Home, that is, a facility devoted to "reclaiming" prostitutes, made it unappealing to women whose pregnancies were not the result of prostitution.)

Yet another possible explanation for the apparent preference of the almshouse over private maternity homes is the poor reputation of some of the private maternity homes in the city. A state investigation into maternity homes conducted around 1910 found that some private maternity homes were "guilty of the most flagrant abuses." "Disgustingly unsanitary," these for-profit homes charged expectant mothers an entry fee; after delivery, they then charged adoptive parents another fee. The state investigation revealed neglected babies, alcoholic proprietors, and drug-addicted patrons. Significantly, the report also noted that "rumors" of high infant mortality had swirled around some of the homes.[70] Such rumors may have caused some mothers to avoid these homes when they could.

Finally, some women may have chosen the almshouse to avoid unappealing policies inside the maternity homes. The private maternity homes were the products of the nineteenth-century moral reform movement, in which conversion and Christian redemption were a major portion of the agenda. Evangelical reform-minded women saw maternity homes as the means to "redeem" and "reclaim" unmarried mothers; they established homes that were places of both rehabilitation and conversion. As Regina Kunzel has demonstrated, the unmarried mothers who entered those maternity homes often resisted the discipline and social control permeating those institutions.[71] Women who were resistant to that kind of forced redemption, or obligatory salvation, may have chosen the less intrusive City Home instead. Run by male bureaucrats rather than female benevolents, the City Home was less interested in working for the forced salvation of its inmates. Although the Richmond almshouse had a decidedly Protestant orientation, and the inmates were regularly encouraged to attend chapel services, women in the almshouse were not subjected to the same kind of maternalistic salvation that permeated the evangelical maternity homes. The Richmond almshouse, under the direction of male administrators of the charity-organization school of thought, attempted to impose the middle-class work ethic on the inmates, but not the "pious example" of "female Christianity."[72]

Similarly, the policies of the evangelical maternity homes regarding adoption may have been a deterrent to some women. Maternity homes such as the Florence Crittenton Homes or those run by the Salvation Army believed that mothers and babies needed to stay together, "one of the most sacred of maternity home policies." They firmly discouraged mothers, even unmarried mothers, from giving their babies up for adoption.[73] Mothers who could not be persuaded to keep their children permanently were encouraged to stay at least a year or eighteen months to nurse them, a sacrifice that Kate Waller Barrett (national president of the Crittenton Homes) considered small, but one that unmarried, working mothers may have considered monumental.[74] Social worker Arthur James observed that it was not the "refuge homes" that separated babies from mothers: "More often it was the mother who insisted upon it, moved by a desperate anxiety to save her reputation."[75]

Mothers-to-be who had already decided to give their babies up for adoption may have chosen to enter the public almshouse, which would facilitate, rather than obstruct, that goal. As shown in table 19, the city almshouse regularly placed children into adoptive homes and arranged for the care of many other children in orphan asylums. Clearly a large minority of almshouse mothers desired to give birth and then give up their babies. Joan Brumberg's study of a maternity home in New York concluded that the young age of the mothers-to-be helps to "explain why they constituted a relatively desperate and docile population, willing to tolerate the exigencies of moral rehabilitation in exchange for their physical care."[76] The relatively older age of the women in the Richmond almshouse may have helped make them more resistant to the controlling maternity homes. They chose the almshouse instead.

After delivery, a large number of almshouse mothers chose to leave their babies at the almshouse. The almshouse did not keep records that would allow us to count precisely the number of babies left behind after their mothers were discharged. However, we can get close to that number by comparing the numbers of births in a given year with the numbers of adoptions the almshouse arranged. Between 1876 and 1895, there were 422 births in the almshouse; during the same period, the almshouse placed 145 babies in private homes or orphanages. That suggests that approximately one-third of the mothers who gave birth in the city facility left without their babies.

A sizable minority of these abandoning mothers were married, or claimed to be so. Since the shame of illegitimacy cannot explain their decision, we can speculate that these were families living on the brink of poverty who divested themselves of a new baby in order to survive.[77] Unmarried women faced a different set of circumstances, but circumstances that led to a similar solution. Joan Brumberg has suggested that illegitimacy became more of a crisis in the late nineteenth century than it had seemed to previous generations, as the Victorian middle class increasingly condemned any kind of premarital sexuality.[78] As a result of this proscription, it was extremely difficult for unmarried mothers to work and keep their children. Those women, black or white, who worked as servants were unlikely to find domestic employment after the birth of their babies. Few employers were willing to allow a servant woman to board her child in their homes. And the taint of illegitimacy prevented some employers from hiring these unmarried mothers. Historian Priscilla Clement notes, "no wonder so many women abandoned their babies in the streets or at the almshouse."[79]

Black mothers, however, were less willing to leave their newborns at the Richmond almshouse than their white counterparts. Much has been said and written about the tolerance of the black community for unmarried mothers and their offspring, both by historians and by contemporary observers. Black Richmonders subjected unmarried mothers to less censure than did their white counterparts.[80] Contemporary racial views about the "mother-love" of black women even affected social workers, who less often pressured black women to give up their babies for adoption.[81] And, as shown in table 19, black mothers in the Richmond almshouse gave up their babies at half the rate of white mothers.

It is also true that the absence of adoption agencies meant that formal adoption was not as easily managed in the black community. With fewer orphanages open to blacks, African American women often built alternative structures to the formal adoption that whites preferred. Black families arranged informal adoptions to care for needy children: one study of Richmond in the late 1920s found that approximately 10 percent of black families in the city were providing care for one or more children for whom they were not legally responsible.[82]

For all the above reasons, then, the Richmond almshouse provided essential services upon which the poor and working class depended. While the middle classes attempted to attach great stigma upon public charities, those who used the services themselves viewed them as important pieces of their families' survival strategies. Women in particular relied on public welfare for medical care and would not have necessarily felt "demoralized" by receiving those services.

The York Family

Most people who received aid from Richmond, or any other city, remained nearly anonymous. The bare details of their lives were recorded when they entered the almshouse; after a short stay, most disappeared back into historical obscurity, leaving behind little for us to analyze. One family, however, surfaced again and again. John York, his wife, Mary Vest, and their two sons appeared repeatedly in the almshouse records; they also showed up in several other public documents. There is sufficient material to sketch together an outline of this family's life during several decades, although it is not a deeply detailed one. By doing so, I do not mean to suggest that this family was the "typical" or "representative" almshouse family; the fact that they appeared so frequently makes them by definition unusual. Instead their story affords us the opportunity to examine the many points of contact that a poor family might have with the welfare system, and to speculate about the world seen through their eyes.

John York was born in Richmond in 1860, to parents who had emigrated from Ireland. His father, Thomas, had died in 1878; his mother's fate is unknown. John's story of poverty and poor relief begins, therefore, as did many others—a family of recent arrivals, who had little in the way of extended family or other kinship networks upon which to rely, and who lose the main breadwinner prematurely. John York's first confirmed contact with the public-welfare system in Richmond occurred in 1888, when he was admitted to the almshouse in May, at the age of twenty-eight.[83] This was to be the first of twenty-nine confirmed admissions to the Richmond city almshouse over a twenty-one-year period (see table 20).[84]

During those twenty-one years, which should have been his prime working years, York spent more time in the City Home than outside it. Gaps in the extant records make it impossible to calculate exactly the dates he went in and out for the entire twenty-one-year period. The records do make it clear that for the ten years from May 1888 to May 1898, York remained in the almshouse all but fifty-three days. For much of these years, York was never out of the institution for more than a few days or occasionally a few weeks before he returned to be readmitted.

The admissions registers offer very little in the way of detail, even though York must have qualified as one of the most egregious recidivists in the institution's history. Nevertheless, the registers treated each of his admissions matter-of-factly, with no editorial comment along the way. In all this time, York was admitted for illness only twice. (Once he was treated for malaria, and once for gastritis.) The remaining entries simply listed him as indigent. The registers noted that he ran away from the City Home once, in 1905, and suggested that he did so a second time, in 1908, when the clerk noted that his discharge date was "unknown." Not once does it appear that he was refused entry, even though he would have been very well known to those in charge of the institution.

A few other details about York can be ascertained from the admissions data. Most of the entries listed him as a "laborer" or having no occupation, although occasionally he identified himself as a "teamster."[85] In 1900, the register noted that he had been appointed "driver," which a later newspaper article clarified by explaining that York had once worked as the driver for the "dead wagon."[86] York alternately reported that he could read and that he had had no education. Both facts could have been true, depending upon how the question was asked and how the literacy had been obtained. In the earliest entries, York identified himself either as having no religious affiliation or as being a Catholic. Beginning in 1897, he listed himself as Protestant. Whether this reflected a religious conversion or a fear of identification as a Catholic cannot be determined, but it is certainly possible that York stopped identifying himself as Catholic in an attempt to keep the city from forcing him onto the Catholic charities. The overseers of the poor would certainly have done so willingly if possible. The various inconsistencies in the admissions records suggest, at a minimum, that York worked to represent himself differently at different times, as part of the "theater of charity" that was nineteenth-century poor relief.

Although York seemed to have little difficulty gaining admission to the almshouse time and again, eventually the local officials began to balk. Authorities complained that, despite being in excellent physical health and able to work with horses as a teamster or a driver, York instead would go from almshouse to almshouse, alternating between Richmond, Henrico County, and Chesterfield County. It was while in the Henrico County almshouse that he met Mary Vest, sometime in 1909.[87]

Mary Vest's family was originally from Henrico County, but her parents had moved to Illinois for a short while, where Mary was born around 1879. When her mother died, Mary's remaining family returned to Virginia. By 1908, Mary, her brother, her father, and her two illegitimate sons were discovered living in a one-room hut, "their manner of living more like animals than human beings." The authorities believed that Mary's two children might have been fathered by her own father, although the public record does not explain what evidence produced this conclusion. They were all sent to the Henrico County almshouse, where she met John York.[88]

The couple gained local notoriety when it was announced in the paper that they had applied for a marriage license, had asked the superintendent to act as "best man," and planned not only to marry but also to remain in the almshouse afterward.[89] The flustered superintendent, after hurriedly consulting with county officials, told the couple that they were free to marry at the almshouse, but they would have to leave the facility if they did. The story initially appeared as an amusing local interest piece, told in lighthearted fashion as a story of love at first sight, and in a patronizing tone about the irresponsibility of the poor. The initial article did not detail some of the seamier details of the family's situation, such as the fact that Mary had two children already or that the couple were both well known to the local welfare authorities.

The tone of condescending humor turned to outrage when the family returned to the city several months later. In June 1910, the Yorks suddenly reappeared and applied to the Associated Charities for bed and board. The AC attempted to find John work, and first placed him at the Richmond Cedar Works. York left there before noon on his first day of work, claiming he had been injured. The AC then placed him at another job that same afternoon, which he also left. The newspaper found nothing funny about a man who quit two jobs in one day while asking for charity for his family. The Associated Charities found no humor in the situation either, especially when it was discovered that another local charity had helped the family without the knowledge of the AC.[90]

A few weeks later, the *Times-Dispatch* picked up their story again. The Associated Charities had taken the York children while John and Mary looked for work. Both adults found jobs, left them abruptly, and continued to ask for assistance. James Buchanan, director of the Associated Charities, turned the children over to the Henrico County poorhouse.[91] Two weeks later, the Associated Charities was again caring for all four members of the family. Mary was described as "a little less intelligent" than John, but "shows a better disposition, and she has been quite industrious in cleaning rooms in the Associated Charities building." John, however, "came into the world with a disinclination and a dislike for work and he has never recovered."[92]

Ominously, this newspaper article raised for the first time the issue of mental ability. With no indication of who made a diagnosis, Mary York was described as "an idiot," her mother and grandfather were termed "weakminded," and her older son was considered "in the last stages of idiocy," and "hardly knows how to close his mouth." Their case, according to the paper, "revives the discussion of the old question of whether the State should make it illegal for feeble-minded persons to marry."[93]

This rather intensive newspaper coverage was likely responsible for bringing the Yorks to the attention of the State Board of Charities and Corrections, which featured the York family in its official annual report for 1911.[94] The article used the Yorks as the symbolic problem family, one that used and abused the welfare system so wantonly as to offend the whole community. Stressing feeblemindedness, in language that previewed the arguments made notorious later in the Carrie Buck case, the board's report insinuated that the only "cure" for such people was a eugenic one.[95]

A photograph of the Yorks, which accompanied the article, quite literally made them a "poster family" for feeblemindedness. While the images of the children might elicit some sympathy from a viewer, with their clear-eyed innocent gazes, the depiction of the parents seemed calculated to produce antipathy. John York looked dull and lifeless, while Mary appeared more brazen. Although we know less about her, the photograph certainly made her appear as the center of the family, as perhaps the driving force behind it all. The Board of Charities believed them all to be feebleminded without question. And in fact, just a few years thereafter, the state successfully committed John York to the Colony for the Feeble-Minded at Lynchburg. He died there in 1931, at the age of seventy, having spent the last fourteen years of his life in confinement.[96] The remaining members of the family appear to have been firmly banned from the City Home—neither Mary nor her two sons were ever admitted again.[97]

From the perspective of the Yorks, the beginning of their downward spiral may have been the local newspaper coverage. Had they not come under such intense public scrutiny, the Yorks might have managed to stay in the almshouse as they wished, keeping together their newly formed family. Instead, their fifteen minutes of fame resulted first in their being removed from the almshouse, next in having their children taken from their custody, and finally in having John institutionalized, permanently severing this family unit.

Although the cynic might wonder how much of a "family" this could be under these circumstances, a more sympathetic analysis of the evidence might question whether Mary Vest York had lost a protective figure when John was committed to the Colony. If the allegations about incest were true, Vest may very well have been a victim, looking for a defender, especially since she had originally been sent to the Henrico County almshouse in the company of her father and her brother. John York would seem a poor choice for a husband if a woman was looking for a traditional "provider," but that may not have been foremost in Mary Vest's mind at the time she chose to marry him. With John gone, and the

The York family, *Virginia Annual Reports*, 1911. This photograph, which made the York family a "poster family" for feeble-mindedness, was especially unsympathetic to Mary Vest York.

rest of the family proscribed from entering the almshouse, Mary Vest's options had narrowed considerably. Even a weak family unit seemed preferable to that with which Mary ended up.

To the local officials in charge of the Associated Charities and the City Home, the York family was a hopeless cause. Unable to break the cycle of dependency and help this family to become self-sustaining, the welfare community of Richmond effectively conceded defeat and turned to the state government for some assistance. In order to pass off the Yorks to the care of the state, one or more members of the family had to be diagnosed as feebleminded. Indeed, it was remarkable how quickly this determination was made once the family surfaced as a problem family. In their many previous years of contact with the city's relief officials, no mention of feeblemindedness or any other incapacity had ever been made.

While the local welfare agencies blamed the Yorks for their own problems, tracing their encounters with these various welfare agencies highlights the gaps and the shortcomings present in the system as it existed during their time of need. John York's long-term relationship with the city almshouse points to the absence of job training and unemployment programs in the early twentieth century. The available records give no indication of the kind of education or training John had had, but there was no indication of any evaluation of mental or physical incapacity until after the newspaper exposé. York's real problem appears to be employment. Since there was no job training offered at the almshouse (or any other city facility), each time he left he was still as underqualified for work as when he had arrived. Nor was there any job bureau offered by the city at the time, which might explain why York returned so quickly after each release. With no follow-up assistance, almshouse residents were on their own after discharge.

In a sense, able-bodied men used the almshouse as a substitute for the unemployment insurance schemes that were still in the future. Unable to pay rent during seasonal or other temporary unemployment, those out of work used the almshouse as a refuge. Women suffered from unemployment too, of course, but this was a highly gendered facet of poverty. Men's unskilled and semiskilled labor was more dependent upon weather and season patterns of production. Construction workers, dockworkers, and the like had far more erratic employment patterns than did factory "girls" or domestic workers.

Mary Vest York suffered from a gendered form of poverty as well. There is no indication in the records anywhere what kind of work she did, though she must have done something, for she had money to pay for the marriage license. Her "problem," by the standards of the day, was having no adequate provider for herself and her children. A father, a brother, and then a husband were all part of her life, yet none of these men was able to keep her and her boys from the poorhouse. Mothers' pensions, available in extremely limited numbers in Richmond, were reserved for the most "deserving" of white women. As an unmarried mother, around whom rumors of incest swirled, Mary would hardly have qualified for such support. (This was largely a moot point, as Mary's children were undoubtedly too old to qualify by the time the Virginia mothers' aid law was passed in 1918.)

The two boys, who remained unnamed in any record uncovered, appeared to be somewhere between six and twelve at the time the photo was taken (c.1910). They had never been admitted to the Richmond almshouse, where schooling was offered but was considered decidedly inferior to the local public schools. If there was any schooling offered at all in the Henrico County almshouse, it would have been of even lower quality than that in Richmond's City Home. Moving about as frequently as the family did, even if the boys were enrolled in public school, their education would have been intermittent, disrupted, and inadequate. The two Vest boys would thereby be positioned to follow their parents and grandparents into lives of unskilled labor and periodic poverty.

Worse still, the Vest boys were in danger of being diagnosed with generational feeblemindedness, as they lived in a Virginia that was increasingly committed to eugenic sterilization as part of its public-welfare policy.[98] They had the misfortune to be contemporaries of Carrie Buck, with the threat of institutionalization and sterilization hovering very close.[99] (John York, as a long-term resident of the Colony at Lynchburg in these very years, undoubtedly knew Carrie Buck personally.) By the mid-1920s, sterilization had in fact become the centerpiece of Virginia's public policy for mental defects.[100] Feeblemindedness, a new category of mental illness in the early twentieth century, was so loosely defined as to permit the state to use it as a tool for dealing with problems like the Yorks.

The York family's story remains incomplete, as the remaining members of the family disappear back into historical invisibility after their brief appearance in the records. But the purpose of this account was not to provide a full history of the York family. Rather, this sketch serves to highlight the shortcomings of the social-welfare system in place in Richmond by the early decades of the twentieth century. Despite the tremendous expenditures of the city and state governments, despite the presence of dozens of private charitable organizations and institutions, despite the emergence of professional social work and the appearance of trained caseworkers, this family still lived as mired in poverty in the 1910s as their parents had a generation earlier. By virtue of fate, the Yorks did not qualify for Virginia's biggest welfare program: no one in the family qualified for a Confederate pension. Without some fundamental change in the welfare system in Richmond, the future for the next generation of Yorks looked equally grim.

WHAT DAILY LIFE was like for the poor in Richmond in the late nineteenth and early twentieth centuries remains part mystery, part speculation. The admissions registers for the city almshouse help to peel back some of the layers obscuring our view of the past, but there still is much we cannot know with certainty until some new source of information becomes available. This much is clear: no simple story of "dread" or "social control" will suffice. Whatever interpretation of their lives we construct must allow for variety and contradictions, as different families evolved different strategies for wrestling with the poor-relief system to extract what they perceived to be their daily needs.

CHAPTER NINE

The End of the Poor Laws

The New Deal and Social Welfare

In October 1933, New Dealer Alan Johnstone attempted to rally support in Richmond for the federal government's new relief programs. "I am sure that we will realize that all of us who are engaged in the field of human welfare are writing history in America today. We may not be putting it down in books and printing it on pages," announced Johnstone, "but we are making records in the minds and hearts and consciences and in the lives of one out of every eight of our fellow citizens." When the depression was finally ended, the welfare administrator predicted, "the American people will know whose responsibility this was."[1]

When the depression was indeed finally ended, responsibility for the poor had shifted and Virginia's welfare system had been overhauled. The poor laws had survived the Civil War, Reconstruction, and the Progressive reform movement, "like flies embalmed in amber, a memorial to a vanished social-economic pattern,"[2] but had finally been dismantled by the New Deal. In their place stood a complicated welfare system that linked local, state, and federal governments in a joint effort to care for certain categories of dependents. Sizable gaps in the system remained, and the United States fell far short of the sort of cradle-to-grave coverage instituted in other Western industrial democracies. Nevertheless, writing from the perspective of 1940, pioneering social worker Edith Abbott could say with much truth that the past decade had witnessed "a social revolution" in public-welfare policy.[3] Nowhere did those changes seem more revolutionary than in the South.

Despite the fact that some important southern political leaders balked at the concept of a welfare state and did their utmost to minimize its impact, the South's system of social provision was fundamentally changed by the New Deal's welfare programs. The federal government poured money into the region, frequently with "strings" attached to the funds that helped to produce far-reaching change in the poor-relief system. Those strings compelled the creation of a modern public welfare bureaucracy in every locality, embedded standards of professional social work in every community, and raised the standards of relief and the expectations of an entire generation. In the South especially, the standards of relief were higher than the old poor-law system had offered, and were in fact high enough to put some upward pressure on wages in the region.[4]

In Virginia, the progressive social-work community cheered the New Deal and embraced the welfare state it envisioned. Several Virginians, such as Frank Bane, joined other young southern liberals and moved up to national positions in the new welfare bureaucracy as they worked to implement the goals of Roosevelt's program of social security.[5] At the same time, however, congressional representatives from the Byrd organization contested the New Deal at every turn and resisted the advent of the welfare state with all its considerable might. The Byrd machine—that "political museum piece"[6]—also dug in its heels in Virginia and worked to forestall the arrival of federal welfare programs in the state. Unable to prevent the creation of a federal welfare system, the Byrd organization did what it could to limit its implementation in Virginia. Thanks to the machinations of the Byrd organization, the Commonwealth would be the last state in the Union to enact the full range of laws necessary to participate in the federal welfare system. As historian Ronald Heinemann wryly noted, "Writing the history of Virginia in the 1930s requires a tolerance for ambiguity."[7]

The Great Depression in Virginia

The initial impact of the Great Depression on Virginia seemed minimal, with little evidence of panic. Some of this relative buoyancy may have been artificial, as newspaper editors and civic boosters kept good news on the front page while minimizing the size of negative local stories.[8] Politicians mustered up optimistic words about Virginia's "bright future," and unemployment and economic statistics were carefully placed in context so that the public would understand how relatively well the state was doing. By 1930, although unemployment in the state had risen to approximately fifty thousand, it stood at a rate lower than the national average; unemployment in Virginia cities was also lower than in comparably sized cities elsewhere. In 1931, industrial unemployment in the Commonwealth stood at 14 percent; but again, this stood in contrast to a national rate of 26 percent.[9]

Virginia's milder depression was the product of several factors. The state's economy was well diversified and not overly dependent on any one area of production. Fewer banks failed in the state, largely because fewer farms were held under mortgage than in other states (which is another way of saying that residents of the state had fewer opportunities to obtain loans and credit). A decade of conservative fiscal policies meant that the state government was not burdened with the level of debts that plagued other states. And the state had fewer investors deep into the speculative markets. All of these things worked to soften the impact of the economic catastrophe. But the other side of the story was the fact that Virginia was already marked by widespread poverty, with large numbers of people living in a permanent state of deprivation, one unaffected by economic fluctuations. The chronic rural poverty that had marked the lives of several generations of Virginians was not a product of the depression and was little changed by fluctuations in the business cycle.[10] Although rural areas suffered most, cities also had problems with chronic unemployment; in Richmond, the YWCA began expressing concern about "this very real social problem" in 1928.[11]

Richmond's own economy weathered the first months of the depression reasonably well. Its more diversified manufacturing sector held up solidly at first. State government, an important employer, remained strong with few layoffs. Tobacco manufacturing seemed almost depression-proof, as demand for cigarettes remained unabated by the upheaval in the economy. Even a year after the stock market crash, unemployment was not considered a significant problem in Richmond.[12] But sizable layoffs began early in 1931, hitting industrial workers in several areas. Flour mills and textile mills closed first; the construction trades were hit next, with business down to half its level of the year before.[13] Even tobacco workers suffered, from underemployment if not unemployment; one study found that the average tobacco worker had only ninety-one days of employment over the course of eleven months.[14]

The signs of economic breakdown were ubiquitous and unmistakable. Crime stories filled the daily papers, as desperate men broke into stores, robbed banks, and mugged citizens on the streets.[15] Local welfare agencies reported that beggars were "appearing on the streets in large numbers" in October 1931.[16] By the winter of 1932–33, Richmond's unemployed were estimated at approximately eleven thousand.[17] IVNA nurses, who served the needy in their homes, reported seeing increased numbers of cases of pellagra, due to malnutrition.[18]

The urban middle classes were soon feeling the impact as well. One memoirist wrote: "I recall the suffering of many old Richmond ladies when the brokerage house of F.E. Nolting & Co., located in the Mutual Building, was forced to close its doors. . . . A 'Nolting Bond' was considered by old Richmonders as equal in value to a United States bond."[19] Workers in the city's service economy suffered from the domino effect: middle-class families tightened their budgets by firing their domestics.[20]

The crisis continued to deepen, testing the abilities of the state's leadership to find good news for the front pages. In 1932, the state's average number of unemployed was 100,000, with a peak level of 145,000 reached in July. Industrial cities like Richmond, Norfolk, and Roanoke had the highest unemployment rates.

"Consumables" industries like processed food, tobacco, and clothing were less affected; industries that produced more durable goods like furniture, lumber, railroads, and automobiles were most affected.[21] As journalist W. J. Cash observed, "Richmond, Greensboro, Charlotte, Atlanta—all along the commercial nerve centers stringing southward along the Southern Railway, took on the air of those old dead towns of Belgium and the Hanseatic League. You could hear your heels ring as you walked in their streets, left to go dirty and unkempt."[22]

Conditions likewise seemed grave to those tens of thousands of Virginians without jobs. Susie Burch of Alexandria reported her family's "great distress. My husband having lost his position two years ago, we have been struggling along, on the little we had saved, now that is about gone, worst of all we have had to mortgage our little home, which we have toiled so hard to get."[23] Unemployed, with a wife and five children to feed, C. E. Miller of Buell begged for work or charity and found neither. "It seems like God and man has both forgotten me," wrote the desperate man. "I have a wife and five little children to support. . . . I have had to ask for charity and they tell me there is none, that the county does not provide anything for a man when they are down & out."[24] Refused admittance to the local almshouse, Michael O'Neil wrote Governor Peery for help. "So I am wating to here So I wish you please see that [I] get in poorhouse so I would be better satisfied."[25]

Designed to care for small numbers of dependents rather than massive unemployment, the depression stretched Virginia's existing poor-relief systems beyond their capacity. Even though the Progressive decades had wrought many changes and improvements in the state's welfare institutions, the system was not flexible enough to absorb so rapidly the vast increases in the number of needy families produced by this kind of crisis. Neither public welfare nor private charities had the means to increase their revenues that quickly. Private charities found their usual donors were often victims of the depression too.[26] Community Chest drives rarely met their goals; even those amounts pledged could often be hard to obtain. In 1930, Lynchburg's Chest failed to meet its goal in the annual fund drive by twenty-five thousand dollars. Making the situation worse, more than eighteen thousand dollars of those pledges was never paid. The following year, the Chest tried setting a lower goal (the lowest in the organization's ten-year history), but the campaign still came up short. By March 1930, the president of Lynchburg's Associated Charities, Mrs. Bessie Woolfolk, acknowledged that the AC could no longer meet the needs of the unemployed in the city. Its caseload had nearly tripled in one year, and it could stretch its resources no further.[27] Private charities themselves succumbed to the depression: between 1929 and 1932, one-third of the private agencies in the United States disappeared for lack of funds.[28]

Volunteers raising money for the Community Fund, ca. 1930. Volunteers such as these had tremendous difficulty collecting donations during the depression. Courtesy of the Valentine Richmond History Center.

The public sector could do little more. Even if they had the will, local governments had little "emergency" resources to enable them to act quickly. Lynchburg, for example, offered up a public-works project in November 1930, a street-widening program. But the city had only ten thousand dollars available, a sum that was quickly exhausted. [29] Understandably, local residents resisted tax hikes when conditions were so bad. Asking the governor for assistance, the city manager of Hopewell, Virginia, described the dire conditions in his town:

> During the coming year the City thru [sic] its relief organization will be expected to carry the total load of the relief to the unemployed as no other organizations are functioning, with the exception of the Salvation Army, to which the City contributes. . . . Therefore, unless outside relief is obtained, it is very probably [sic] that the City, in face of its present financial condition, due to non-payment of taxes, will have to cease relief work before the winter is over. . . . In the face of these conditions, it is imperative that the City of Hopewell receive outside aid in the caring for its unemployed, or the City will be forced to discontinue relief work before the end of winter. [30]

At the same time that tax revenues were in decline, the state's constitution limited the ability of the municipalities to raise money in other ways. During the 1920s, the state had "segregated" tax revenues, reserving taxes on real estate and personal property for local use, while assigning income taxes and a variety of user fees to the state government. While rural county governments seemed to raise adequate revenue under this system, city governments had considerable difficulty doing so. Nor could local governments borrow extensively to cover a crisis. The state constitution also limited the ability of municipal governments to incur bonded indebtedness, while county governments had no such restrictions.[31] Cities like Lynchburg and Hopewell had few options for raising emergency funds.

Faced with these conditions, local welfare officials in many Virginia counties began to reconsider the wisdom of consolidating almshouses. The movement to consolidate county almshouses into larger "district" homes, which had been building momentum during the 1920s, was derailed by the depression. With new demands for relief on the counties, few saw the desirability of closing their much-needed almshouses. Other counties that had already closed their facilities, such as Campbell County, began asking to reverse their earlier "consolidation" agreements.[32]

As in earlier economic crises, the poor and unemployed turned to any source of help available and seemed not to care whether it was public or private. Despair pushed aside concerns over which level of government was rightly responsible for poor relief, and Virginians asked for help from all governments. Poignant letters flooded government offices, begging for help. Typical was the letter Mrs. Ella Gallion of Salem wrote the governor: "I kindly request of you if possible to send me some money to get coal & other neaisities [sic] for the winter. . . . I don't see any way through the winter & couldn't think of any better place than yours to ask for an accommodation & any assistance you see best to give if any I will be more than thankful to you."[33] Mrs. Ina Duncan of Edinburg was more explicit: "I am very much in distress and trouble will you please be so kind as to help me raise $992.00 to take care of my land note I am supposed to pay off April 12th next month."[34] J. R. Forsyth of Staunton had a simpler request; he asked the governor for a cow, since the "place I live on has plenty of pasture for a cow, if I was able to get a cow [it] would be quite a help to my family."[35]

Confederate welfare recipients, the only group of citizens then receiving any kind of state-level direct relief, besieged the capital with requests for additional aid. Veterans like J. T. Walters of East Radford demanded an increase in the Confederate pension: "When you were campaigning through this section last fall," he prodded Governor Pollard, "you promised me that you would 'go the limit' in helping to increase the Confederate veteran's pensions. I am writing to remind you of this promise, and to request that you at this time do all you can to carry this promise into effect."[36] Sons of Confederate veterans also wrote for help, only to be advised, "[W]e have no law by which we can pay sons of Confederate veterans."[37]

Some needy correspondents tried to shame the state government into action by comparing Virginia's small Confederate pensions to those of the federal government. Comptroller E. R. Combs attempted to explain to one such complainant that, although the state could not pay as much as the federal government did, "Virginia is paying now about as much as other Southern States who have as large a roll as we have. Some of the southern States are paying more than Virginia but in most cases they have a very much smaller pension roll."[38] Confederate widows presented some of the most vexing petitions, as Comptroller Combs struggled unsuccessfully to explain why women received smaller pensions than men: "You are asking why Confederate soldiers receive $30.00 per month, while Confederate widows only receive $10.00. The amount of pension . . . is fixed by the pension law. The law provides $30.00 per month to soldiers and $10.00 per month to widows. This is the very reason we are only paying widows $10.00 per month."[39]

To put these pension figures into a context, a study of the standard of living in Virginia conducted in 1929 concluded that the rural poor expended an average of $892 per year per family, while the urban poor spent an average of $977 per year per family.[40] Those figures come to $74 and $81 per month respectively. At these rates, neither veterans nor widows could survive on Confederate pensions alone. The depression thereby highlighted one of the great flaws of the Confederate welfare system in Virginia: although means-tested, the pensions were not then scaled to meet the individual's needs. Each veteran or widow received a flat (small) grant, irrespective of how many people lived in the home and without regard to any other factors that influenced levels of need. Confederate welfare was public welfare exercised without modern standards of relief for public welfare.

In addition to asking for cash assistance, other Virginians barraged the state government with requests for work relief. The chairwoman of the Charlotte County Red Cross wrote Governor Pollard to "urge upon you, first and foremost, the need of employment or some form of relief for these people."[41] The local chairman of the Red Cross in Buchanan County reported, "We have hundreds of families who can not put their children in school for the want of clothing. Can not get work. Men begging for any thing to do at any price. We must have some relief in some way." He asked the governor for "some work on roads . . . if you could see the condition in this county I am sure you would come to our relief."[42]

The impoverished showed no lack of initiative or imagination in seeking to help themselves. B. M. Beckham of Ferrum tried to get assistance from the federal government first, as he explained in his letter to Governor Pollard: "I wrote to Mr. Hoover about the matter, and he referred me to you. Will you kindly advise me how to secure clothing?"[43] Melessa Hazelwood of Danville wrote the governor requesting a pardon for her son so that he could be released from the reformatory and work to support the family: "[I]f you see a possible [way?] to pardon him do for Mother & Father sake he promised never to do any bad thing any more he's joined the church."[44]

The state government, under the firm control of the Byrd organization, re-buffed these and all other requests, insisting that its fiscal orthodoxies remained the best solution to a temporary economic downturn. While several industrial states began to experiment with state-funded unemployment relief,[45] Virginia's leadership continued to adhere to the Byrd philosophy that keeping a balanced budget would make the state attractive to business. A vibrant business sector would cure whatever ailed the economy, in time. Expenditures on relief, espe-cially if they would require increased taxation, would be counterproductive. In-stead, Governor Pollard recommended cuts in the state budget to avert a deficit. He reduced his own salary by 10 percent and recommended the same for all state employees.[46]

Pollard's only initiative for relief came in 1930, when he obtained short-term loans for $2.4 million to match federal advances on highway funds, offered to the states to put unemployed men to work on road construction.[47] This measure provided work relief without requiring a state appropriation, although the loans did increase the state's indebtedness.[48] This action also set a precedent of sorts, that of using highway construction as work relief, a policy that would become the cornerstone of the relief program of the next administration. This one ex-ception highlighted the firmness of the state's commitment to its philosophy of political economy. Even the most devastating depression of the nation's history could not shake the resolve of the state's political leadership.

Despite intense criticism by Carter Glass, Virginia also applied for and re-ceived federal funds from the Reconstruction Finance Corporation. The RFC was largely intended to provide loans for businesses struggling to survive, but it also had a much smaller pool of money to aid states in providing relief. The program was fraught with problems, including a bureaucracy opposed to its involvement in direct relief, which slowed the distribution of those funds to a miserly trickle. By September 1932, Virginia had received grants (meaning loans) totaling $283,367 from the RFC.[49]

As conditions worsened, many Virginians began to question the state's fis-cal policies and inadequate response to the crisis. In November 1932, the Na-tional Unemployed Council set up shop in several Virginia cities, including Richmond, and demanded more government assistance for the unemployed. The Richmond local office, headed by Thomas H. Stone, wanted the city coun-cil to appropriate $750,000 for relief for the winter, a figure that would have constituted nearly twice the annual welfare budget in the mid-1920s (see table

10). A panicky Mayor J. Fulmer Bright cracked down on protesters conducting a hunger march on city hall. The police arrested local leaders of the protests, fearing the alleged communism of the left-leaning group. Historian Ronald Heinemann terms this one of few public demonstrations of dissatisfaction to appear in Virginia throughout the entire depression.[50]

Mayor Bright was not the only one worried about the restlessness of the unemployed, as they began "using the word 'revolution'. Very cloudy was their wishing," wrote journalist W. J. Cash, "and very unclear was every one of them as to precisely whom and what it was he meant to rebel against. Nevertheless, there the word was, marching about in the open."[51] C. P. Spaeth, a labor leader from Norfolk, reported "murmurs among groups in the streets, to the effect, if this situation continues to prevail, the outcome may result in a condition detrimental to peaceful operation, of Law and order."[52]

Local Relief in Richmond

In the absence of state-level assistance, the poor and unemployed in Richmond had no option but to turn to whatever local resources were available to them. Both public and private charities expanded their already existing programs and experimented with new ones. But all such efforts were limited by the financial resources of the city, which were substantially undermined by the effects of the depression. Even early in the crisis, local charitable groups were already strained beyond their capacity. During the winter of 1930, the Community Fund started a work relief program but ran out of funds by the summer of 1931.[53] In January 1930, the Sheltering Arms Hospital, the private charity where Ellen Glasgow had once worked as a volunteer, reported that it was entirely full and had a waiting list of seventy-five. Only emergency cases were being accepted.[54] In the fall of 1933, the Community Fund failed to reach its fundraising goal by more than fifty thousand dollars, which resulted in budget cuts to all member agencies.[55] Charitable organizations such as the IVNA had to cut back staff and slash wages, all the while trying to meet the greatly increased demand for their services.[56]

Donations to many private charities declined, some precipitously. In 1928, for example, the Ladies' Hebrew Benevolent Society had reported receipts of $7,466; in 1933, their income was down to $6,594, while they tried to care for 200 additional cases.[57] The Salvation Army reported that its street collections declined from $1,338 in 1928 to $359 in 1933, while the numbers of people the charity was assisting increased five-fold. Other private charities reported steady income, or even slight increases, while the demand for their services doubled or even tripled. The Children's Department of the Bureau of Catholic Charities took in $7,830 in 1928, while caring for 136 children. In 1933, when the bureau's receipts climbed to $9,846, the organization cared for 339 children. Similarly, in 1928, the Family Service Society had income of $103,307 and cared for 1,796 cases; in 1933, although the society's receipts rose to $176,855, its caseload had risen to 6,819. In an attempt to spread the relief out to as many needy as possible, the Family Service Society reduced its allowance for food to $1.10 per person per week.[58]

One new initiative in the private sector proved enormously popular, partly because it operated with very little funding. In 1933, the Richmond Council of Social Agencies established the Citizens' Service Exchange under the direction of A. H. "Dutch" Herrman. The unemployed could gain credits toward goods and services through work at the Exchange. It operated sewing rooms, a cobbler shop, and a barbershop, where participants could earn work credits or redeem them. Workers at the Exchange also gathered wood, did home repairs, and provided medical and dental services, in exchange for their own supplies. This new private agency remained in operation until 1945, when it became the Richmond branch of Goodwill Industries.[59]

Despite the popularity of this new venture, it was no panacea. Contemporaries could see clearly that the city's private charities were sinking under the weight of the depression and urged greater efforts by the city government.[60] Even those who had once attempted to push public institutions aside to make welfare the arena of the private sector now changed positions: the Community Fund "expressed the belief that the City of Richmond should be asked to contribute a larger amount than it is now contributing toward welfare work, especially toward providing funds to meet the unemployment emergency."[61] The City Council agreed to increase its role in poor relief but insisted on working through its own Social Service Bureau. The Social Service Bureau, established in 1922 as the casework agency of the city welfare department, was expanded in 1931 and given responsibility for unemployment relief. The Family Service Society (formerly the Associated Charities) turned over more than three hundred families, whose breadwinners were unemployed, to the city in July 1931.[62] The city's expenses necessarily skyrocketed: appropriations for relief went from $50,000 in 1931 to $235,000 in 1932. The caseload doubled, with each caseworker averaging 645 cases.[63] The city took on even more of the private sector's caseload in January 1933, when the city's Social Service Bureau agreed to take over the "surplus" caseload of the Family Service Society and the Bureau of Catholic Charities, both of which had been forced to suspend their intake of new clients.[64]

Thus even before the advent of the New Deal, the working relationships between the private and public charities in the city had shifted. The tensions that had been growing in the 1920s had made the municipal agencies less willing to cooperate with groups such as the Family Service Society. When the financial crisis undermined the strength of the private sector, the municipal welfare offices emerged as the central relief distributor in the city. The private charities were pushed into a more auxiliary position, performing investigations and referrals.

This reconfiguration of local relief programs forced private charities to re-evaluate their place in the larger scheme of welfare policy. Increasingly the private charities redirected their efforts toward what were often called "character building" programs, institutions designed to strengthen families, and "preventative" efforts, while leaving direct relief to the city. The Family Service Society, for example, began to argue that its purpose was "to work toward bringing about adjustments in individuals and families for restoration to the normal—the upbuilding of family life."[65] Unemployment relief did not fall within the realm of activities that family-welfare agencies began to see as their specialization. The temporarily unemployed, "so obviously competent and accustomed to managing his own affairs and supporting himself in a normal way," did not require the kind of assistance and counseling given by family-welfare groups. Welfare workers began to recognize that the unemployed were in fact a special category of "the poor" with special needs. The common practice of sending a social worker out shopping with her "clients" to teach them budgeting and money management simply was inappropriate for such formerly independent and self-sufficient families, who clearly were not in financial difficulty due to their inability to shop properly.[66]

Thus one of the early effects of the depression on social-welfare policy was to begin to push public and private agencies away from their previously intertwined relationships and into more distinctly different areas of activity. Another impact of the depression was to put pressure on the state and federal governments to take up responsibilities to the poor that were going unmet by local communities. A handful of state welfare officials agreed that the crisis required an expansion of government relief. While Hoover argued that private charities could and should carry the full burden of relief, Virginia's commissioner of public welfare, Frank Bane, disagreed. "Government has a responsibility in this matter. We cannot and should not expect these private organizations to handle alone a problem far beyond their capacity because of their limited resources. It is the duty of the government to work with them and to carry its portion of the increased load."[67]

Bane did not speak for the "organization," however. The state's political leadership remained opposed to any state-level expansion in poor relief, and in fact included Bane's department in the across-the-board appropriations cuts of 30 percent announced for the year 1933. This difference in philosophy may explain why Bane left the Department of Public Welfare shortly after speaking out in favor of government relief, to become executive director of the American Public Welfare Association in 1931.[68]

Instead, Virginia's state relief efforts would focus on Harry Byrd's highway proposal. In 1932, former governor Byrd had proposed a scheme that would increase the amount of relief money available to the county governments without having the state spend anything on direct relief. Byrd suggested that the state government take over the entire county road-building system, which would save the counties millions of dollars in expenses that could then be spent on relief. To borrow a quip that circulated in Mississippi, Virginians would be able to "ride to the poorhouse on the best roads in the country."[69] Rural legislators, who dominated the state assembly, passed the measure enthusiastically despite protests from urban representatives who pointed out that cities got nothing at all from this scheme.[70]

The highway work-relief plan also offered nothing for needy women, who would have been considered ineligible for such jobs by contemporary gender norms. The state's only concession to poor women during the depression took the form of a small subsidy to the already-existing mothers' aid program. Beginning in 1932, local governments could be reimbursed by the state for one-third of their mothers' aid expenditures. (In 1934, the amount was raised to one-half.) The numbers funded by this program remained pitifully small: for the year 1933, a total of 98 families were aided, with the state contributing just over $12,000. In a city the size of Richmond—with more than 180,000 residents—only 13 families received mothers' aid. As of April 1934, there were still only 122 families in the entire state on the rolls of mothers' aid.[71]

State-level relief policies in Virginia therefore consisted of the highway-building program and the minuscule mothers' aid plan, making it one of the few states in the nation that failed to enact some form of state unemployment-relief program.[72] Pollard's administration instead concentrated on balanced budgets. The 1933 across-the-board budget cut produced "loud complaints" from state administrators like the superintendent of public education.[73] The public, however, registered more concern about the appropriations reductions for the Confederate pension program. (Virginia was still paying pensions to some thirteen hundred Confederate veterans and to forty-one hundred widows.)[74] Veteran J. O. Hall begged, "Please do not reduce my little pension. I am an old man not able to work and look to that source for a living."[75] Mrs. Q. T. Davies wrote from Norfolk, "I make bold to beg of you to restore the cut [made to] the Confederate widows married after 1880. We have suffered much privation due to this cut. Make us happy July 1st by giving it back to us."[76] These letters of desperation poured into the governor's office.

Compared to the thousands of letters requesting assistance or offering encouragement to proposals for state relief, there were only a handful of correspondents opposed to public welfare. One of those rare letters came from Mr. E. L. Dudley of Redwood, who wrote the governor in February 1934 to explain his opposition to state relief expenditures: "[I]t will be a burden on the tax payers, and besides what has been appropriated hasn't been used properly. More than that it influences people of good standing not to work. The prominent men of the County advocating the relief aid is [sic] getting more of it than the needy."[77]

Other letters criticized the application of relief, rather than the principle itself. In December 1934, James Cooly of Quicksburg complained to the state comptroller that one of his neighbors, William Baily, was drawing a pension he did not deserve, since Baily had worked through the recent apple harvest.[78] R. E. Ankers wrote from Falls Church his opinion that "those in actual need of relief in Virginia can be well taken care of with a total outlay not to exceed one-third of the amount we have been putting out." The correspondent did not suggest ending public relief, but rather cutting its expense.[79] Another criticism was directed at the nature of work relief rather than the concept. Plummer Jones, secretary of the Buckingham County Chamber of Commerce, wrote the governor, "I can't see that the construction of roads here would help to any extent. We now have a fairly good system of roads. The building of additional roads would render no material service." Jones asked the governor to consider some other kind of work relief for his district.[80] Such criticisms—of the method, not the principle—of relief predominated.

Still, the Byrd machine refused to budge. One federal observer summed it up this way: "There is considerable sentiment in the press in support of the State making an appropriation for relief. I believe the majority of the legislature would appropriate funds before it would see a cessation of relief in the state. What is known as the 'Machine' in Virginia headed by the able and astute Senator Byrd has, however, complete control of the situation and will resist an appropriation for relief even to the extent of abandoning a relief program."[81]

Federal Relief

The manifest shortcomings of local and state relief efforts led to widespread calls for federal assistance. C. P. Spaeth of Norfolk wrote, "I make the sweeping indictment that the Virginia officials are not only incompetent, but show a callous disregard to human suffering. . . . I could point a great need here for more adequate relief, and employment. It begins to appear that the only salvation for Virginia lies with the Federal Government taking over all relief activities throughout the state."[82] Even the conservative *Lynchburg News* demanded that the federal government do something more for relief, although the paper was quite restrained in its vision of federal activism. "Payment of fixed sums to the unemployed in normal times is one thing and is called a 'dole,' but . . . lending of money for food for the farmer, his wife and babies, victims of a natural cataclysm is emergency relief and no more of a dole than an appropriation for relief of starving Europeans."[83]

Such sentiments did not mean that a consensus had emerged in favor of a federal welfare state. Virginia's U.S. senator Carter Glass, for one, remained unalterably opposed to the kind of activist federal government that would be required to provide national relief. Glass believed that even Hoover's cautious policies had "largely transformed the United States Treasury into an eleemosynary institution which practically puts us on the British dole system."[84] Relief measures would not solve the unemployment crisis, Glass contended. Besides, if anyone was going to tax Virginians, he preferred that it be the people of Virginia rather than those in Washington. "I would rather trust the people of Virginia to levy their own taxes and take care of their own unemployed than to have them taxed and their money brought here to Washington and doled back to them for political purposes."[85] (Even as he spoke, Glass knew that the Virginia political machine would never impose such taxes, making his rhetoric disingenuous at best.)

Like the nation as a whole, Virginians turned to Democratic candidate Franklin D. Roosevelt in the presidential election of 1932, with his vaguely worded but nevertheless reassuring promises of a new deal for the American people. Although Roosevelt had made no commitments as to policies, many people nevertheless were already convinced that only the federal government—with its ability to tax corporations and incomes—had the power to confront the unprecedented economic crisis.[86] As one Richmonder put it, "Our powerful central government has wealth and an unlimited credit."[87] Roosevelt's record in relief while governor of New York gave many people confidence that, despite the absence of promises, Roosevelt was more likely than Hoover to use the as-yet-untested power of federal government to deal with the depression. As William Leuchtenburg phrased it, Roosevelt "suggested that beneath his cautious platitudes lay the promise of an audacious program."[88]

W. J. Cash contended that "no section of the country greeted Franklin Roosevelt and the New Deal with more intense and unfeigned enthusiasm than did the South."[89] As a Democratic president, Roosevelt benefited by the South's traditional party allegiance; as the region that was soon labeled the nation's number one economic problem, the South hoped to benefit by whatever form this vague "new deal" might take. Southern politicians determined to bring back as many of those benefits to the region as possible but remained alert to the possibility that relief legislation might have undesirable ramifications. As a result southern regional mores made a great deal of difference in national welfare policy. That is to say, regional differences were more than just interesting variations on the national theme; southern distinctiveness could profoundly affect national policies. Thanks to the seniority system, Roosevelt's first Congress was dominated by southerners. They chaired nine of the fourteen most important committees in the Senate and twelve of seventeen in the House.[90] Southern views on federal activism, welfare policy, race, and employment would profoundly shape the future of the New Deal and of social welfare in America.

Southerners could also be among the most powerful opponents of the New Deal, and Virginia's Carter Glass joined the ranks of the opposition from the beginning. "Roosevelt is driving the country to destruction faster than it has ever moved before," Glass fumed. "Congress is giving this inexperienced man greater power than that possessed by Mussolini and Stalin, put together."[91] Glass, so conservative that he even considered Hoover's mild relief efforts to be "tainted with State socialism,"[92] earned a record of voting against the New Deal more than any other Democratic senator, opposing the administration on four out of every five votes. Glass voted with the administration only on bills that could be considered "economizing" measures, such as a refusal to pay veterans' bonuses.[93]

With powerful foes like Byrd and Glass, Roosevelt had to craft federal relief policies very carefully. Rather than antagonize the southern Democratic leadership upon which he so heavily relied, the president had to compromise on numerous details. Southern congressmen, holding positions of considerable strength, very effectively asserted themselves in a variety of ways, including regional wage differentials. New Deal relief legislation showed the marks of their presence. As one recent study put it, "Southern political power was enhanced by a tacit deal between Roosevelt and the Southern contingent: Support for the New Deal was exchanged for a relatively free hand in writing and rewriting legislation to fit the peculiarities of the South."[94]

Roosevelt's first relief program was the "tradition-shattering" Federal Emergency Relief Administration, with former settlement-house worker Harry Hopkins at the helm.[95] As set up by Congress in May 1933, the FERA had an initial budget of $500 million. The money was divided into two equal funds, one given to the states as direct grants, the other set up as a "matching grant"—states had to come up with money to match the federal funds. (The FERA thus established a precedent for this new "fiscal relationship" between the states and the federal government.)[96] Hopkins put great pressure on the states to do their part, and occasionally cut off funds from states that failed to contribute. Kentucky and West Virginia both felt the power of Hopkins's purse strings when they lost FERA appropriations after their legislatures refused to supply relief money from their own coffers.[97] At the same time, Hopkins had considerable sympathy for the situation in the South. He told Roosevelt bluntly in 1933, "The financial condition of the South is such that we are going to have to pay a much larger percentage of the relief bill than in other States. . . . Relief in the South has been wofully [sic] inadequate and it is going to be necessary to almost double it to aven [sic] give a minimum livelihood."[98]

FERA money was to be spent in one of two ways: direct relief, where necessary, and work relief, where possible. Although frequently condemned as nothing but a dole, the FERA in fact emphasized work relief from its inception. Hopkins repeatedly spotlighted public works projects in his messages to the states but settled for lesser projects—including raking leaves and shoveling snow—rather than have the unemployed go entirely without relief.[99] The legislation creating the FERA had dictated that the agency use professionally trained social workers in each local unit, in an attempt to avoid politicizing the distribution of relief. At Hopkins's insistence, FERA money was also to be funneled only through public agencies, necessitating the building of public-welfare systems where none existed. This requirement effectively ended the traditional public subsidies to private agencies.[100] It also helped to spread professional social work more evenly throughout the country; as a result, social work was no longer solely an urban occupation.[101]

With an underdeveloped public-welfare system, Virginia was ill equipped to distribute FERA relief monies when they came. Before the depression crisis, forty counties had created welfare boards, but the state board of public welfare concluded that they really operated in only ten or twelve of them.[102] Since no statewide welfare department was operating, a separate entity, called the Virginia ERA (VERA), was created to administer the federal funds. Established in June 1933, the VERA was headed by William A. Smith, an engineer from Petersburg. Smith (like other state ERA administrators) answered to the governor rather than to Washington. A federal relief supervisor sent to study conditions in Virginia observed that Smith had "personal qualities which make for constructive leadership in a state as conservative as Virginia." Still, as an appointee of the Byrd machine, Smith was unlikely to respond to FERA pressures on the state to contribute to the relief effort.[103]

Within months of the establishment of federal relief through the FERA, it became clear that Virginia was not participating to the degree that other states were.[104] Initially, officials in the FERA were not sure whether this indicated "that Virginia's unemployment situation is better than other states" or whether it was "an indication of the fact that it has been more difficult to get on the relief rolls in Virginia than in many of the other states."[105] In September 1933, the state had the second-lowest percentage of people on relief in the nation. Between July 1934 and June 1935, Virginia ranked behind only two states—Delaware and Vermont—as the smallest percentages of population on relief, with only 8.6 percent of its people on the relief rolls. This was partly because of a milder depression, partly because of a low standard of living in the state, and partly because of the absence of state funds.[106] As one would expect, the percentages of population on relief were higher in urban areas: in Richmond, 9.6 percent; in Norfolk, 11.6 percent; and in Portsmouth, 13.6 percent of the population were on the relief rolls in June 1935.[107]

Local officials insisted the situation could be explained. Where the localities had no existing welfare apparatus, "it was necessary to set up an organization equipped to meet the needs of each locality. It will thus be realized," explained a local bureaucrat, "that where no agency previously existed there were no records whatsoever, and as a result the office, as well as all records, had to be built from the beginning." In addition, in rural counties, the cases were scattered, with "slow relief resulting."[108] Federal officials, however, soon concluded that it was really opposition from the Byrd machine that was responsible for slowing down the flow of federal money to Virginia. FERA field-worker Gertrude Gates reported, "There is definite opposition to relief as such in this state—a feeling that it is not needed in rural counties and an unwillingness to admit the extent of its unemployed numbers."[109] Harry Hopkins, who had once held sanguine hopes about southerners' "determination to cooperate with the Government in whatever measures are applied to gain a complete recovery,"[110] realized that in Virginia, at least, cooperation was at a minimum.

Despite the overwhelming evidence of need, the Virginia "organization" actually discouraged the FERA from sending money to the state. Arthur James, appointed state commissioner of public welfare in 1932, was more in sync with the machine than his predecessor and spoke the party line quite clearly. James informed the FERA that he was "quite disturbed" over the minimum wage of thirty cents per hour, which was higher than the prevailing wages in most of Virginia and therefore would likely put pressure on landowners to raise their wages. James suggested that, as a result, "work relief would assume a minor importance" in Virginia, and "he looked forward to having practically all their funds expended on direct relief very shortly." Under the circumstances, James "questioned very seriously receiving the first $800,000 allotment from the Federal government," and he did not believe that the state required any further federal funds.[111]

James also complained about the centralizing pressure of the federal aid. The

FERA required that the local governments adopt a uniform accounting system so that all local reports could be compared. But James "questioned the advisability" of having the state relief authorities dictate policies to the county welfare departments. "He pointed out that traditionally the counties and cities of Virginia adhered to local autonomy and disliked strong central State supervision." James predicted that, even if the state tried to extend control over the county units, "it would undoubtedly fail in its objectives."[112] The state department of welfare had no intention of becoming "a department of control over local government."[113] James effectively announced his allegiance to the state system rather than the federal plans.

In the fall of 1933, federal welfare authorities began what would prove to be an unsuccessful two-year effort to push Virginia to expand the relief program in the state and to provide matching funds. In October, Alan Johnstone informed the VERA that the FERA would not grant further money to Virginia because the state had used federal aid "to prosecute a program of relief so inadequate as to be absolutely indefensible."[114] State welfare commissioner James disagreed. The state had taken reasonable action to deal with the depression, James argued, by reducing the state budget, reducing the local tax burden, and providing highway construction jobs for the jobless. These continued to be the defenses mounted by Virginia throughout the life of the FERA.[115]

Harry Hopkins threatened again in September 1934 to withhold all funds from Virginia if the legislature did not contribute something to direct relief efforts. Governor Peery responded that this was unfair since Virginia was already receiving less aid than states with comparable populations, like North Carolina and West Virginia. The increasingly irritated Hopkins explained that the federal government distributed aid based on the state's ability to bear the burden, not its population. A state should exhaust its own resources, according to Hopkins, before turning to the federal funds. Since Virginia had a more "solvent" financial condition than other states, it should provide greater allocations.[116] Senator Harry Byrd retorted that the federal government was not giving the state sufficient credit for holding down its expenses: "Those states that are the most extravagant and waste money are the ones that are rewarded by the Federal government."[117]

Not giving in to the threats by Hopkins, the state assembly refused to raise taxes to fund direct relief, despite the fact that Virginia had one of the lowest tax rates in the nation.[118] The rural-dominated legislature, content with the road-building plan of work relief, was "not going to come across with an appropriation for the cities, particularly, if it means a sale's tax or a sur tax on incomes."[119] The state's leadership believed that its fiscal conservatism had already been vindicated, as evidenced by lower levels of unemployment, fewer bank closings, and other positive measures of the economy. The Byrd machine believed that balanced budgets and reduced expenditures had produced this happier situation, and it saw no reason to tinker with "success."[120]

Meanwhile critics of the state's relief policies grew more vocal. The *Times-Dispatch* editorialized in December 1934 that "our statement that Virginia is not doing her part to relieve the suffering of her urban jobless, is as true as it ever was. . . . But it is perhaps worth while to point out in this connection that the State's sole contribution to relief since the beginning of the depression has gone to the rural areas in the form of work on the highways, and that it is about time the cities were treated as though they too were parts of the Commonwealth. Their unemployment problem is far more acute than that of the country districts."[121]

Virginia never authorized funds for direct relief during the life of the FERA, and the federal government continued to cover Virginia's due portion (see table 21). Perhaps fearful of antagonizing the powerful Virginia delegation in Congress, Hopkins never made good on his financial threats, despite his willingness to do so in the case of other recalcitrant states. FERA field-worker Gertrude Gates contended that Virginia's leadership was "playing poker with Washington and they say in effect—we have always been able to get money—Washington is not going to cut us off." Gates wrote, "The conservative element, which is predominate, apparently, in this state, does not, from all I can gather, want help in meeting its relief cost, because it does not believe relief is necessary, but there is a willingness to accept F.E.R.A. funds as long as they can get funds without putting up money themselves."[122] In the end, the FERA spent some $26 million in Virginia; an estimated four to five hundred thousand people had some form of contact with the agency, despite the state government's considerable opposition to its activities. The localities had appropriated over $2 million during the same period. In contrast, the state government had provided only $34,452, mainly for administrative costs.[123]

Work Relief

Federal relief strategists had conceived of the FERA as a short-term program to keep people from starving while the planning for more sweeping relief and reform programs proceeded. A second work relief program, the Civil Works Administration, was similarly designed as a temporary measure to employ millions of workers in public works projects during the critical winter of 1933–34. The more permanent work relief programs included smaller efforts such as the Civilian Conservation Corps and the National Youth Administration, and the larger ones such as the Public Works Administration, under the direction of

Harold Ickes, and the Works Progress Administration, headed by Harry Hopkins. Like his boss, Hopkins was eager to end the federal government's "dole," and he celebrated "the transfer of millions of able-bodied Americans from the dole to self-respect-restoring jobs." Hopkins added that he hoped "that this country never will return to the dole on a nation-wide basis."[124]

Virginia's Governor Peery interpreted these new federal programs as a victory for the machine's philosophies and for the state in its contest with the federal government. As plans for the new work relief programs were developing, Peery suggested that "Washington is turning toward a new relief policy that may resemble in many respects the plan which the Commonwealth has followed since 1931, and for which the federal relief administration has criticized Virginia on a number of occasions. If the federal government adopts a general policy of work relief in place of a direct dole, Virginia can claim to be four years ahead of the country." Peery presented this as a vindication of "the Virginia plan" of work instead of a dole.[125]

Even though the proposed programs were based on work rather than a dole, Virginia's senators Harry Byrd and Carter Glass nevertheless led the fight against the WPA in Congress. They were opposed to the open-ended appropriations, as well as to power given the executive in spending the funds.[126] The WPA gave responsibility for "employables" to federal government while turning "unemployables" back over to the states. This division of labor highlighted the underlying philosophy of Roosevelt's work program: massive unemployment was a national problem of a temporary nature, for which the federal government would step in with emergency relief for the duration of the crisis. The poverty of "unemployables" was not a product of the emergency, but was rather the same kind of problem that local and state governments had long handled, and therefore they should continue to do so.[127] Although not designed with Virginia in mind, this division of labor effectively forced Virginia's hand. Since employable laborers would be on federal payrolls, Virginia could no longer claim its road-building plan was work relief. Virginia would have to go into the direct relief business as a result.[128]

Ironically, once the WPA legislation passed over their objections, Virginia's senators then worked to get Virginia its full share of WPA money, even as they criticized the program for its "excesses." Since WPA projects did not require matching funds, the Byrd organization did less to obstruct its activities in Virginia than they did other federal agencies. Aware of Byrd's tremendous political clout, Washington officials approved most of Byrd's pet projects, and Byrd was relatively muted in his criticisms of the WPA. This more cooperative stance resulted in WPA jobs for an estimated ninety-five thousand Virginians, who earned sixty-six million dollars over the eight years of the program.[129]

There can be no doubt that the federal work relief programs pumped desperately needed money into Virginia's communities. The National Youth Administration provided forty-five thousand Virginians with jobs in the "out of school" program. (Richmond had the largest NYA enrollment in the state, with an average of 175 people per month in 1938).[130] In its first year of operation, the Public Works Administration approved $90 million worth of projects for Virginia, including a $663,000 public housing project for Richmond. By 1937, the Civilian Conservation Corps had more than eighty camps in Virginia, twelve of which were for blacks. Monthly payrolls ranged from five thousand to twenty thousand recipients. In nine years, the CCC spent over $100 million in Virginia, the fifth largest amount in the country.[131]

The CCC was undoubtedly one of the best liked of the New Deal programs. As one Richmonder observed, "I appreciate most highly the CCC act for taking young men from idleness to teach them not to fight to kill as in military service, but learn how to create; how to build not how to destroy. . . . The future will appreciate it much more than the present, I am sure of that."[132] The WPA was even more important for pumping money and jobs into the state. By mid-1935, between 40,000 and 50,000 Virginians were employed on more than 2,500 WPA projects. In January 1938, there were still over 19,000 WPA workers in the state, including 1,719 in Richmond.[133]

Unlike the state's highway-building program, which had benefited rural counties at the expense of urban centers, the federal work programs offered much to places like Richmond. The WPA had multiple projects, small and large, in the city. By 1939, for example, a WPA project at the city airport had spent four hundred thousand dollars. More than six miles of city streets had been paved, almost entirely with federal funds, and more federal money went to improvements at Chimborazo Park, Battery Park, and William Byrd Park.[134] Educational opportunities, included in FERA, WPA, CCC, and NYA programs, may have benefited city dwellers more often than rural residents. The WPA's educational programs in Richmond, including courses in history, public speaking, and English, hired dozens of teachers and provided educational opportunities to hundreds of residents. Adult education classes were held at the State Penitentiary, the YWCA, the YMCA, community centers, and the City Home.[135] By October 1936, Virginia had 756 teachers and 22,277 students enrolled in federally funded educational programs.[136] The amounts of money could be truly astonishing by contemporary standards. In 1938, the WPA expenditures in Richmond, combined with the required matching funds from the state and city sources, totaled nearly two million dollars.[137]

There can also be no doubt that the federal work relief efforts in Virginia were riddled with problems, including charges of nepotism and other forms of favoritism. A Warrenton woman complained that she could not get a work relief job because "Nepotism is rife in this country and our little town is full of it in the P.W.A. and the C.W.A."[138] Rev. R. W. Vanderberry reported similar problems: "I have had dozens of people who were entitled to help from this source [the works programs] say that it is almost impossible for one who has not some political influence to get a job. This is naturally aggravated by the presence of so many sons, daughters, and relatives of congressmen holding highly remunerative positions under the Works Program."[139] Many job applicants assumed that their political affiliations mattered and volunteered such information, as did Nena Foster: "If politics are to be taken into consideration in such employment, I can assure you that I am faithful to the Administration. Having grown up in a home where the father has been most loyal to the democratic principles, and even now, in his eighty-second year, boasts of never having voted any other ticket, I, too, can cheerfully say that these same principles have been good enough for me."[140]

In addition to nepotism, other problems stemmed from the state leadership's continuing conservative views on relief, race, and gender. Federal and state relief officials held differing views of what constituted an "adequate" level of relief. Alan Johnstone, field director for the southern states, reported to Harry Hopkins his belief that "[r]elief has been very inadequate in Virginia, ranging in the country districts from $10 to $15 per month per family, and in the cities $18 to $20."[141] To put these numbers into some kind of context, a study of women factory workers in Richmond in 1932 found that the typical factory wage was $666 per year, or $55.50 per month.[142] A 1934 survey of African American domestic workers in the South found their average weekly wage to be just over $6.[143] Virginia's relief payments, then, were lower than what a black female domestic worker might expect to earn with steady work.

The lack of enthusiasm for relief at the state level would continue through the remainder of the New Deal years and would continue to produce very low levels of benefits in Virginia (even when state money was not involved). Although fiscal conservatism explains much of the state's skimpy welfare programs, concerns over race also played a part in keeping relief levels low. Black leaders frequently pointed out the racial discrimination in federal relief efforts. The *Norfolk Journal and Guide* pointed out that blacks were more often assigned inferior jobs, such as ditch digging. Even when given jobs identical to those of whites, blacks were nevertheless paid lower wages.[144] Skilled laborers especially resented the hiring policies in work programs. Local contractors were allowed to hire as local conditions permitted, which often meant that African American workers were not hired, even on construction jobs in their own neighborhoods.[145]

Other African Americans protested that the white supervisors on work projects actively worked to see that black employees failed and could then be fired.

Catherine Johnson, a black woman from Petersburg who received a WPA job working on a park project, complained that her supervisor assigned her work that was too strenuous for her, and then fired her for doing it poorly. "[W]e had to carry large trees, two workers to a tree; carry gravel in a bushel basket. . . . I had to dig, and dig shrubbery, and go up very steep hills. This made my breath short. My weight is 200 pounds, I just had to stop to rest between digs. It was for this reason the Supervisor cut me off. She put on my slip 'Careless Worker.' " Johnson felt she and other black women workers had nowhere to take their grievances: "We wanted to tell someone but didn't know where to go, because all the supervisors were white."[146]

New Deal programs made no attempt to challenge Jim Crow orthodoxies. Blacks were not excluded from the New Deal: African Americans were appointed to the staffs of various federal agencies in the state and received money from the FERA, WPA, and other New Deal programs. African American communities also received lasting benefits in the form of new schools, hospitals, and community centers.[147] Richmond, for example, received a new "negro swimming pool" and recreation center from WPA funds.[148] But Washington set the tone in race relations, which local administrators gladly followed, for few were willing to take on segregation and the depression too. The result was a tacit toleration of discrimination in hiring, in work conditions, and in pay scales.

Nor were many New Dealers in the South eager to challenge traditional gender roles. The specialized nature of women's work was one of the earliest concerns of federal relief authorities, and a women's work division was formed under the VERA in December 1933.[149] The director was Ellen Agnew of Richmond, who had been the first "home demonstration" agent in the nation. Agnew wrote to local relief directors throughout the state, urging them to create jobs for women in libraries and clerical and recreational programs. But as was the case in other states, the single most important work relief program for women was in the sewing room. (Table 23 summarizes the kinds of women's work projects operating in Virginia and highlights the relative importance of sewing rooms in the group.) Virginia eventually had over one hundred sewing centers where women produced thousands of garments for distribution to relief families.[150]

The official reports from the sewing rooms could sometimes be glowing. An anonymous CWA report on Virginia described "a group of happy looking negro women gathered in a large, well lighted and ventilated room, sewing diligently on all sorts of bright colored material. In one corner a group was busy making sheets and pillow cases. Two women were supervising. All were happy in making money for their own needs and providing clothes for people on relief rolls."[151] Even Lorena Hickok, who could offer biting criticisms of local programs, praised the sewing rooms: "I don't think you have any idea of what [the sewing room projects] have done to the women themselves. The results are marvelous. They came in, sullen, dejected, half starved. Working in pleasant surroundings, having some money and food have done wonders to restore their health and their morale." [152]

In truth, welfare officials had difficulty coming up with any other work relief programs for women besides sewing. [153] While men on work relief were often given job training to boost their skill levels, women were seldom trained to do anything beyond traditional domestic work. [154] The NYA in Virginia established sixteen "home-making centers" where "girls are trained to be capable housewives." [155] Women's projects under the FERA, CWA, and WPA focused on food preparation, canning, nursing, and even house cleaning. [156] The "visiting housekeepers" project, sponsored by the CWA and directed by a social worker from the IVNA, hired unemployed women "with wide housekeeping experience" to work in the homes of relief families who had illness or other emergencies requiring domestic assistance. [157] Virginia's CWA tried to put the best possible face on the "cleaning" projects: "In far-away corners of many counties there are scores of women—desperately poor, living from hand to mouth with hardly a dollar in their possession from one year's end to another. Because they have had no chance to broaden their lives, they are qualified to fill only those places calling for physical labor. . . . With the advent of CWS [sic] these women saw a light. The fifteen hour job a week bringing in five shining dollars for cleaning local school houses, meant warmth, food and shelter." [158]

The federal work relief programs were limited by their conceptions of women's work. In 1934, the FERA tried to create a women's version of the CCC's resident camps. Nicknamed the "she, she, she," the camps enrolled small numbers of young women to do light work such as bandage rolling, while taking classes in home economics. In contrast to the widely popular men's CCC, the women's camps proved expensive to operate, and even the FERA never evinced much enthusiasm for them. [159] In one of the rare cases in which women were given training in an entirely new skill, the Virginia CWA selected forty women to work under a bookbinder, repairing books for public libraries. [160] Unlike most women on relief, this small group of workers received training in a skill outside the traditional categories of women's work.

For black women, the narrow vision of women's work was compounded by the contemporary proscriptions of race. Lorena Hickok reported that the director of women's projects in Georgia suggested a project to have white "gentlewomen" train "Negresses" for domestic service. Hickok understood what the state director did not: "The only trouble . . . is that the Negresses won't go in for it. They don't want to learn how to be servants." [161] In Virginia, the FERA hired black women to clean public buildings, a job viewed as unsuited for white women.[162] Virginia's sewing rooms were also segregated by race. Even the clothing made by work relief women was sometimes segregated, with articles made by black women sent to the "needy of their own race."[163]

Thus traditional regional understandings of race, gender, and relief served to circumscribe the potential of the New Deal's welfare programs to effect widespread social reform. Even so, many conservative southerners believed that the New Deal had in fact done just that, contending that the federal government's welfare policies endangered both the economy and traditional social relations in the region. Some southern farmers complained that wage rates were too high and therefore put inflationary pressure on private sector wages. Farmers in South Carolina told investigator Lorena Hickok that the "CWA has created dissatisfaction among their Negroes. They all want to be on CWA, working for 30 and 40 cents an hour. Their hearts are no longer in the work on the farms."[164] A sympathetic W. J. Cash agreed: "[P]oor as was the stipend paid Federal relief clients in the South, it still afforded a more attractive standard of living, or at least one considered so, than that provided by such jobs as hoeing and picking cotton, stemming tobacco, and gathering strawberries, fruit, and truck in season."[165]

Conservative southern whites feared that New Deal relief policies were tearing at the foundation of white supremacy. Even those working for the federal agencies themselves could continue to hold this opinion. Lorena Hickok reported that the Federal Reemployment director in Georgia confided to her his belief that "[a]ny Nigger who gets over $8 a week is a spoiled Nigger, that's all."[166] Such critics claimed that relief work "ruined" workers by teaching them to expect easy work and high wages and by ending the deference southern employers had long demanded from their workers, whether white or black. "Relief has ruined more men than any one thing I know of," believed Virginia landowner John E. Bess.

> I know men who were good, honest laborers, who never knew anything but to
> do an honest day's work when they were hired. And they were on the lookout for
> work all the time and got it, too, and since they went on relief, they aren't worth a
> darn. If you succeed in hiring one of these fellows, they consider it an insult if their
> employer or boss tells them what to do. No, they think they should tell the owner
> how to farm and manage his affairs. They would rather have a little food doled out
> to them than to work at a fair wage and be independent. Yes sir, relief has had that
> effect on more people than you would think.[167]

Hickok's extensive travels in the South convinced her that "thousands of those Negroes are living much better on relief than they ever did while they were working. You hear the same stories over and over again—Negroes quitting their jobs or refusing to work because they can get on relief. Perhaps only half of those stories are true, but that's bad enough. And God knows the wages they receive are low, and that their standards of living ought to be raised."[168]

In fact, New Deal work relief policies did raise the standard of living in the South, although it took some time before federal officials recognized that "temporary unemployment" and the low standard of living were two different problems. As early as the 1890s depression, some observers had begun to understand that unemployment was a continuing problem rather than a periodic one: "Evidence is too clear that even in so-called normal times there is an amount of non-employment which occasions suffering."[169] But this observation was slow to gain widespread acceptance. By the second year of the New Deal, some welfare authorities were beginning to argue for a much broader welfare policy, one that would include nonemergency poverty. When the CWA work relief program was about to be shut down, Lorena Hickok warned her boss, "From all I hear we are by no means through with this relief job in the South. Everywhere I hear the same thing. A tremendous labor surplus that is not an emergency surplus, but CHRONIC."[170]

State welfare administrators in the South wrestled with this issue. Gay Shepperson, in charge of federal relief efforts in Georgia, observed in January 1934 that "the $7,000,000 a month we've been spending in Georgia has been largely wasted, outside the cities, where an emergency DOES exist. Wasted, in that outside the cities it ISN'T an emergency, and relief and CWA don't do anything to remedy the situation permanently."[171] Similarly, VERA director William Smith explained: "We recognize that for many of these families the economic depression has not brought about a financial emergency, and that the condition under which they are living at the time of applying for relief is more or less the standard to which they have been accustomed. However, their need for assistance is obvious, and it is most difficult for the most astute case worker to say in many such cases that their condition is not due at this time to lack of work opportunities."[172]

Some state officials had already known about the chronic rural poverty in Virginia, having been informed by an official study in 1926 that five hundred thousand families lived below a subsistence level in rural areas. But, according to Gertrude Gates of the FERA, the state's political leaders responded, " '[T]hese people have always lived so' and that was that. Why should they be disturbed in 1934 and 1935 about those same people, plus a few more."[173] The presence of chronic poverty came as more of a surprise to others, whose attentions had understandably been directed to the problem of emergency unemployment. The later widespread recognition of chronic poverty helped gained support for a broadened federal welfare policy. Rather than just a temporary program for unemployment relief, the depression triggered support for the creation of a much more substantial welfare state to address problems of chronic poverty.

From Relief to Social Security

Several basic components of a welfare state were combined together in the Social Security Act, passed by Congress in 1935. The complex legislation attempted to battle the poverty produced by unemployment, old age, childhood dependency, and blindness and other debilities. Again, southerners in Congress intervened to weaken the administration's proposed legislation considerably, and Roosevelt accepted their amendments because he needed southern support for passage. Southern politicians prevented the coverage of most agricultural and domestic workers, effectively eliminating most southern blacks from the benefits of the new welfare state. Likewise, southern delegates insisted that the states be given complete freedom to set benefit levels; and again, Roosevelt compromised.[174] Moreover, the federal system relied upon the states to administer the programs, offering a further opportunity for obstreperous southern opponents to dilute the final outcome. As one recent scholar has interpreted it, American federalism allowed a division not only of governmental functions, but also of ideology. The more liberal ideals intended by the federal government were not always shared by the states; New Deal federalism "actually empowered state governments . . . to extend the reach of their non-liberal rule."[175]

Southern opposition to the Social Security Act stemmed from several regional concerns. Planters in particular worried about the effect that the welfare programs would have on their labor supply. For decades, southern landowners had practiced their own kind of personalized "welfare," called planter paternalism by a recent study, which served to tie the workers to the landlords. The product of this personalized welfare was loyalty, obedience, and a guarantee of hard work. That entire system was in danger of breaking up if federal welfare benefits came between the planters and their laborers.[176]

Regional concerns about race, often expressed in terms of "states' rights," also stimulated southern opposition to the proposed Social Security bill. Virginia's Congressman Howard W. Smith, trying to cut back the size of the Old-Age Assistance program, argued, "My objection . . . would be answered by a provision in the bill which took away from some person in Washington the power to say when the State of Virginia could participate; in other words, for someone in Washington to say what was a reasonable and decent subsistence down in the Blue Ridge Mountains of Virginia." That race was the underlying issue in Smith's defense of states' rights was clarified in the same speech: "Of our 116,000 [persons over age 65 in Virginia] practically 25 percent are of one class that will probably qualify 100 percent. I am interested . . . [in] a provision in this law that permits the State to govern itself on that proposition." When queried about this by another congressman, Smith replied, "[I]n the South we have a great many colored people, and they are largely of the laboring class."[177]

The collective pressure by southern delegates in Congress would modify the final Social Security bill, in much the same way they had reigned in the New Deal's relief measures. The states gained the ability to control benefit levels and were guaranteed federal matching money no matter how low the benefit levels were set. States would not be penalized either for imposing additional qualifications on applicants for assistance. With these kinds of modifications in place, southern congressmen finally let the bill pass.[178]

Offered as a long-term solution to the problem of unemployment, one part of the Social Security Act established an unemployment insurance system, with "premiums" paid through a payroll tax. The federal legislation required the states to pass a "parallel" measure by 31 December 1936 in order to share in the unemployment benefits. A state that remained outside the system stood to lose millions of dollars each year, as the federal government would collect the premiums regardless of whether the state participated. The Virginia "organization" rallied to oppose the federal unemployment plan. State senator W. Stuart Muffet of Staunton argued that passing the required state unemployment bill would be yielding to the coercion of the federal government and would be voluntarily giving up "the last vestige of State sovereignty we have."[179] William Munford Tuck, state senator from South Boston, complained that the Social Security Act "is not only undemocratic in that it places in the hands of a bureaucrat in Washington a stick to whip over our heads and tell us what and how much we shall do, but it also penalizes frugality and economy in government."[180]

Governor Peery believed that Virginia could safely hold out against the program since so many other states had also hesitated to act. In mid-1936, those states still represented a majority of the whole, and Peery contended that Congress would be forced to grant an extension to the deadline with so many states still in noncompliance. But in early December, several states hurriedly passed their enabling legislation, bringing the majority of states into the system. There no longer appeared much possibility that Congress would extend the deadline. Even then, Peery refused to call a special session of the legislature until he had secured assurances from a majority of the assembly that they would confine their activities to the proposals sent them by the governor. Peery could be certain that other parts of the social security plan—namely the much-hated old-age pensions—would not sneak in during the session. The special session passed the enabling bill in December 1936, and more than three hundred thousand Virginians were covered immediately.[181]

The state was even slower to see the advantage of old-age assistance, despite the public support of labor unions and advocacy groups such as the Old-Age Pension League, the Virginia Homemakers' Association, and the "Three-Score-and-Ten Club" of Norfolk.[182] Work relief or unemployment insurance could do little for elderly women like Emily Allison, "now 68 years of age," who once supported herself "as far as my health would permit yet now . . . I am dependent on others for what I get and it is hard, needing the necessities of life and nothing to look to."[183] Like unemployment insurance, the federal old-age insurance plan required the states to pass enabling legislation. But while other states implemented the necessary infrastructure quickly and began enrolling their elderly poor, Virginia stalled. Mrs. Sarah Lupton of Berkley, Virginia, wrote the First Lady asking her "influence in seeking the passage of similar legislation in our state."[184] Another resident believed that Eleanor Roosevelt was "the head of the Old Ladys Pension" and was in charge of the distribution of money to women.[185]

Such widespread enthusiasm did not penetrate the Byrd machine, however. Senator Byrd had established the organization's position in his opposition to the original social security legislation. Publicly, Byrd complained that the federal government would be dictating to the states both the size and the recipients of the pensions.[186] Privately, Byrd attacked the plan because "negroes will be placed on the same basis as white people. The result will be that practically all negroes over sixty-five years will be pensioned, receiving from $30.00 to $40.00 per month, and all their children and grandchildren, cousins and aunts will live on them. . . . It will simply mean that nearly all the colored population of the South will stop working."[187]

Race was a concern for Governor Peery as well, although he thought that race might indirectly help the state in one way. Publicly he stressed his opposition to raising taxes and to old-age pensions because he believed they would double taxes.[188] Privately he "expressed fear that the old age pension plan . . . will throw too heavy a burden on State finances. . . . Proof of age will be one of the primary qualifications of any old age pension bill which may be proposed in Virginia, and as matters stand, it will be impossible for all persons listed by the Census as over 65 to prove their age because of lack of birth records, particularly those of negroes, prior to 1870, and this may keep thousands off the pension rolls."[189]

The Virginia legislature refused to pass an old-age pension in 1936—despite the fact that the federal contribution would be 90 percent.[190] Welfare commissioner Arthur James claimed the state needed additional time to investigate the program thoroughly to avoid the problems experienced in other states. Former governor Westmoreland Davis, a longtime critic of the Byrd organization, condemned the machine's obstinacy: "The explanation for Virginia's lag [in implementing old-age pensions] lies not in a lack of need for her aged, but in a lack of interest of a machine-controlled legislature in matters of human welfare."[191]

Unable to hold out any longer, and in danger of losing millions of dollars in federal contributions, Virginia passed the final pieces of the Social Security program 1 September 1938, the last state in the Union to join the basic old-age pension program.[192] By October 1939, 818 Richmond residents had qualified for Old-Age Assistance, receiving an average grant of $13.76 per month. There were still pending another 200 applications. At the same time, 37 families were receiving grants from Aid to Dependent Children, averaging $40.24 per month per family.[193] Ironically, after opposing the Social Security program with all its might, Virginia tried to turn its Confederate pensioners over to the new Old-Age Assistance program in 1938. After great public outcry about this "insult to Confederate heroes," Governor Price had to drop the proposal. Virginia continued to fund its own Confederate pension program until the end of the century.[194]

To provide required state funds for all these programs, the legislature passed the Public Assistance Act of 1938 to provide assistance to the aged needy and other categories of dependents. William Brock has termed this the "*annus mirabilis* in Virginia's welfare legislation," as the law required every city and county to provide sufficient funds to support a welfare program.[195] Even then, Governor Peery argued that the old-age assistance program should be considered a temporary relief measure during an economic crisis, not a permanent welfare system. His successor, Price, agreed: "The Act must be conservatively administered, and should be made perfectly clear that Old Age Assistance, as the term implies, is intended to be based upon the actual needs of the individual case and is not to be regarded as a pension. It is in the last analysis a relief measure."[196]

Despite the wishful thinking by Virginia's leadership, the limited-welfare state crafted by the Social Security Act was a permanent entity. The state's department of welfare, which had greatly expanded in order to administer the federal work programs, might have been expected to retract again after the emergency was over. Instead, the department would administer Aid to Dependent Children, Old-Age Assistance, and other federal welfare programs, making its expanded size and functions a permanent trend. Before the New Deal, the state's welfare department had a very limited program and little power over the localities. By 1938, it supervised a large domain of welfare activities and its authority had become substantial.[197]

VIRGINIA'S CONSERVATIVE POLITICAL leaders did their utmost to prevent it, but the federal welfare state arrived in the Commonwealth nevertheless. After three centuries of resilience, the old poor laws finally were dismantled. The new system in their place blended funds from local, state, and federal coffers and offered a combination of direct relief programs and contributory insurance schemes to several categories of the "deserving" poor. In many ways, it seemed a new day.

Still, the implementation of the Social Security Act did not mean that the Byrd machine stood vanquished or that the state legislature suddenly grew sympathetic to the poor. The depression and New Deal years had helped to highlight how great the distance was between the demands of the people and the philosophies of the Byrd machine. Yet the machine remained in power, continuing its rear guard defense against further federal intrusions for years to come.

Nor did the implementation of the Social Security Act mean that poverty disappeared from Virginia. The abolition of the poor laws did not equal the abolition of poverty. As Bruce Schulman has observed, the 1938 *Report of Economic Conditions* identified the South as the nation's number one economic problem; the federal government would subsequently focus on wages rather than welfare in its attempts to solve these problems.[198] Still poverty continued to plague the state and the region for decades, resisting the forces of the post–World War II economic boom, the civil rights movement, the War on Poverty, and the trickle-down 1980s. The establishment of the federal protowelfare state can only be considered a partial victory, a compromised system that represented an imperfect improvement over the poor laws.

CONCLUSION

By the close of the 1930s, the "welfare/industrial complex" in Richmond had changed dramatically since its origins in the colonial poor laws. In many ways, poor relief appeared so different as to be incomparable to the past. No longer rooted solely in local government, the welfare system now included state and federal governments in the complex protowelfare state ushered in by the New Deal. The sums expended on the poor seemed enormous. The locus of control had shifted (if imperfectly) away from the local authorities. Funding (necessarily) came from a wide variety of sources rather than a simple poll tax. Concerns about legal "settlement" or residency no longer dominated the question of entitlement to relief. Public welfare and private charity had developed a cooperative, complementary working relationship. The gatekeepers to both charity and welfare had become professional women rather than elected or appointed men.

Yet many other features of Richmond's post–New Deal welfare system remained consistent with past practices. The system continued to struggle with defining who was deserving of assistance, as well as with keeping costs low. Potential charity and welfare recipients still had to perform in the "theater of charity," and the most skillful presentations garnered the most aid from the widest range of sources. Women, children, and the elderly continued to gain the most sympathy and the most support. Racial segregation and discrimination continued as hallmarks of both public and private welfare practices. Confederate veterans continued to benefit from a parallel regional welfare system privileging the honored soldiers of the Lost Cause. Poor families continued to combine assistance from a variety of sources and to use those services in ways that they believed benefited them best. And finally, the city almshouse continued to offer care to hundreds of people, as it had every year since 1810.

In both change and continuity, Richmond's welfare history bore the marks of national trends with a regional accent. The New Deal served to standardize many social-welfare policies, helping to bring the South ever closer to national norms in provision for the poor. At the same time, loathe to give up regional traditions regarding states' rights and white supremacy, Virginia's leadership fought alongside other southerners in Congress to protect those mores and in fact to incorporate them into federal programs. The two processes operated simultaneously, as both the Americanization of southern welfare policy and the southernization of national welfare policy.[1] As a result, racial disparities permeated the federal welfare system, and "states' rights" lived on to fight another day, reemerging in the 1990s as a rallying cry for the partial dismantling of the welfare state.[2]

It has been suggested that the New Deal did little to change southern attitudes about relief, especially federal government provision of relief.[3] I think it is important here to be specific about exactly which southerners we mean. In the case of Virginia, the political elites, representing agricultural and manufacturing interests, maintained their traditional opposition to generous relief expenditures, especially if it came from the federal government. But other southerners—middle-class workers, relief recipients, unemployed workers—indicated time and again their willingness to have government, at any level, provide assistance. In the Great Depression, like the Civil War crisis earlier, the masses of people held a view of welfare very different from that of their political leaders. For southern workers, "the feeling that 'Uncle Sam' had somehow become their champion had an enormous influence upon them."[4] There were grassroots critics of federal activism, to be sure, such as the Charlottesville minister who complained that the New Deal was "taxing the poor to pay the rich not to work."[5] But a far more common reaction by non-elites was the observation by Walter Sparks of Richmond: "there is a wide spread feeling among thinking people everywhere that not only on account of the need revealed by the depression but also because of the tendency of the age toward communism, makes absolutely necessary something like the Social Security Legislation."[6]

During the 1930s, even private charities came to conclude that government, not the private sector, held ultimate responsibility for the poor. In the spring of 1932, the president of Lynchburg's Associated Charities pointedly told the city council, "It is your job to take care of these needy people."[7] In 1938, at a meeting of Virginia social workers, Harry Greenstein of the American Association of Social Workers acknowledged that "the day long has passed when private charities can care for the problem of relief. Community chests are finding it an impossible task to carry the burden of financing social agencies." Greenstein insisted that "responsibility rests upon the local, State and Federal government."[8] Where control over poor relief had been a source of tension between public and private entities in previous generations, the New Deal had helped to sort out those tensions and find a more cooperative system.

And although nearly everyone hated the dole, there were also those who recognized its temporary necessity. Churchill Gibson of Richmond believed that the federal government withdrew the direct-relief program too quickly: "The employables have been listed for weeks waiting for some project to be developed to give them work for which they may be paid. This lapse between direct relief and employment is, I know, not according to your wishes, but direct relief is being withdraw[n] too rapidly."[9] Similarly, the Instructive Visiting Nurses

Association sent a resolution to the federal authorities asking that the direct-relief program for transients not be withdrawn immediately.[10] The depression, unprecedented in its depth, and the New Deal, unprecedented in its scope, could not help but influence southerners' views on poverty and its relief.

In addition, the depression and New Deal affected public opinion about the poor themselves. Much like in the 1860s, the 1930s saw a "softening" of opinion about the poor. In 1938, for example, social workers for Richmond's Social Service Bureau attempted to live on the weekly allowance given to relief recipients. The director of the experiment, Georgiana Sinclair, believed that the experience would help caseworkers "know how our clients feel when they must restrict their diet to 7-cent meals." Like real relief recipients, the social workers were allowed to supplement their diets with federally distributed "surplus products," which were, at the time, apples. One of the caseworkers in the experiment, Irene M. Lapsley, reported, "I will be glad when this is over, and I hope I never see another apple."[11] This experiment, unimaginable in an earlier era, indicates just how profoundly the depression and New Deal had affected public sensibilities. The good will toward the poor would be temporary, as harsher assessments began to reoccur after World War II, but for a short time Americans softened their views on the poor.

The New Deal produced in Richmond a clearer articulation of the need for public welfare. A minister in Richmond, deeply involved in local charitable efforts, came to believe that "No social legislation would be too drastic, in my opinion, to provide people with some form of active work and the assurance of food, clothing, and shelter, when their physical strength is exhausted."[12] By 1948, the Committee on Public Welfare, appointed to study social problems in the city and make recommendations for their redress, could state unequivocally, "public assistance has as its purpose the alleviation by government of need among those citizens whose basic needs for food, shelter, and clothing cannot otherwise be met. [The committee] recognized the right of individuals to the necessities for decent existence, the responsibility of these individuals for helping themselves insofar as possible, the responsibility of government for the basic welfare of its people, and the responsibility of public welfare to administer public assistance economically and effectively."[13] Moreover, the broadening of public-welfare policy had also led to a bureaucratic sea change in welfare philosophies in Richmond. By 1939, the city's Social Service Bureau could report:

> Cash relief has certainly been of great benefit to the numbers of families receiving it during the year. Some of the visitors who had practically no experience in granting cash relief went into it hesitantly but have been delighted with the results. The families do not feel as if they are labeled, making them different from other people.

They feel more independent and can buy to better advantage. There are not so many evictions. There has been comparatively little criticism from City Council and the community. We are hoping to get all cases, with a few exceptions, on cash relief during next year. We believe it the more economical and efficient plan.[14]

Such changes in thinking may not be quantifiable, but they were real nevertheless.

At the same time, the New Deal had indirect impact on the world of private charities. As public welfare came to carve out more clearly its place, taking over some functions for which private charity had once competed, it left the private sector to try new functions and experiment with new programs. The Family Service Society of Richmond, for example, began planning for a Legal Aid Department in 1934 and contacted the local bar association about the effort.[15] With the federal government moving to cover unemployment relief and other areas, the FSS looked for services still unprovided.

The New Deal, in the words of Frank Freidel, "represented a giant, nationwide cornucopia from which federal aid poured into the desperately depression-ridden South."[16] That money, wrapped in federal regulations for its expenditure, helped to produce a thoroughly revamped welfare system in the region. On one level, the New Deal's social-welfare programs were not so very new. Work relief, direct relief, mothers' aid, and old-age pensions had all existed at the local or state level before the depression. (Unemployment insurance was arguably an innovation, since only one state had enacted such a plan before the federal one was created. But with that one exception, the New Deal essentially expanded and refined already known policies.)[17] However, many of those already known policies were not so well known in the South. Southern states had lagged behind other regions in the creation of old-age pensions, unemployment relief, and mothers' aid.[18] The implementation of these welfare programs was indeed innovation for southern communities previously unfamiliar with them.

There were limits to the impact the federal welfare state had in the South. The establishment of a welfare state did not automatically end southern opposition to it, and once passed by Congress the federal programs still had to be implemented at the state and local levels. The federal government did not, and could not, compel generosity; southern states continued to be as stingy as possible with the distribution of relief. Virginia's intransigence, although extreme, was not unique. Despite their greater poverty, southern states generally were among the slowest to adopt the Social Security programs. After adopting the programs, the South established the lowest benefits levels as well, with Mississippi taking the "honor" of offering the lowest rate in the country: $4.79 per month for old-age assistance.[19]

This tendency toward low benefits levels, based partly on regional biases, was reinforced by professional caseworkers. Although the poor themselves often expressed the sentiment that "it ain't going to hurt the government to feed and clothe them that needs it,"[20] social workers frequently had a different perspective. Long accustomed to viewing casework as the process by which the undeserving were weeded out, social workers continued to see part of their function as limiting the numbers of people who had access to relief. Social worker Josephine Brown observed that even public welfare caseworkers "seemed to think in terms of how many applicants they could reject, not of how many they could possibly accept under the eligibility requirements. Theoretically they believed in high standards of relief," Brown complained, "but in practice they figured out not how much they could give but on how little a family could possibly manage and how many items could be cut out of the budget."[21]

The New Deal, then, despite its tremendous importance for social-welfare policy, did not end poverty in Richmond or the rest of the South. Old-age assistance, aid to dependent children, and other New Deal programs clearly improved the quality of life for many people. WPA and CCC jobs clearly sustained many people through the crisis. But poverty did not disappear as a result. Instead, New Deal programs offered families additional resources, new sources of income, to the range of possibilities already available to them. Poor families still had to work to find the right combination of resources—public and private—to suit their needs at any given time. Aid to dependent children might help some families through a temporary crisis; others continued to turn to orphanages and occasionally to the City Home to deposit children during a family emergency. Poor families still had to practice their dramatic skills as they approached new gatekeepers of relief in the "theater of charity." Face to face, the applicant and caseworker hashed out the terms of relief. Whether at the office of the Family Services Society, the front door of the City Home, or the intake center for ADC, applicants for assistance still had to present a convincing case to those who controlled the resources. Ultimately, welfare remained an intensely local affair. While policy might be set in Washington, and bureaucrats might attempt to channel policy at the state level, welfare was still a process that took place in a local setting.

Poor and working-class families also continued to insist on their rights to control their own affairs, to pick and choose which services they wanted and what restrictions on their activities they were willing to accept in return. Charlotte Anderson, a young working "girl" who had been given free passes to swim at the YWCA with her sister, reacted strongly in 1937 when her caseworker recommended she see a psychiatrist. Charlotte told her caseworker that "she would like us to understand that they were not paupers, and that if the Y.W.C.A. was not willing to give C. free swimming unless they were allowed to meddle in her private life that C. did not have to swim at the 'Y' even though it was all the pleasure she got out of life." Charlotte was willing to forego one of her only pleasures in order to resist the "meddling" in her private life. Carolyn Barnes threatened even more dire action to maintain control over her life. While living at the YWCA, Carolyn developed a large phone bill. When the "Y" threatened to have her wages garnished if she did not immediately pay off the balance, Carolyn counterthreatened to quit her job so there would be no wages to garnish. The caseworker quietly worked out a longer term payment plan, and Carolyn continued to reside at the YWCA.[22]

Richmond, as an urban and industrial center, experienced both the Great Depression and New Deal in ways different from the rural South. With a functioning public-welfare department already in place, including a small mothers' pension program, Richmond already had a more comprehensive welfare system than most rural counties even before the advent of the New Deal. Nevertheless, the 1930s wrought many changes in Richmond's social-welfare system, capping decades of evolving public policy in the city. One of the most important of these changes was to define more distinctly different roles for public and private charitable efforts. For more than a century, public and private efforts at poor relief had overlapped in Richmond, with duplicated efforts being commonplace. The two often had nearly identical functions, which had contributed to frequent tensions and "turf wars." By 1940, public and private charitable efforts had become more clearly distinct from one another. Public charity, channeled by federal directives, focused more attention on categorical poverty: programs to alleviate and prevent need for the elderly, dependent children, the unemployed, and other categories such as the blind. Private charity specialized more in family relations and personal development, in attempts to prevent a range of conditions that often produced destitution: family breakdown, juvenile delinquency, marital discord, substance abuse. Public and private agencies might still overlap at points, and might be assisting one family simultaneously, but the imaginary line dividing them seemed more visible by 1940.

Along with more specialized functions had come more cooperative relations between the public and private parts of the welfare system. The tensions that flared repeatedly in the past were smoothed over, not only by the separation of their activities, but also by the mutual acceptance of modern standards of social casework. Both public and private charities practiced nearly identical forms of casework, operating under a common set of assumptions about poverty, poor relief, and the recipients of poor relief. Caseworkers, whether employed by the city's Social Service Bureau or the private Family Welfare Society, had often trained at the same School of Social Work in Richmond. Professional staff frequently moved from one agency to another, shifting from public to private charities (and vice versa) and helping to standardize practice between them in the process.

Federal programs resulted in an expansion of the responsibilities and the power of Richmond's city welfare department (see table 22). Richmond's small mothers' aid program, now incorporated into the federal program Aid to Dependent Children, expanded its coverage and raised its benefits. In the first months of operation of ADC, the number of Richmond families receiving assistance rose to thirty-seven, and the average grant per family rose to more than forty dollars per month.[23]

The New Deal's social-welfare programs also had important ramifications for Richmond's almshouse. Although a few contemporaries thought the New Deal might be used to sustain the almshouse system—such as the correspondent from Herdon, Virginia, who had attempted to get federal funds for "making over the Poorhouse in Fairfax County"[24]—most of the social-welfare community saw the demise of the poorhouse as a happy outcome of the New Deal. While the New Deal had not necessarily targeted almshouses for closure, many of its programs (old-age insurance, old-age assistance, and aid to dependent children) provided funds to people who had traditionally been consigned to the almshouses. Many such people were able to withdraw from the almshouse and live independently with the federal aid. (Richmond's almshouse population peaked in 1935, with 503 residents, and declined every year thereafter.)[25] The previously existing national movement to close almshouses thereby received an indirect boost from the federal programs.

Those almshouses that remained open, like the one in Richmond, saw their populations change, as the chronically ill and the infirm became the bulk of the remaining residents. (Old-age assistance and old-age insurance did little to help the elderly who were physically incapacitated or needed extensive medical care.) More clearly than before, almshouses became public infirmaries, often with elderly patients as their clientele. Too feeble to care for themselves in their own homes, with chronic conditions that could not always be cured by hospitalization, this group of elderly poor helped to turn almshouses into public nursing homes.[26]

In Richmond, this transition was made official in 1959, when the name of the City Home was changed to the Richmond Nursing Home.[27] Once the centerpiece of the city's welfare program, the almshouse came to play a reduced role in a much-enlarged public-welfare system. For generations, the poorhouse/almshouse/City Home had been an important civic institution, central to the lives of many families. Thousands of babies had entered the world there; thousands of other Richmonders had left the world there, some of whom were buried on

Richmond City Home, undated photograph. The home served as a monument to a community's civic ideal. Courtesy of the Library of Virginia.

the grounds in the "potter's field." Despite the former importance of the city almshouse, few mourned its passing.

The almshouse, after all, represented the thinking of an earlier age. It symbolized as nothing else did the old poor laws, which had finally been swept away by the welfare state with an emphatic "good riddance" behind them. The fact that subsequent generations have come to be as critical of the welfare state as we once were of the poor laws should not rekindle any former appreciation for the old facilities. A return to the almshouse will not fix what is wrong with our current welfare system.

I would suggest, however, that there was still something positive lost with the passing of the almshouse. In Richmond, at least, if not in other communities, the almshouse was not only a symbol of the flawed poor laws. The City Home also stood as a visible reminder of community responsibility to the poor. It embodied a community's civic ideal and stood as testament to a society's mutual obligations. Twenty-first-century Americans have no such monuments. Our welfare state is an amorphous bureaucracy with no marble statuary or granite pillars to represent mutual responsibilities. While we build monuments by the hundreds to honor military service to one's country, we have no equivalent memorial to our communal obligations to one another.

The City Home, designed to impress visitors and residents alike with the gravity of the city's response to need, stood as just that kind of monument. Like a good monument should, it could inspire (or shame) observers to action. Its presence offered unabated reproach to those who ignored poverty in the community. Unlike the tax deductions taken from a paycheck and used for anonymously provided services, the City Home was something tangible and concrete. Taxpayers could see what their money did, and perhaps even feel good about its effect. The modern welfare state offers few such positive reinforcements to taxpayers, and few positive reminders of a society's mutual obligations to its members.

APPENDIX

Table 1A. Population of Richmond, 1790–1940 (by race)

Year	Total	White	%	Black	%
1790	3,761	2,017	53.6%	1,694	45.0%
1800	5,737	2,837	49.5%	2,900	50.5%
1810	9,735	4,798	49.3%	4,937	50.7%
1820	12,067	6,622	54.9%	5,622	46.6%
1830	16,060	7,755	48.3%	8,305	51.7%
1840	20,153	10,718	53.2%	9,435	46.8%
1850	27,570	15,274	55.4%	12,296	44.6%
1860	37,910	23,635	62.3%	14,275	37.7%
1870	51,038	27,928	54.7%	23,110	45.2%
1880	63,600	35,705	56.2%	27,832	43.7%
1890	81,388	49,034	60.3%	32,354	39.8%
1900	85,050	52,798	62.1%	32,230	37.9%
1910	127,628	80,879	63.4%	46,733	36.6%
1920	171,667	117,574	68.5%	54,041	31.5%
1930	182,929	125,825	68.8%	52,988	29.0%
1940	193,042	131,706	66.5%	61,251	31.7%

Source: U.S. census returns.

Table 1B. Population of Richmond, 1790–1940 (by nativity)

Year	Total	Foreign-born	%
1790	3,761	*	
1800	5,737	*	
1810	9,735	*	
1820	12,067	324	2.7%
1830	16,060	117	0.7%
1840	20,153	*	
1850	27,570	2,101	7.6%
1860	37,910	4,956	13.1%
1870	51,038	3,778	7.0%
1880	63,600	3,340	5.3%
1890	81,388	3,473	4.3%
1900	85,050	2,834	3.3%
1910	127,628	4,084	3.2%
1920	171,667	4,713	2.7%
1930	182,929	4,046	2.2%
1940	193,042	3,487	1.8%

Source: U.S. census returns.
*Not reported.

Table 2. City of Richmond, Public Poor Relief, 1818–1829

Year[*]	No. Receiving Aid			Indoor Poor				Outdoor Poor				Total Relief Costs
	White	Black	Total	No.	Expenditures	Cost per Pauper		No.	Expenditures	Cost per Pauper		
1818	350	10	360	60	$3,850.00	$64.17		300	$2,402.58	$8.01		$6,253
1819	350	10	360	60	$3,920.00	$65.33		300	$2,868.00	$9.56		$6,788
1820	350	10	360	60	$3,811.60	$63.53		300	$2,946.78	$9.82		$6,758
1821	354	9	363	63	$3,964.56	$62.93		300	$2,591.68	$8.64		$6,556
1822	418	10	428	78	$4,550.00	$58.33		350	$3,111.38	$8.89		$7,661
1823	426	12	438	88	$5,700.00	$64.77		350	$2,300.00	$6.57		$8,000
1824	440	12	452	102	$5,300.00	$51.96		350	$2,297.31	$6.56		$7,597
1825	359	12	371	71	$4,049.47	$57.03		300	$3,160.18	$10.53		$7,210
1826	352	12	364	64	$4,424.09	$69.13		300	$3,155.37	$10.52		$7,579
1827	409	15	424	78	$5,011.35	$64.25		356	$3,221.54	$9.05		$8,233
1828	411	14	425	69	$3,976.50	$57.63		356	$3,078.50	$8.65		$7,055
1829	390	12	402	66	$3,898.59	$59.07		336	$2,682.17	$7.98		$6,581

Sources: Auditors of Public Accounts, State of Virginia; Annual Reports, Overseers of the Poor, Richmond City, 16 June 1829.

[*]Year ending in May.

Table 3. City of Richmond, Public Poor Relief, 1830–1860

Year (ending)	Indoor Poor						Outdoor Poor			Total Relief Costs
	White	Black	Total	Avg. Daily Attendance	Expenditures	Cost per Pauper	No.	Expenditures	Cost per Pauper	
May 1830	57	10	67	*	$4,380	$65.38	356	$2,316.43	$6.51	$6,697
1831	67	17	84	*	$4,581	$54.54	334	$2,289.00	$6.85	$6,899
1832	68	18	86	*	$4,359	$50.69	359	$2,110.56	$5.88	$6,470
1833	116	15	131	65	$4,791	$36.57	66	$501.92	$7.60	$6,000
1834	52	18	70	*	$4,059	$57.99	0	*	*	$5,000
1842 †	128	30	158	79	$5,223	$33.06	*	*	*	*
1843	164	18	182	79	$5,061	$27.81	23	$266.00	$11.57	$5,327
1844	155	24	179	*	$4,607	$25.74	35	$333.00	$9.51	$4,940
1845	183	24	207	*	$5,247	$25.35	8 to 10	$67.02	*	$5,314
1846	161	41	202	*	$5,804	$28.73	8 to 10	$109.00	*	$5,913
1847	196	44	240	107	$5,813	$24.22	20 to 25	$155.50	*	$5,969
1849	246	45	291	102	$5,359	$18.42	*	*	*	*
1850	217	49	266	99	$5,606	$21.07	12	$53.95	$4.50	$5,659
March 1851	205	31	236	*	$5,286	$22.40	6	*	*	*
1852	245	41	286	117	$7,079	$24.75	6	*	*	*
1853	282	38	321	124	*	*	7	$114.50	$16.36	$8,197
1855	325	51	376	132	$8,064	$21.45	7	$132.56	$18.94	$8,197
1856	389	46	435	141	$9,673	$22.24	6	$105.00	$17.50	$9,778
1857	376	32	408	133	$9,825	$24.08	7	$103.00	$14.71	$9,928
1858	446	43	489	161	$11,221	$22.95	4	$140.12	$35.03	$11,361
1859	396	28	424	157	$9,959	$23.49	6	$137.25	$22.88	$10,096
1860	386	29	415	133	$10,393	$25.04	*	$151.12		$10,544

Sources: Auditors of Public Accounts, State of Virginia; Annual Reports, Overseers of the Poor, Richmond City (broken series).

* Not reported.

† Records from 1835 to 1841 are lacking.

Table 4. Poorhouse Residents in Antebellum Richmond

	1836–37 Report[§]		1850–51 Report[‖]		1850 Census[#]		1860 Census[#]	
	No.	%	No.	%	No.	%	No.	%
Total	183		236		99		123	
Male	102	56%	113	48%	43	43%	70	57%
Female	81	44%	123	52%	56	57%	53	43%
White	145	79%	205	87%	78	79%	108	88%
Black	38	21%	31	13%	21	21%	15	12%
Illness [†]	52	28%	64	27%	n/a		n/a	
Injury	18	10%	19	8%	n/a		n/a	
Old Age	8	4%	77	33%	n/a		n/a	
Dependent [‡]	7	4%	48	20%	n/a		n/a	
Alcohol Related	10	5%	111	47%	n/a		n/a	
Runaways	9	5%	21	9%	n/a		n/a	
Unable to Work	*		155	66%	n/a		n/a	
Able to Work	*		81	34%	n/a		n/a	
Avg. No. Days Worked	*		64.62	n/a	n/a		n/a	
Native-born	*		*		90	91%	62	50%
Foreign-born	*		*		9	9%	61	50%
Average Age	*		*		41.1	n/a	39.8	n/a

* Not reported.

[†] Includes pregnancy.

[‡] Includes insane, crippled, orphans.

[§] As reported to the Auditor of Public Accounts. Numbers are cumulative, from 1 June 1836 to 1 June 1837.

[‖] As reported to the Auditor of Public Accounts. Numbers are cumulative, from 1 June 1850 to 31 March 1851.

[#] Census figures are not cumulative; lists only those present on census day.

Table 5. State of Virginia, Expenditures on Non-Confederate Welfare, 1871–1941

Year Ending	Total State Expenditures	Total Expenditures on Non-Confederate Welfare	Non-Confederate Welfare as % of Budget	Categories of Non-Confederate Welfare Reported				
				Asylums‡	Reformatories	State Board of Charities	Comm. for the Blind	Misc. Public Outlays
Sep. 30, 1871	$1,505,650	$192,775	12.8%	$192,349				$426#
Sep. 30, 1872	$2,146,276	$238,095	11.1%	$238,095				
Sep. 30, 1873	$2,459,543	$221,538	9.0%	$221,538				
Sep. 30, 1874	$3,301,620	$179,255	5.4%	$179,255				
Sep. 30, 1875	$2,814,614	$224,670	8.0%	$224,670				
Sep. 30, 1876	$3,773,502	$240,278	6.4%	$240,278				
Sep. 30, 1877	$3,044,865	$207,951	6.8%	$207,951				
Sep. 30, 1878	$2,997,067	$212,095	7.1%	$212,095				
Sep. 30, 1879	$2,811,860	$227,020	8.1%	$227,020				
Sep. 30, 1880	$2,718,550	$303,792	11.2%	$303,792				
Sep. 30, 1881	$2,281,890	$379,072	16.6%	$379,072				
Sep. 30, 1882	$3,585,612	$395,081	11.0%	$395,081				
Sep. 30, 1883	$2,714,431	*	[insufficient data]	*				
Sep. 30, 1884	$3,369,577	$285,350	8.5%	$285,350				
Sep. 30, 1885	$2,931,908	$435,032	14.8%	$435,032				
Sep. 30, 1886	$2,755,036	$416,145	15.1%	$416,145				
Sep. 30, 1887	$2,626,713	$380,753	14.5%	$380,753				
Sep. 30, 1888	$2,891,730	$381,013	13.2%	$381,013				
Sep. 30, 1889	$2,648,675	$342,965	12.9%	$342,965				

(continued)

Table 5. (continued)

Year Ending	Total State Expenditures	Total Expenditures on Non-Confederate Welfare	Non-Confederate Welfare as % of Budget	Categories of Non-Confederate Welfare Reported				
				Asylums‡	Reformatories	State Board of Charities	Comm. for the Blind	Misc. Public Outlays
Sep. 30, 1890	$2,695,659	$378,811	14.1%	$378,811				
Sep. 30, 1891	$2,491,177	$377,010	15.1%	$377,010				
Sep. 30, 1892	$3,350,123	$428,880	12.8%	$428,880				
Sep. 30, 1893	$3,754,629	$381,797	10.2%	$381,797				
Sep. 30, 1894	$3,602,571	$385,730	10.7%	$385,730				
Sep. 30, 1895	$3,404,097	$406,332	11.9%	$406,332				
Sep. 30, 1896	$3,347,399	$348,187	10.4%	$348,187				
Sep. 30, 1897	$3,151,282	$346,139	11.0%	$346,139				
Sep. 30, 1898	$3,200,258	$328,712	10.3%	$328,712				
Sep. 30, 1899	$3,111,431	$336,872	10.8%	$336,872				
Sep. 30, 1900	$3,535,343	$406,331	11.5%	$406,331				
Sep. 30, 1901	$3,597,881	$377,615	10.5%	$377,615				
Sep. 30, 1902	$3,948,267	$482,218	12.2%	$472,001	$10,217			
Sep. 30, 1903	$4,076,716	$467,389	11.5%	$467,389				
Sep. 30, 1904	$4,239,396	$453,862	10.7%	$453,862				
Sep. 30, 1905	$4,428,776	$422,400	9.5%	$422,400				
Sep. 30, 1906	$4,954,693	$452,055	9.1%	$441,264	$10,791			
Sep. 30, 1907	$5,063,430	$461,047	9.1%	$461,047				
Sep. 30, 1908	$5,786,019	$545,232	9.4%	$542,232	$3,000			
Sep. 30, 1909	$5,795,191	$549,094	9.5%	$525,056	$15,888	$8,149		
Sep. 30, 1910	$6,099,480	$567,021	9.3%	$559,929	$2,500	$4,592		
Sep. 30, 1911	$6,530,040	$498,000	7.6%	$491,500		$6,500		

Year Ending	Total State Expenditures	Total Expenditures on Non-Confederate Welfare	Non-Confederate Welfare as % of Budget	Categories of Non-Confederate Welfare Reported				
				Asylums‡	Reformatories	State Board of Charities	Comm. for the Blind	Misc. Public Outlays
Sep. 30, 1912	$7,183,468	$668,924	9.3%	$594,276	$67,273	$7,375		
Sep. 30, 1913	$7,118,578	$770,877	10.8%	$717,552	$46,783	$6,542		
Sep. 30, 1914	$7,645,357	$789,989	10.3%	$752,258	$30,495	$7,237		
Sep. 30, 1915	$7,994,572	$815,338	10.2%	$761,836	$42,574	$10,928		
Sep. 30, 1916	$8,353,992	$843,185	10.1%	$791,251	$41,944	$9,990		
Sep. 30, 1917	$9,094,126	$804,533	8.8%	$695,596	$99,758	$9,179		
Sep. 30, 1918	$9,176,603	$1,040,286	11.3%	$911,645	$119,462	$9,179		
Sep. 30, 1919	$12,651,765	$1,022,960	8.1%	$856,962	$154,074	$11,924		
Sep. 30, 1920	$16,517,994	$1,416,827	8.6%	$1,214,103	$197,191	$5,533		
Sep. 30, 1921	$22,065,405	$1,355,509	6.1%	$1,345,813		$5,696		$4,000 ‖
Sep. 30, 1922	$23,702,202	$1,363,572	5.8%	$1,104,914	$251,568	$7,091		
Sep. 30, 1923	$26,562,013	$1,382,789	5.2%	$1,146,659	$195,668	$8,438	$10,171	$21,853 §
June 30, 1925 †	$33,108,973	$1,286,039	3.9%	$1,062,213	$160,284	$27,584	$9,650	$26,308 §
June 30, 1926	$32,371,261	$1,344,412	4.2%	$1,092,922	$185,023	$29,170	$17,819	$19,478 §
June 30, 1927	$41,282,826	$1,624,555	3.9%	$1,332,494	$201,712	$39,022	$22,441	$21,325 §	$7,561 ‖
June 30, 1928	$38,361,851	$1,492,933	3.9%	$1,204,914	$222,974	$44,979	$20,066	
June 30, 1929	$41,690,997	$70,158	0.2%	$2,212,364	$263,212	$70,158		
June 30, 1930	$46,635,575	$1,692,502	3.6%	$1,350,264	$204,079	$94,013	$44,146	
June 30, 1931	$53,238,371	$1,796,303	3.4%	$1,449,315	$218,605	$87,105	$41,278	
June 30, 1932	$47,334,110	$1,679,931	3.5%	$1,328,607	$218,609	$97,122	$35,593	
June 30, 1933	$43,431,645	$1,486,490	3.4%	$1,172,106	$208,876	$77,963	$27,545	
June 30, 1934	$44,987,273	$1,530,631	3.4%	$1,214,707	$187,530	$100,326	$28,068	

(continued)

Table 5. (continued)

Year Ending	Total State Expenditures	Total Expenditures on Non-Confederate Welfare	Non-Confederate Welfare as % of Budget	Categories of Non-Confederate Welfare Reported				
				Asylums‡	Reformatories	State Board of Charities	Comm. for the Blind	Misc. Public Outlays
June 30, 1935	$56,956,367	$1,754,645	3.1%	$1,404,428	$221,014	$99,981	$29,222	
June 30, 1936	$60,705,931	$1,595,601	2.6%	$1,241,628	$231,038	$106,622	$16,314	
June 30, 1937	$71,614,336	$2,872,958	4.0%	$1,553,028	$282,665	$977,610	$58,156	$1,500**
June 30, 1938	$84,459,660	$6,266,826	7.4%	$1,652,140	$258,595	$189,672	$58,250	$808,527†† $3,299,642‡‡
June 30, 1941	$90,684,744	$6,542,094	7.2%	$287,526	$21,968	$4,886,983	$376,114	$969,504‡‡

Source: Annual reports, Auditor of Public Accounts, State of Va., various years.

* Not reported.
† Report for 21 months ending June 30.
‡ Includes "lunatics" in county jails, state insane hospitals, Colony for Feeble-Minded, and Asylum for Deaf, Dumb, and Blind.
§ State maternity fund.
‖ Home for Incurables.
For transport of colored paupers.
** Negro Organization Society.
†† Public Assistance Act of 1938.
‡‡ Unemployment Compensation.

Table 6. State of Virginia, Expenditures on Confederate Welfare, 1871–1938

| | Categories of Confederate Welfare Reported | | | | | | | Total Confederate Welfare | Total State Expenditures | Confederate Welfare as % of Whole |
| | Veterans | | | Widows | | Other | | | | |
Year Ending	Limbs/Medical	Pensions†	Home	Home	Pensions	Memorial Associations	Misc.			
Sep. 30, 1871								$0	$1,505,650	0.0%
Sep. 30, 1872	$7,092	$7,920					$1,500§	$15,012	$2,146,276	0.7%
Sep. 30, 1873	$2,483	$18,000						$20,483	$2,459,543	0.8%
Sep. 30, 1874	$1,424	$4,326						$5,750	$3,301,620	0.2%
Sep. 30, 1875	$490	$3,120						$3,610	$2,814,614	0.1%
Sep. 30, 1876		$6,000						$6,000	$3,773,502	0.2%
Sep. 30, 1877		$9,900						$9,900	$3,044,865	0.3%
Sep. 30, 1878		$15,100						$15,100	$2,997,067	0.5%
Sep. 30, 1879		$13,950						$13,950	$2,811,860	0.5%
Sep. 30, 1880	$320	‡						$320	$2,718,550	0.0%
Sep. 30, 1881	$40	‡						$40	$2,281,890	0.0%
Sep. 30, 1882	$150	$39,330						$39,480	$3,585,612	1.1%
Sep. 30, 1883	$150	‡						$150	$2,714,431	0.0%
Sep. 30, 1884	$30	$59,340						$59,370	$3,369,577	1.8%
Sep. 30, 1885		$60,150						$60,150	$2,931,908	2.1%
Sep. 30, 1886		$83,040	$5,460					$88,500	$2,755,036	3.2%
Sep. 30, 1887		$71,880	$10,600			$1,000		$83,480	$2,626,713	3.2%
Sep. 30, 1888		$65,223	$9,820					$75,043	$2,891,730	2.6%
Sep. 30, 1889		$65,607	$10,420					$76,027	$2,648,675	2.9%
Sep. 30, 1890		$116,190	$11,410					$127,600	$2,695,659	4.7%
Sep. 30, 1891		$85,680	$8,950					$94,630	$2,491,177	3.8%

(continued)

Table 6. (continued)

| Year Ending | Veterans | | Widows | | Other | | Total Confederate Welfare | Total State Expenditures | Confederate Welfare as % of Whole |
	Limbs/Medical	Pensions†	Home	Pensions	Memorial Associations	Misc.			
Sep. 30, 1892		$99,205	$15,221				$114,426	$3,350,123	3.4%
Sep. 30, 1893		$97,100	$27,038				$124,138	$3,754,629	3.3%
Sep. 30, 1894	$422	$109,705	$37,388				$147,515	$3,602,571	4.1%
Sep. 30, 1895	$86	$110,260	$30,000				$140,346	$3,404,097	4.1%
Sep. 30, 1896	$65	$110,800	$32,500				$143,365	$3,347,399	4.3%
Sep. 30, 1897		$108,125	$32,500				$140,625	$3,151,282	4.5%
Sep. 30, 1898		$108,095	$35,000				$143,095	$3,200,258	4.5%
Sep. 30, 1899		$106,235	$35,000				$141,235	$3,111,431	4.5%
Sep. 30, 1900		$125,373	$35,000			$1,000"	$160,373	$3,535,343	4.5%
Sep. 30, 1901		$130,553	$35,000				$165,553	$3,597,881	4.6%
Sep. 30, 1902		$204,591	$45,000		$1,220		$250,811	$3,948,267	6.4%
Sep. 30, 1903		$346,616	$35,000		$1,435		$383,051	$4,076,716	9.4%
Sep. 30, 1904		$310,854	$35,000	$5,000	$1,550		$352,404	$4,239,396	8.3%
Sep. 30, 1905		$313,499	$35,000				$348,499	$4,428,776	7.9%
Sep. 30, 1906		$346,008	$35,000		$1,505		$382,513	$4,954,693	7.7%
Sep. 30, 1907		$339,617	$35,000		$1,695		$376,312	$5,063,430	7.4%
Sep. 30, 1908		$430,035	$41,000		$4,145		$475,180	$5,786,019	8.2%
Sep. 30, 1909		$438,369	$47,000		$2,645		$488,014	$5,795,191	8.4%
Sep. 30, 1910		$369,373	$46,667	$280	$2,710		$419,030	$6,099,480	6.9%
Sep. 30, 1911		$520,000	$46,000		$2,540		$568,540	$6,530,040	8.7%

| | | Categories of Confederate Welfare Reported | | | | | | Total | | |
| | Veterans | | | Widows | | Other | | Confederate | Total State | Confederate Welfare |
Year Ending	Limbs/Medical	Pensions†	Home	Home	Pensions	Memorial Associations	Misc.	Welfare	Expenditures	as % of Whole
Sep. 30, 1912	$2,345	$718,248	$45,667	$743		$3,220	$1,779	$770,222	$7,183,468	10.7%
Sep. 30, 1913		$455,439	$45,667		$2,830	$3,155	$1,388#	$508,869	$7,118,578	7.1%
Sep. 30, 1914		$516,016	$52,533	$5,000	$3,813	$2,275	$1,001	$579,638	$7,645,357	7.6%
Sep. 30, 1915		$498,864	$49,488	$5,000	$5,305	$2,590		$562,248	$7,994,572	7.0%
Sep. 30, 1916	$1,836	$547,993	$56,480	$4,000	$6,063	$2,190		$618,562	$8,353,992	7.4%
Sep. 30, 1917		$520,954	$61,420	$9,000	$6,538	$3,030	$1,251.30#	$600,941	$9,094,126	6.6%
Sep. 30, 1918		$726,750	$89,392	$5,833	$8,084	$2,220	$765#	$832,279	$9,176,603	9.1%
Sep. 30, 1919		$699,561	$86,950	$10,000	$10,162	$2,490	$600#	$809,163	$12,651,765	6.4%
Sep. 30, 1920		$839,278	$80,166	$11,167	$10,100	$2,450	$610#	$943,160	$16,517,994	5.7%
Sep. 30, 1921		$823,018	$78,572	$12,000		$2,695	$660#	$916,285	$22,065,405	4.2%
Sep. 30, 1922	$1,767	$777,768	$88,182	$12,000	$10,025	$2,520		$892,262	$23,702,202	3.8%
Sep. 30, 1923	$979	$970,057	$96,476	$12,000	$9,875	$2,580		$1,091,967	$26,562,013	4.1%
June 30, 1925*	$1,395	$957,675	$95,068	$12,000	$10,088	$2,595		$1,078,821	$33,108,973	3.3%
June 30, 1926	$898	$947,508	$93,202	$12,333	$10,488	$4,195		$1,068,624	$32,371,261	3.3%
June 30, 1927		$966,066	$95,320	$15,167	$11,288	$3,665	$714.90#	$1,091,505	$41,282,826	2.6%
June 30, 1928		$1,075,090	$87,598			$3,620	$1,250	$1,167,558	$38,361,851	3.0%
June 30, 1929		$1,118,546	$86,910			$3,880		$1,209,336	$41,690,997	2.9%
June 30, 1930		$944,901	$90,304	$10,623	$8,288	$4,690	$1,875	$1,060,680	$46,635,575	2.3%
June 30, 1931		$1,118,974	$75,882	$14,334	$14,863	$4,650	$1,625	$1,230,328	$53,238,371	2.3%
June 30, 1932		$998,011	$60,187	$20,213	$14,063	$4,050		$1,096,524	$47,334,110	2.3%

(continued)

Table 6. (continued)

	Categories of Confederate Welfare Reported							Total Confederate Welfare	Total State Expenditures	Confederate Welfare as % of Whole
	Veterans		Widows		Other					
Year Ending	Limbs/Medical	Pensions[†]	Home	Home	Pensions	Memorial Associations	Misc.			
June 30, 1933		$756,034	$36,633	$15,663	$21,138	$3,670		$833,137	$43,431,645	1.9%
June 30, 1934		$666,634	$27,571	$18,738	$17,518	$4,853		$735,314	$44,987,273	1.6%
June 30, 1935		$656,168	$33,400	$22,296	$24,970	$4,894		$741,728	$56,956,367	1.3%
June 30, 1936		$569,824	$31,481	$27,185	$25,025	$4,877		$658,392	$60,705,931	1.1%
June 30, 1937		$530,485	$23,534	$24,326	$27,988	$6,180		$612,513	$71,614,336	0.9%
June 30, 1938		$494,836	$27,039	$25,273	$28,013	$6,015	$1,280	$582,456	$84,459,660	0.7%

Source: Annual reports, Auditor of Public Accounts, State of Va.

* Report for 21 months ending June 30.

† Includes "commutations."

‡ There were no line item reports of pensions for these years. Pensions may have been included in other budget lines.

§ Listed as "removal and reburial."

‖ Ladies Auxiliary, Lee Camp.

Listed as "misc. needy veterans."

Table 7. Comparative Data on Confederate Welfare in Southern States, 1914

State	Year Soldiers' Home Established	No. of Inmates in Home, 1914	Appropriation for Home, 1914	Year Pensions First Paid	Pensions Paid in 1914	Annual Pensions to Veterans and Widows	Total Expended on Pensions and Home Since 1865	No. of Veterans on Pension Rolls	No. of Widows on Pension Rolls
Ala.	1902	86	$12,000	1889	$925,000	$64	$10,718,000	8,000	6,500
Ark.	1891	108	$37,500	1892	$625,000	$50	$5,500,000	4,985	4,985
Fla.	1891	23	$5,850	1885	$624,000	$120	$6,514,000	2,646	2,542
Ga.	1901	132	$30,000	1889	$1,125,000	$60	$17,750,000	10,000	7,000
Ky.	1892	210	$38,850	1913	$281,000	$120	$985,000	1,800	900
La.	1882	125	$48,000	1898	$550,000	$96	$3,567,000	3,234	2,256
Md.	1888	87	$15,500	none	none	none	$360,500	none	none *
Miss.	1904	230	$40,000	1888	$450,000	$40	$5,504,000	9,635	*
Mo.	1895	309	$60,000	none	none	none	$730,000	none	none
N.C.	1891	160	$35,000	1885	$450,000	$32	$6,000,000	9,274	6,242
Okla.	1911	95	$17,500	1915	none	$120	$125,000	none	none
S.C.	1909	90	$16,600	1887	$258,528	$36	$3,625,000	4,130	4,732
Tenn.	1889	92	$16,000	1891	$800,000	$100	$7,500,000	5,094	3,189
Tex.	1891	365	$96,000	1899	$850,000	$90	$6,300,000	18,000	*
Va.	1884	274	$50,000	1888	$540,000	$30	$6,645,000	9,207	5,013
W.Va.	none	none	none	none	none	none	none	none	none
Total		2386	$518,800		$7,478,528		$81,823,500	86,005	43,359

Source: *Confederate Veteran* 23 (June 1915): 155. N.B.: *I have corrected math errors in original totals.*

* "Both sexes."

Table 8. State of Virginia, Combined Expenditures on Welfare, 1871–1938

Year Ending	Total State Expenditures	Total Confed. Welfare	Confed. Welfare as %	Total Non-Confed. Welfare	Non-Confed. Welfare as %	Total of Confed. and Non-Confed. Welfare	All Welfare as %
Sep. 30, 1871	$1,505,650	$0	0.0%	$192,775	12.8%	$192,775	12.8%
Sep. 30, 1872	$2,146,276	$16,512	0.8%	$238,095	11.1%	$254,607	11.9%
Sep. 30, 1873	$2,459,543	$20,483	0.8%	$221,538	9.0%	$242,021	9.8%
Sep. 30, 1874	$3,301,620	$5,750	0.2%	$179,255	5.4%	$185,005	5.6%
Sep. 30, 1875	$2,814,614	$3,610	0.1%	$224,670	8.0%	$228,280	8.1%
Sep. 30, 1876	$3,773,502	$6,000	0.2%	$240,278	6.4%	$246,278	6.5%
Sep. 30, 1877	$3,044,865	$9,900	0.3%	$207,951	6.8%	$217,851	7.2%
Sep. 30, 1878	$2,997,067	$15,100	0.5%	$212,095	7.1%	$227,195	7.6%
Sep. 30, 1879	$2,811,860	$13,950	0.5%	$227,020	8.1%	$240,970	8.6%
Sep. 30, 1880	$2,718,550	$320	0.0%	$303,792	11.2%	$304,112	11.2%
Sep. 30, 1881	$2,281,890	$136	0.0%	$379,072	16.6%	$379,208	16.6%
Sep. 30, 1882	$3,585,612	$39,330	1.1%	$395,081	11.0%	$434,411	12.1%
Sep. 30, 1883	$2,714,431	$150	0.0%	$0	0.0%	$150	0.0%
Sep. 30, 1884	$3,369,577	$59,370	1.8%	$285,350	8.5%	$344,720	10.2%
Sep. 30, 1885	$2,931,908	$60,150	2.1%	$435,032	14.8%	$495,182	16.9%
Sep. 30, 1886	$2,755,036	$88,500	3.2%	$416,145	15.1%	$504,645	18.3%
Sep. 30, 1887	$2,626,713	$83,480	3.2%	$380,753	14.5%	$464,233	17.7%
Sep. 30, 1888	$2,891,730	$75,043	2.6%	$381,013	13.2%	$456,056	15.8%
Sep. 30, 1889	$2,648,675	$76,027	2.9%	$342,965	12.9%	$418,992	15.8%
Sep. 30, 1890	$2,695,659	$127,600	4.7%	$378,811	14.1%	$506,411	18.8%
Sep. 30, 1891	$2,491,177	$94,630	3.8%	$377,010	15.1%	$471,640	18.9%
Sep. 30, 1892	$3,350,123	$114,426	3.4%	$428,880	12.8%	$543,306	16.2%
Sep. 30, 1893	$3,754,629	$124,138	3.3%	$381,797	10.2%	$505,935	13.5%

Year Ending	Total State Expenditures	Total Confed. Welfare	Confed. Welfare as %	Total Non-Confed. Welfare	Non-Confed. Welfare as %	Total of Confed. and Non-Confed. Welfare	All Welfare as %
Sep. 30, 1894	$3,602,571	$147,515	4.1%	$385,730	10.7%	$533,245	14.8%
Sep. 30, 1895	$3,404,097	$140,346	4.1%	$406,332	11.9%	$546,678	16.1%
Sep. 30, 1896	$3,347,399	$143,365	4.3%	$348,187	10.4%	$491,552	14.7%
Sep. 30, 1897	$3,151,282	$140,625	4.5%	$346,139	11.0%	$486,764	15.4%
Sep. 30, 1898	$3,200,258	$143,095	4.5%	$328,712	10.3%	$471,807	14.7%
Sep. 30, 1899	$3,111,431	$141,235	4.5%	$336,872	10.8%	$478,107	15.4%
Sep. 30, 1900	$3,535,343	$161,373	4.6%	$406,331	11.5%	$567,704	16.1%
Sep. 30, 1901	$3,597,881	$165,553	4.6%	$377,615	10.5%	$543,168	15.1%
Sep. 30, 1902	$3,948,267	$250,811	6.4%	$482,218	12.2%	$733,029	18.6%
Sep. 30, 1903	$4,076,716	$383,051	9.4%	$467,389	11.5%	$850,440	20.9%
Sep. 30, 1904	$4,239,396	$352,404	8.3%	$453,862	10.7%	$806,266	19.0%
Sep. 30, 1905	$4,428,776	$348,499	7.9%	$422,400	9.5%	$770,899	17.4%
Sep. 30, 1906	$4,954,693	$382,513	7.7%	$452,055	9.1%	$834,568	16.8%
Sep. 30, 1907	$5,063,430	$376,312	7.4%	$461,047	9.1%	$837,359	16.5%
Sep. 30, 1908	$5,786,019	$475,180	8.2%	$545,232	9.4%	$1,020,412	17.6%
Sep. 30, 1909	$5,795,191	$488,014	8.4%	$549,094	9.5%	$1,037,108	17.9%
Sep. 30, 1910	$6,099,480	$419,030	6.9%	$567,021	9.3%	$986,051	16.2%
Sep. 30, 1911	$6,530,040	$568,540	8.7%	$498,000	7.6%	$1,066,540	16.3%
Sep. 30, 1912	$7,183,468	$770,222	10.7%	$668,924	9.3%	$1,439,146	20.0%
Sep. 30, 1913	$7,118,578	$508,869	7.1%	$770,877	10.8%	$1,279,746	18.0%
Sep. 30, 1914	$7,645,357	$581,026	7.6%	$789,989	10.3%	$1,371,015	17.9%
Sep. 30, 1915	$7,994,572	$562,248	7.0%	$815,338	10.2%	$1,377,586	17.2%
Sep. 30, 1916	$8,353,992	$618,562	7.4%	$843,185	10.1%	$1,461,747	17.5%
Sep. 30, 1917	$9,094,126	$602,182	6.6%	$804,533	8.8%	$1,406,715	15.5%

(continued)

Table 8. (continued)

Year Ending	Total State Expenditures	Total Confed. Welfare	Confed. Welfare as %	Total Non-Confed. Welfare	Non-Confed. Welfare as %	Total of Confed. and Non-Confed. Welfare	All Welfare as %
Sep. 30, 1918	$9,176,603	$833,044	9.1%	$1,040,286	11.3%	$1,873,330	20.4%
Sep. 30, 1919	$12,651,765	$809,763	6.4%	$1,022,960	8.1%	$1,832,723	14.5%
Sep. 30, 1920	$16,517,994	$943,770	5.7%	$1,416,817	8.6%	$2,360,587	14.3%
Sep. 30, 1921	$22,065,405	$916,945	4.2%	$1,355,509	6.1%	$2,272,454	10.3%
Sep. 30, 1922	$23,702,202	$892,262	3.8%	$1,363,572	5.8%	$2,255,834	9.5%
Sep. 30, 1923	$26,562,013	$1,091,967	4.1%	$1,382,789	5.2%	$2,474,756	9.3%
June 30, 1925*	$33,108,973	$1,078,821	3.3%	$1,286,039	3.9%	$2,364,860	7.1%
June 30, 1926	$32,371,261	$1,068,624	3.3%	$1,344,412	4.2%	$2,413,036	7.5%
June 30, 1927	$41,282,826	$1,092,220	2.6%	$1,624,555	3.9%	$2,716,775	6.6%
June 30, 1928	$38,361,851	$1,167,558	3.0%	$1,492,933	3.9%	$2,660,491	6.9%
June 30, 1929	$41,690,997	$1,209,336	2.9%	$70,158	0.2%	$1,279,494	3.1%
June 30, 1930	$46,635,575	$1,060,680	2.3%	$1,692,502	3.6%	$2,753,182	5.9%
June 30, 1931	$53,238,371	$1,230,328	2.3%	$1,796,303	3.4%	$3,026,631	5.7%
June 30, 1932	$47,334,110	$1,096,524	2.3%	$1,679,931	3.5%	$2,776,455	5.9%
June 30, 1933	$43,431,645	$833,137	1.9%	$1,486,490	3.4%	$2,319,627	5.3%
June 30, 1934	$44,987,273	$735,314	1.6%	$1,530,631	3.4%	$2,265,945	5.0%
June 30, 1935	$56,956,367	$741,728	1.3%	$1,754,645	3.1%	$2,496,373	4.4%
June 30, 1936	$60,705,931	$658,392	1.1%	$1,595,601	2.6%	$2,253,993	3.7%
June 30, 1937	$71,614,336	$612,513	0.9%	$2,872,958	4.0%	$3,485,471	4.9%
June 30, 1938	$84,459,660	$582,456	0.7%	$6,266,826	7.4%	$6,849,282	8.1%

Source: Annual reports, Auditor of Public Accounts, State of Va.

* Report for 21 months ending June 30.

Table 9. City of Richmond, Indoor Relief, 1874–1935

Year Ending	Total Admissions for Year	Avg. No. Present per Day	Cost per Capita per Annum
Jan. 31, 1874	471	228	$50.00
Jan. 31, 1875	446	245	$129.22
Jan. 31, 1877	691	258	$118.53
Dec. 26, 1879	584	*	*
Dec. 26, 1880	659	*	*
Jan. 31, 1881	704	244	$104.37
Jan. 31, 1883	834	261	$113.66
Jan. 31, 1885	785	296	$102.93
Dec. 31, 1886	707	*	*
Dec. 31, 1888	698	255	$111.72
Dec. 31, 1889	655	252	$109.26
Dec. 31, 1890	804	282	$110.51
Dec. 31, 1891	741	279	$107.53
Dec. 31, 1892	722	263	$115.99
Dec. 31, 1893	726	235	$125.67
Dec. 31, 1895	843	256	$99.52
Dec. 31, 1896	847	251	$93.44
Jan. 31, 1898	908	235	$95.63
1901 [May 1?]	1,272	228	$99.78
1910 [May 1?]	1,466	236	$149.19
Jan. 31, 1919	1,232	269	$238.26
Year 1920	*	228	$0.74/day
Year 1921	913	245	*
Year 1922	*	*	$0.855/day
Year 1923	574	*	*
Year 1926	*	261	*
Year 1927	*	293	*
Year 1928	*	332	*
Year 1929	*	351	*
Year 1930	993	364	*
Year 1934	*	470	*
Year 1935	1,417	503	$163.89

Source: Annual reports, supt. of almshouse/public welfare, broken series.

* Not reported.

Table 10. City of Richmond, Annual Welfare Expenditures, 1870–1940

| Year Ending | Public Welfare | | | Grants to Private Charities | Total City Expenditures on Public and Private Welfare | Total City Budget | Public and Private Charity as % of Total Expenditures |
	For Almshouse	For Outdoor Poor	Total				
Jan. 31, 1870	$27,000	$14,850	$41,850	$4,000	$45,850	$582,149	8%
Jan. 31, 1874	$33,003	$7,888	$40,891	$4,375	$45,266	$2,049,599	2%
Jan. 31, 1875	$31,660	$14,328	$45,988	$4,000	$49,988	$1,495,718	3%
Jan. 31, 1876	$34,246	$9,565	$43,811	$4,000	$47,811	$1,480,588	3%
Jan. 31, 1877	$30,581	$9,965	$40,546	$4,125	$44,671	$1,309,188	3%
Jan. 31, 1880	$23,376	$8,500	$31,876	$6,715	$38,591	$1,077,175	4%
Jan. 31, 1881	$25,376	$7,500	$32,876	$5,890	$38,766	$1,255,720	3%
Jan. 31, 1882	$24,300	$7,500	$31,800	$9,750	$41,550	$1,528,344	3%
Dec. 31, 1885	$31,000	$7,000	$38,000	$4,650	$42,650	$1,471,499	3%
Dec. 31, 1886	$23,699	$5,501	$29,200	$6,248	$35,448	$1,555,180	2%
Dec. 31, 1888	$27,614	$7,099	$34,713	$9,272	$43,985	$2,139,543	2%
Dec. 31, 1889	$27,645	$6,499	$34,144	$9,188	$43,332	$2,098,464	2%
Dec. 31, 1890	$30,094	$6,466	$36,560	$5,638	$42,197	$2,258,345	2%
Dec. 31, 1891	$32,707	$7,000	$39,707	$10,568	$50,275	$2,594,355	2%
Dec. 31, 1892	$27,707	$7,000	$34,707	$8,863	$43,570	$2,127,887	2%
Dec. 31, 1893	$27,713	$9,534	$37,247	$9,288	$46,535	$2,423,689	2%
Jan. 31, 1901	$23,789	$8,284	$32,073	$7,750	$39,823	$1,638,514	2%
Jan. 31, 1902	$34,824	$8,749	$43,573	$12,300	$55,873	$1,535,620	4%
Jan. 31, 1903	$27,241	$9,656	$36,897	$12,371	$49,268	$1,834,694	3%
Jan. 31, 1904	$18,083	$9,894	$27,977	$1,003	$28,980	$2,425,940	1%

Year Ending	Public Welfare			Grants to Private Charities	Total City Expenditures on Public and Private Welfare	Total City Budget	Public and Private Charity as % of Total Expenditures
	For Almshouse	For Outdoor Poor	Total				
Jan. 31, 1911	$42,900	$16,000	$58,900	$4,400	$63,300	$3,000,000	2%
Dec. 31, 1912	$55,842	$16,465	$72,307	$20,750	$93,057	$4,303,517	2%
Dec. 31, 1913	$56,890	$18,675	$75,565	$12,375	$87,940	$4,730,066	2%
Dec. 31, 1914	$53,476	$14,255	$148,595		$148,595	$5,768,637	3%
Dec. 31, 1915	$49,624	$16,000	$157,555		$157,555	$6,160,401	3%
Dec. 31, 1919†	$59,928	$10,834	$625,224	$16,050	$641,274	$6,148,816	10%
Dec. 31, 1920	$62,520	$8,533	$670,400	$14,950	$685,350	$6,700,300	10%
Dec. 31, 1921	$65,995	$9,017	$734,066	$15,450	$749,516	$7,278,565	10%
Dec. 31, 1922	$66,843	$11,235	$352,785	$16,175	$368,960	$6,509,578	6%
Dec. 31, 1923	$67,913	‡	$422,070	$16,725	$438,795	$7,031,207	6%
Jan. 31, 1926	$69,000		$420,440	$19,000	$439,440	$7,006,901	6%
Jan. 31, 1927	$73,545		$443,743	$19,000	$462,743	$7,937,729	6%
Jan. 31, 1928	$79,717		$479,022	$19,000	$498,022	$8,242,215	6%
Jan. 31, 1929	$79,717		$479,022	$23,000	$502,022	$8,081,208	6%
Jan. 31, 1930	$86,625		$511,147	$23,000	$534,147	$8,139,332	7%

(continued)

Table 10. (continued)

Year Ending	Public Welfare			Grants to Private Charities	Total City Expenditures on Public and Private Welfare	Total City Budget	Public and Private Charity as % of Total Expenditures
	For Almshouse	For Outdoor Poor	Total				
[Dec. 31, 1930]							
Jan. 31, 1931	$89,247		$530,892*	$23,000	$553,892	$8,096,547	7%
[Dec. 31, 1932]							
Jan. 31, 1933	$79,428	$166,980§	$865,162	$26,881	$892,043	$7,740,794	12%
[Dec. 31, 1933]							
Jan. 31, 1934	$76,724	$255,661	$845,045	$23,920	$868,965	$6,985,245	12%
[Dec. 31, 1934]							
Jan. 31, 1935	$81,997	$202,359	$823,776	$21,770	$845,546	$7,210,804	12%
[Dec. 31, 1935]							
Jan. 31, 1936	$81,800	$164,044	$769,192	$23,540	$792,732	$6,969,866	11%
[Dec. 31, 1936]							
Jan. 31, 1937	$89,337	$288,055	$945,971	$25,078	$971,049	$7,815,286	12%
[Dec. 31, 1937]							
Jan. 31, 1938	$92,262	$257,248	$989,119	$27,261	$1,016,380	$7,788,737	13%
[Dec. 31, 1938]							
Jan. 31, 1939	$88,272	$361,422	$1,115,113	$23,229	$1,138,342	$8,279,809	14%
[Dec. 31, 1939]							
Jan. 31, 1940	$83,918	$345,762	$1,020,549	$20,710	$1,041,259	$8,055,403	13%

Sources: Combined from annual reports, city mayor; annual reports, city comptroller.

*Includes $10,035 for mothers' aid.

†The city created the Dept. of Public Welfare and moved other city functions to this dept. that were not previously included in welfare figures.

‡After this date, there were no more reports listed for "outdoor poor."

§Beginning with this year, the city made a "special appropriation for the unemployed."

Table 11. Richmond City Almshouse Admissions Registers: Admissions Data Overview

	Vol. A White Males and Females 1872–77	Vol. B White Males 1887–1902	Vol. C White Males 1902–7	Vol. D White Females 1903–7	Vol. E White Males and Females 1907–13	Vol. F Black Males 1903–7	Vol. G Black Females 1902–7	Vol. H Black Males and Females 1907–13	Totals
Males	737	4,120	1,913	13	2,931	1,510	9	2,677	13,910
Females	676		2	710	1,045	1	1,030	2,048	5,512
Sex Not Reported			1	54	9				64
Totals	1,413	4,120	1,916	777	3,985	1,511	1,039	4,725	19,486

Table 12A. Richmond City Almshouse Admissions Registers: Nativity—Summary

	Vol. A White Males and Females 1872–77	Vol. B White Males 1887–1902	Vol. C White Males 1902–7	Vol. D White Females 1903–7	Vol. E White Males and Females 1907–13	Vol. F Black Males 1903–7	Vol. G Black Females 1902–7	Vol. H Black Males and Females 1907–13
Native-born	1,384	3,310	1,460	661	3,327	1,399	956	4,533
Foreign-born	0	728	298	39	509	7	1	11
Nativity Not Reported	29	82	158	77	149	105	82	181
Total Admissions	1,413	4,120	1,916	777	3,985	1,511	1,039	4,725
Foreign-born as Percentage of Admissions	0%	17.67%	15.55%	5.02%	12.77%	0.46%	0.10%	0.23%

Table 12B. Richmond City Almshouse Admissions Registers: Nativity by State

	Vol. A White Males and Females 1872–77	Vol. B White Males 1887–1902	Vol. C White Males 1902–7	Vol. D White Females 1903–7	Vol. E White Males and Females 1907–13	Vol. F Black Males 1903–7	Vol. G Black Females 1902–7	Vol. H Black Males and Females 1907–13
Va.—Richmond	329	1,161	372	97	296	375	298	284
Va.—other	968	1,308	616	479	2,250	732	587	3,459
Ala.		11	4	3	2	12		10
Alaska		1			1	1	1	1
Ariz.					3			
Calif.		5	2		2			2
Colo.		1						
Conn.		16	4		6			3
D.C.	5	30	19	4	25	10	5	20
Del.	1	2	8	4	11	1		1
Fla.	2	10	4	1	3			13
Ga.	1	25	14	5	27	26	2	49
Ill.		13	7		11			2
Ind.		5	6		13			4
"Indian territory"			1			1		1
Iowa		6	1		2	1		
Kans.		2			2			
Ky.	2	33	14	2	15	4		10
La.		24	8	1	5	1	1	6
Maine		8	5		1			
Mass.	2	31	22	2	21	5		3
Md.	11	93	56	2	43	14		28
Mich.		9	7	1	16			1
Minn.		2			2			

(continued)

Table 12B. *(continued)*

	Vol. A White Males and Females 1872–77	Vol. B White Males 1887–1902	Vol. C White Males 1902–7	Vol. D White Females 1903–7	Vol. E White Males and Females 1907–13	Vol. F Black Males 1903–7	Vol. G Black Females 1902–7	Vol. H Black Males and Females 1907–13
Miss.		5	2	2	0	1	1	4
Mo.		8	7		6	2	1	2
Mont.		1	1					
N.C.	27	72	71	29	196	139	48	445
N.D.		1	1					
Nebr.								
Nev.					2			
N.H.		2	6		2			
N.J.		11	12	4	25	11	2	5
N.Y.		157	78	7	104		1	27
Ohio	1	45	15	1	33	1		10
Oreg.					1			
Pa.	4	120	50	7	95	9	3	30
R.I.		5	4		8			
S.C.	15	23	12	1	24	34	2	70
S.Dak.				1	0			
Tenn.		11	11	2	16	12		17
Tex.		8	2		7	2		3
Utah					1			
Vt.		3		1	2			
W.Va.	11	37	15	5	35	6	4	23
Wash.		3	1		2			
Wis.		2	1		6			
"U.S."	5		1		5			

Table 12C. Richmond City Almshouse Admissions Registers: Foreign-born

	Vol. A White Males and Females 1872–77	Vol. B White Males 1887–1902	Vol. C White Males 1902–7	Vol. D White Females 1903–7	Vol. E White Males and Females 1907–13	Vol. F Black Males 1903–7	Vol. G Black Females 1902–7	Vol. H Black Males and Females 1907–13
"Africa"								1
Aragon		3			1			
Armenia		5						
Australia					4	1		1
Austria		8	9		14			
Bohemia		1	1		3			
Canada		29	26	4	24	1	1	
China					1			
Cuba			1		1	3		
Denmark		7	1		5			
Egypt		1						
England		102	41	5	74			2
Europe		1	1		7			
Finland		1	1		1			
foreign					7			
France		13	3	1	8			
Germany		130	35		69			
Greece		4	5		26			
Holland		5	1					
Hungary			1		8			
Ireland		254	75	22	91			
Italy		36	22		29			

(continued)

Table 12C. (continued)

	Vol. A White Males and Females 1872–77	Vol. B White Males 1887–1902	Vol. C White Males 1902–7	Vol. D White Females 1903–7	Vol. E White Males and Females 1907–13	Vol. F Black Males 1903–7	Vol. G Black Females 1902–7	Vol. H Black Males and Females 1907–13
Jamaica						1		
Mexico		2						
Newfoundland		2						
Norway		6	2		7			
P.E. Island		1		1				
Poland		4	9		7			
Prussia		3	3					
Puerto Rico			1		2			
Romania			1		1			
Russia		23	25	2	75			1
Scotland		51	15	2	29			2
S. Africa		1						
S. America		1						
S. Wales		1						
Spain		1	3		2			
Sweden		13	7		3			
Switzerland		8	4		3			
Syria		8	1	2	4			
Turkey		1	1		2			
Wales		4	3		1			
West Indies						1	1	4
Total	0	728	298	39	509	7	1	11

Table 13. Richmond City Almshouse Admissions Registers: Mortality

	Vol. A White Males and Females 1872–77	Vol. B White Males 1887–1902	Vol. C White Males 1902–7	Vol. D White Females 1903–7	Vol. E White Males and Females 1907–13	Vol. F Black Males 1903–7	Vol. G Black Females 1902–7	Vol. H Black Males and Females 1907–13
Total Admissions	1,413	4,120	1,916	777	3,985	1,511	1,039	4,725
Deaths	490	363	146	69	359	291	182	890
Deaths as Percentage of Admissions	34.7	8.8	7.6	8.9	9.0	19.3	17.5	18.8
Avg. Age at Admission of Those Who Subsequently Died in Almshouse	48	44	43.1	47	51	43.5	34.9	40
Avg. Age of All Admissions	36.7	40.5	42.5	36.6	39.8	33.4	26.1	28.3

Table 14A. Richmond City Almshouse Admissions Registers: Runaways

	Vol. A White Males and Females 1872–77	Vol. B White Males 1887–1902	Vol. C White Males 1902–7	Vol. D White Females 1903–7	Vol. E White Males and Females 1907–13	Vol. F Black Males 1903–7	Vol. G Black Females 1902–7	Vol. H Black Males and Females 1907–13
Males	19	81	44	0	139	6	0	11
Females	11	0	0	24	46	0	3	8
Total	30	81	44	24	185	6	3	19
Runaways as Percentage of Admissions	2	2	2	3	4.6	0.4	0.3	0.4
Avg. Age of Runaways	38	43.5	46.1	48	45.5	27.8	30.7	26.42
Age Range of Runaways	11–75	10–77	1–79	21–77	1–84	17–45	19–38	12–52

Table 14B. Runaways Listed in Annual
Reports of Superintendent, 1874–1893

Year Ending	White	Black	Total
Jan. 31, 1874	*	*	25
Jan. 31, 1875	*	*	14
Jan. 31, 1877	*	*	35
Dec. 31, 1886	*	*	11
Dec. 31, 1888	*	*	17
Dec. 31, 1889	*	*	10
Dec. 31, 1890	7	25	32
Dec. 31, 1891	5	14	19
Dec. 31, 1892	12	10	22
Dec. 31, 1893	5	10	15

Source: Annual reports, supt. of almshouse/public
welfare, broken series.

*Not reported

Table 15A. Richmond City Almshouse Admissions Registers: Recidivism, Detailed

	Vol. A White Males and Females 1872–77	As %	Vol. B White Males 1887–1902	As %	Vol. C White Males 1902–7	As %	Vol. D White Females 1903–7	As %	Vol. E White Males and Females 1907–13	As %	Vol. F Black Males 1903–7	As %	Vol. G Black Females 1902–7	As %	Vol. H Black Males and Females 1907–13	As %
Total Admissions	1,413		4,120		1,916		777		3,985		1,511		1,039		4,725	
1x	1,301	92.1	3,648	88.5	1,683	87.8	679	87.4	3,552	89.1	1,351	89.4	929	89.4	4,288	90.8
2x	92	6.5	243	5.9	120	6.3	52	6.7	237	6.0	106	7.0	86	8.3	318	6.7
3x	14	1.0	88	2.1	54	2.8	16	2.1	75	1.9	32	2.1	13	1.3	61	1.3
4x	3		31	0.8	25	0.01	13	1.7	37	0.9	14	0.9	6		26	
5x	1		24		14		5		30		3		3		15	
6x	1		20		6		3		14		2		2		5	
7x	1		13		2		1		15		1				5	
8x			11		5		2		6		1				3	
9x			12				4		3		1				1	
10x			6		2				4						2	
11x			6		2		1		2						0	
12x			5		1				4						0	

	Vol. A White Males and Females 1872–77	As %	Vol. B White Males 1887–1902	As %	Vol. C White Males 1902–7	As %	Vol. D White Females 1903–7	As %	Vol. E White Males and Females 1907–13	As %	Vol. F Black Males 1903–7	As %	Vol. G Black Females 1902–7	As %	Vol. H Black Males and Females 1907–13	As %
13x			1		1		1		2						0	
14x			1						1						0	
15x			2		1				1						1	
16x									1							
17x									0							
18x			1						1							
19x			1													
20x																
21x			1													
22x			3													
25x			1													
28x			1													
38x			1													

Table 15B. Richmond City Almshouse Admissions Registers: Recidivism, Concise

	Vol. A White Males and Females 1872–77	As %	Vol. B White Males 1887–1902	As %	Vol. C White Males 1902–7	As %	Vol. D White Females 1903–7	As %	Vol. E White Males and Females 1907–13	As %	Vol. F Black Males 1903–7	As %	Vol. G Black Females 1902–7	As %	Vol. H Black Males and Females 1907–13	As %
Total Admissions	1,413		4,120		1,916		777		3,985		1,511		1,039		4,725	
1 Entrance Only	1,301	92.1	3,648	88.5	1,683	87.8	679	87.4	3,552	89.1	1,351	89.4	929	89.4	4,288	90.8
2 or More Entrances	112	7.9	472	11.5	233	12.2	98	12.6	433	10.9	160	10.6	110	10.6	437	9.3

Table 16. Richmond City Almshouse Admissions Records: Children (age 13 and under)

	Vol. A White Males and Females 1872–77	Vol. B White Males 1887–1902	Vol. C White Males 1902–7	Vol. D White Females 1903–7	Vol. E White Males and Females 1907–13	Vol. F Black Males 1903–7	Vol. G Black Females 1902–7	Vol. H Black Males and Females 1907–13	Totals
Arrived as Foundlings	5	30	13	9	23	9	3	29	121
Born in Almshouse	67	82	26	29	83	82	87	397	853
By Regular Admission	59	180	42	81	219	67	51	294	993
Total No. Children	131	292	81	119	325	158	141	720	1,967
Children as Percentage of Admissions	9.3	7.1	0.04	15.3	8.2	10.5	13.6	15.2	10.1

Table 17. Richmond City Almshouse Admissions Registers: Numbers of Pregnancies

	Vol. A White Males and Females 1872–77	Vol. D White Females 1903–7	Vol. E White Males and Females 1907–13	Vol. G Black Females 1902–7	Vol. H Black Males and Females 1907–13	Totals
No. of Women 14 and older	581	646	909	879	1,722	4,737
No. of Pregnancies	96	85	88	224	261	754
Pregnancies as Percentage of Women Admitted	16.5	13.2	9.7	25.5	15.2	15.9
Avg. Age of Pregnant Women at Admission	22.6	24.1	24	21.5	21.5	22.74

Table 18. Richmond City Almshouse Admissions Registers: Profiles of Pregnant Women

	Vol. A White Males and Females 1872–77	Vol. D White Females 1903–7	Vol. E White Males and Females 1907–13	Vol. G Black Females 1902–7	Vol. H Black Males and Females 1907–13
Number Listed	96	85	88	224	261
Avg. Age (in years)	22.6	24.1	24.0	21.5	21.5
Age Range (in years)	15–69	16–43	15–40	14–52	15–70
Born in Richmond	13	11	15	42	37
Born in Virginia (but not Richmond)	76	55	49	162	178
Born out of State	5	18	17	20	43
Foreign-born	0	1	7	0	0
Nativity Unknown	2	0	0	0	3
Protestant	*	75	*	168	*
Catholic	*	6	*	2	*
Jewish	*	0	*	0	*
Other/none/unknown	*	4	*	54	*
Illiterate	*	2	*	62	*
Single	*	40	47	193	191
Married	*	28	34	18	47
Widowed	*	14	6	11	20
Marital Status Unknown	*	3	1	2	3

* Not reported.

Table 19. Richmond City
Almshouse: Adoptions Arranged,
1876–1895

Year	White	Black	Total
1876	3	0	3
1877	6	6	12
1881	*	*	12
1883	4	9	13
1885	0	2	2
1886	1	0	1
1888	2	2	4
1890	0	10	10
1891	2	4	6
1892	1	2	3
1893	6	2	8
1895	4	3	7

Source: Annual Reports, Superintendent
(broken series)
* Race not reported.

Entrance No.	Date Admitted	Date Discharged	Age	Religion	Occupation	Remarks
1	5/15/1888	9/13/1892	18	none	laborer	
2	2/9/1892	8/4/1896	22	none	laborer	malaria
3	8/6/1896	8/1/1897	30	none	none	
4	8/6/1897	10/29/1897	32	Catholic	laborer	
5	11/2/1897	11/4/1897	32	Catholic	none	
6	11/10/1897	3/18/1898	32	Catholic	none	
7	4/28/1898	4/29/1898	33	Catholic	laborer	
8	5/4/1898	2/20/1898	33	Protestant	none	
9	5/2/1899	6/14/1899	34	Protestant	none	
10	7/10/1899	7/14/1899	34	Protestant	laborer	
11	7/17/1899	7/24/1899	34	Protestant	laborer	
12	7/26/1899	8/2/1899	38	Protestant	none	
13	11/17/1899	12/1/1899	*	Protestant	laborer	returned to city today
14	12/7/1899	1/8/1900	21	Protestant	none	
15	1/9/1900	1/30/1900	about 30	Protestant	laborer	
16	2/2/1900	8/1/1900	about 30	Protestant	none	made driver
17	2/4/1902	3/31/1903	40	Protestant	none	
18	4/6/1903	4/2/1904	about 40	Protestant	none	
19	4/8/1904	4/9/1904	60	Protestant	none	
20	4/21/1904	4/18/1905	about 30	Protestant	none	
21	4/23/1905	6/30/1905	*	*	none	
22	7/4/1905	"out"	about 40	Catholic	laborer	
23	2/7/1907	3/11/1907	about 35	*	none	
24	2/24/1908	3/10/1908	38	*	laborer	
25	3/20/1908	3/26/1908	48	*	laborer	
26	5/2/1908	5/3/1908	*	*	*	
27	5/13/1908	unknown	*	*	*	
28	7/8/1909	7/22/1909	48	*	teamster	gastritis
29	9/2/1909	11/20/1909	48	*	laborer	

*Not reported.

Table 21. Sources of Public Emergency Relief Funds (July 1933–June 1935)

State	Local—%	State—%	Federal—%	State	Local—%	State—%	Federal—%
Ala.	5.0	0.1	94.9	Nev.	5.9	1.2	92.9
Ariz.	0.7	14.8	84.5	N.H.	22.1	24.8	53.1
Ark.	3.1	0.8	96.1	N.J.	6.5	17.0	76.5
Calif.	20.0	15.9	64.1	N. Mex.	1.2	0.1	98.7
Colo.	10.9	5.5	83.6	N.Y.	27.6	17.3	55.1
Conn.	41.3	9.7	49.0	N.C.	1.6	0	98.4
Del.	22.9	20.5	56.6	N.D.	9.2	0	90.8
Fla.	4.3	0	95.7	Ohio	4.7	17.1	78.2
Ga.	4.7	0	95.3	Okla.	12.9	0.7	86.4
Idaho	10.5	2.9	86.6	Oreg.	10.7	11.4	77.9
Ill.	4.1	25.4	70.5	Pa.	6.1	20.6	73.3
Ind.	31.9	0.2	67.9	R.I.	33	24.8	42.2
Iowa	30.7	9.7	59.6	S.C.	2.2	0	97.8
Kans.	25.0	0.3	74.7	S.Dak.	8.6	0	91.4
Ky.	9.3	5.8	84.9	Tenn.	3.3	3.2	93.5
La.	2.7	0	97.3	Tex.	0.2	23.0	76.8
Maine	35.3	8.3	56.4	Utah	7.2	14.3	78.5
Md.	2.8	18.2	79.0	Vt.	36.6	0.9	62.5
Mass.	42.6	0.2	57.2	**Va.**	**9.2**	**0.2**	**90.6**
Mich.	10.5	18.8	70.7	Wash.	6.0	14.1	79.9
Minn.	15.2	6.0	78.8	W.Va.	2.4	9.4	88.2
Miss.	1.6	0.7	97.7	Wis.	21.8	2.4	75.8
Mo.	10.6	9.8	79.6	Wyo.	2.6	1.5	95.9
Mont.	9.6	1.6	88.8	National			
Nebr.	21.8	<0.1	78.2	Avg.	15.0	12.6	72.4

Source: Edith Abbott, *Public Assistance* (Chicago: University of Chicago Press, 1940), 868.

Table 22. Family Welfare and Relief Agencies in Richmond, Expenditures for 1939–1940

| Date of Report | Private Agencies | | | | | | Public | Total Public and Private | Public as % of Total |
	Red Cross	Bureau Catholic Charities	Family Service Society	Ladies Hebrew Benevolent Society	Salvation Army	Total Private Agencies	Social Service Bureau (City of Richmond)		
1939 (Feb.)	$24.80	$686.94	$4,991.92	$236.24	$52.39	$5,992.29	$31,096.58	$37,088.87	84%
1939 (June)	$46.03	$857.85	$4,303.48	$286.40	$15.70	$5,509.46	$35,307.00	$40,816.46	87%
1940 (Feb.)	$28.75	$662.79	$6,006.58	$375.90	$37.73	$7,111.75	$24,477.51	$31,589.26	77%
1940 (June)	$10.10	$801.43	$4,266.53	$349.70	$41.96	$5,469.72	$35,087.22	$40,556.94	87%

Source: *Social Statistics Bulletin*, no. 2, February 1940, Research Bureau of the Richmond Community Council, L.V.

Table 23. Women's Work Relief in Virginia, 1934

Type of Project	No. of Projects	As %	No. of Women Employed	As %
Nursing	20	11.3%	309	11.3%
Home Visiting	18	10.2%	103	3.8%
Recreation	7	4%	274	10.0%
School Lunches	11	6.2%	63	2.3%
Home Demonstration	4	2.3%	39	1.4%
Sewing Rooms	46	26%	1,379	51.0%
Other	71	40.1%	565	20.7%
Total	177		2,732	

Source: "Brief Objective Analysis of Women's Work Projects by States," typescript by Anna T. Winecoff, February 1934.

ER Papers, "Correspondence with Government Departments," box 277, folder "1934 Wo," FDR Library.

NOTES

Introduction

1. Message to Congress, 4 January 1935, in Rosenman, ed., *Public Papers*, 4:19–20. Roosevelt was not the only one to speak of the "business of relief" during the 1930s, as it became a quite common phraseology among New Dealers. Harry Greenstein of the American Association of Social Workers argued that "the business of relief must be viewed on a national perspective" ("Social Workers Hear Appeal by Greenstein," *Richmond Times-Dispatch*, 21 January 1938, 5). Virginia's emergency relief administrator, William A. Smith, wrote, "Relief is, I suppose, the only 'business' in the world which proceeds by orderly design to destroy itself. It attains its highest degree of perfection only when it has overcome the necessity for its existence" ("VERA's Campaign," 28).

2. Ellen Ross has described charity as "big business" in Victorian and Edwardian Britain ("Hungry Children: Housewives and London Charity, 1870–1918," in Mandler, ed., *Uses of Charity*, 164).

3. A good starting point for this vast body of literature would include Katz, *Price of Citizenship*; Koven and Michel, eds., *Mothers of a New World*; Berkowitz, *Creating the Welfare State*; and Gordon, *New Feminist Scholarship*.

4. *Vengeance and Justice*, 76.

5. Dailey, *Before Jim Crow*, 112.

6. *Solidarities of Strangers*, 6–7.

7. Franklin, "Public Welfare," 383; Grantham, *Southern Progressivism*, 217–18; Noll, *Feeble-Minded*, 157; Wisner, *Social Welfare*, 9, 45.

8. Skocpol, *Protecting Soldiers and Mothers*, 17.

9. Katz, *In the Shadow*, 15.

One. Colonial Origins

1. Beverley, *History and Present State*, 275.

2. Kulikoff, *Tobacco and Slaves*, 24–25; Darrett B. and Anita H. Rutman, *A Place in Time, Middlesex County, Virginia, 1650–1750* (New York: W. W. Norton, 1984), chapters 5 and 6; and Winthrop D. Jordan, *White over Black: American Attitudes toward the Negro, 1550–1812* (Chapel Hill: University of North Carolina Press, 1968).

3. The literature on the English poor laws is enormous. Useful recent works include Boyer, *Economic History*; Driver, *Power and Pauperism*; and King, *Poverty and Welfare in England*. Important "classic" studies include Bridenbaugh, *Vexed and Troubled Englishmen*.

4. Lees, *Solidarities of Strangers*, 3.

5. Wisner, *Social Welfare in the South*, 23–31.

6. Jernegan, *Laboring and Dependent Classes*, 175.

7. Trattner, *From Poor Law to Welfare State*, 19.

8. Residency requirements were not completely abolished until 1969, with a Supreme Court decision that finally ended the settlement provision. Wisner, *Social Welfare in the South*, 5.

9. Lees, *Solidarities of Strangers*, 32.

10. Quoted in Watkinson, "Rogues, Vagabonds, and Fit Objects," 23.

11. Porter, *County Government in Virginia*, 38–39. Virginia's counties were created in 1634 and in 1641 they were divided into parishes. Jernegan, *Laboring and Dependent Classes*, 178.

12. Katz, *In the Shadow*, 17.

13. Like their English counterparts, Virginia poor laws assumed that the local overseers and guardians were the most effective judges of destitution and the needs of local people. No standards were set from above. Little consideration was given to complaints from below. Lees, *Solidarities of Strangers*, 14.

14. Rothman, *Discovery of the Asylum*, 31, 5. Later, "younger" states like Arkansas, Mississippi, and Alabama fixed much shorter residency laws. In unsettled, frontier areas, short settlement requirements would have served to attract needed settlers. Wisner, *Social Welfare in the South*, 27–28.

15. Beverley, *History and Present State*, 312.

16. Mackey, "Operation of the English Old Poor Law," 39; C. G. Chamberlayne, ed., *The Vestry Book of Petsworth Parish, Gloucester County, Virginia, 1677–1793* (Richmond: Division of Purchase and Printing, 1933), 26 (entry for 9 September 1684); and 187 (entry for 6 October 1725).

17. In England, settlement could be acquired by serving an apprenticeship there, by being hired for a year, by holding local office, by paying local taxes, or by renting or owning local property. Women acquired their husbands' settlement upon marriage, and legitimate children inherited settlement rights from their parents. As Lees notes, these requirements gave access to settlement rights more easily to men than to women, and most easily of all to those with property who could buy their way in with little difficulty. Lees, *Solidarities of Strangers*, 28.

18. Chamberlayne, *Vestry Book of Petsworth Parish*, 19 (entry for 11 October 1681).

19. Ibid., 42 (entry for 7 October 1695).

20. Ibid., 36 (entry for 29 October 1693); and 59 (entry for 24 April 1700).

21. Cassel, "Analysis of the Poor Relief System," 43.

22. Mackey, "Operation of the English Old Poor Law," 36, 38.

23. Cassel, "Analysis of the Poor Relief System," 66–72, notes several instances of poor-relief recipients owning land and other property.

24. J. Staunton Moore, ed., *History of Henrico Parish*, "Vestrybook for Henrico Parish," 41–42 (entry for 8 October 1737). In that one year, 25 percent of the parish's expenditures went to the support of the indigent. One recent study has found that Natchez, Mississippi, spent one-third of its annual budget on poor relief in the period 1807–17. Vogt, "Poor Relief in Frontier Mississippi," 184. In size and development, Henrico Parish in 1737 could be considered roughly similar to Natchez in 1807.

25. Kulikoff, *Tobacco and Slaves*, 215; Guest, "Boarding of the Dependent Poor," 98–99.

26. Chamberlayne, *Vestry Book of Petsworth Parish*, 154 (entry for 7 October 1720); and 58–59 (entry for 24 April 1700).

27. Ibid., 63 (entry for 2 October 1700); and 17 (entry for 11 October 1681).

28. Ibid., 69 (entry for 1 October 1701); and 76 (entry for 26 October 1703).

29. Rutman and Rutman have found the same thing to be true elsewhere in colonial Virginia. See *Place in Time*, 196.

30. Chamberlayne, *Vestry Book of Petsworth Parish*, 70, 72 (entries for 1 October and 26 October 1701). Again, the Rutmans have found similar examples in Middlesex County, Virginia. See *Place in Time*, 196.

31. Chamberlayne, *Vestry Book of Petsworth Parish*, 29, 44 (entries for 1 October 1690 and 14 October 1696).

32. It may be the case that only a few of the local elites were willing to take on such responsibilities. Elena Daly Cassel found that, of the sixty-three men who served as vestrymen in Truro Parish before the Revolution, only seven were listed in the records as having directly cared for the poor of the parish. "Analysis of the Poor Relief System," 14. Robert Cray has speculated that locally prominent people in New York might have also been willing to take in the poor since they had servants or slaves to do the actual work. *Paupers and Poor Relief*, 60.

33. Mackey, "Operation of the English Old Poor Law," 32, 33.

34. Trattner, *From Poor Law to Welfare State*, 20–22.

35. Edmund S. Morgan, *American Slavery, American Freedom*, 338.

36. Cray, *Paupers and Poor Relief*, 34. Lynn Hollen Lees has pointed out that English local governments were inconsistent in their application of the demands for work that were embedded in the poor laws. Parishes supplied work "intermittently and ineffectively." Lees, *Solidarities of Strangers*, 19.

37. Lees, *Solidarities of Strangers*, 57; Levine-Clark, "Engendering Relief," 107–30.

38. Richard L. Morton, *The Tidewater Period, 1607–1710*, vol. 1 of *Colonial Virginia* (Chapel Hill: University of North Carolina Press, 1960), 53.

39. Paul, "Rural Almshouse of Virginia," 15–16.

40. Ibid., 17; MacLeod, "Case Study of Poor Relief," 57; Porter, *County Government in Virginia*, 39.

41. Rothman, *Discovery of the Asylum*, 25, 32, 36.

42. Edmund S. Morgan, *American Slavery, American Freedom*, 340–41.

43. Abramovitz, *Regulating the Lives of Women*, 93.

44. Chamberlayne, *Vestry Book of Petsworth Parish*, 7 (entry for 13 November 1677).

45. Mackey, "Operation of the English Old Poor Law," 30, 37.

46. In Christ Church Parish, between 1666 and 1700, only seventeen bastard children received parish care. MacLeod, "Case Study of Poor Relief," 87.

47. Mackey, "Operation of the English Old Poor Law," 31. Priscilla Clement has found the same reduction of relief taxes over time in antebellum Philadelphia. *Welfare and the Poor*, 63. The Rutmans calculated that welfare costs increased as a percentage of the entire amount of public expenditures over time, 2 percent of total in 1668 up to 19 percent

of total in 1724. They did not calculate the rate per tithable over time. *Place in Time*, 196–99.

48. J. Staunton Moore, *History of Henrico Parish*, see entries for 1735, 1755, and 1770.

49. For examples of diligence in removal from New England, see Trattner, *From Poor Law to Welfare State*, 20–23. See also Alan D. Watson, "Public Poor Relief," 349–50.

50. Chamberlayne, *Vestry Book of Petsworth Parish*, 106 (entry for 7 July 1711). It does appear that the vestry reversed itself in at least one of these cases, for George Stickel shows up again on subsequent poor lists (pp. 132, 134, 139).

51. Quoted in Watkinson, "Rogues, Vagabonds, and Fit Objects," 20.

52. Although few scholars have yet investigated these issues, there is some corroborating evidence for other colonies/states. Alan D. Watson counted 134 people cared for over a seventy-three-year period in one North Carolina parish, or less than two per year. "Public Poor Relief," 349. Geoffrey Guest similarly found a very low number of poor-relief recipients in colonial Somerset County, Maryland. Between 1725 and 1759, 456 individuals received assistance; in any given year, the number was between 16 and 40, numbers that never exceeded 1 percent of the total free white adult population. "Boarding of the Dependent Poor," 97. According to Brenda Stevenson, Loudon County, Virginia, supported 40 to 50 indigents in 1800. *Life in Black and White: Family and Community in the Slave South* (New York: Oxford University Press, 1996), 29.

53. Cassel, "Analysis of the Poor Relief System." See the table on pages 24–25. Cassel excluded blacks from the calculations since they were not counted as tithables or eligible for assistance.

54. MacLeod, "Case Study of Poor Relief," 140.

55. Jernegan, *Laboring and Dependent Classes*, 181.

56. MacLeod, "Case Study of Poor Relief," 91, 137.

57. Cassel, "Analysis of the Poor Relief System." See the table on pages 32–33. During the Revolutionary War, it should be noted, the figures change dramatically, rising to more than two-thirds of annual expenditures. For comparison's sake, England's national relief costs have been estimated at less than 1.5 percent of national income in 1690; 1.5 percent in 1755; and 2 percent by 1802. Lees, *Solidarities of Strangers*, 44–45.

58. MacLeod, "Case Study of Poor Relief," 103, 135.

59. Chamberlayne, *Vestry Book of Petsworth Parish*, 16 (entry for 14 October 1680); 54 (entry for 9 February 1698).

60. Jernegan, *Laboring and Dependent Classes*, 181.

61. MacLeod, "Case Study of Poor Relief," 97.

62. Trattner has suggested that planters in the colonial South, with their Anglican religion and their emulation of the English gentry, engaged in "especially large-scale" private charity. His identification of George Washington as "typical" in this respect is, I think, questionable. *From Poor Law to Welfare State*, 35.

63. Richard L. Morton, *Colonial Virginia*, 1:14. Morton does not view this from the perspective of "charity."

64. See for example Vogt, "Poor Relief in Frontier Mississippi," 181; and Alan D. Watson, "Public Poor Relief," 347.

65. Dabney, *Richmond,* 39; Shelburne, "Brief History," 25.

66. Very little is known about the Amicable Society. It continued to exist until at least the 1850s, when Samuel Mordecai described it in his memoirs. The society apparently evolved into a more general-purpose charity: Mordecai noted that it gave donations to the Female Humane Association and the Male Orphan Asylum, and during a severe winter in 1855–56, the society distributed relief to the poor. *Richmond in By-Gone Days,* 258–59. An account book for the society is at the Virginia Historical Society.

67. Wisner, *Social Welfare in the South,* 19. Not surprisingly, the more developed and more diverse colony of New York had more early private charities. See Cray, *Paupers and Poor Relief,* 38–39; Mohl, *Poverty in New York,* chapters 8 and 9.

68. Randolph S. Klein, "Medical Expenses," 261.

69. Increasing levels of poverty were not unique to Virginia in the late colonial period. Gary Nash has argued that the rising economic stresses of the 1750s and 1760s, which had different origins in cities like Boston than that of Virginia, were one of the major contributing factors in the coming of the American Revolution. See *The Urban Crucible: Social Change, Political Consciousness, and the Origins of the American Revolution* (Cambridge: Harvard University Press, 1979). New York experienced a similar rise in poverty in the decades just prior to the Revolution and responded with a toughened poor-relief system. See Cray, *Paupers and Poor Relief,* chapter 2.

70. Kulikoff, *Tobacco and Slaves,* 298.

71. Cassel, "Analysis of the Poor Relief System," 27. The figures dropped dramatically after 1765, but this was caused by the division of the parish into two smaller units. Cassel, 28.

72. Shifflett, *Patronage and Poverty,* 70; Richard L. Morton, *Westward Expansion and Prelude to Revolution, 1710–1763,* vol. 2 of *Colonial Virginia* (Chapel Hill: University of North Carolina Press, 1960), 676.

73. Cray, *Paupers and Poor Relief,* 41.

74. Fredricksville Parish (Louisa County) in 1756; Petsworth Parish (Gloucester County) in 1764; Christ Parish (Lancaster County) in 1767; Augusta Parish (Augusta County) in 1767; Elizabeth City Parish (Elizabeth City County) in 1771; and Stratton Major Parish (King and Queen County) in 1772. Paul, "Rural Almshouse of Virginia," 28.

75. Chamberlayne, *Vestry Book of Petsworth Parish,* 326–28 (entries for 13 November 1764, 4 November 1765, and 13 November 1765). The vestry book for Stratton Major Parish remained equally quiet on the reasons for its decision to build a poorhouse. In 1766, the vestry ordered two of its members to begin making inquiries for a "Convenient Piece of Land to Build a House on to keep and Entertain the Poor People of this Parish," but no explanations were recorded. C. G. Chamberlayne, ed., *The Vestry Book of Stratton Major Parish, King and Queen County, Virginia, 1729–1783* (Richmond: Division of Purchase and Printing, 1931), 157 (entry for 29 September 1766). The vestry book contained a more detailed description of the planned building than that of Petsworth Parish. The Stratton Major vestrymen ordered that the house be "Thirty six foot long, sixteen foot wide, nine foot Pitch, with a Brick Chimney in the Middle, with two good fire places,

to be fram'd of good Oak Timber Underpinn'd with Stone or Brick and cover'd with Cypress of Chestnut Singles, 18 Inches long to shew [*sic*] six inches, a Shedd on one side, Ten foot wide with two Petitions [*sic*] & convenient Doors thereto." Entry for 3 June 1767, p. 159.

76. This absence of detail is maddeningly common for these records. For example, the vestry book for Stratton Major Parish mentioned poorhouse inmates by name only once. "Ned Shepherd and his family are allowed to live at the poorhouse during the pleasure of the Vestry." Entry for 13 December 1783, p. 230.

77. Dain, *Disordered Minds*, 19. A second asylum would open in western Virginia in 1828. Virginia was clearly very early in funding such a program. Not until 1824 would the next southern state do so (Kentucky), followed by South Carolina in 1828. Wisner, *Social Welfare in the South*, 55.

78. Josephine Chapin Brown, *Public Relief*, 4.

79. For a similar observation on New York, see Cray, *Paupers and Poor Relief*, 44.

80. Jernegan, *Laboring and Dependent Classes*, 188.

81. Porter, *County Government in Virginia*, 147. All southern states followed this model, replacing the vestries with county overseers of the poor. This change made southern states more consistent with northern practices in that poor relief now was invested in a secular authority. Trattner, *From Poor Law to Welfare State*, 43. Elizabeth Wisner has suggested that this change was meaningless to the recipients of poor relief, who were no better cared for by the civil authorities than they had been by the parish vestrymen. *Social Welfare in the South*, 22.

82. Dorman, ed., *Virginia Revolutionary War*, v–vii. Examples of state pensions being paid in the 1850s include Mrs. Sally Arthur (p. 3), Moses Rollins (p. 103), and Peter Triplett (pp. 124–25).

83. It should be acknowledged that this "innovation" drew upon earlier English examples. In 1593 Parliament had provided for disabled soldiers and sailors, and English colonies (including Virginia) had followed this precedent. Axinn and Levin, *Social Welfare*, 21.

84. Stanard, *Richmond*, 37; Tyler-McGraw, *At the Falls*, 64.

Two. Poor Relief in Early Richmond

1. Tyler-McGraw, *At the Falls*, 48–49; Dabney, *Richmond*, 13.

2. Sidbury, *Ploughshares into Swords*, 158; Stanard, *Richmond*, 25; Takagi, "Rearing Wolves," 9; Kulikoff, *Tobacco and Slaves*, 125.

3. Tyler-McGraw, *At the Falls*, 65, 69, 90; Takagi, "Rearing Wolves," 10–11; Dabney, *Richmond*, 62–63; Stanard, *Richmond*, 78.

4. Dabney, *Richmond*, 31–32; Tyler-McGraw, *At the Falls*, 64.

5. Dabney, *Richmond*, 39–40, 61; Tyler-McGraw, *At the Falls*, 67.

6. Mandler, *Uses of Charity*, 2–3.

7. Sidbury, *Ploughshares into Swords*, 223. By 1810, the sex ratio had improved some. There were then three men for every two women.

8. Takagi, *"Rearing Wolves,"* 64; Sidbury, *Ploughshares into Swords,* 160–62.

9. Richmond City Common Hall Records, 1:90 (entry for 26 January 1785) and 177 (entry for 22 July 1788), LoV. Unfortunately for the researcher, no such list was recorded in the minute book.

10. Ibid., 269 (entry for 11 October 1792), and 2:42 (entry for 21 December 1793); vol. 1, see representative entries for 8 February 1790, 16 September 1790, 20 January 1791, and vol. 2, 19 January 1795.

11. Ward and Greer, *Richmond during the Revolution,* 6, 18.

12. The most recent treatments of Gabriel's revolt include Sidbury, *Ploughshares into Swords;* Takagi, *"Rearing Wolves";* and Douglas R. Egerton, *Gabriel's Rebellion: The Virginia Slave Conspiracies of 1800 and 1802* (Chapel Hill: University of North Carolina Press, 1993).

13. Sidbury, *Ploughshares into Swords,* 162–73.

14. Takagi, *"Rearing Wolves,"* 64–67; Tyler-McGraw, *At the Falls,* 80.

15. The city council had begun laying plans for the establishment of a workhouse as early as 1786. Richmond City Common Hall Records, vol. 1, 9 April 1786. It cannot be determined from the extant records when a workhouse was opened. A workhouse is referred to indirectly in at least one source: Ward and Greer, *Richmond during the Revolution,* 113.

16. Mississippi's legislature authorized county poorhouses in 1818. Callaway, "Poor Relief in Mississippi," 40.

17. Clement, *Welfare and the Poor,* 96.

18. Mutual Assurance Society of Virginia. Declaration, vol. 52, policy 438, LoV.

19. Rothman, ed., *Almshouse Experience,* 1104. (The information came from Robert Greenhow, president of the Overseers of the Poor for Richmond, in a letter included in the "Report of the Secretary of State in 1824 on the Relief and Settlement of the Poor" from New York state.)

20. Untitled article, *Richmond Enquirer,* 26 February 1816, 3.

21. Mary Wingfield Scott, *Old Richmond Neighborhoods,* 291.

22. There are no records indicating why the Hustings Court ordered the investigation. Given the criticisms that came out of the subsequent report, we can only surmise that there had been complaints about the facility.

23. Report of the committee appointed by the Hustings Court respecting the poorhouse, 16 March 1811 (hereafter cited as "Report of 16 March 1811"). Appended in Richmond City Common Hall Records, vol. 3, LoV. Quote from p. 12.

24. Ibid., 8; "Streets, Poor-house, &c.&c.," *Richmond Enquirer,* 19 March 1811, 3. Enclosing of the grounds would continue to be recommended regularly for the next forty years without result.

25. Report of 16 March 1811, 8.

26. Richmond City Common Hall Records, vol. 3, 22 January 1808.

27. Report of 16 March 1811, 9, 10. If such records were indeed ever kept, they have not survived.

28. Ibid., 8–11.

29. Ibid., 11–12.

30. Callaway, "Poor Relief in Mississippi," 44.

31. Cray, *Paupers and Poor Relief,* 96–97.

32. On the English workhouse model, see Piven and Cloward, *Regulating the Poor,* 33–34; "Streets, Poor-house, &c.&c.," 3.

33. Rothman, *Almshouse Experience,* 1104 (emphasis in original).

34. Report of 16 March 1811, 8, 9.

35. Rothman, *Almshouse Experience,* 1107.

36. Report of 16 March 1811, 11.

37. Rothman, *Almshouse Experience,* 1107. Charlestonians perceived similar difficulties that stemmed from the "necessary mingling of the honest but unfortunate sick with the degraded and vicious reprobates sent to the same house for temporary punishment." "Proceedings of Council," *Charleston Courier,* 6 July 1849, 2.

38. Stanard, *Richmond,* 39, 56–57, 113; Dabney, *Richmond,* 66.

39. Stanard, *Richmond,* 50–57.

40. Mordecai, *Richmond in By-Gone Days,* 157.

41. Mary Wingfield Scott, *Old Richmond Neighborhoods,* 30.

42. Dabney, *Richmond,* 67; Tyler-McGraw, *At the Falls,* 68–69.

43. Tyler-McGraw, *At the Falls,* 68, 86; Berman, *Richmond's Jewry,* 58; Varon, " 'We Mean to Be Counted,' " 15.

44. Barber, "Anxious Care and Constant Struggle," 121–23.

45. Lebsock, *Free Women of Petersburg,* 199–201; Varon, "We Mean to Be Counted," 8. Other southern towns produced similar institutions. Women in New Bern, North Carolina, formed the Female Charitable Society for the relief of the poor and the education of poor female children, incorporated by the state legislature in 1812. The Female Orphan Asylum Society of Fayetteville was incorporated the following year. Roy M. Brown, *Public Poor Relief,* 152.

46. Mordecai, *Richmond in By-Gone Days,* 284, 291.

47. Mary Wingfield Scott, *Houses of Old Richmond,* 163.

48. Tyler-McGraw, *At the Falls,* 93; Dabney, *Richmond,* 103; Steger, " 'United to Support,' " 37.

49. Steger, " 'United to Support,' " 71.

50. Richmond City Overseers of the Poor, Minutebook, 1817–28, LoV (entries for 1 June 1818, 3 June 1822, and 14 December 1822).

51. Rothman, *Almshouse Experience,* 1105.

52. Although the reports for these years did not specify that only whites received outdoor relief, records from later years indicate that outdoor relief went exclusively to whites. How much public relief went to free blacks is hard to document, given the extant records. Free blacks were admitted to the Williamsburg Asylum, for example, whenever space permitted. But we have no numbers available. Wisner, *Social Welfare in the South,* 57. Mississippi had a unique provision for the relief of free blacks: they were allowed to bind themselves into slavery for life, with their new owners bound to care for them. Callaway, "Poor Relief in Mississippi," 57.

53. Lebsock, *Free Women of Petersburg,* 213–14.

54. Richmond City Overseers of the Poor, Minutebook, 1817–28, 28–32 (entry for 5 June 1820).

55. Ibid., 8 March, 3 April, and 11 July 1821.

56. For example, see the Common Council Minutes for 19 July 1819; 9 December 1822; 13 January 1823; 14 July 1826; and 25 January 1831.

57. Common Council Minutes, 8:253 (entry for 14 July 1826).

58. Greenhow was a former mayor of Richmond and served as president of the over-seers of the poor from 1817 to the early 1830s. A brief obituary in the *Richmond Enquirer,* 3 July 1840, neglected to mention his role in poor relief.

59. Common Council Minutes, 8:190 (entry for 15 June 1825); Ibid., 194 (entry for 17 June 1825).

60. Ibid., 248 (entry for 26 June 1826).

61. Newspaper clipping from *Richmond Enquirer,* 7 August 1827. Found pasted into Richmond City Overseers of the Poor, Minutebook, 1817–28.

62. Newspaper clipping from *Richmond Enquirer,* 8 August 1827. Found pasted into Richmond City Overseers of the Poor, Minutebook, 1817–28. A gill would have been approximately five ounces.

63. Common Council Minutes, 9:131 (entry for 13 June 1828); and 132 (entry for 8 June 1828).

64. Richmond City Overseers of the Poor, Minutebook, 1817–28, 14 February 1822.

65. Of the eighty-three residents on 1 December 1822, twenty-four were children. Richmond City Overseers of the Poor, Minutebook, 1817–28, 14 December 1822.

66. Common Council Minutes, 6:297 (entry for 15 February 1819); 7:48 (entry for 30 November 1819).

67. See Sander, *Business of Charity;* and Dufour, *Women Who Cared.*

68. Common Council Minutes, 7:156 (entry for 15 June 1821).

69. As late as 1835, some Richmond ministers were trying to restrain the charitable activities of their female congregants. See Tyler-McGraw, *At the Falls,* 86, for an account of a "celebrated fight" at St. Paul's Episcopal Church over women's missions.

70. Clement, *Welfare and the Poor,* 47.

71. Here I am following the logic of Clement, *Welfare and the Poor,* 89.

72. Richmond City Overseers of the Poor, Minutebook, 1817–28, 14 December 1822.

73. Ibid., 29 December 1823; and 19 March 1824.

74. By 1836, it appears that some separate facilities had been arranged, although there are no records of any new buildings being approved. Overseer of the poor records include a receipt dated 16 July 1836 for work done at the poorhouse, including "white washing the poor house and negro huts." From the phrasing, we can only assume that there were some kind of separate facilities on the premises. Hustings Court, Poor Accounts (1836–37), Richmond City Records, LoV. A later record also refers to the "huts for the accommodation of the blacks, which are situated in rear of the main building." Common Council Minutes, 11:167 (entry for 26 June 1843).

75. Richmond City Overseers of the Poor, Minutebook, 13 October 1822.

76. Ibid.

77. Katz, *In the Shadow*, 31.

78. I have found no records for these years that suggest any complaints from women inmates or resistance to these tasks. This may, of course, be a product of the limited extant records. Or, such complaints may never have been recorded by those administrators who kept the books. Complaints did surface in later years, as discussed in chapter 5.

79. Richmond City Overseers of the Poor, Minutebook, 29 December 1823.

80. Ibid., 13 August 1824.

81. Ibid., 10 June 1818.

82. W. J. Rorabaugh, *The Alcoholic Republic, An American Tradition* (New York: Oxford University Press, 1979).

Three. Antebellum Richmond

1. Goldfield, *Urban Growth*, 27.

2. Steger, " 'United to Support,' " 80–81.

3. Tyler-McGraw, *At the Falls*, 110.

4. Takagi, "*Rearing Wolves*," 11, 12.

5. Goldfield, *Urban Growth*, 114; Takagi, "*Rearing Wolves*," 79.

6. Kimball, *American City, Southern Place*, 35, 44, 84–85.

7. The shortages of labor during the 1840s caused wages to rise dramatically: "mechanics" in the city earned one dollar per day in 1848, a rate higher than the national average. Goldfield, *Urban Growth*, 123.

8. Tyler-McGraw, *At the Falls*, 110–12.

9. Steger, " 'United to Support,' " 156.

10. Tyler-McGraw, *At the Falls*, 114.

11. McLeod, "Not Forgetting," 37.

12. Ibid., 40–41; Steger, " 'United to Support,' " 192–93.

13. Out of a total of 123 inmates. The growth of foreign-born population as poorhouse residents occurred throughout the urban South. In Charleston, the numbers were even greater than in Richmond, as Irish immigrants outnumbered native-born in that city's poorhouse by 1839. Bellows, *Benevolence among Slaveholders*, 105. In Alexandria, Virginia, fourteen of the eighteen inmates in the poorhouse in 1854 were immigrants. Goldfield, *Urban Growth*, 164. In Mobile in 1860, eight out of the eighteen inmates of the poorhouse were from Ireland. Amos, *Cotton City*, 172. Edward L. Ayers has also pointed out that immigrants were overrepresented in the region's penitentiaries. While the foreign-born constituted less than 3 percent of the total population in most southern states, they made up anywhere from 8 to 27 percent of the prison population. *Vengeance and Justice*, 75.

14. Edward L. Ayers, *Vengeance and Justice*, 95.

15. Dabney, *Richmond*, 153; Mordecai, *Richmond in By-Gone Days*, 246. Similar trends occurred in other southern cities. In Norfolk, immigrants constituted 17 percent of the white male workforce in 1850. And the figure rose to 27 percent by 1860, making the Irish

the largest ethnic group in the city. Irish were 68 percent of the white unskilled labor force in the city. Bogger, *Free Blacks*, 71–72. In Savannah, immigrants and their children comprised half of the city's white population by 1860. Edward L. Ayers, *Vengeance and Justice*, 77. In Memphis, the population was 30 percent foreign-born in 1860, again chiefly Irish and German. Biles, *Memphis in the Great Depression*, 10.

16. Schuricht, *History of the German Element*, 29.

17. Steger, " 'United to Support,' " 162.

18. Tyler-McGraw, *At the Falls*, 113–14; Bell, "German Immigrant Community," 42.

19. The *Richmond Anzeiger* began publication in 1853, followed by the *Virginische Zeitung* in 1859. Schuricht, *History of the German Element*, 40; Steger, " 'United to Support,' " 159–61.

20. Bell, "German Immigrant Community," 66.

21. Mordecai, *Richmond in By-Gone Days*, 246.

22. Goldfield, *Urban Growth*, 125; McLeod, "Not Forgetting," 38–39; *Richmond Republican* quoted by Steger, " 'United to Support,' " 194.

23. Steger, " 'United to Support,' " 166, 196; Bell, "German Immigrant Community," 86.

24. The Freie Gemeinde, or German Free Society, founded in 1850, "excited suspicion and severe critique" with its advocacy of "radical" ideas. The society "frightened the slaveholders and church-goers" of the city with its call for universal suffrage, taxation of church property, emancipation of slaves, and state ownership of railroads. The society's radical proposals for full public education, the abolition of the presidency, and the eight-hour day further convinced natives that the flow of immigration threatened many of their most cherished institutions. Schuricht, *History of the German Element*, 33–36. Although the Free Society never appealed to the majority of Germans in the city and had very little impact on the city's politics, it nevertheless inspired much fear and nativist reaction from native-born Richmonders. In the mid-1850s, the local press whipped itself up into a frenzy over the "Red Republican societies that purpose to pull down our government." Germans spent much time explaining through the press that they found these radicals as distasteful as did the rest of Richmond. As one recent scholar has noted, the vignette said more about the fears of native whites than about radicalism of German immigrants. Steger, " 'United to Support,' " 169–70; Kimball, *American City, Southern Place*, 53.

25. McLeod, "Not Forgetting," 41; Schuricht, *History of the German Element*, 46–47.

26. *Penny Post* of 15 March 1855, quoted by Steger, " 'United to Support,' " 186. The rising nativist fears of the 1850s produced at least one mob action, directed at Germans. On 20 June 1853, a mob of stone-throwing white Richmonders attacked a group of Germans returning from a day's picnic outside the city. Word had spread through town that "the whole German population had risen en masse upon our native citizens, and were about to take entire possession of the city." This same fear would result in another mob action at the outbreak of the Civil War, when a mob looted the meeting hall of the Richmond Turnverein after it was rumored that the Germans, long suspected of abolitionist sentiments, would support the Union. Steger, " 'United to Support,' " 185, 390.

27. "The Poor, We Have Always with Us," *Richmond Enquirer*, 8 January 1856, 1.

28. Samuel Mordecai noted in the winter of 1855–56 that "our poor-houses and other receptacles for the destitute or dissipated whites, are crowded to overflowing, chiefly with foreign paupers." *Richmond in By-Gone Days*, 358.

29. Jefferson Wallace, quoted by Kimball, *American City, Southern Place*, 15.

30. Mordecai, *Richmond in By-Gone Days*, 358. Elites in Charleston similarly described their city poorhouse and charity hospital as "mostly filled by strangers." "Proceedings of Council," *Charleston Courier*, 6 July 1849, 2.

31. Katz, *In the Shadow*, 17–18.

32. "The Poor, We Have Always With Us."

33. The classic analysis of free-labor ideology is Eric Foner's *Free Soil, Free Labor, Free Men: The Ideology of the Republican Party before the Civil War* (New York: Oxford University Press, 1970).

34. Abramovitz, *Regulating the Lives of Women*, 146; Trattner, *From Poor Law to Welfare State*, 55–56.

35. The literature on antebellum evangelicalism and social reform is substantial. See, for example, Alice Felt Tyler, *Freedom's Ferment: Phases of American Social History to 1860* (Minneapolis: University of Minnesota Press, 1944); Paul Boyer, *Urban Masses and Moral Order in America, 1820–1920* (Cambridge: Harvard University Press, 1978); Richard J. Carwardine, *Evangelicals and Politics in Antebellum America* (New Haven: Yale University Press, 1993); Michael Barkun, *Crucible of the Millennium: The Burned-Over District of New York in the 1840s* (Syracuse, N.Y.: Syracuse University Press, 1986); Douglas M. Strong, *Perfectionist Politics: Abolitionism and the Religious Tensions of American Democracy* (Syracuse, N.Y.: Syracuse University Press, 1999).

36. Bellows, *Benevolence among Slaveholders*, 54; Anne C. Loveland, *Southern Evangelicals and the Social Order, 1800–1860* (Baton Rouge: Louisiana State University Press, 1980), 161.

37. Quoted by Loveland, *Southern Evangelicals*, 171.

38. Varon, "'We Mean to Be Counted,'" 77.

39. Loveland, *Southern Evangelicals*, 169.

40. The literature on women's antebellum benevolent activities has grown extensive. See for example Ginzberg, *Women and the Work of Benevolence*; Nancy Hewitt, *Women's Activism and Social Change: Rochester, N.Y., 1822–1872* (Ithaca: Cornell University Press, 1984); Mary P. Ryan, *Women in Public: Between Banners and Ballots, 1825–1880* (Baltimore: Johns Hopkins University Press, 1990); and Anne Firor Scott, *Natural Allies: Women's Associations in American History* (Urbana: University of Illinois Press, 1991).

41. The literature on southern women and antebellum voluntary associations remains much thinner than that on northern women, and there remains much work to be done here. A few examples include Gail S. Murray, "Charity within the Bounds of Race and Class: Female Benevolence in the Old South," *South Carolina Historical Magazine* 96 (January 1995), 54–70; Priscilla Ferguson Clement, "Children and Charity: Orphanages in New Orleans, 1817–1914," *Louisiana History* 27 (1986), 337–51; Carole Stanford Bucy,

"Quiet Revolutionaries: The Grundy Women and the Beginnings of Women's Volunteer Associations in Tennessee," *Tennessee Historical Quarterly* 54 (1995), 40–53; and Harriet E. Amos, " 'City Belles': Images and Realities of the Lives of White Women in Antebellum Mobile," *Alabama Review* (1981), 3–19.

42. Bellows, *Benevolence among Slaveholders*, 166–67.

43. Tyler-McGraw credits the famous theater fire of 1811, in which seventy-two people died, as providing an opening wedge for evangelicalism in Richmond. Evangelical ministers attacked "the stage, the race track, and the dance floor and advanced their vision of a church that emphasized a personal salvation and promoted missions." *At the Falls*, 84. Contemporary observer Samuel Mordecai concurred: "the disaster at the theater gave a better tone to society and a death-blow to female gambling." *Richmond in By-Gone Days*, 267.

44. Suzanne Lebsock has noted similar events in Petersburg. In the 1830s, in the wake of a series of revivals, there was an "explosion" of private charitable organizations in the city. *Free Women of Petersburg*, 218. Other cities saw the same multiplication of organizations: Alexandria's Orphan Asylum of 1832, Lynchburg's Orphan Asylum of 1846.

45. Bellows, *Benevolence among Slaveholders*, 21.

46. Loveland, *Southern Evangelicals*, 171.

47. *Second Annual Directory for the City of Richmond to Which Is Added a Business Directory for 1860* (Richmond: W. Eugene Ferslew, 1860). See listings for organizations.

48. Tyler-McGraw, *At the Falls*, 115–16; Varon, " 'We Mean to Be Counted,' " 60–61.

49. *Second Annual Directory for the City of Richmond*. See listings for organizations.

50. Lebsock, *Free Women of Petersburg*, 216.

51. Loveland, *Southern Evangelicals*, 167.

52. Tyler-McGraw, *At the Falls*, 116; Irons, "And All These Things," 28–29, 34; Takagi, "Rearing Wolves," 106.

53. Takagi, "Rearing Wolves," 106; Kimball, *American City, Southern Place*, 71. Sallie B. Putnam recorded an incident in which two servant women deceived their mistress by professing "to be seriously exercised on the vital subject of religion, and the unsuspecting mistress, much gratified at the disposition evinced by her maids, permitted them from day to day to go out, ostensibly to attend religious meeting of the friends of their own race, but she had afterwards abundant reason to believe that these were only subterfuges invented by them and their guilty coadjutors, the betters to carry out their nefarious intentions [that is, to rob the mistress]." *In Richmond*, 265.

54. Irons, "And All These Things," 35; Bogger, *Free Blacks*, 152.

55. The extant records occasionally note the presence of a slave in the Richmond poorhouse. But it is clear that such an occurrence was rare, and against official policy. In one instance, when it came to the attention of the city council that an elderly slave was in the poorhouse, the council ordered "that said negro be immediately sent by the proper authorities to his Mistress, and that hereafter no slaves be received in the Poor House." Common Council Minutes, 26 June 1856, 13:528. Small numbers of slaves received public relief in other southern states as well. One study from North Carolina, for example,

found ten slaves in Orange County received assistance from the wardens of the poor between 1838 and 1856, Roy M. Brown, *Public Poor Relief*, 52. It may very well be that rural counties offered more aid to slaves than was the case in urban centers like Richmond. This is an area that needs more detailed study.

56. O'Brien, "Factory, Church, and Community," 512–16.

57. Barbara Bellows has found similar religious competition in Charleston. *Benevolence among Slaveholders*, 38.

58. That some Richmonders shared anti-Semitic sentiments is clear, and those prejudices surfaced during crises. During the Civil War, Sallie Putnam's memoirs were filled with criticism of Jews for what she believed was their role in speculation, which drove up prices. See Putnam, *In Richmond*, 271, for one of many such observations.

59. During the antebellum years, the poorhouse records are remarkably quiet on the issue of religious instruction, in contrast to the postbellum period, in which the administrators worried constantly about the religion of the inmates. See chapter 6.

60. Berman, *Richmond's Jewry*, 145.

61. Keiley, *Memoranda of the History*, 8.

62. Varon, " 'We Mean to Be Counted,' " 48. The explosion of sectarian benevolencies occurred in other cities as well. On Mobile, for example, see Amos, *Cotton City*, 173–79.

63. Extant records do not clarify whether this organization was related to or affiliated with the Union Benevolent Association of Philadelphia, established in 1831. Given the similarity of names, functions, and chronology, I think it quite likely there were connections between the two organizations.

64. Varon, " 'We Mean to Be Counted,' " 31.

65. Ibid., 31–32. Women in Mobile operated a similar charity, called the Protestant Episcopal Church Employment Society, beginning in 1860. Amos, *Cotton City*, 179.

66. Loveland, *Southern Evangelicals*, 167.

67. Board of Managers of the Gentlemen's Benevolent Society, letter dated January 1845. Virginia Historical Society.

68. On Norfolk, see Goldfield, *Urban Growth*, 160–61. On Petersburg, see Lebsock, *Free Women of Petersburg*, 227. On the New York AICP, see Trattner, *From Poor Law to Welfare State*, 70–74.

69. Moses Drury Hoge quoted by Loveland, *Southern Evangelicals*, 173.

70. Barber, "Anxious Care and Constant Struggle," 121.

71. On the more aggressive proslavery thought, see especially Drew Gilpin Faust, ed., *The Ideology of Slavery: Proslavery Thought in the Antebellum South, 1830–1860* (Baton Rouge: Louisiana State University Press, 1981); and Eugene D. Genovese, *The World the Slaveholders Made: Two Essays in Interpretation* (New York: Pantheon Books, 1969).

72. Bellows, *Benevolence among Slaveholders*, 36.

73. "Modern Philanthropy and Negro Slavery," *DeBow's Review* 16 (January 1854), 274.

74. "Emancipation of Villiens in England," *Richmond Enquirer*, 3 July 1855, 1.

75. Bellows, *Benevolence among Slaveholders*, 21.

76. Varon, " 'We Mean to Be Counted,' " 58, 87–92.

77. Common Council Minutes, 23 December 1846, 11:520; and 11 January 1847, 11:525.

78. Varon, " 'We Mean to Be Counted,' " 34–35.

79. Common Council Minutes, 26 August 1843, 11:186.

80. Bellows, *Benevolence among Slaveholders*, 69.

81. Peter Mandler, "Poverty and Charity in the Nineteenth Century Metropolis," in Mandler, ed., *Uses of Charity*, 1.

82. Common Council Minutes, 13 June 1842, 11:67; 16 May 1846, 11:427; 11 January 1847, 11:570; 29 August 1842, 11:86–87.

83. Ibid., 29 March 1855, 13:339.

84. Goldfield, *Urban Growth*, 174.

85. Common Council Minutes, 13 February 1860, 14:336. These figures are from the city auditor's report to the council and cover an eleven-month period. This is why the numbers do not match up exactly with the twelve-month figures for 1860 as recorded in table 2.

86. Goldfield, *Urban Growth*, 177.

87. Overseers of the Poor, Annual Reports, Richmond City, years ending 31 March 1852 and 31 March 1858, Auditors of Public Accounts, State of Virginia, LoV.

88. Abramovitz, *Regulating the Lives of Women*, 148. Both cities restored outdoor relief shortly thereafter. See also Trattner, *From Poor Law to Welfare State*, 58–61.

89. The 1836–37 list comes from the Richmond City Hustings Court Records, Overseers of the Poor Reports, Richmond City Records. The 1850–51 list comes from the Auditor of Public Accounts, State of Virginia, Annual Reports of the Overseers of the Poor. Both in the LoV.

90. The 1850–51 report listed multiple conditions for individuals. One person could be considered elderly, sick, and intemperate at the same time. The result is 319 "causes" for only 236 admissions. The 1836–37 report listed a single condition for each individual. Since these two reports used different methodologies, they cannot be directly compared.

91. Here, I am following the observations (and language) of Peter Mandler "Poverty and Charity," 23.

92. Catharina Lis and Hugo Soly, " 'Total Institutions' and the Survival Strategies of the Laboring Poor in Antwerp, 1770–1860," in Mandler, *Uses of Charity*, 41–42. In Antwerp, the pawning of poor-relief goods came to be such a "problem" that the city outlawed it, hence leaving a paper trail of court cases for the authors to read. They also note that the underground market in sales of these goods remains undocumentable.

93. Overseers of the Poor Annual Reports, years ending 31 March 1853 and 31 March 1855.

94. Here it might be useful to point out that the statistics on race and imprisonment were quite different. In the 1850s, according to Edward L. Ayers, over a third of the inmates of Virginia's penitentiary were free blacks. *Vengeance and Justice*, 61.

95. Common Council Minutes, 11 January 1858, 14:126–27.

96. Ibid., 10 June 1844, 11:255–56; 9 June 1845, 11:338.

97. Ibid., 8 January 1855, 13:323; 9 July 1849, 12:195.

98. Ibid., 11 January 1847, 11:570.

99. Ibid., 10 June 1839, 10:445; 9 September 1839, 10:460; 29 August 1842, 11:86–87.

100. Ibid., 12 June 1843, 11:154; 10 June 1844, 11:255.

101. Bellows, *Benevolence among Slaveholders*, 73.

102. Common Council Minutes, 14 June 1841, 11:5–6; 13 June 1842, 11:67; 12 December 1842, 11:107; 22 September 1845, 11:376; 20 January 1852, 12:614.

103. Ibid., 12 February 1855, 13:333; 29 March 1855, 13:339; 15 September 1856, 13:557–58.

104. Ibid., 29 March 1855, 13:340.

105. "Insubordination at the Work House," *Charleston Courier*, 14 July 1849, 2. The story continued for several weeks and culminated in the execution of one slave and the punishment of several others. Untitled article, 2 August 1849, 2.

106. Edward L. Ayers, *Vengeance and Justice*, 55. Southerners were also exposed to northern reform movements while traveling for pleasure. Samuella Curd of Virginia attended a women's rights convention in Philadelphia, while on her honeymoon trip. Rable, *Civil Wars*, 16.

107. For the frequency of correspondence and closeness of ties, see for example Varon, " 'We Mean to Be Counted,' " 62–63, 105–6, 140.

108. Kimball, *American City, Southern Place*, 99.

109. Anne Firor Scott, *Southern Lady*, 20.

110. When a local committee tried to eliminate gambling in Richmond in the 1830s, for example, it wrote to a New York City district attorney for advice and information. Kimball, *American City, Southern Place*, 46. When the city council considered how to build and operate a workhouse, it wrote letters of inquiry to other cities, including Philadelphia. Common Council Minutes, 29 August 1842, 11:86–87.

111. Edward L. Ayers, *Vengeance and Justice*, 58.

112. In 1832, Mary Blackford obtained three thousand copies of a procolonization essay she read in the *American Quarterly Review*, which she then circulated throughout the state. Varon, " 'We Mean to Be Counted,' " 123.

113. Copies of Dix's publications are found in archives and libraries across the region. A list of her reports from the South is found in the bibliography. The most recent treatments of Dix are Thomas J. Brown, *Dorothea Dix: New England Reformer* (Cambridge: Harvard University Press, 1998); and David Gollaher, *Voice for the Mad: The Life of Dorothea Dix* (New York: Free Press, 1995).

114. Katz, *In the Shadow*, 26.

115. Ibid., 3. Charleston practiced the same official neglect of its city poorhouse with similar results. By 1849, local citizens complained that the building was on the verge of collapse: "its dilapidated condition calls for extensive repairs." "Proceedings of Council," *Charleston Courier*, 6 July 1849, 2.

116. Common Council Minutes, 12 June 1843, 11:154; 26 June 1843, 11:166–67; 11 September 1843, 11:187.

117. Ibid., 13 June 1859, 14:279.

118. Ibid., 13 June 1859, 14:280. Peachy Grattan had once been a visitor with the Gentlemen's Benevolent Society. Board of Managers of the Gentlemen's Benevolent Society, letter dated January 1845, Virginia Historical Society.

119. Common Council Minutes, 10 October 1859, 14:307.

120. This changing nomenclature appears to have been regional. In the 1850s, Charleston had also closed its old poorhouse, opened a new building, and formally changed its name to the "almshouse." Hope and Silverman, *Relief and Recovery*, 258.

121. "Proceedings of Council," *Charleston Courier*, 6 July 1849, 2.

122. See, for example, working-class outrage over the commutation of the sentence of Jordan Hatcher, a slave convicted of murdering his boss at a local tobacco factory. Kimball, *American City, Southern Place*, 119–20.

123. Bass, *History of the Education*, 33–35.

124. The year's total state expenditures amounted to a little more than $2,750,000. Richard Edwards, comp., *Statistical Gazetteer*, 107–9.

125. Ellen Ross, "Hungry Children: Housewives and London Charity, 1870–1918," in Mandler, *Uses of Charity*, 175.

126. Ibid., 167.

127. Mandler, "Poverty and Charity," in Mandler, *Uses of Charity*, 15.

128. Lynn Hollen Lees, "The Survival of the Unfit: Welfare Policies and Family Maintenance in Nineteenth-Century London," in Mandler, *Uses of Charity*, 88.

Four. The Civil War

1. Trattner, *From Poor Law to Welfare State*, 79. Trattner referred to a national trend, not a regional one.

2. Putnam, *In Richmond*, 210.

3. See for example Rable, *Civil Wars*; Richard E. Beringer et al., *Why the South Lost the Civil War* (Athens: University of Georgia Press, 1986); and Paul D. Escott, *After Secession: Jefferson Davis and the Failure of Confederate Nationalism* (Baton Rouge: Louisiana State University Press, 1978).

4. Pvt. A. J. Craddock to Governor Letcher, 28 March 1863, Executive Papers, John Letcher, box 26, folder 2, LoV.

5. Escott, "'Cry of the Sufferers,'" 230.

6. Barber, "Quiet Battles," 12; Chesson, "Harlots or Heroines?" 136.

7. Blair, *Virginia's Private War*, 39–40.

8. Unidentified from King George County to Governor Smith, 25 February 1864, Executive Papers, William Smith, box 2, folder 5, LoV.

9. Dr. W. H. Syme to Governor Smith, 1 March 1864, Executive Papers, William Smith, box 2, folder 1, LoV.

10. Judith C. Marr to Governor Smith, 30 March 1864, Executive Papers, William Smith, box 2, folder 5, LoV.

11. Elizabeth Marshall to Governor Smith, 28 March 1864, Executive Papers, William Smith, box 2, folder 5, LoV.

12. Blair, *Virginia's Private War*, 95. This is not to suggest that no local governments had ever paid rents before, but rather to emphasize that local communities now adopted policies that were new to them.

13. Emory M. Thomas, *Confederate State of Richmond*, 147.

14. Rable, *Civil Wars,* 103, 248. See also Laura F. Edwards, *Gendered Strife and Confusion,* 163–64.

15. Mrs. Lucy A. Cardwell et al., "a few of the many widows of Clarksville," to Governor Letcher, 13 January 1863, Executive Papers, John Letcher, box 25, folder 2, LoV.

16. W. A. Little to Governor Smith, 27 February 1864, Executive Papers, William Smith, box 2, folder 1, LoV.

17. Overseers of the Poor to Governor Smith, 13 March 1865, Executive Papers, William Smith, box 5, folder 8, LoV.

18. Escott, " 'Cry of the Sufferers,' " 231–32.

19. Wallenstein, *From Slave South to New South,* 102–4.

20. Zornow, "Aid for Indigent Families," 455.

21. Blair, *Virginia's Private War,* 74.

22. Zornow, "Aid for the Indigent Families," 456; Blair, *Virginia's Private War,* 95.

23. Emory M. Thomas, *Confederate State of Richmond,* 148, 170.

24. Zornow, "Aid for the Indigent Families," 457.

25. Escott, " 'Cry of the Sufferers,' " 231; Blair, *Virginia's Private War,* 96–97.

26. Putnam, *In Richmond,* 273.

27. Escott, " 'Cry of the Sufferers,' " 233.

28. Emory M. Thomas, *Confederate State of Richmond,* 81–84, 105–6.

29. Escott, " 'Cry of the Sufferers,' " 235–36.

30. Brig. Gen. Thomas L. Rosser to Major Barker, 8 December 1863, Executive Papers, John Letcher, box 28, folder 7, LoV.

31. Escott, " 'Cry of the Sufferers,' " 234; Blair, *Virginia's Private War,* 117–18.

32. Blair, *Virginia's Private War,* 6.

33. Escott, " 'Cry of the Sufferers,' " 238.

34. Ibid., 231.

35. Ibid., 236–37.

36. Edward L. Ayers, *Vengeance and Justice,* 147.

37. Tyler-McGraw, *At the Falls,* 139; Putnam, *In Richmond,* 40.

38. Emory M. Thomas, "To Feed the Citizens," 22. Quote by Putnam, *In Richmond,* 27. Since there was no census taken during the war years, all population figures are necessarily speculative. Estimates have been as high as one hundred thousand people by 1865.

39. Woodward, ed., *Mary Chesnut's Civil War,* 430. On refugees in general, see Massey, *Refugee Life.*

40. Barber, "Quiet Battles," 20.

41. Putnam, *In Richmond,* 320.

42. George W. Duesberry Jr. to Governor Letcher, 15 December 1863, Executive Papers, John Letcher, box 28, folder 7, LoV.

43. Putnam, *In Richmond,* 78.

44. Emory M. Thomas, "To Feed the Citizens," 27.

45. "A Case of Destitution," *Richmond Examiner,* 12 December 1862, 1.

46. "An Object of Pity," *Richmond Sentinel,* 21 March 1863, 1.

47. Emory M. Thomas, *Confederate State of Richmond,* 69, 106.

48. Putnam, *In Richmond,* 343.

49. Jones, *Rebel War Clerk's Diary,* 1:277 (entry dated 20 March 1863).

50. See for example the editorial in *Richmond Examiner,* "Paupers of Richmond," 30 December 1861, 3. The editor noted, "we have not yet found any one who could enlighten us on" the location of the temporary quarters.

51. "The City Almshouse," *Richmond Examiner,* 31 December 1861, 3.

52. Manarin, ed., *Richmond at War,* 44. The shell of the building had been completed, but the facility had not yet been furnished. The army could use the empty building by supplying its own furnishings. The city, by contrast, would still have had to spend considerable amounts of its own money before it could use the building for its intended purposes.

53. "The City Almshouse," *Richmond Examiner,* 31 December 1861, 3.

54. Manarin, *Richmond at War,* 262, 373, 438.

55. Ibid., 136.

56. Emory M. Thomas, "To Feed the Citizens," 23–27. (Thomas misstated the amount of welfare expenditures.)

57. Younger, ed. *Inside the Confederate Government,* 43 (entry dated 7 March 1863).

58. Emory M. Thomas, "To Feed the Citizens," 27.

59. Jones, *Rebel War Clerk's Diary,* 1:266 (entry dated 1 March 1863).

60. Quoted by Blair, *Virginia's Private War,* 73.

61. Jones, *Rebel War Clerk's Diary,* 1:275 (entry dated 16 March 1863).

62. Oregon Hill was a working-class neighborhood, within walking distance of the Tredegar Ironworks, where many of its residents were employed. Mary Wingfield Scott, *Old Richmond Neighborhoods,* 205–6. The most detailed analysis of rioters is found in Barber, "Quiet Battles." Her research in court records and newspapers uncovered some descriptions of some rioters. Francis Brown was a shoemaker who worked for the government. Mary Butler's family owned real estate in the city. Martha Cardona was the wife of a cabinetmaker. Mary Duke, forty years old, had a husband in the Confederate navy. Andrew Hawkins, also age forty, was a shoemaker for the government. Barbara Idoll, pregnant at the time of the riot, made tents. Mary Jackson, considered a leader in the riot, was a huckster at the Second Street Market and had a son in the Confederate army. Virgil Jones had been dismissed from his job in the city battalion for attempting to steal Confederate notes. John D. Lowry, a fifty-year-old Irishman, ran a brothel. Robert Mckinney, also Irish, was a member of the city battalion. Melissa Jane Palmeter was a fourteen-year-old prostitute. Margaret Pomfrey, who had two sons in Confederate service, owned slaves and land. Benjamin Slemper, German, was a member of the city battalion. We know even less than these scant details about most of those arrested in the riot.

63. Chesson, "Harlots or Heroines?" 143–44. As Chesson noted, determining the numbers of people involved in the Bread Riot is impossible given the inadequate, and often contradictory, evidence.

64. Ibid., 145–48; "Crowds of women, Marylanders and foreigners" were still hovering

on downtown streets the next day, demanding food. The city police dispersed the crowd. Jones, *Rebel War Clerk's Diary*, 1:286 (entry dated 3 April 1863). On the "tradition" of food riots, see Jack Tager, *Boston Riots: Three Centuries of Social Violence* (Boston: Northeastern University Press, 2001); Cynthia A. Bouton, *The Flour War: Gender, Class, and Community in Late Ancien Régime French Society* (University Park: Pennsylvania State University Press, 1993); and Jon Bohstedt, *Riots and Community Politics in England and Wales, 1790–1810* (New York: Cambridge University Press, 1983).

65. Emory M. Thomas, "To Feed the Citizens," 27.

66. Quoted by Furgurson, *Ashes of Glory*, 196.

67. "City Council—Provision for the Poor," *Richmond Examiner*, 10 April 1863, 2.

68. "The Poor of the City," *Richmond Sentinel*, 10 April 1863, 1.

69. *Richmond Examiner*, 4 April 1863, quoted by Chesson, "Harlots or Heroines?" 132.

70. Putnam, *In Richmond*, 208.

71. The Fleet family, of King and Queen County, heard of the riot a week after the event and believed it to be the work of "Yankees . . . aided by . . . the Dutch and the Irish." Fleet and Fuller, eds., *Green Mount*, 216–17.

72. Emory M. Thomas, "To Feed the Citizens," 27; "The City Poor," *Richmond Examiner*, 14 April 1863, 1. On the New Orleans market, see Massey, "Free Market of New Orleans," 202–20.

73. Blair, *Virginia's Private War*, 75.

74. The *Richmond Whig* issued such warnings, beginning in August 1863. Cited by Emory M. Thomas, *Confederate State of Richmond*, 146.

75. Younger, *Inside the Confederate Government*, 98 (entry dated 21 August 1863).

76. Emory M. Thomas, *Confederate State of Richmond*, 156.

77. The "Meat House" article, *Richmond Whig*, 4 April 1864, was quoted by Emory M. Thomas, *Confederate State of Richmond*, 168. The burglary at Winder's was reported in the *Richmond Whig*, 21 November 1863, cited in Thomas, 154.

78. Untitled, *Richmond Examiner*, 9 June 1863, 1.

79. "Henrico County," *Richmond Sentinel*, 25 March 1864, 1. On the private efforts, see "The Poor of Church and Union Hills," *Richmond Sentinel*, 19 November 1863, 1.

80. "The Meeting on Saturday Night," *Richmond Sentinel*, 12 October 1863, 1.

81. Blair, *Virginia's Private War*, 97–98.

82. "The Poor of the City," *Richmond Sentinel*, 10 October 1863, 1.

83. Blair, *Virginia's Private War*, 99.

84. Emory M. Thomas, "To Feed the Citizens," 28.

85. "Supplies for the Poor," *Richmond Sentinel*, 13 January 1864, 1.

86. Tyler-McGraw, *At the Falls*, 157.

87. "City Supplies for the Poor," *Richmond Sentinel*, 15 June 1864, 1.

88. "Richmond Soup Association," *Richmond Examiner*, 26 November 1864, 2.

89. Untitled, *Richmond Examiner*, 7 December 1864, 2.

90. See for example, "Young Men's Christian Association," *Richmond Sentinel*, 3 April 1863, 1.

91. "Relief of the Poor in Western Henrico," *Richmond Sentinel*, 25 November 1864, 1.

92. Barber, "Anxious Care and Constant Struggle," 127.

93. Woodward, *Mary Chesnut's Civil War*, 747.

94. Putnam, *In Richmond*, 344.

95. Undated newspaper clipping, quoted by Faust, "Altars of Sacrifice," 197.

96. Jones, *Rebel War Clerk's Diary*, 2:101 (entry dated 20 November 1863).

97. "Robbing an Asylum," *Richmond Examiner*, 11 April 1864, 1. See also Laura F. Edwards, *Gendered Strife and Confusion*, 164–65.

98. William S. Fowler of Thompson's Crossroads to Governor Letcher, 25 November 1863, Executive Papers, John Letcher, box 28, folder 4, LoV.

99. Quoted in "Relief for the Suffering," *Richmond Sentinel*, 29 September 1864, 1.

100. "To the Public," *Richmond Sentinel*, 23 January 1865, 1.

101. "Remember the Poor," *Richmond Sentinel*, 6 March 1865, 1.

102. "A Good Work," *Richmond Sentinel*, 26 November 1864, 1.

103. "To Disabled Soldiers," *Richmond Sentinel*, 1 December 1864, 1.

104. Jones, *Rebel War Clerk's Diary*, 2:100–101 (entry dated 20 November 1863).

105. Ibid., 2:388 (entry dated 16 January 1865). Emphasis original.

106. Rable, *Civil Wars*, 200. Mary Chesnut recorded how well she and her entourage ate while in Richmond, late in 1863: "We lived well—kept open house indeed. . . . We had sent us from home wine, rice, potatoes, hams, eggs, butter, pickles. About once a month a man came on with all that the plantation could furnish us." Her husband seemed more concerned than she about the appearance that such indulgences made, since a few months later he ordered her to hold no more parties. "The country is in danger. There is too much levity here." Woodward, *Mary Chesnut's Civil War*, 434, 508.

Five. Reconstruction

1. McDaid, "With Lame Legs," 15. See also Mark Grimsley, *And Keep Moving On: The Virginia Campaign, May–June 1864* (Lincoln: University of Nebraska Press, 2002); Noah Andre Trudeau, *Bloody Roads South: The Wilderness to Cold Harbor, May–June 1864* (Boston: Little, Brown, 1989).

2. Lynda J. Morgan, *Emancipation in Virginia's Tobacco Belt*, 128–29.

3. Tyler-McGraw, *At the Falls*, 159; Chesson, *Richmond after the War*, 58.

4. Dabney, *Richmond*, 196.

5. Tyler-McGraw, *At the Falls*, 165.

6. Chesson, *Richmond after the War*, 72–73. The army used this method—a civilian relief committee—in other cities as well. See Hope and Silverman, *Relief and Recovery*, 27.

7. C. Thorton Chase to Brig. General A. R. Hawley, 14 August 1865, Freedmen's Bureau Papers, Unregistered Letters and Telegrams Received, from Northern Charitable Societies, May 1865 to January 1869 (microfilm, reel 36, NARA).

8. Joe M. Richardson, *Christian Reconstruction*, 63; Rabinowitz, *Race Relations*, 129.

9. Quote by Trattner, *From Poor Law to Welfare State*, 85; Colby, "Freedmen's Bureau," 221.

10. W. E. B. Du Bois, *Black Reconstruction*, 223.

11. Colby, "Freedmen's Bureau," 222.

12. Allen Richardson, "Architects of a Benevolent Empire," 126, 119.

13. Colby, "Freedmen's Bureau," 226. By 1869, the bureau had issued twenty-one million rations in the South, with approximately five million going to whites. Franklin and Moss, *From Slavery to Freedom*, 229.

14. "Rations for the Poor," *Daily Dispatch*, 23 January 1867, 1.

15. These other activities of the Freedmen's Bureau are outside the scope of the present study. Recent scholarship on the bureau includes Paul A. Cimbala, *Under the Guardianship of the Nation: The Freedmen's Bureau and the Reconstruction of Georgia, 1865–1870*; Donald G. Nieman, ed., *The Freedmen's Bureau and Black Freedom* (New York: Garland Publishing, 1994); and McFeely, *Yankee Stepfather*.

16. Burr, ed., *Secret Eye*, 277.

17. "The Freedmen's Bureau," *Atlantic Monthly* 87 (March 1901): 354–65.

18. W. K. Kean to superintendent, 29 March 1866, Freedmen's Bureau Papers, Records Relating to Policies of Local Boards of Overseers of the Poor toward Destitute Freedmen, March–June 1866 (microfilm, reel 57).

19. Ben L. Leavell to superintendent, 2 April 1866, Records Relating to Policies, March–June 1866 (microfilm, reel 57).

20. Younger, ed., *Inside the Confederate Government*, 210 (entry dated 1 June 1865). It should be noted that Kean made these remarks by way of criticizing manumission "as the greatest social crime ever committed on the earth."

21. C. A. Holcomb, clerk, to superintendent, 2 April 1866, Freedmen's Bureau Papers, Records Relating to Policies, March–June 1866 (microfilm, reel 57).

22. R. S. Boulwang to superintendent, 2 April 1865 [*sic*], Records Relating to Policies, March–June 1866 (microfilm, reel 57).

23. J. T. Wilson, Lynchburg, to General O. Brown, 3 September 1868, Freedmen's Bureau Papers, Monthly Lists of Unemployed Freedmen, March 1866–December 1868 (microfilm, reel 58).

24. Whitelaw, *After the War*, 328.

25. John Clift to superintendent, 31 March 1866, Freedmen's Bureau Papers, Records Relating to Policies, March–June 1866 (microfilm, reel 57).

26. G. F. Harrison to superintendent, 31 March 1866 (emphasis original), Freedmen's Bureau Papers, Records Relating to Policies, March–June 1866 (microfilm, reel 57). It should also be noted that there were a few localities that reported their willingness to care for the freedmen on equal terms with whites. See for example Thomas N. Welch, Caroline County, to superintendent, 26 March 1866.

27. Chesson, *Richmond after the War*, 94.

28. H. Merill, forwarding correspondence from the Richmond Committee on Relief of the Poor, to General O. Brown, 23 May 1866, Freedmen's Bureau Papers, Monthly

Narrative Reports of Operations and Conditions, January–June 1866 (microfilm, reel 44).

29. "The Freedmen of Virginia," *Daily Dispatch*, 1 January 1866, 1.

30. Benjamin C. Cook to General O. Brown, 31 October 1868, Freedmen's Bureau Papers, Monthly Lists of Unemployed Freedmen, March 1866–December 1868 (microfilm, reel 58).

31. Wisner, *Social Welfare in the South*, 82–83.

32. "Suffering Freedmen," *Daily Dispatch*, 9 January 1867, 1.

33. "Died of Starvation," *Daily Dispatch*, 4 October 1866, 1.

34. "Negroes at the Souphouse," *Daily Dispatch*, 18 January 1868, 1.

35. "Rations," *Daily Dispatch*, 6 February 1868, 1.

36. Foner, *Reconstruction*, 152.

37. P. S. Evans to Capt. J. A. Rosekranz, 14 July 1865, Freedmen's Bureau Papers, Letters and Telegrams Sent, 1:49 (microfilm, reel 1).

38. Report from Greene County, 14 May 1866, Freedmen's Bureau Papers, Monthly Lists of Destitute Whites, May–September 1866 (microfilm, reel 58).

39. J. W. Hall, assistant superintendent, subdistrict C, report for June 1866, Freedmen's Bureau Papers, Monthly Lists of Destitute Whites, May–September 1866.

40. Henry K. W. Ayers, assistant superintendent for Westmoreland and Richmond Counties, to Major James Johnson, 31 May 1866 (emphases original), Freedmen's Bureau Papers, Monthly Lists of Destitute Whites, May–September 1866.

41. Undated report, labeled "Destitute and suffering white citizens who do not receive relief from the civil authorities Richmond City," Freedmen's Bureau Papers, Monthly Lists of Destitute Whites, May–September 1866. (Although this list is undated, the names and numbers are identical to a list dated 22 May 1866.)

42. William N. Felt, Report of the Number of Freedmen Issued Rations, October 1865, Freedmen's Bureau Papers, Unregistered Letters and Telegrams Received.

43. Report from Richmond Bureau Staff, George O. White, for months of December 1865 and January and February 1866, Freedmen's Bureau Papers, Unregistered Letters and Telegrams Received.

44. Du Bois, *Black Reconstruction*, 225. To put this figure into some kind of perspective, the federal government spent an estimated three billion dollars on the direct costs of the Civil War (excluding pensions and other indirect expenditures). Roger L. Ransom, "The Economic Consequences of the American Civil War," in *The Political Economy of War and Peace*, edited by M. Wolfson, (Norwell, Mass.: Kluwer Academic Publishers, 1998), 51.

45. Franklin and Moss, *From Slavery to Freedom*, 231.

46. For example, New Jersey–born Cornelia Hancock, who had served as a nurse during the war, volunteered to work with Laura Towne to start schools for the freedmen. Ten years of service in South Carolina led her to a career with the Society for Organizing Charity, the Children's Aid Society, and community organizing. Jaquette, ed., *South after Gettysburg*, x–xii. See also Giesberg, *Civil War Sisterhood*, chapter 7.

47. O. Brown to Lt. H. L. Merrill, 15 June 1865, Freedmen's Bureau Papers, Letters and Telegrams Sent, 1:9–10.

48. Quoted by Foner, *Reconstruction,* 153.

49. Bremner, *Public Good,* 116.

50. Mary J. Farmer, " 'Because They Are Women,' " 163–65.

51. Lt. Col. U. B. Scott to Capt. Stuart Barnes, 24 October 1865, Freedmen's Bureau Papers, Letters and Telegrams Sent, 1:265.

52. Whitelaw, *After the War,* 18.

53. F. T. Massey to Gen. S. C. Armstrong, 22 September 1866, Freedmen's Bureau Papers, Monthly Lists of Unemployed Freedmen, March 1866–December 1868.

54. F. T. Massey to Gen. S. C. Armstrong, 30 November 1866, Freedmen's Bureau Papers, Monthly Lists of Unemployed Freedmen, March 1866–December 1868.

55. Younger, *Inside the Confederate Government,* 213 (entry dated 7 July 1865).

56. S. C. Armstrong to Gen. O. Brown, 1 April 1867, Freedmen's Bureau Papers, Monthly Lists of Unemployed Freedmen, March 1866–December 1868. Armstrong's sympathies went only so far. This same letter described these poor, widowed women as "too weak-minded and ignorant to discern and act according to their best interests. This class demand sympathy, firm but tender and patient treatment."

57. Capt. B. C. Cook, report for August 1867, Freedmen's Bureau Papers, Reports Relating to Temperance (microfilm, reel 67).

58. Benjamin C. Cook to Gen. O. Brown, 31 October 1868, Freedmen's Bureau Papers, Monthly Lists of Unemployed Freedmen, March 1866–December 1868.

59. O. Brown to Major Turner, 14 June 1865, Freedmen's Bureau Papers, Letters and Telegrams Sent, 1:8.

60. Alex Dudley to Maj. Gen. Turner, 20 November 1865, Freedmen's Bureau Records, Registers of Letters and Telegrams Received, 1:59 (microfilm, reel 7).

61. J. J. DeLamater to superintendent, 8 February 1866, Freedmen's Bureau Records, Registers of Letters and Telegrams Received, 1:63.

62. Lt. Col. H. B. Scott to Capt. Stuart Barnes, 12 September 1865, Freedmen's Bureau Papers, Letters and Telegrams Sent, 1:166.

63. On the gendered nature of poverty for freedwomen in Virginia, see Farmer, " 'Because They Are Women.' "

64. S. C. Armstrong to Gen. O. Brown, 31 May 1867, Freedmen's Bureau Papers, Monthly Lists of Unemployed Freedmen, March 1866–December 1868.

65. Benjamin C. Cook to Gen. O. Brown, 30 November 1868, Freedmen's Bureau Papers, Monthly Lists of Unemployed Freedmen, March 1866–December 1868.

66. S. P. Lee to Gen. O. Brown, 2 January 1868, Freedmen's Bureau Papers, Monthly Lists of Unemployed Freedmen, March 1866–December 1868.

67. Lt. E. B. Townsend to superintendent, 8 February 1866, Freedmen's Bureau Records, Registers of Letters and Telegrams Received, 1:318.

68. P. S. Evans to Lt. H. S. Merrell, 29 July 1865, Freedmen's Bureau Records, Letters and Telegrams Sent, 1:79.

69. James A. Bates to Lt. J. S. Merrill, 28 October 1865, Freedmen's Bureau Records, Letters and Telegrams Sent, 1:277.

70. "Relief for the Poor," *Daily Dispatch,* 6 May 1867, 1.

71. "The Colored Paupers Who Flocked to Richmond after the Evacuation Not to Be Supported by the City," *Daily Dispatch,* 27 August 1867, 1.

72. "The Alms-House Affair," *Daily Dispatch,* 13 March 1866, 1.

73. Extant records do not clarify just when or why Bigger took the place of Phillips.

74. "The Richmond Alms-house," *Daily Dispatch,* 30 January 1867, 1.

75. Common Council Minutes, 16:114–15 (entry for 10 May 1867), LoV.

76. "Removal of Capt. Charles P. Bigger," *Daily Dispatch,* 23 July 1867, 1. The newspaper article claimed to have "been unable to learn the cause assigned for the removal."

77. "City Alms-House," *Daily Dispatch,* 11 July 1868, 1.

78. "Distribution of Wood to the Poor," *Daily Dispatch,* 9 January 1866, 1.

79. See "Local Matters" and "The Bureau and the Poor of the City," both in *Daily Dispatch,* 1 April 1868, 1. The city council appears to have been divided in opinion on how to cooperate with the Freedmen's Bureau. In July, Mr. Yale offered a resolution in support of cooperating; it was tabled by the rest of the council. "City Council–Called Meeting," *Daily Dispatch,* 8 July 1868, 1. The discussion continued 15 July 1868, 1.

80. "City Council," *Daily Dispatch,* 2 December 1868, 1.

81. Committee on Relief of the Poor, Minutebook 1870–75, 6 (entry for 6 December 1870), Richmond City Records, LoV.

82. "A Meeting of Citizens Yesterday," *Daily Dispatch,* 6 January 1866, 1.

83. "Meeting for the Relief of the Poor," *Daily Dispatch,* 12 January 1866, 1. Many other such organizations formed, such as Rocketts Relief Association, Humane Association of Church Hill, and the Colored YMCA. An interdenominational women's group formed a Dorcas society the following winter for the purpose of aiding orphans of soldiers, especially those in the northwestern parts of the city. "An Association of Ladies," *Daily Dispatch,* 6 December 1866, 1. New groups continued to appear in subsequent years, such as one by the women of the Third Presbyterian Church, formed in January 1868. "Clothing for the Poor," *Daily Dispatch,* 3 January 1868, 1. A "St. George's Society," for the mutual aid of English immigrants, formed in February 1868. "Organization of a St. George's Society," *Daily Dispatch,* 21 February 1868. A Catholic Beneficial Society, organized in 1871, had more than two hundred members by 1875. "Catholic Societies," *Daily Dispatch,* 1 January 1875, 1.

84. "List of Visitors of the Richmond Relief Association," *Daily Dispatch,* 3 February 1866, 1; "Humane Association of Church Hill and Union Hill," *Daily Dispatch,* 12 February 1866, 1.

85. "About Poor People," *Daily Dispatch,* 9 January 1867, 1.

86. Board of Managers of the Gentlemen's Benevolent Society, letter dated January 1845, Virginia Historical Society.

87. At different times, Parker served on the Board of Domestic Missions of the Virginia Methodist Conference, as president of the Male Orphan Society, and in several other such positions.

88. "Homes for the Orphans of Confederate Soldiers," *Daily Dispatch,* 15 May 1866, 1.

89. "A New Plan to Aid the Destitute Sick of Richmond," *Daily Dispatch,* 11 October 1867, 1. Three weeks later, the newspaper called attention to the fact that names were in

the sick box, "some cases of great distress, to which no one seems disposed to give heed." "Need Help," *Daily Dispatch*, 6 November 1867, 1.

90. See for example "Cheap Wood," *Daily Dispatch*, 21 January 1868, 1; "For the Poor," *Daily Dispatch*, 4 February 1868, 1; "Cheap Wood," 21 February 1868, 1.

91. See for example "To the Editor," *Daily Dispatch*, 2 January 1868, 1; 24 January 1868, 1; 25 February 1868, 1.

92. "Help the Poor," *Daily Dispatch*, 21 November 1870, 1.

93. "Episcopal Free School" and "Incorporation of St. Joseph's Academy and Orphan Asylum," both in *Daily Dispatch*, 5 October 1868, 1.

94. "Orphans," *Daily Dispatch*, 1 February 1866, 1.

95. "An Appeal to the Young Ladies of Richmond," *Daily Dispatch*, 15 February 1866, 1.

96. "City Council," *Daily Dispatch*, 27 February 1866, 1.

97. "Appropriations to the Orphan Asylums," *Daily Dispatch*, 16 December 1868, 1.

98. "City Council," *Daily Dispatch*, 1 January 1869, 1.

99. "Male Orphan Asylum," *Daily Dispatch*, 28 January 1869, 1.

100. "Charitable Appropriations," *Daily Dispatch*, 9 December 1868, 1.

101. Benjamin C. Cook to Lt. Paul R. Hambrick, 20 September 1868, Freedmen's Bureau Papers, Monthly Lists of Unemployed Freedmen, March 1866–December 1868.

102. "Necessity of Aid for the Poor," *Daily Dispatch*, 7 January 1867, 1.

103. "City Council," *Daily Dispatch*, 1 January 1869, 1. This article reported the number in the almshouses as 160. An article on 12 January 1869 reported the number had increased to 266.

104. See *Daily Dispatch*, 5 February 1868, 6 February 1868, 7 March 1868, and 25 March 1868 for examples of criticisms of the bureau's soup house.

105. "City Council. Soup House," *Daily Dispatch*, 9 February 1869, 1.

106. "The Almshouse," *Daily Dispatch*, 8 July 1870, 1. Again, the records do not make clear exactly when Bigger was reappointed. In the mid-1880s, Bigger was appointed superintendent of the Lee Camp Soldiers' Home for Confederate Veterans, a setting where his particular management style was undoubtedly more appreciated.

107. Margaret Neary found fifteen mutual-aid groups with deposits in the Freedmen's Bank. "Some Aspects," 114.

108. Trattner, *From Poor Law to Welfare State*, 86.

Six. The New South, Part I

1. Weller, "Charity and Social Developments," 466.

2. Tyler-McGraw, *At the Falls*, 180–81, 189–90.

3. Foner, *Reconstruction*, 535.

4. Rachleff, *Black Labor*, 71.

5. Neary, "Some Aspects," 114–17.

6. Chesson, *Richmond after the War*, 145; Tyler-McGraw, *At the Falls*, 182.

7. *Annual Message and Accompanying Documents of the Mayor of Richmond to the City Council for the Fiscal Year Ending January 31, 1876* (Richmond: City Printer, 1876), xv.

8. "Help the Poor," *Daily Dispatch*, 12 November 1873, 1.

9. Dailey, *Before Jim Crow*, 29.

10. Pulley, *Old Virginia Restored*, 33.

11. "Meeting of the Special Committee," *Daily Dispatch*, 21 November 1873, 1. (The newspaper coverage did not make clear whether these jobs would be open to both black and white workers.) Other city governments took a similar approach to public works, with identical reasoning. Using language that virtually duplicated Richmond's city council, the Indianapolis Trades Assembly in 1873 requested public works "which are a necessity to the city, and which can be done cheaper now than the same labour can be done in the spring." Quoted by Feder, *Unemployment Relief*, 67.

12. "Lodgings for the Homeless," *Daily Dispatch*, 14 November 1873, 1. Using empty jail space for nightly lodging appears to have been a common urban response to homelessness. During the first months of 1874, New York reported thirty thousand such "lodgers" each month. Feder, *Unemployment Relief*, 64. See also Vandal, "Nineteenth-Century Municipal Responses," 30–59.

13. "Relief of the Poor," *Daily Dispatch*, 9 December 1873, 1.

14. *Third Annual Message and Accompanying Documents of the Mayor of Richmond* (Richmond: Evening News Steam Press, 1873), 322; *Annual Message and Accompanying Documents of the Mayor of Richmond to the City Council for the Fiscal Year Ending January 31, 1876*, 43, 232.

15. "From *Petersburg News*," *Daily Dispatch*, 12 February 1875, 1. Quoting a letter from Richmond, in the *Petersburg News*.

16. "Aiding the Poor," *Daily Dispatch*, 5 December 1873, 1.

17. Ibid.

18. "Relief of the Poor," *Daily Dispatch*, 23 December 1873, 1.

19. Shelburne, "Brief History," 26–27. Extant records do not clarify the details, but it seems that the City Mission began as something like a women's auxiliary to the Richmond Relief Committee. The City Mission immediately took over the district visiting of the RRC; and by the 1880s, the RRC had moved more into the background, raising money for the City Mission. The organizations clearly worked in close cooperation from the beginning.

20. "Annual Report of Work Done by the City Mission from May 1888 to May 1889," Broadside, Virginia Historical Society.

21. "City Mission," *Daily Dispatch*, 4 February 1885, 1. The extent of the mission's activities is illustrated by a report for the month of February 1885. It reported the distribution of 1,200 "sick rations," 2,250 quarts of soup, 4,500 "pones" of bread, 125 yards of red flannel, 30 blankets, 200 yards of unbleached cotton and flannel, 100 pairs of donated shoes, 600 donated garments, and 200 coal tickets. In one month, the visitors reported 500 home visits. "Monthly Report of City-Mission Work," *Daily Dispatch*, 4 March 1885, 1.

22. "Knights of Honor," *Daily Dispatch*, 22 April 1876, 1.

23. "A Benevolent Association," *Daily Dispatch*, 6 December 1885, 1.

24. Levine, "Single Standard," 54–55; Gordon, *Pitied but Not Entitled*, 118.

25. Rachleff, *Black Labor*, 25, 71.

26. "The Colored Home," *Daily Dispatch*, 10 June 1873, 1; 7 July 1873, 1; and 9 July 1873, 1.

27. Lynn, "Social Functions," 49–50.

28. Rabinowitz, *Race Relations*, 144. This was the standard arrangement the city made with all orphanages: a small subsidy in exchange for taking several children a year who were public charges.

29. Report of Superintendent of Public Charities, *Annual Message and Accompanying Documents of the Mayor of Richmond to the City Council for the Fiscal Year Ending December 31, 1886* (Richmond: Public Printing, 1887), 6. Increased public appropriations for private charities was a national trend during the 1870s. See for example Feder, *Unemployment Relief*, 50.

30. "Asking for Money," *Daily Dispatch*, 23 January 1901, 1; "Pleas for Charities," *Daily Dispatch*, 26 January 1901, 6.

31. On January 1 every year, the *Richmond Dispatch* listed charitable organizations, mutual-aid associations, and social groups. Information on individual organizations can also be found in the published annual reports to the State Board of Charities and Corrections.

32. " 'Bell Day' Wins Big Sum for Home," *Times-Dispatch*, 17 March 1910, 14.

33. "The City's Poor Are Suffering," *Times-Dispatch*, 30 January 1904, 8.

34. "Money for the Ice Mission," *Daily Dispatch*, 9 July 1893, 7.

35. Cities throughout the country were experimenting with new forms of finance during these years. See for example Feder, *Unemployment Relief*, 54.

36. Barber, "Anxious Care and Constant Struggle," 129–31.

37. Frank Dekker Watson, *Charity Organization Movement*, 53. See also Leiby, "Charity Organization Reconsidered," 523–38.

38. Lubove, *Professional Altruist*, 1–9. Charity-organizing groups took a variety of names. To avoid confusion, I will refer to them as charity-organizing societies, or COS, which is the "generic" name for the movement.

39. Lubove, *Professional Altruist*, 16.

40. Frank Dekker Watson, *Charity Organization Movement*, 94, 100–101, 61.

41. Feder, *Unemployment Relief*, 131, 44.

42. In an example of the extremes to which charity organization might reach: the London COS opposed free school meals for children. Ellen Ross, "Hungry Children: Housewives and London Charity, 1870–1918," in Mandler, ed., *Uses of Charity*, 178.

43. "State Aid to the Unemployed," *Forum* 17 (May 1894), quoted by Feder, *Unemployment Relief*, 132.

44. Charles R. Henderson of the University of Chicago, 1897, quoted by Josephine Chapin Brown, *Public Relief*, 45.

45. Josephine Chapin Brown, *Public Relief*, 55–56. The survey was taken in 1928.

46. Frank Dekker Watson, *Charity Organization Movement*, 348–49.

47. "An Imposter," *Daily Dispatch*, 14 March 1885, 1.

48. In 1895, Philip W. Ayers reported the operation of COS locals in New Orleans, Louisville, Memphis, Nashville, Chattanooga, Richmond, Charleston, and Wilmington (N.C.). He noted the absence of such a society in Atlanta at the time. "Charity Organization," 260–61. The communication between northern and southern reformers was clear. Charleston's Associated Charities Society, formed in 1888, noted it had received valuable materials from organizations in New York, Boston, and other cities. Laylon Wayne Jordan, " 'Method of Modern Charity,' " 36–37.

49. Hunter, "Relations between Social Settlements," 75.

50. See Kogut, "Negro and the Charity Organization," 11–21.

51. Philip W. Ayers, "Charity Organization," 260.

52. Frank Dekker Watson, *Charity Organization Movement*, 357 n.

53. Laylon Wayne Jordan, " 'Method of Modern Charity,' " 43.

54. Ibid.

55. Frank Dekker Watson, *Charity Organization Movement*, 357 n.

56. Laylon Wayne Jordan, " 'Method of Modern Charity,' " 42; *Fourth Annual Report, Conference of Charities* (1886–87), 24–25, Louisiana Collection, Howard-Tilton Library, Tulane University.

57. Nellie R. Secrest to Maurice Willows, 12 March 1913, box 84, folder 75, "Virginia Correspondence, Prior to 1928," Family Service Association of America Records, Social Welfare History Archives, University of Minnesota.

58. Laylon Wayne Jordan, " 'Method of Modern Charity,' " 38; Lubove, *Professional Altruist*, 10.

59. For a clear example of this process at work, see Whites, "Charitable and the Poor," 601–15.

60. Glasgow, *Woman Within*, 81.

61. "The City Mission—Its Work and Prospects," *Daily Dispatch*, 11 December 1881, 1.

62. "Richmond City Mission," *Daily Dispatch*, 4 June 1901, 7.

63. *Richmond State* of 1881 quoted by Moger, *Virginia*, 126.

64. Laylon Wayne Jordan, " 'Method of Modern Charity,' " 39.

65. *Twelve Months of Constructive Service, Seventeenth Annual Report of the Associated Charities of Richmond* (Richmond: n.p., 1922), 6.

66. Philip W. Ayers, "Charity Organization," 263. Ayers was criticizing Richmond specifically here.

67. Feder, *Unemployment Relief*, 59.

68. Extant records do not make clear when the first charity organization disappeared. The impetus for the reorganization may have come from the outside. In 1903, the Virginia Conference of Charities and Corrections annual meeting in Richmond hosted a speaker from the National Conference of Charities and Corrections, John M. Glenn. He spoke on the need for organized charities and specifically mentioned conditions in Richmond. *Proceedings of the Virginia Conference of Charities and Corrections* (1903), (Petersburg: Frank Owen, 1903), 85–91. Officially representing their organizations at that meeting were Mrs. Charles E. Bolling and Miss Virginia Jones of the City Mission, both of whom became officers of the Associated Charities. *Proceedings*, 102–3. John Stewart

Bryan and Horace Hawes were also members of the conference who became officers of the AC (104–5).

69. Shelburne, "Brief History," 28–29.

70. *The Associated Charities of Richmond* (Richmond: Capitol Printing, 1906), 3 (a copy of this pamphlet is found in the Virginia Historical Society).

71. Quoted by Shelburne, "Brief History," 30; "Associated Charities of Richmond" (1906), 5.

72. Shelburne, "Brief History," 36–37. A list of volunteers' names can be found in the pamphlet *Associated Charities of Richmond* (1906), 13–17.

73. "Associated Charities of Richmond" (1906), 2.

74. Ibid., 17, 19–28.

75. Committee on Relief of the Poor, Minutebook 1875–85, entry for 8 February 1881, Richmond City Records, LoV.

76. Shelburne, "Brief History," 41.

77. "Public Charities," *Times-Dispatch*, 8 March 1910, 4.

78. Other regional social-welfare groups were powerfully influenced by charity organizing as well. The Southern Sociological Conference, which focused much of its attention on religious charities, strongly urged charity organization to the private sector. See for example "Sociology's Welcome," 213. On the Southern Sociological Conference in general, see McCulloch, ed., *Battling for Social Betterment*; Chatfield, "Southern Sociological Congress: Organization of Uplift," 328–47; and Chatfield, "Southern Sociological Congress: Rationale of Uplift."

79. First annual report of the Virginia Conference, quoted by Pulley, *Old Virginia Restored*, 146–47.

80. For example, the New York Charity Organization Society founded the first training program in social work in 1898. Trattner, *From Poor Law to Welfare State*, 241. The Boston School for Social Workers was organized in 1904 by Jeffrey Brackett, formerly of the COS of Baltimore. Lubove, *Professional Altruist*, 141.

81. School of Social Work, Virginia Commonwealth University, *Past, Present, and Future*, 10, 16.

82. Shelburne, "Brief History," 52.

83. Lynn, "Social Functions," 45, 33.

84. Bremner, *Public Good*, 145–46.

85. Young, "Confederate Pensions," 47.

86. Skocpol, *Protecting Soldiers and Mothers*, 65. See also McClintock, "Civil War Pensions," 456–80.

87. Ervin L. Jordan Jr., *Black Confederates*, 267.

88. Krowl, " 'Her Just Dues,' " 70. No source available gives an accounting of how much money was expended in each state, making it impossible to evaluate the relative economic impact of these pensions.

89. Axinn and Levin, *Social Welfare*, 82.

90. *Eleventh Census of the United States, 1890. Schedules enumerating Union veterans and widows of Union veterans of the Civil War.* (Although the population schedules of the

1890 census for Virginia burned, this special schedule survived the fire.) This schedule of the census did not ask for the race of the enumerated, nor did it ask whether they received a pension. In five cases, the enumerator volunteered the information that the persons being listed were black. In three cases, the enumerator volunteered the information that the persons being listed were recipients of federal pensions. These were undoubtedly not the only ones.

91. Article in 1898 Southern Historical Society papers, quoted by Rodgers, *Tracing the Civil War,* 22–23.

92. In 1867, the Alabama legislature provided $100 each to Civil War veterans who were so maimed as to be unable to use artificial limbs. Alabama added payments of $150 to blind Confederate veterans in 1879. Alabama Department of Pensions and Security, "Brief History," 3. Georgia's 1877 "redeemer" constitution, despite its "reputation for retrenchment," nevertheless specifically authorized the legislature to provide artificial limbs for veterans. Wallenstein, *From Slave South to New South,* 137–39. In 1881, the Texas legislature granted land certificates of 1,280 acres for every permanently disabled and indigent Confederate veteran living in the state. The act had to be repealed two years later, when the state ran out of public lands to distribute. Rosenburg, *Living Monuments,* 33. Virginia passed its first Confederate relief legislation during the war, with a state law that offered relief benefits to soldiers disabled or killed in military service. In January 1867, Virginia's legislature appropriated $20,000 to purchase artificial limbs for maimed veterans. Rodgers, *Tracing the Civil War,* 2, 4; McDaid, "With Lame Legs," 17.

93. Skocpol, *Protecting Soldiers and Mothers,* 139.

94. Teipe, *America's First Veterans,* 11–30.

95. Skocpol, *Protecting Soldiers and Mothers,* 139–42.

96. Young, "Confederate Pensions," 49 (table 1).

97. Alabama funded pensions for veterans by levying a half-mill property tax in 1891. The state provided pensions to veterans and unremarried widows, ranging from thirty to sixty dollars per year, in 1899. The property tax was raised to one mill for this purpose. Alabama Department of Pensions and Security, "Brief History," 3. In 1886, Georgia added pensions to disabled veterans as part of the state's welfare obligation. Wallenstein, *From Slave South to New South,* 137–39. Legislation in the 1890s provided pensions to indigent soldiers, regardless of past injury, and for their widows. Young, "Confederate Pensions," 48.

98. The classic studies of the Lost Cause are Charles Reagan Wilson, *Baptized in Blood: The Religion of the Lost Cause, 1865–1920* (Athens: University of Georgia Press, 1980); and Foster, *Ghosts of the Confederacy.* On Richmond in particular, see Parrott, " 'Love Makes Memory Eternal' "; and Hamburger, "We Take Care."

99. Edward L. Ayers, *Promise of the New South,* 333–38; Tyler-McGraw, *At the Falls,* 186–87. See also van Zelm, "Virginia Women."

100. Rodgers, *Tracing the Civil War,* 5, 7; McDaid, "With Lame Legs," 18.

101. Rodgers, *Tracing the Civil War,* 17, 19; McDaid, "With Lame Legs," 20.

102. Rodgers, *Tracing the Civil War,* 25–26, 43, 48.

103. North Carolina's legislature provided for a Confederate soldiers' home in 1891.

Roy M. Brown, *Public Poor Relief*, 96–97. See also Poole, "Final Encampment," 10–17. Georgia opened such a facility in 1898. Young, "Confederate Pensions," 48.

104. Rosenburg, *Living Monuments*, 32, 50.

105. Rodgers, *Tracing the Civil War*, 8–9. See also Emily J. Williams, "Home . . . for the Old Boys," 40–47.

106. North Carolina opened a Confederate Woman's Home in 1913. Roy M. Brown, *Public Poor Relief*, 96–97.

107. Hamburger, "We Take Care," 63–65.

108. Young, "Confederate Pensions," 49–50 (tables 2 and 3).

109. Gorman, "Confederate Pensions," 29–31.

110. Rosenburg, *Living Monuments*, 82–83.

111. Gorman, "Confederate Pensions," 31, 34–36.

112. Ervin L. Jordan Jr., *Black Confederates*, 185.

113. McDaid, "With Lame Legs," 19.

114. Virginia was one of several southern states to institute "servants'" pensions in the early 1920s. Rodgers, *Tracing the Civil War*, 53, 58. The earliest record of pensions for servants appears to be in Mississippi legislation of 1888, "an act for the relief of certain soldiers and sailors and servants of officers, soldiers and sailors of the late war between the States." *Laws of the State of Mississippi, Passed at a Regular Session of Mississippi Legislature . . . Ending March 8, 1888* (Jackson: State Printer, 1888), 30. My thanks to Frank Deserino for bringing this citation to my attention.

115. Report of the State Auditor, Fiscal Year Ending June 1925, table 42, p. 169; Rodgers, *Tracing the Civil War*, 60. The twenty-five dollars each "servant" pensioner received was substantially lower than that of whites, which were up to seventy-five dollars per year by then (48).

116. Rodgers, *Tracing the Civil War*, 26, 28.

117. Kousser, *Shaping of Southern Politics*, 171–81; Edward L. Ayers, *Promise of the New South*, 305–9; Dailey, *Before Jim Crow*, 156–65.

118. Key, *Southern Politics*, 20.

Seven. The New South, Part II

1. Report of Chief Nurse [Nannie J. Minor], Annual Report 1909–10, p. 15. Instructive Visiting Nurses Association Papers. Archives and Special Collections, Tompkins-McCaw Library, Medical College of Virginia, VCU.

2. On a national level, the depression of the 1890s was far worse than its predecessor in the 1870s. As with any depression, however, some places were affected more than others and some sectors of the economy fared better than others. Textile manufacturing in the South managed to prosper even while the same industry in New England declined. Edward L. Ayers, *Promise of the New South*, 112. In Virginia, cotton, tobacco, and wheat farmers suffered the most, as falling crop prices sent much of the southside into depression. Other farmers, especially truck farmers, weathered the depression better. Virginia's industrial sector was also unevenly affected. The state lost fewer businesses and banks

than did most other southern states. Woodward, *Origins of the New South*, 269; Moger, *Virginia*, 130–31, 151–53. Still, some important companies succumbed to the pressure, like the venerable Haxall-Crenshaw flour mills in Richmond. Tyler-McGraw, *At the Falls*, 227.

3. Journals that specialized in "muckraking," such as *McClure's Magazine*, appealed to a national audience. Important exposés in book form, which also helped to create a sense of a national movement, included Upton Sinclair, *The Jungle* (New York: Doubleday, Page and Co., 1906); Ray Stannard Baker, *Following the Color Line: An Account of Negro Citizenship in the American Democracy* (New York: Doubleday, Page and Co., 1908); and Lincoln Steffens, *The Shame of the Cities* (New York: McClure, Phillips and Co., 1904).

4. The literature on the national progressive movement is vast, and only a few works, representative of the most important recent trends, can be listed here. See Lissak, *Pluralism and Progressives;* Odem, *Delinquent Daughters;* James J. Connolly, *The Triumph of Ethnic Progressivism: Urban Political Culture in Boston, 1900–1925* (Cambridge: Harvard University Press, 1998).

5. Rothman, *Conscience and Convenience*, 5–6.

6. Ibid., 6. See also Kathryn Kish Sklar, *Florence Kelley and the Nation's Work* (New Haven: Yale University Press, 1995); and Muncy, *Creating a Female Dominion*.

7. Chambers, "Women in the Creation"; Walkowitz, *Working with Class;* Trolander, *Professionalism and Social Change;* Lubove, *Professional Altruist.*

8. Crocker, *Social Work and Social Order;* Lasch-Quinn, *Black Neighbors.*

9. Minutes for the Council of Social Agencies for 16 May 1922 noted that a representative for *Survey* magazine had recently been in town addressing a group of social workers and encouraging them to subscribe to the magazine. United Way Archives, box 14, folder "Council of Social Agencies, 1919–1925."

10. Lubove, *Professional Altruist*, 15.

11. Social-welfare progressives would be an example of the tendency of some voluntary associations to begin favoring public social legislation, as described by Theda Skocpol. She points out that not all members of voluntary associations were inherently or morally opposed to governmental activism, even when they placed great value on voluntary activism. *Protecting Soldiers and Mothers*, 17.

12. Important works on southern progressivism not cited elsewhere in this work include Bailey, *Liberalism in the New South;* Evan Anders, *Boss Rule in South Texas: The Progressive Era* (Austin: University of Texas Press, 1982); Lewis Gould, *Progressives and Prohibitionists: Texas Democrats in the Wilson Era* (Austin: University of Texas Press, 1973); Janette Thomas Greenwood, *Bittersweet Legacy: The Black and White "Better Classes" in Charlotte, 1850–1910* (Chapel Hill: University of North Carolina Press, 1994); Sheldon Hackney, *Populism to Progressivism in Alabama* (Princeton: Princeton University Press, 1969); Mary Martha Thomas, *The New Woman in Alabama: Social Reforms and Suffrage, 1890–1920* (Tuscaloosa: University of Alabama Press, 1992); Elizabeth Hayes Turner, *Women, Culture, and Community: Religion and Reform in Galveston, 1880–1920* (New York: Oxford University Press, 1997).

13. On black progressivism, see for example Higginbotham, *Righteous Discontent,*

171–84; O'Donnell, "Care of Dependent African American Children," 763–76; and Ross, "Black Heritage," 297–307.

14. See Elna C. Green, *Southern Strategies: Southern Women and the Woman Suffrage Question* (Chapel Hill: University of North Carolina Press, 1997).

15. Quoted by Moger, *Virginia*, 155.

16. See William A. Link, *Paradox of Southern Progressivism.*

17. See Mazie Hough, "Are You or Are You Not Your Sister's Keeper? A Radical Response to the Treatment of Unwed Mothers in Tennessee," in *Before the New Deal: Social Welfare in the South, 1830–1930,* edited by Elna C. Green (Athens: University of Georgia Press, 1999); Eggener, "Old Folks, New South," 251–80; and Speizman, "Movement of the Settlement House," 237–46.

18. Tindall, *Emergence of the New South,* 283, 284.

19. Ibid., 276. On the public-health crusades in the South, see Humphreys, *Yellow Fever;* Elizabeth Etheridge, *The Butterfly Caste: A Social History of Pellagra in the South* (Westport, Conn.: Greenwood Press, 1972); John Ettling, *The Germ of Laziness: Rockefeller Philanthropy and Public Health in the New South* (Cambridge: Harvard University Press, 1981); and William A. Link, *Paradox of Southern Progressivism.* On northern philanthropy in the South during the Progressive era, see Anderson and Moss, *Dangerous Donations.*

20. Grantham, *Southern Progressivism,* 218.

21. See especially Moger, *Virginia;* and Pulley, *Old Virginia Restored.* Published in the period before the rise of women's history, these works did not include women's reform activism in their coverage of progressivism, which narrowed the definition of progressivism considerably.

22. The quoted phrase comes from Ibid.

23. Moger, *Virginia,* 174, 214–15. See also Larsen, *Montague of Virginia.*

24. See Henry C. Ferrell Jr., *Claude A. Swanson of Virginia: A Political Biography* (Lexington: University Press of Kentucky, 1985).

25. "Epileptic Home Will be Erected," *Times-Dispatch,* 12 May 1910, 3. See also Noll, *Feeble-Minded.*

26. By 1923, forty-three states had established institutions for the feebleminded; and by 1931, thirty states permitted the sterilization of the feebleminded. Odem, *Delinquent Daughters,* 98. On sterilization in general, see Schoen, " 'Great Thing for Poor Folks.' " On sterilization at the Lynchburg Colony, see Lombardo, "Eugenic Sterilization in Virginia."

27. *Annual Report of Auditor of Public Accounts to the Governor and General Assembly of Virginia for the Fiscal Year Ending September 30, 1910* (Richmond: Public Printing, 1910).

28. *Annual Report of Auditor of Public Accounts to the Governor of Virginia for the Fiscal Year Ending September 30, 1920.* It should be noted that the private organizations that had originally created many of these institutions were fully supportive of the state's action in taking over responsibility for them. In some cases, that had been the goal from the outset. When the state had initially refused to establish such institutions, private groups built them instead, hoping to prove their worth and convince the state to continue to operate them.

29. The active lobbying of COS advocates appears to be behind the movement to create state boards. Philip W. Ayers suggested that the United Charities of Memphis had "taken steps toward the formation of a Board of State Charities for Tennessee." "Charity Organization," 262.

30. James, *Virginia's Social Awakening*, ix, 2–4. As an advisory board only, the State Board was limited to publicity, education, and influencing public opinion on behalf of positive reforms. DeWitt, "Present Charitable Needs," 433.

31. James, *Virginia's Social Awakening*, 50–52. By contrast, North Carolina enacted a mothers' aid law in 1923; and by 1926, seventy-one counties were participating in the program. Roy M. Brown, *Public Poor Relief*, 145. On mothers' pensions, see especially Skocpol, *Protecting Soldiers and Mothers*; Tuttle, *Mothers' Aid*; Leff, "Consensus for Reform; Bullock, comp., *Selected Articles*; Gordon, *Pitied but Not Entitled*; Joanne L. Goodwin, *Gender and the Politics of Welfare Reform: Mothers' Pensions in Chicago, 1911–1929* (Chicago: University of Chicago Press, 1997); and Robert Halpern, *Fragile Families, Fragile Solutions: A History of Supportive Services for Families in Poverty* (New York: Columbia University Press, 1999).

32. McLean and Mills, *Survey of the Social Agencies*, 61.

33. Key, *Southern Politics*, 19.

34. Kirby, *Westmoreland Davis*, 159.

35. Tyler-McGraw, *At the Falls*, 260–61.

36. Key, *Southern Politics*, 19.

37. Pulley, *Old Virginia Restored*, 180–83.

38. Shepherd, "Churches at Work," 16–17, 22.

39. City Board of Health quoted by Tyler-McGraw, *At the Falls*, 202.

40. Negro Welfare Survey Committee, *Negro in Richmond Virginia*, 73.

41. Tyler-McGraw, *At the Falls*, 222. See also Treadway, *Women of Mark*.

42. Ironmonger and Phillips, *History of the Woman's Christian Temperance Union*; Chappell and Gilchrist, "History of the YWCA"; Curtis, "Juvenile Court Movement."

43. Shepherd, "Churches at Work," 155.

44. On juvenile courts, see Knupfer, *Reform and Resistance*; Getis, *Juvenile Court*; Leroy Ashby, *Saving the Waifs: Reformers and Dependent Children, 1890–1917* (Philadelphia: Temple University Press, 1984); and Eric C. Schneider, *In the Web of Class: Delinquents and Reformers in Boston, 1810s–1930s* (New York: New York University Press, 1992). On juvenile courts in the South, see Trost, "Gateway to Justice."

45. Allen F. Davis, *Spearheads for Reform*.

46. Shepherd, "Churches at Work," 101–2.

47. McLean and Mills, *Survey of the Social Agencies*, 90. On the settlements in Richmond, see "Nurses Settlement in Richmond"; Minor and Cabiness, "Nurses' Settlement in Richmond," 624–26; Sibert, "Development of the Community Houses"; Nadler, "History of the Instructive Visiting Nurses Association."

48. "Governor's Wife Is Guest at Neighborhood House," *Times-Dispatch*, 3 March 1920, 9. On southern settlements, see Speizman, "Movement of the Settlement House," 237–46; Stuart, "Kingsley House Extension Program," 112–20; Dubroca, *Good Neighbor*; Berry, "Plymouth Settlement House"; and Lasch-Quinn, *Black Neighbors*.

49. Manuscript census returns, 1920.

50. "Orphans of Virginia," *Daily Dispatch,* 24 November 1900, 1.

51. *A Year of Service, Sixteenth Annual Report of the Associated Charities of Richmond,* 5.

52. *Annual Message and Accompanying Documents of the Mayor of Richmond to the City Council for the Fiscal Year Ending December 31, 1914* (Richmond: City Printer, 1915), 16.

53. Warner, *American Charities,* 192. See also Murray A. Auerbach, "Almshouses: Existing Conditions and Needed Reforms," *Proceedings of the National Conference of Charities and Corrections* (1914), 465–73; and Bardwell, "Standards of Almshouse Administration," 357–64.

54. For example, *Second Annual Report of the State Board of Charities and Corrections to the governor of Virginia for the year ending September 30, 1910.*

55. *Calendar of the Richmond Neighborhood Association, 1919–1920,* LoV.

56. Curtis, "Juvenile Court Movement," 75. Richmond's black community was certainly not unique in this, and there are numerous organizations in other cities. A handful of examples will suffice: In Hampton, Virginia, Amelia Perry Pride, a graduate of Hampton Institute, founded the Dorchester Home for aged black women in 1897. Primarily funded by private donations, Pride successfully lobbied the city council for support (Levine, "Single Standard," 67). Also in Hampton was Janie Porter Barrett's settlement house, the Locust Street Settlement (Janie Porter Barrett, *Locust Street Social Settlement*). On the Neighborhood Union in Atlanta, see Rouse, *Lugenia Burns Hope.*

57. Brigadier W. H. Barrett, quoted by Lynn, "Social Functions," 22.

58. Higginbotham, *Righteous Discontent,* 2, 196; Odem, *Delinquent Daughters,* 47. See also Gordon, "Black and White Visions," 559–90.

59. Negro Welfare Survey Committee, *Negro in Richmond Virginia,* 26.

60. Perdue, Barden, and Phillips, eds., *Weevils in the Wheat,* 170.

61. Elsa Barkley Brown, "Womanist Consciousness," 610–33.

62. In 1936, the Southern Aid Society advertised itself as "the oldest existing Insurance company owned and operated by colored people in this country." *The Acorn of 1893 Is the Spring Oak of Today* (pamphlet in the LoV).

63. "The Irish Relief Fund," *Daily Dispatch,* 14 January 1880, 1.

64. *Die Virginische Zeitung,* 16 June 1923, 8.

65. Ibid., 8 September 1923, 8.

66. Berman, *Richmond's Jewry,* 227. The Ladies Hebrew Benevolent Association reported in 1928 that it "handled" three hundred "cases" (285).

67. See Mary J. Oates, *The Catholic Philanthropic Tradition in America* (Bloomington: Indiana University Press, 1995); Robert Wuthnow and Virginia Ann Hodgkinson, eds., *Faith and Philanthropy in America: Exploring the Role of Religion in America's Voluntary Sector* (San Francisco: Jossey-Bass, 1990); and Debra Susan Block, "Virtue Out of Necessity: A Study of Jewish Philanthropy in the United States, 1890–1918" (Ph.D. diss., University of Pennsylvania, 1997). In some northeastern urban centers, the creation of Jewish charity organizations and financial federations came quite early—Philadelphia's

United Hebrew Charities was formed in 1868. The strength of these movements can be seen in the formation of schools of social work designed specifically for Catholics and Jews, both in New York. Warner, Queen, and Harper, *American Charities*, 567–68. Catholic training in social work was also established at the Jesuit Schools of Loyola, Chicago, Boston College, and St. Louis University. Brown and McKeown, *Poor Belong to Us*, 6. Catholic laymen of the Society of St. Vincent de Paul had long practiced "home visitation" that paralleled "friendly visiting" of the COS. Brown and McKeown, 25–26.

68. "Aid for the Jewish Refugees from Russia," *Daily Dispatch*, 30 November 1881, 1.

69. Berman, *Richmond's Jewry*, 286, 266.

70. Ibid., 206.

71. Brown and McKeown, *Poor Belong to Us*, 3.

72. For a similar pattern in another major southern city, see my essay "National Trends."

73. Glasgow, *Woman Within*, 80–81.

74. "Monthly Meeting of Woman's Christian Association," *Daily Dispatch*, 13 November 1900, 5.

75. "The Infants' Home," *Daily Dispatch*, 11 November 1900, 2.

76. Lynn, "Social Functions," 23

77. See my forthcoming article "Big Stories in Little Places: The Nurses' Settlement of Richmond during the Progressive Era."

78. Southern Woman's Educational Alliance, *Social Work*, 3; School of Social Work, Virginia Commonwealth University, *Past, Present, and Future*, 15. Several other institutions similarly claimed to be the oldest in the South.

79. *School of Social Work and Public Health, Second Annual Catalog* (1918–19), 9.

80. School of Social Work, Virginia Commonwealth University, *Past, Present, and Future*, 9, 11. Similar sentiments were behind the proposal by the Red Cross to establish social-work training at Tulane University, in June 1920: "Up to now, Southern communities were forced to accept Northern or Eastern social service workers, else manage to get along with untrained, poorly equipped and unsatisfactory service. No Southern University has brought this field of thought and service adequately into their programs. . . . The advantages of developing and training Southern leadership needs no explanation. It is fundamental and essential to the progress and rapid development of the South." "Tulane New Bulletin, 1921," quoted in Campbell, ed., *Making a Difference*, 7.

81. Louise McMaster to Miss Margaret Rich, 18 December 1924, box 84, folder "Richmond, Virginia, 1912–27," Family Service Association of America Records, Social Welfare History Archives, University of Minnesota.

82. Board of Charities and Corrections, Minutes 1908–48, 2:161 (entry dated 4 March 1927), LoV.

83. School of Social Work, Virginia Commonwealth University, *Past, Present, and Future*, 10, 16. Interestingly enough, Hibbs had trained at the Boston School of Social Work and held a Ph.D. from Columbia University. But throughout his years at the School of Social Work, he consistently reinforced the regional preference for native-born social workers.

84. *Richmond School of Social Work and Public Health, 1921–22, Fifth Annual Catalog,* 8.

85. McLean and Mills, *Survey of the Social Agencies,* 116. In 1925, the school affiliated with the College of William and Mary; it later became a part of the Virginia Commonwealth University.

86. School of Social Work, Virginia Commonwealth University, *Past, Present, and Future,* 16.

87. Negro Welfare Survey Committee, *Negro in Richmond,* 96.

88. *Not Alms, but Opportunity. Annual Report of Associated Charities of Richmond, for Year Ending November 1, 1923* (Richmond: n.p., 1923), 3, 7–9, 12–13.

89. Auerbach, "Almshouses," 473.

90. *A Year of Service, Sixteenth Annual Report of the Associated Charities of Richmond,* 8.

91. Ibid., 14.

92. H. MacComb to Margaret Byington, 15 March 1918, box 84, folder "Richmond, Virginia, 1912–17," Family Service Association of America Records, Social Welfare History Archives, University of Minnesota.

93. *Not Alms, but Opportunity,* 7.

94. *Twelve Months of Constructive Service, Seventeenth Annual Report of the Associated Charities of Richmond* (Richmond: 1922), 6–7. These tensions between public welfare and private charitable agencies were not unique to Richmond, but rather were part of a national struggle between the advocates of each. For the national scene, see Feder, *Unemployment Relief,* 245–47.

95. Marguerite Watson Farmer, "Analysis of Applications," 14–15; *Twelve Months of Constructive Service,* 6.

96. Shelburne, "Brief History," 47.

97. Marguerite Watson Farmer, "Analysis of Applications," 10.

98. *A Quarter Century of Service, Richmond Area Community Chest Twenty-fifth Anniversary, 1924–1948* (Richmond: n.p., 1948), unpaginated pamphlet, LoV. "History of the Richmond Community Fund, 1924–1936" (typescript, unidentified author). Although Catholic charities in some other cities resisted joining the Community Chests/Funds, those in smaller sized cities were more enthusiastic about financial federations. Brown and McKeown, *Poor Belong to Us,* 58–60. Richmond's Bureau of Catholic Charities joined the fund shortly after its organization.

99. Community Fund Budget Committee Minutes, 17 October 1924, box 7, United Way of Greater Richmond Archives (M247), Special Collections, Cabell Library, VCU.

100. Community Fund Budget Committee Minutes, 20 April 1927, box 7, United Way of Greater Richmond Archives, VCU.

101. "Citizenship Unified by Community Fund," *Times-Dispatch,* 12 March 1925, 11.

102. "City's Budget Goes before Finance Body," *Times-Dispatch,* 4 February 1925, 1.

103. Report of Superintendent of Public Charities, *Annual Message and Accompanying Documents of the Mayor of Richmond to the City Council for the Fiscal Year Ending December 31, 1905* (Richmond: Public Printing, 1906), 2.

104. See for example "Some Children Still in the Poorhouse," 147.

105. Foundling Hospital (1891); Friends Asylum for Colored Orphans (1872); Memorial Home for Girls (formerly the Female Humane Association's Asylum); Virginia Conference Orphanage (1900); Spring Street Home (1874).

106. Belle Bryan Day Nursery (1890); Fulton Day Nursery; Fulton Colored Day Nursery; Sunnyside Day Nursery. In 1928, these four nurseries reported a total of ninety-eight children cared for. Annual Report, State Board of Charities and Corrections, year ending 1928.

107. Average age for 1860 comes from data in table 4. Average age for 1907 comes from Admissions Register, Volume E (White Males and Females, 1907–13). The registrar began the new book with a listing of all those present on 26 August 1907. (These are whites only; the volume for the black almshouse did not begin with the same listing.)

108. See Green, "Infanticide and Infant Abandonment," 187–211.

109. On the history of adoption, see Barbara Melosh, *Strangers and Kin: The American Way of Adoption* (Cambridge: Harvard University Press, 2002); E. Wayne Carp, *Family Matters: Secrecy and Disclosure in the History of Adoption* (Cambridge: Harvard University Press, 1998); and Marilyn Irvin Holt, *The Orphan Trains: Placing Out in America* (Lincoln: University of Nebraska Press, 1992).

110. *Annual Message and Accompanying Documents of the Mayor of Richmond to the City Council for the Fiscal Year Ending December 31, 1913* (Richmond: City Printer, 1914), 17–18.

111. Randall, "Admissions and Records," 524.

112. See Charles E. Rosenberg, "From Almshouse to Hospital: The Shaping of Philadelphia General Hospital," *Health and Society* 60 (1982): 108–54; Charles E. Rosenberg, *The Care of Strangers: The Rise of America's Hospital System* (New York: Basic Books, 1987); and Dowling, *City Hospitals.*

113. Report of Lena R. Waters, to Mr. F. H. McLean, dated 2 January 1923, p. 9, box 84, folder "Richmond, Virginia, 1912–27," Family Service Association of America Records, Social Welfare History Archives, University of Minnesota.

114. The grants ranged in size from $42.40 to the Fulton Day Nursery up to $3,000 to the Instructive Visiting Nurses Association. The city spent $420,439.95 in its own poor-relief programs that year. *Annual Report of the Comptroller, City of Richmond, Year Ended January 31, 1926* (Richmond: City Printing, 1926), 36, 48, 67.

115. "Move to Abolish the Poorhouse," 10–11.

116. *Fifth Annual Report of the State Board of Charities and Corrections to the Governor of Virginia for the Year Ending September 30, 1913* (Richmond: Public Printing, 1913), 40.

117. *Eleventh Annual Report of the State Board of Charities and Corrections to the Governor of Virginia for the Year Ending September 30, 1919* (Richmond: Public Printing, 1919), 7.

118. James, *Virginia's Social Awakening*, 13.

119. "The Almshouse Contracts," *Daily Dispatch*, 15 August 1893, 1.

120. *Second Annual Report of the State Board of Charities and Corrections to the Governor of Virginia for the Year Ending September 30, 1910*, 22.

121. Stewart, *Cost of American Almshouses*, 51–52; *Second Annual Report of the State*

Board of Charities and Corrections to the Governor of Virginia for the Year Ending September 30, 1910, 15.

122. *Tenth Annual Report of the State Board of Charities and Corrections to the Governor of Virginia for the Year Ending September 30, 1918* (Richmond: Public Printing, 1918), 6.

123. *Sixteenth Annual Report of the State Board of Public Welfare for Virginia for the Year Ending June 30, 1925* (Richmond: Public Printing, 1925), 10.

124. "Sociology's Welcome," 212.

125. As early as 1900, the city paid for the superintendent of the almshouse to attend the meeting of the National Conference of Charities, held that year in Topeka, Kansas. "Relieve Distress," *Daily Dispatch,* 16 December 1900, 1. This became an annual trip for the superintendent. See for example Report of Superintendent of Public Charities, *Annual Message and Accompanying Documents of the Mayor of Richmond to the City Council for the Fiscal Year Ending December 31, 1905* (Richmond: Public Printing, 1906), 7.

126. Nannie Minor and Elizabeth Dinwiddie published articles in national welfare journals. Kate Waller Barrett, who entered social work during her years in Richmond, became a nationally known leader in work with maternity homes and unmarried mothers. Gay Shepperson and Frank Bane went on to hold key positions in New Deal welfare agencies.

Eight. On the Margins

1. Assuming that "behavior" demonstrates "opinion" is an exercise fraught with problems, which I am the first to acknowledge. Recognizing the limitations of this methodology, I have tried to read the aggregate data cautiously. I do not believe I have pushed the analysis further than the evidence can support.

2. The admissions registers, located at the Library of Virginia, run from 1872 to 1913, with an apparent gap in the 1880s. (There are volumes extant for the years after 1913; however, they contain different categories of information and cannot be used for the same purposes as the earlier volumes.) I have entered the entire text, some twenty thousand entries, into spreadsheets created with Microsoft Excel. There has been no sampling.

3. Administrators in Confederate veterans' homes, for example, noted that some of the inmates, having never had modern conveniences, did not know how to care for them. Rosenburg, *Living Monuments,* 98.

4. By the early twentieth century, the administrators were less often concerned with discipline and order in the almshouse. The records reflect a much less contentious atmosphere.

5. Glasgow, *Woman Within,* 21–22.

6. *First Annual Report of the State Board of Charities and Corrections to the Governor of Virginia for the Year Ending September 30, 1909* (Richmond: Public Printing, 1909), 39.

7. "The City Almshouse," *Daily Dispatch,* 3 April 1873, 3.

8. "The City Almshouse," *Daily Dispatch,* 24 April 1871, 1.

9. *Rules and Regulations for the Government of the Officers and Employees of the Almshouse of Richmond, Va.,* 6.

10. Although the almshouse superintendents made clear their intention to be nonsectarian, I have not seen evidence that Jewish or Catholic services were held at the facility. This was despite the presence of small populations of both Catholics and Jews in the almshouse, as well as substantial and established congregations of Jews and Catholics in the city. The attention to religious services by Richmond was not universal in Virginia's almshouses. An investigation by the State Board of Charities and Corrections in 1910 noted that "in many of our almshouses no religious service is ever held." *Second Annual Report of the State Board of Charities and Corrections to the Governor of Virginia for the Year Ending September 30, 1910* (Richmond: Public Printing, 1910), 27. A subsequent report found that, of the ninety-eight almshouses in use in the state, sixty-three had no religious services, twenty-eight had religious services occasionally, and seven had services weekly. Services were usually conducted by the Salvation Army or members of the WCTU. *Seventh Annual Report of the State Board of Charities and Corrections to the Governor of Virginia for the Year Ending September 30, 1915* (Richmond: Public Printing, 1915), 12.

11. "Entertainment at Almshouse," *Daily Dispatch,* 20 February 1901, 5.

12. "Music for the Poor," *Daily Dispatch,* 21 December 1901, 10.

13. Report of Superintendent of Public Charities, *Annual Message and Accompanying Documents of the Mayor of Richmond to the City Council for the Fiscal Year Ending December 31, 1903* (Richmond: Public Printing, 1904), 8.

14. *First Annual Report of the State Board of Charities and Corrections to the Governor of Virginia for the Year Ending September 30, 1909* (Richmond: Public Printing, 1909), 108.

15. Report of Superintendent of Public Charities, *Annual Message and Accompanying Documents of the Mayor of Richmond to the City Council for the Fiscal Year Ending December 31, 1907* (Richmond: Public Printing, 1908), 8.

16. "Inspect City Almshouse," *Daily Dispatch,* 3 February 1901, 6.

17. Committee on Relief of the Poor, Minutebook 1885–96, entry for 12 April 1887, Richmond City Records, LoV.

18. Ibid., entry for 10 May 1887.

19. Ibid., entry for 28 December 1890.

20. Ibid., Minutebook 1896–99, entry for 10 February 1897.

21. Ibid., Minutebook 1904–8, entry for 28 November 1906.

22. Ibid., Minutebook 1896–99, entry for 24 February 1897.

23. Ibid., entry for 19 April 1897.

24. Ibid., Minutebook 1897–99, entry for 10 February 1897.

25. Listed in volume White Males, 1887–1902.

26. Committee on Outdoor Poor, Minutebook 1904–8, entries for 10 December 1907 and 2 January 1908.

27. Committee on Relief of the Poor, Minutebook 1870–75, entry for 6 February 1871.

28. Ibid., Minutebook 1885–96, entry for 10 September 1889.

29. Ibid., Minutebook 1896–99, entry for 17 May 1897.

30. Ibid., Minutebook 1899–1904, entry for 15 May 1899.

31. Similar problems with alcohol plagued other institutions. Confederate veterans

living at the Soldiers' Home in Richmond also posed the problem. According to one inmate, any veteran who wanted a drink could go downtown and be "treated" to all the whiskey he wished. The board of directors appealed to local merchants and citizens to refrain from selling or giving whiskey to inmates in town. Rosenburg, *Living Monuments,* 112–14.

32. The superintendent, two assistant superintendents, two resident physicians, and the matron were required to live in the almshouse. *Rules and Regulations,* 3. In addition, most superintendents had family members living with them in the facility; other resident staff, including the matron, occasionally had family members living with them in their almshouse quarters. The 1880 census, for example, listed superintendent Charles Bigger living at the almshouse with his wife, five children, mother-in-law, and sister-in-law. The assistant superintendent, William Eppes, had a wife and daughter living on site with him. The "matron," Lucy Macon, also had a child with her in the almshouse.

33. *Rules and Regulations,* 3.

34. Committee on Relief of the Poor, Minutebook 1885–96, entry for 10 November 1891.

35. Ibid., entry for 14 July 1885.

36. Ibid., Minutebook 1875–85, entries for 12 September 1876 and 10 October 1876.

37. *Forty-fourth Annual Report of the Male Orphan Society* [1887] (Richmond: Whittet and Shepperson, 1887), 7.

38. The Children's Aid Society reported in 1931 that the depression was affecting the ability of parents to make partial support payments for the children they were boarding. Twenty-seven of the thirty-nine white children currently boarded were taken with the understanding that the parents would pay something toward their support. By the time of the report, only thirteen were continuing to contribute to their upkeep. Minutes, Richmond Community Fund, 26 August 1931, United Way of Greater Richmond Archives (M247), box 7, folder "minutes 1928–31," Special Collections, Cabell Library, VCU.

39. Committee on Relief of the Poor, Minutebook 1896–99, entry for 17 August 1896. Notation about transfer to payroll in volume White Males, 1887–1902.

40. Committee on Relief of the Poor, Minutebook 1896–99, entries for 14 November 1896 and 16 August 1897.

41. Listed in volume White Males, 1887–1902.

42. Stewart, *Cost of American Almshouses,* iii.

43. "Anything but the 'Po'-house," *Daily Dispatch,* 9 December 1900, 10.

44. Abramowitz, *Regulating the Lives of Women,* 164.

45. *A Year of Service, Sixteenth Annual Report of the Associated Charities of Richmond* (Richmond: Associated Charities, 1921), 10.

46. Cooley, "Substitute for the Poorhouse," 910.

47. Listed in the volume White Males and Females, White Males, 1887–1902.

48. Listed in the volume White Males, 1887–1902.

49. It is impossible, based on extant records, to reconstruct the exact composition of the medical staff. However, there are many instances in the records in which the same doctors or midwives were paid to treat both black and white patients. It seems, therefore,

that the quality of medical care for African Americans in the almshouse was similar to that of whites.

50. "Ambulance Calls," *Daily Dispatch*, 11 June 1885, 1.

51. Department of Public Welfare, *An Introduction to the Richmond Nursing Home* (Richmond: The Department, 1962), 3 (pamphlet in the VHS).

52. Mrs. Elizabeth Cramer to Governor Pollard, 10 December 1931, Executive Papers, John Garland Pollard, box 32, folder "Family Service Society," LoV.

53. Stewart, *Cost of American Almshouses*, 38.

54. Roy M. Brown, *Public Poor Relief*, 78.

55. Rachleff, *Black Labor*, 72.

56. Gordon, *Pitied but Not Entitled;* Higginbotham, *Righteous Discontent.*

57. For an introduction to these issues, see E. Anthony Rotundo, *American Manhood: Transformations in Masculinity from the Revolution to the Modern Era* (New York: Basic Books, 1993); Gail Bederman, *Manliness and Civilization: A Cultural History of Gender and Race in the United States, 1880–1917* (Chicago: University of Chicago Press, 1995); and Kristin Hoganson, *Fighting for American Manhood: How Gender Politics Provoked the Spanish-American War* (New Haven: Yale University Press, 1998).

58. Rosenburg, *Living Monuments*, 73, 31.

59. See Chambers, "Women in the Creation"; Walkowitz, "Making of a Feminine Professional Identity," 1051–75.

60. Cavan and Ranck, *Family and the Depression*, 159.

61. Erskine Caldwell, *Tragic Ground* (New York: Grosset and Dunlap, 1944).

62. American Public Welfare Association, *Survey of the Department of Public Welfare and Social Service Bureau of the City of Richmond* (Chicago: The Association, 1936), 11.

63. This trend was not unique to Richmond. Similar evolutions took place at other city almshouses. See Morton, *And Sin No More*, 21, 26.

64. There are no birth records for most of the maternity homes. In the census year of 1910, three facilities reported the births from their homes. The City Almshouse thus far exceeded any of them.

65. This figure comes from the registers of admissions. Since this does not match the numbers reported in the Annual Reports of the Superintendent of the Almshouse, I must conclude that there are registers or parts of registers lacking from the holdings in the Library of Virginia.

66. A report on 115 illegitimate births in Richmond in 1922 noted that only 30 were residents of Richmond. "The rest came from Virginia and North Carolina, mostly. This is as might be expected. Other cities are carrying in the same way the burden of unmarried mothers originally coming from Richmond." McLean and Mills, *Survey of the Social Agencies*, 36.

67. Maternity homes seemed to have short life expectancy; many folded after a brief existence. The only record of them is a listing in the City Directory, like the Faith Home, listed in 1898 and 1900, but not afterward. In 1916, there appear to have been six different homes caring for mothers and babies, in addition to the almshouse. *Eighth Annual Report*

302 · Notes to Chapter Eight

of the State Board of Charities and Corrections to the Governor of Virginia for the Year
Ending September 30th, 1916 (Richmond: Public Printing, 1917), 104–40.

68. Bureau of the Census, *Benevolent Institutions, 1910.* The other two homes did not
report entry fees that year.

69. Kunzel, *Fallen Women,* 8.

70. James, *Virginia's Social Awakening,* 35–39. Regina Kunzel argues that social workers
began a campaign to professionalize maternity homes during the 1910s. Social workers formed a united front against the maternity homes and were harshly critical of the
women who ran them. *Fallen Women,* 49. The tone of James's account supports this assessment, which suggests that the report cited here may be overly critical of the maternity
homes in Richmond. This investigation did result in the regulation of these homes by
both the state and the city governments. The Richmond city council passed an ordinance
in 1910 requiring the licensing of "lying-in hospitals." *Ordinances and Certain Joint Resolutions of the City of Richmond from September 1, 1908 to September 1, 1910* (Richmond:
city printer, 1910), 236.

71. Kunzel, *Fallen Women,* 1–2, 26; Morton, *And Sin No More,* 37.

72. Quoted phrases are from Morton, *And Sin No More,* 44. The administrators of
the Richmond almshouse, although not "professional social workers" during the period
under review, nevertheless were participants in the Virginia Conference on Charities and
Corrections, which was the forerunner of the Virginia Conference of Social Work. Heavily influenced by charity-organization methods and philosophies, the Virginia Conference was the clearinghouse for contemporary social work techniques and theories.

73. Kunzel, *Fallen Women,* 33–34.

74. "Is it too much to ask of a woman, who has brought a child into the world under
such conditions that it must always remaine handicapped because of the circumstances
of its birth, to remain with it at least for a year or eighteen months and give it the food
which God has placed in her keeping?" Kate Waller Barrett, "Unmarried Mother," 97–98.

75. James, *Virginia's Social Awakening,* 48.

76. Brumberg, "Ruined Girls," 253.

77. Fuchs, *Abandoned Children,* 11. David Ransel has made another thoughtful observation about married women who gave up their babies in Moscow, in a line of reasoning
that could apply to women in Richmond as well. Since husbands and wives often worked
in different homes, it was just as difficult for these women to keep their children as for
their unmarried counterparts. He suggests that this may have been the source of many
of the legitimate children who entered orphanages and foundling homes. It was the conditions of employment as much as poverty per se that interfered with the ability of these
women to keep their children. Ransel, *Mothers of Misery,* 173.

78. Brumberg, "Ruined Girls," 247, 249.

79. Clement, *Welfare and the Poor,* 30.

80. Although whites disapproved, they recognized that their black neighbors held different cultural conventions regarding "illegitimacy." See *Illegitimacy in Richmond, Va.*

81. Kunzel, *Fallen Women,* 140.

82. Negro Welfare Survey Committee, *Negro in Richmond Virginia,* 43. The report

noted that black families took in other children, while white children filled the orphanages instead.

83. There is certainly the possibility that John York had earlier contact with the welfare system, but no extant records confirm it.

84. Admissions registers for the almshouses in Henrico and Chesterfield, if extant, would likely produce evidence of even further institutionalization. I have been unable to locate any other registers.

85. The registers appear to have recorded what type of work an individual had done most recently, as opposed to the kind of work done most frequently.

86. "Man in Poorhouse to Wed Girl There," *Times-Dispatch,* 18 December 1909, 1.

87. Since York was in the Richmond almshouse from 2 September to 20 November, I think it is likely that the couple met after the latter date. That would mean that they married just a month after they met.

88. Mary Vest does not appear in the Richmond City Almshouse admission registers. There are two Vests, Joseph and Phillip, admitted to the almshouse in 1911, who might be Mary's brothers.

89. "Man in Poorhouse," 1. According to the Henrico County Marriage Register, a marriage was performed for John York and Mary Vest on 17 December 1909. John York was listed as a forty-nine-year-old plumber; Mary listed herself as thirty years old and single. Legally speaking, there was no reason why marriage would have affected their eligibility for admission to the almshouse. Married people were not excluded by law. The local authorities took advantage of the situation, hoping to rid themselves of a long-vexing problem. They counted on the Yorks not knowing their legal rights, and it appears they were correct. It is also possible that the overseers took advantage of the mobility of the York family and used the settlement laws to prohibit their reentry.

90. "Honeymoon Ends in Call for Help," *Times-Dispatch,* 5 June 1910, 1.

91. "To County Poor House," *Times-Dispatch,* 10 July 1910, sec. D, p. 4.

92. "Still Unable to Place Children," *Times-Dispatch,* 22 June 1910, 3.

93. Ibid.

94. *Third Annual Report of the State Board of Charities and Corrections for the Year Ending September 30, 1911* (Richmond: Public Printing, 1911), 26–27.

95. On Carrie Buck and sterilization at the Colony for the Feeble-Minded, see Lisa Lindquist Dorr, "Arm in Arm," 143–66; Sally A. Webb, Mary Faith Marshall, and Paul A. Lombardo, "Eugenics in the South: The Carrie Buck Case," *The Journal of the South Carolina Medical Association* 94 (1998): 389–92; Lombardo, "Eugenic Sterilization in Virginia"; and Gregory Michael Dorr, "Segregation's Science."

96. John York's death certificate, from 1931, reported that he had lived at the Colony for fourteen years. I have not been able to confirm the exact date of admission. Death Certificate 11405, Amherst County, 28 May 1931.

97. In fact, the moratorium seems to have applied to any extended family as well. Before the exposé of 1910, there were several other Vests in the admissions registers (presumably one of whom was Mary's brother). But no one with the last name Vest or York was admitted after that date.

98. Virginia mental health officials accepted as fact the generational transmission of feeblemindedness. The biennial reports of the Colony at Lynchburg matter-of-factly tabulated the numbers of patients whose feeblemindedness was caused by heredity. See for example, *First Biennial Report of the Board of Directors and Superintendent of the State Colony for Epileptics and Feeble-Minded* (Richmond: Public Printing, 1921), 38. Systematic sterilizations began in November 1927.

99. Mental health officers of the Progressive era considered sterilization to be the more humane solution to the problem of feeblemindedness. The alternative was to keep such people "in institutions and supported at the expense of the State for the child-bearing period covering at least thirty years, to prevent them from bearing children to increase the population of mental and physical defectives and dependents. . . . it certainly seems more humane and just to them to give them the benefit of a milder and less severe method of attaining the desired end." *Second Biennial Report of the Board of Directors and Superintendent of the State Colony for Epileptics and Feeble-Minded* (Richmond: Public Printing, 1923), 27.

100. "[O]ur plan is to increase our hospital facilities as rapidly as is possible, and make this part of our institution a sort of clearing house for these cases; that is, they will simply pass through the institution for the purpose of sterilization." *Nineteenth Annual Report of the Board of Directors and Superintendent of the State Colony for Epileptics and Feeble-Minded* (Richmond: Public Printing, 1928), 8.

Nine. The End of the Poor Laws

1. "Report on a Relief Meeting at Richmond, Virginia," 11 October 1933. Records of the Works Progress Administration, NARA (Archives II), RG 69, Federal Emergency Relief Administration Central Files (1933–36), "State" series (1933–35), Virginia (May 1933–December 1935), box 301, folder "Field Reports." This collection cited hereafter as "FERA Papers."

2. Colcord, *Cash Relief*, 11.

3. Edith Abbott, *Public Assistance*, vii.

4. The impact on wage levels was significant enough to bring a backlash. Southern Democrats demanded, and received, a reduction in regional pay rates. Wages that had been as high as 40 cents an hour dropped as low as 12 cents an hour. Schulman, *From Cotton Belt to Sunbelt*, 32.

5. Ibid., 42.

6. Key, *Southern Politics*, 19.

7. Heinemann, *Depression and New Deal*, ix.

8. See for example Jeffrey S. Cole, "Impact of the Great Depression," 165.

9. Heinemann, *Depression and New Deal in Virginia*, 4, 7, 13.

10. Ibid., 7–10.

11. Mary D. McClellan to the Council of Social Agencies, 12 December 1938, United Way Archives, box 14, folder "Council of Social Agencies, 1928–1932," Cabell Library, Special Collections, VCU.

12. Tyler-McGraw, *At the Falls*, 261.

13. Heinemann, *Depression and New Deal*, 12.

14. "Relief Administered to Workers in the Tobacco Industry in Winston-Salem, Durham, and Richmond January 1, 1934 to November 1, 1934," FERA Research Bulletin, series 1, no. 9, p. 5.

15. For example, "Hold Up Man Is Foiled at Theatre; Got $200 at Paul's," *Times-Dispatch*, 28 December 1930, 1; "Negro Is Charged in Theft of Clothes," *Times-Dispatch*, 29 December 1930, 2; "Accused of Theft," *Times-Dispatch*, 30 December 1930, 3.

16. Community Fund Budget Committee Minutes, 21 October 1931, box 7, United Way of Greater Richmond Archives (M247), Special Collections, Cabell Library, VCU.

17. Dabney, *Richmond*, 313.

18. Minutes, October 12, 1932, Instructive Visiting Nurses Association Papers, box 4, Virginia Commonwealth University, Tompkins-McCaw Library Medical College of Virginia, Archives and Special Collections, Richmond. Cited hereafter as IVNA Papers.

19. Cutchins, *Memories of Old Richmond*, 326.

20. Tyler-McGraw, *At the Falls*, 262–63.

21. Heinemann, *Depression and New Deal*, 19, 30.

22. Cash, *Mind of the South*, 368.

23. Mrs. Susie E. Burch, Alexandria, Virginia, to ER 25 June 1934, ER Papers, "Positions Sought through Mrs. Roosevelt" series, box 2381 (alphabetically arranged), FDR Library.

24. Mr. C. E. Miller to Governor Pollard ("Beloved Brother and Friend"), 5 October 1933, Pollard Executive Papers, box 34, folder "Federal Emergency Relief," LoV.

25. Michael O'Neil to Governor Peery, 4 January 1935, Peery Executive Papers, box 74, folder "Public Welfare Commissioner, 1," LoV. A note appended from welfare commissioner Arthur James informed the governor: "This is one of the few instances I have encountered of a person displeased because he cannot get into the poorhouse."

26. This was nothing unique to the Great Depression. Private charities had learned this lesson nearly a century earlier: Philadelphia's Union Benevolent Association found the 1850s depression had "fallen with most fatal force upon many of the best friends of this society and some of its most liberal subscribers." Feder, *Unemployment Relief*, 27.

27. Charles Scott Wright, "Creating a New Deal," 44–45; Jeffrey S. Cole, "Impact of the Great Depression," 166, 169, 176.

28. Trattner, *From Poor Law to Welfare State*, 274.

29. Jeffrey S. Cole, "Impact of the Great Depression," 172.

30. Lamar Johnson, city manager of Hopewell, Virginia, to Governor Pollard, 17 August 1932, Pollard Executive Papers, box 38, folder "RFC, relief, local."

31. Humbert et al., eds., *Virginia*, 316–17, 355. Not surprisingly, most of Virginia's city governments carried the maximum bonded debt they could, with Richmond being the largest debtor municipality in the state. (It should be noted that Virginia was not the only state with constitutional limitations in dealing with the depression. Josephine Chapin Brown, *Public Relief*, 117.)

32. *Twenty-seventh and Twenty-eighth Annual Reports of the State Department of Public Welfare of Virginia for the Two Years Ending June 30, 1937* (Richmond: Public Printing,

1937), 37; "County Seeks Amendment to Almshouse Act," *Times-Dispatch*, 17 January 1930, 1.

33. Mrs. Ella V. Gallion to Governor Pollard, 4 October 1933, Pollard Executive Papers, box 34, folder "Federal Emergency Relief." Despite Gallion's deferential tone, she received a reply from the governor informing her that the state had no fund for direct relief, and referring her to her local welfare office.

34. Mrs. Ina P. Duncan to Governor Peery, 9 March 1934, Peery Executive Papers, box 79, folder "Relief."

35. J. R. Forsyth to Governor Pollard, 1 June 1933, Pollard Executive Papers, box 34, folder "Federal Emergency Relief."

36. J. T. Walters to Governor Pollard, 13 February 1930, Pollard Executive Papers, box 17, folder "Confederate Veterans."

37. E. R. Combs, comptroller, to J. G. Jackson, 13 April 1931, Pollard Executive Papers, box 17, folder "Confederate Veterans." This is one of many dozens of letters from "sons" hoping for assistance.

38. E. R. Combs to Mrs. Eva L. Shoemaker, 27 February 1931, Pollard Executive Papers, box 17, folder "Confederate Veterans."

39. E. R. Combs to Mr. James C. Harding, 11 March 1931, Pollard Executive Papers, box 17, folder "Confederate Veterans."

40. Gee and Stauffer, *Rural and Urban Living Standards*, 11.

41. Mrs. Joel H. Watkins to Governor Pollard, 30 August 1932, Pollard Executive Papers, box 38, folder "RFC, relief, local."

42. J. H. Stinson to Governor Pollard, 12 August 1932, Pollard Executive Papers, box 38, folder "RFC, relief, local."

43. B. M. Beckham to Governor Pollard, 27 July 1932, Pollard Executive Papers, box 38, folder "RFC, relief, local."

44. Melessa Hazelwood to Governor Pollard, 18 February 1933, Pollard Executive Papers, box 98, folder "Public Welfare Commissioner, 2."

45. Josephine Chapin Brown, *Public Relief*, 96.

46. Heinemann, *Depression and New Deal*, 6, 13.

47. Ibid., 5.

48. Like the municipal governments, the state government's ability to issue bonds was also limited by restrictions in the constitution, thanks to a 1928 amendment. Humbert et al., *Virginia*, 353.

49. Singleton, *American Dole*, 95–107; Grace Abbott, *From Relief to Social Security*, 141 n. The amount obtained from the RFC increased the next year. By May 1933, Virginia had secured a total of $3,485,711. Of that amount, $183,825 was used for direct relief. James, *State Becomes a Social Worker*, 251, 256.

50. Tyler-McGraw, *At the Falls*, 263; Heinemann, *Depression and New Deal*, 18.

51. Cash, *Mind of the South*, 372.

52. C. P. Spaeth to Harry Hopkins, 10 April 1934, FERA Papers, box 299. Other southern states also experienced fearful disorder. Mississippi, for example, reached a point at which "food riots and looting were an almost daily occurrence." As an agent for the RFC

during the Hoover administration, Aubrey Williams attempted to hold public meetings with the unemployed in Mississippi but had to suspend those plans when several such meetings "ended in uproar and near riot." Salmond, *Southern Rebel*, 37–38.

53. Marguerite Watson Farmer, "Analysis of Applications," 17.

54. "Board Will Plan Founders' Day at Sheltering Arms Hospital," *Times-Dispatch*, 17 January 1930, 14.

55. Marguerite Watson Farmer, "Analysis of Applications," 18.

56. Annual Reports 1932, Director's Report, 3; Annual Reports 1933, Director's Report, 1, IVNA Papers, box 10.

57. Figures for 1928 and 1933 in this paragraph come from "Reports on Private Philanthropy," Annual Reports of Comptroller, Commonwealth of Virginia, years ending 1928 and 1933.

58. Heinemann, *Depression and New Deal*, 17, 40.

59. Ibid., 76; Dabney, *Richmond*, 315.

60. On the national level, even the Association of Community Chests and Councils "became a strong advocate of greater amounts of public relief as a necessary means of preventing hysteria and panic." Josephine Chapin Brown, *Public Relief*, 132. One recent study has argued that this trend actually began in the 1920s, and by 1931, "the resistance to public welfare had almost completely broken down." Singleton, *American Dole*, 58. (If this was true, I found little evidence of it in Richmond.)

61. Community Fund Budget Committee Minutes, February 11, 1931, box 7, United Way of Greater Richmond Archives (M247), Special Collections, Cabell Library, VCU.

62. Shelburne, "Brief History," 70.

63. Heinemann, *Depression and New Deal*, 41.

64. Marguerite Watson Farmer, "Analysis of Applications," 15, 17–18.

65. Shelburne, "Brief History," 60.

66. Josephine Chapin Brown, *Public Relief*, 227; McJimsey, *Harry Hopkins*, 55–56. The use of the term "client" itself indicated the "diagnostic and counseling role" of social workers. William R. Brock, *Welfare*, 37.

67. Quoted by Heinemann, *Depression and New Deal*, 11.

68. Bane later joined the Roosevelt administration, serving on the staff of the FERA, the CWA, and finally the Social Security Board. See the biographical sketch in *Dictionary of Virginia Biography*. Carter Glass appears not to have forgiven Bane's outspokenness and worked to have him removed from the Social Security Board in 1937. McKinley and Frase, *Launching Social Security*, 88.

69. Quoted by Schulman, *From Cotton Belt to Sunbelt*, 11.

70. Heinemann, *Depression and New Deal*, 14–15.

71. William A. Smith, state administrator, to Harry Hopkins, 27 April 1934, FERA Papers, box 299. As late as January 1936, a survey of mothers' aid in Virginia found that although 3,500 families were eligible for mothers' assistance, only 124 were then receiving the grants. The small state appropriation remained part of the explanation: only $23,500 was included for that year. "Only 124 of 3,500 Eligibles Get Mother's Aid in Virginia," *Times-Dispatch*, 5 January 1936, 1. The small state support for mothers' aid meant that

the program did not qualify for federal matching funds. The state program granted aid to only 4 percent of the eligible, rendering it among the "most inadequate" in the country in the assessment of the federal government. Heinemann, *Depression and New Deal*, 156.

72. By the end of 1935, Virginia, Georgia, North Carolina, South Carolina, and Vermont were the only states without unemployment relief plans. Geddes, *Trends in Relief Expenditures*, 5.

73. Heinemann, *Depression and New Deal*, 48.

74. Rodgers, *Tracing the Civil War*, 65.

75. J. O. Hall to Governor Pollard, undated (but the governor's reply is dated 9 December 1931), Pollard Executive Papers, box 17, folder "Confederate Veterans."

76. Mrs. Q. T. Davies to Governor Peery (undated, but the governor's reply is dated 4 June 1936), Peery Executive Papers, box 16, folder "Confederate Pensions."

77. E. L. Dudley to Governor Peery, 26 February 1934, Peery Executive Papers, box 79, folder "Relief."

78. The comptroller replied that there was no one on the state's pension rolls by the name of William Baily, so he "is probably drawing a Federal pension, for service rendered in the World War or Spanish American war. If so, the State of Virginia has nothing to do with that." E. R. Combs to Mr. James Cooly, 12 December 1934, Peery Executive Papers, box 16, folder "Confederate Pensions."

79. Mr. R. E. Ankers to Governor Peery, 17 April 1935, Peery Executive Papers, box 155, folder "FERA, General."

80. Plummer F. Jones to Governor Pollard, 29 September 1932, Pollard Executive Papers, box 38, folder "RFC, relief, local."

81. Alan Johnstone to Dear Aubrey [Williams], 7 March 1934, Harry Hopkins Papers, FERA-WPA Narrative Reports, box 60, folder "Virginia," FDR Library.

82. C. P. Spaeth to Harry Hopkins, 10 April 1934, FERA Papers, box 299. (Although written after the establishment of the New Deal, this letter was written while the state of Virginia was still obstructing its implementation.)

83. Quoted by Heinemann, *Depression and New Deal*, 5 (emphasis mine).

84. Glass to Harry Byrd, 1931, quoted by Koeniger, " 'Unreconstructed Rebel,' " 31.

85. Quoted by Koeniger, " 'Unreconstructed Rebel,' " 41.

86. Josephine Chapin Brown, *Public Relief*, 114.

87. J. S. Keene, Richmond, Virginia, to FDR, 9 October 1935, FDR Papers, President's Personal File, series 21A: Clergy Letters, box 32, folder "Virginia," FDR Library.

88. Leuchtenburg, *Perils of Prosperity*, 265.

89. Cash, *Mind of the South*, 373.

90. Biles, *South and the New Deal*, 127.

91. Quoted by Heinemann, *Depression and New Deal*, 47.

92. Jeffrey S. Cole, "Impact of the Great Depression," 21.

93. Heinemann, *Depression and New Deal*, 139. The owner of two daily newspapers in Lynchburg, Glass steadfastly refused to display the NRA's Blue Eagle, which he compared to "a bird of prey," on his papers. Jeffrey S. Cole, "Impact of the Great Depression," 4, 74.

94. Alston and Ferrie, *Southern Paternalism*, 44.

95. Trattner, *From Poor Law to Welfare State*, 285.

96. Axinn and Levin, *Social Welfare*, 178.

97. McJimsey, *Harry Hopkins*, 53–54.

98. Memo to the President, 29 August 1933, FDR Papers, Official files, series 444, FERA, box 1, folder "July-Aug 1933."

99. Josephine Chapin Brown, *Public Relief*, 145–65.

100. Trattner, *From Poor Law to Welfare State*, 286. This policy grew out of both philosophical positions and practical experience: during the Hoover administration, some money loaned to private agencies had disappeared with no record of its disposition. Administrators came to believe that public agencies could better be held accountable than private ones. Salmond, *Southern Rebel*, 40.

101. Trattner, *From Poor Law to Welfare State*, 298.

102. *Sixteenth Annual Report of the State Board of Public Welfare for the Year Ending June 30, 1925* (Richmond: Public Printing, 1925), 31.

103. Gertrude S. Gates, "Report on Special Study of Virginia, December 4, 1934 to January 4, 1935," 3, FERA Papers, box 301, folder "Field Reports"; William R. Brock, *Welfare*, 225.

104. See Federal Emergency Relief Administration, *Unemployment Relief Census, October 1933*, tables A and B, pp. 6–7.

105. Report titled "Unemployment and Obligations Incurred from Emergency Relief from Public Funds throughout the United States during Six Months Ending September 30, 1934," FERA Papers, box 299.

106. Heinemann, *Depression and New Deal*, 49, 80–81.

107. Sato, "Senator Harry F. Byrd," 40.

108. Gordon Bennett to Corrington Gill, May 17, 1932, FERA Papers, box 299.

109. Gates, "Report on Special Study," 12.

110. Harry L. Hopkins to FDR, 29 August 1933, FDR Papers, Official Files, series 444: FERA, box 1, folder "July–Aug 1933."

111. Robert B. Watson [field statistician for FERA] to Mr. Gill, 26 August 1933, FERA Papers, box 301, folder "Watson."

112. Ibid.

113. Quoted by William R. Brock, *Welfare*, 312.

114. Quoted by ibid., 227.

115. Heinemann, *Depression and New Deal*, 77.

116. Hopkins and Peery correspondence from Peery's Executive Papers, as quoted by Fry, "George Campbell Peery," 63.

117. Quoted by Heinemann, *Depression and New Deal*, 80.

118. Ibid., 78. In 1924, Virginia had been ranked forty-first in the nation in tax burden per capita. ("Tax burden" here was defined as the combination of federal, state, and local taxes.) Gee and Corson, *Statistical Study of Virginia*, 93, 101.

119. Gertrude Gates to Aubrey Williams, 14 December 1934, FERA Papers, box 301, folder "Field Reports."

120. Heinemann, *Depression and New Deal*, 132.

121. "Virginia's Relief Problem," *Times-Dispatch*, 14 December 1934. Clipping in FERA Papers, box 301, folder "Field Reports."

122. Gertrude S. Gates to Aubrey Williams, 14 December 1934. Federal programs that did not require state matching funds were more acceptable to the state's leadership. Virginia embraced the Civil Works Administration, which funneled federal money into the state without demanding state expenditures. Heinemann, *Depression and New Deal*, 71.

123. Heinemann, *Depression and New Deal*, 76; Sato, "Harry F. Byrd," 34.

124. "Hopkins Lauds End of Dole for Millions in U.S.," *Times-Dispatch*, 1 January 1936, 2.

125. "New Deal Seen Going toward Virginia Relief Plan," *News-Leader*, 10 December 1934. Clipping in FERA Papers, box 301, folder "Field Reports."

126. Heinemann, *Depression and New Deal*, 89.

127. Josephine Chapin Brown, *Public Relief*, 166.

128. Heinemann, *Depression and New Deal*, 88.

129. Ibid., 102; Heinemann, *Harry Byrd of Virginia*, 171.

130. "Richmond First in NYA Benefits," *Times-Dispatch*, 9 January 1938, 10.

131. Heinemann, *Depression and New Deal*, 97, 61, 65.

132. Stamo S. Spathey, Richmond, Virginia, to FDR, 24 September 1935, FDR Papers, President's Personal File, series 21A: Clergy Letters, box 32, folder "Virginia."

133. Heinemann, *Depression and New Deal*, 72; "State WPA Rolls List 19,824 Workers," *Times-Dispatch*, 27 January 1938, 5.

134. *Annual Report of the Director of Public Works for the Year Ending December 31, 1939* (Richmond: city printer, 1940), 9–13.

135. Hilda W. Smith, "Report on Richmond Trip, December 18–22, 1933," Hilda W. Smith Papers, box 17, Workers' Service Programs, WPA, state files, folder "Virginia," FDR Library.

136. "The Works Program," news release dated 13 December 1936, 5. Hilda W. Smith Papers, box 27, folder "Background of FERA and WPA Programs."

137. Richmond Department of Public Welfare, *Annual Report for the Year Ending December 31, 1938* (Richmond: city printing, 1939), 13.

138. Betty (Mrs. A. M.) Randolph, Warrenton, Virginia, to ER, 10 February 1934, ER Papers, series: Positions Sought through Mrs. Roosevelt, box 2383 (alphabetically arranged).

139. R. W. Vanderberry of the Virginia Conference Board of Christian Education, to FDR, 8 October 1935, FDR Papers, President's Personal File, series 21A: Clergy Letters, box 32, folder "Virginia."

140. Mrs. Nena Helen Foster, Ballston, Virginia, to ER, 17 January 1934, ER Papers, series: Positions Sought through Mrs. Roosevelt, box 2381 (alphabetically arranged).

141. Alan Johnstone, field representative, memo to Harry Hopkins, 26 January 1935, 2, FERA Papers, box 301, folder "Field Reports."

142. "Cost of Living of Wage-Earning Women in Richmond, Va.," *Monthly Labor Report* 35 (October 1932), 974. The report also noted that most female factory workers in the study had to rely upon additional sources of income beyond their wages.

143. YWCA survey cited by Mettler, *Dividing Citizens*, 73.

144. Heinemann, *Depression and New Deal*, 82.

145. Lorena Hickok reported a complaint to her boss that the WPA was building schools for black children but the contractors refused to hire black laborers for the project. Lorena Hickok to Harry Hopkins, 14 January 1934, in Lowitt and Beasley, eds., *One Third*, 149.

146. Martin-Perdue and Perdue, eds., *Talk about Trouble*, 200.

147. Heinemann, *Depression and New Deal*, 185.

148. *Annual Report of the Director of Public Works for the Year Ending December 31, 1939* (Richmond: city printer, 1940), 13.

149. In October 1933, Hopkins announced the appointment of Ellen Woodward as director of the women's work division and asked each state to appoint "a properly qualified woman" to work with her. Hopkins thus effectively ordered the states to put women at the head of state relief agencies. Harry Hopkins to All Governors and State Emergency Relief Administrations, 10 October 1933, FDR Papers, Official Files, series 444: FERA, box 1, folder "Sept-Oct 1933."

150. Heinemann, *Depression and New Deal*, 74–75. Agnew agitated unsuccessfully for a wide variety of work relief jobs for women, including attempting to gain a CCC camp for women. See the biographical sketch in *Dictionary of Virginia Biography*.

151. *A Review of CWA Activities in Virginia* (Richmond: Federal Civil Works Administration of Virginia, 1934), 12 (typescript in LoV).

152. Lorena Hickok to Harry Hopkins, 5 February 1934, in Lowitt and Beasley, *One Third*, 173.

153. See Swain, *Ellen S. Woodward*, chapters 3–6.

154. Mettler, *Dividing Citizens*, 45.

155. "Richmond First in NYA Benefits," *Times-Dispatch*, 9 June 1938, 10.

156. Federal Works Agency, *Final Report*, 67–70.

157. Minutes, 9 January 1934, IVNA Papers, box 4. According to subsequent minutes, the project lasted only until May 1934.

158. *Review of CWA Activities*, 13.

159. Salmond, *Southern Rebel*, 75.

160. *Review of CWA Activities*, 16.

161. Lorena Hickok to Harry Hopkins, 11 January 1934, in Lowitt and Beasley, *One Third*, 145.

162. Asher W. Harman [director of work division, state ERA] to Jack Baker [assistant administrator, FERA], 10 September 1934, FERA Papers, box 299.

163. Jeffrey S. Cole, "Impact of the Great Depression," 214.

164. Lorena Hickok to Harry Hopkins, 8 February 1934, in Lowitt and Beasley, *One Third*, 181.

165. Cash, *Mind of the South*, 418.

166. Lorena Hickok to Harry Hopkins, 16 January 1934, in Lowitt and Beasley, *One Third*, 154.

167. Martin-Perdue and Perdue, *Talk about Trouble*, 229.

168. Lorena Hickok to Harry Hopkins, 13 April 1934, in Lowitt and Beasley, *One Third*, 220.

169. Report of the Massachusetts Board to Investigate the Subject of the Unemployed, March 13, 1895, quoted by Feder, *Unemployment Relief*, 76.

170. Lorena Hickok to Harry Hopkins, 5 February 1934, in Lowitt and Beasley, *One Third*, 172.

171. Lorena Hickok to Harry Hopkins, 23 January 1934, in ibid., 158.

172. Heinemann, *Depression and New Deal*, 84.

173. Gertrude S. Gates [field relief supervisor] to Aubrey Williams [FERA assistant administrator], 14 December 1934, FERA Papers, box 301, folder "Field Reports."

174. Quadagno, *Color of Welfare*, 21.

175. Mettler, *Dividing Citizens*, 7.

176. Alston and Ferrie, *Southern Paternalism*, 58–59.

177. Quoted by Mettler, *Dividing Citizens*, 75.

178. Ibid., 77; Alston and Ferrie, *Southern Paternalism*, 61–74.

179. Quoted by Fry, "George Campbell Peery," 71.

180. Quoted by Sato, "Harry F. Byrd," 57–58.

181. Fry, "George Campbell Peery," 72–73; Heinemann, *Depression and New Deal*, 160.

182. Sato, "Harry F. Byrd," 63.

183. Miss Emily K. Allison, Delton, Virginia, to ER, 28 February 1935, ER Papers, series: Old Age Pensions Correspondence, box 433.

184. Mrs. Sarah L. Lupton, Berkley, Virginia, to ER, 4 January 1935, ER Papers, series: Old Age Pensions Correspondence, box 433.

185. Mrs. Fal Hubbard, Bedford, Virginia, to ER, 5 February 1934, ER Papers, box 267 "Correspondence with Government Departments," folder "1934 Hu-Hy."

186. Alston and Ferrie, *Southern Paternalism*, 69.

187. Byrd to William Tuck, January 1935, quoted by Sato, "Harry F. Byrd," 58.

188. Fry, "George Campbell Peery," 67–69.

189. "Virginia, 2/1/13," Harry Hopkins Papers, FERA-WPA Narrative Reports, box 60, folder "Virginia."

190. Heinemann, *Depression and New Deal*, 159.

191. James, *State Becomes a Social Worker*, 297; Davis quoted by Kirby, *Westmoreland Davis*, 192–93.

192. Heinemann, *Depression and New Deal*, 161–62.

193. Virginia Department of Public Welfare, *Public Assistance Statistics*, 7, 10.

194. Rodgers, *Tracing the Civil War*, 68. In 1998, the state was still paying six Confederate widows thirty dollars per month. Rodgers, 72.

195. William R. Brock, *Welfare*, 313.

196. Sato, "Harry F. Byrd," 66–67.

197. *Twenty-seventh and Twenty-eighth Annual Reports of the State Department of Public Welfare of Virginia for the Two Years Ending June 30, 1937* (Richmond: Public Printing, 1937), 14; Heinemann, *Depression and New Deal*, 155, 162. The state was compelled to meet federal standards in order to get federal money. For example, in the fall of 1936 the fed-

eral Social Security Board rejected Virginia's application for funds for Aid to Dependent Children, because Virginia's Mothers' Aid act gave too much control to the localities. State Department of Public Welfare, *Progress Report* (June 1937), unpaginated.

198. Schulman, *From Cotton Belt to Sunbelt,* especially 6–8.

Conclusion

1. I am borrowing language from John Egerton, *The Americanization of Dixie: The Southernization of America* (New York: Harper's Magazine Press, 1974).

2. On the "war on welfare," see Albelda and Withorn, eds., *Lost Ground*; Katz, *Price of Citizenship*; Adolph L. Reed, ed., *Without Justice for All*; Quadagno, *Color of Welfare*, especially chapter 8; and Katz, *Undeserving Poor.*

3. Biles, *South and the New Deal,* 58.

4. Cash, *Mind of the South,* 395.

5. Rev. R. C. Barbour, Charlottesville, Virginia, to FDR, 25 September 1935, FDR Papers, President's Personal File, series 21A: Clergy Letters, box 32, folder "Virginia," FDR Library.

6. Rev. Walter J. Sparks, Richmond, Virginia, to FDR, 12 October 1935, FDR Papers, President's Personal File, series 21A: Clergy Letters, box 32, folder "Virginia," FDR Library.

7. Quoted by Jeffrey S. Cole, "Impact of the Great Depression," 180.

8. "Social Workers Hear Appeal by Greenstein," *Times-Dispatch,* 21 January 1938, 5.

9. Rev. Churchill Gibson, Richmond, Virginia, to FDR, 28 September 1935, FDR Papers, President's Personal File, series 21A: Clergy Letters, box 32, folder "Virginia," FDR Library.

10. Minutes, 16 October 1935, IVNA Papers, box 4, folder 4, Tompkins-McCaw Library, Medical College of Virginia, Archives and Special Collections, VCU.

11. "Relief Workers Try Eating on $1.50 Weekly Allotment," *Times-Dispatch,* 12 February 1938, 2.

12. Rev. J. Blanton Belk, Richmond, Virginia, to FDR, 25 September 1935, FDR Papers, President's Personal File, series 21A: Clergy Letters, box 32, folder "Virginia," FDR Library.

13. *Report of the Committee on Public Welfare, City of Richmond* (Richmond: The Committee, 1948), 2–3.

14. *Annual Report of the Social Service Bureau for the Year Ending December 31, 1939* (Richmond: city printer, 1940), 179.

15. Council of Social Agencies, minutes for 11 December 1934, United Way Archives, box 14, folder "Minutes 1928–1932," Special Collections, Cabell Library, VCU.

16. Frank Freidel, *F.D.R. and the South* (Baton Rouge: Louisiana State University Press, 1965), 48.

17. Trattner, *From Poor Law to Welfare State,* 291.

18. For example, at the end of 1935, five states had not created any kind of unemployment relief programs; four of them were in the South. Geddes, *Trends in Relief Expenditures,* 5.

19. Mettler, *Dividing Citizens,* 87–89.

20. Couch, ed., *These Are Our Lives*, 366. The anonymous speaker here was a relief recipient who had himself been hired by the WPA to help in the distribution of relief to others.

21. Josephine Chapin Brown, *Public Relief*, 252–53.

22. Richmond YWCA Archives (M177), box 19, case files (alphabetically arranged), Special Collections, Cabell Library, VCU. In accordance with the terms of use, I have applied a pseudonym when publishing from these case records. Researchers wishing to consult these records will find that I maintained the person's actual initials in the pseudonym; that is, "Charlotte Anderson" will be found under a name with the initials "C.A."

23. Department of Public Welfare, *Public Assistance Statistics* (Richmond: city printing, 1939), 10.

24. Ellen G. Agnew to Mrs. Mary Cockerille, 12 December 1933, ER Papers, series: Correspondence with Government Departments, box 277, folder "1934, Ellen Woodward, Jan–Mar," FDR Library.

25. Department of Public Welfare, *Annual Report for the Year Ending December 31, 1938* (Richmond: city printing, 1939), 10.

26. "Effect of Social-Security Program on Almshouses," 518–24. See also Tyson, "Poorhouse Persists," 77.

27. Department of Public Welfare, *The Richmond Nursing Home* (Richmond: The Department, 1962), 3.

BIBLIOGRAPHY

Manuscript Collections

Confederate Museum (Richmond)
  Richmond Soup Association Papers
Franklin D. Roosevelt Library (Hyde Park)
  Eleanor Roosevelt Papers
  Franklin Roosevelt Papers
  Harry Hopkins Papers
  Hilda W. Smith Papers
Library of Virginia (Richmond)
  State agency records
    Board of Charities and Corrections, Minutes
    Executive Papers of John Letcher, John Garland Pollard, George C. Peery, James
      Price, and William Smith
  Richmond city records
    Overseers of the Poor, Annual Reports and Checklist, 1871–81, 1884–1907, 1909
    Overseers of the Poor, Minutes, 1817–28
    Admissions Registers, City Home (Almshouse):
      Vol. A (White Males and Females 1872–77)
      Vol. B (White Males 1887–1902)
      Vol. C (White Males 1902–7)
      Vol. D (White Females 1903–7)
      Vol. E (White Males and Females 1907–13)
      Vol. F (Black Males 1903–7)
      Vol. G (Black Females 1902–7)
      Vol. H (Black Males and Females 1907–13)
  Organizational records
    R. E. Lee Camp Confederate Soldiers' Home. Board of Visitors, General Records,
      Minutes and Applications for Admission
    Home for Needy Confederate Women, Records
National Archives (Washington, D.C.)
  Freedmen's Bureau Papers, Virginia (RG 109)
  Works Progress Administration (RG 69)
  Confederate Secretary of War Papers (Confederate Archives) (RG 109). Letters
    received.
Social Welfare History Archives, University of Minnesota (Minneapolis)
  Florence Crittenden Association Papers
  Family Service Association of America Papers

University of Virginia, Alderman Library, Rare Books and Manuscripts
(Charlottesville)
Kate Waller Barrett Papers
Mary Johnston Collection
Virginia Commonwealth University, Cabell Library, Special Collections (Richmond)
United Way of Greater Richmond Archives (M247)
Richmond YWCA Archives (M177)
Virginia Commonwealth University, Tompkins-McCaw Library at the Medical College
of Virginia, Archives and Special Collections (Richmond)
Instructive Visiting Nurses Association Papers
Virginia Historical Society (Richmond)
Papers of the Richmond Ice and Milk Mission
Amicable Society of Richmond, Minutebook, 1788–1819

Manuscript Federal Census Records for Virginia

Seventh census of the United States, 1850. Population Schedule, Social Statistics
Schedule
Eighth census of the United States, 1860. Population schedule, Social Statistics
Schedule
Ninth census of the United States, 1870. Population Schedule, Social Statistics Schedule
Tenth census of the United States, 1880. Population Schedule, Special Schedule of
Defective, Dependent, and Delinquent Classes
Eleventh Census of the United States, 1890. Special Schedule Enumerating Union
Veterans and Widows of Union Veterans of the Civil War

Newspapers

Charleston Courier, 1849
Richmond Dispatch (Daily Dispatch, Times-Dispatch), 1860–1940
Richmond Enquirer (1804–20, 1850–60)
Richmond Examiner (1861–64)
The *Idea* (Richmond) (1906–11)
The *Jewish South* (Richmond) (1893–99)
The *Live Wire* (Richmond) (1902)
Richmond Planet (1885–1900)
Richmond Sentinel (1863–65)
Richmond Virginia Star (4 June 1881)
Richmond Virginian (1915)
Die Virginische Zeitung (1919–25)

Printed Primary Materials

Abbott, Edith. "Education for Social Work." Washington, D.C.: GPO, 1915.

————. *Public Assistance*. Vol. 1, *American Principles and Policies*. Chicago: University of Chicago Press, 1940.

"Almshouses: Existing Conditions and Needed Reforms." In *Proceedings of the National Conference on Charities and Corrections* (1914). Ft. Wayne, Ind.: Ft. Wayne Printing Company, 1914.

"Almshouses Go." *Survey* 72 (1936): 86.

Altman-Gottheimer, Elizabeth. "Foundling Hospitals." *Survey* 49 (1 December 1922): 320–21.

Annual Catalogs, Richmond School of Social Economy/School of Social Work, Richmond Professional Institute of the College of William and Mary.

Annual Reports, Associated Charities, Richmond. Richmond: privately printed, various years.

Annual Reports of the Auditor of Public Accounts/Comptroller, State of Virginia. Richmond: public printing, various years.

Annual Reports of the Board of Charities and Corrections/Department of Public Welfare, State of Virginia. Richmond: public printing, various years.

Annual Reports, Superintendent of Public Charities, City of Richmond. Richmond: city printer, various years.

Arnold, G. B. "The Feeble-Minded in Virginia from an Institutional Standpoint." [Richmond?]: n.p., 1935.

Ayers, Philip W. "Charity Organization in Southern Cities." *Charities Review* 4 (1895): 259.

Bardwell, F. "Standards of Almshouse Administration." In *Proceedings of the National Conference on Social Work* (1917). Chicago: The Conference, 1917.

Bardwell, Francis G. "Almshouse Boarders." *Survey* 55 (15 March 1926): 687.

Barrett, Janie Porter. *Locust Street Social Settlement*. Hampton, Va.: n.p., 1912.

Barrett, Kate Waller. *Some Practical Suggestions on the Conduct of a Rescue Home*. 1903. Reprint, New York: Arno Press, 1974.

————. "Unmarried Mother and Her Child." *Proceedings of the National Conference on Charities and Corrections* (1910): Ft. Wayne, Ind.: Press of the Archer Printing Company, 1910.

Barstow, M. "Bethlehem House, Nashville." *World Outlook* 4 (May 1918): 25.

Becknell, Ernest P. "State Control of Almshouses." *Charities* 13 (15 October 1904): 72–74.

Betts, L. W. "Richmond of Today." *Outlook* 65 (25 August 1900): 972–79.

Beverley, Robert. *The History and Present State of Virginia*. Edited by Louis B. Wright. London: 1705. Reprint, Chapel Hill: University of North Carolina Press, 1947.

Biennial Reports of the State Colony for Epileptics and Feeble-Minded, State of Virginia. Richmond: public printing, various years.

Bledsoe, M. L. "Best Negroes in the World." *Colliers* 77 (6 February 1926): 23.

Boyd, Leroy Stafford. *The Depression in Virginia—How It May Be Cured.* Arlington, Va.: n.p., 1934.

Brandt, Lillian. "The Causes of Poverty." *Political Science Quarterly* 23 (1908): 637–51.

Brock, R. A., ed. *The Vestry Book of Henrico Parish, 1730–1773.* Bowie, Md.: Heritage Books, 1991.

Bullock, Edna, comp. *Selected Articles on Mothers' Pensions.* White Plains, N.Y.: Wilson Co, 1915.

Bureau of the Census. *Benevolent Institutions, 1910.* Washington, D.C.: GPO, 1913.

———. *Children under Institutional Care and in Foster Homes, 1933.* Washington, D.C.: GPO, 1935.

———. *Fifteenth Census of the United States: 1930, Unemployment.* Vol. 1. Washington, D.C.: GPO, 1931.

———. *Financial Statistics of Cities Having a Population of Over 100,000, 1911–1931.* Washington, D.C.: GPO, 1932.

———. *Historical Statistics on State and Local Government Finances, 1902–1953.* Washington, D.C.: GPO, 1955.

———. *Paupers in Almshouses, 1910.* Washington, D.C.: GPO, 1915.

———. *Relief Expenditures by Governmental and Private Organizations, 1929 and 1931.* Washington, D.C.: GPO, 1932.

———. *Report on Crime, Pauperism, and Benevolence in the United States at the Eleventh Census, 1890.* Washington, D.C.: GPO, 1896.

———. *Report on the Social Statistics of Cities.* Part 2, *The Southern and the Western States.* Washington, D.C.: GPO, 1887.

———. "Soldiers and Widows." *Compendium of the Eleventh Census (1890).* Part 3, *Population.* Washington, D.C.: GPO, 1897.

Burr, Virginia Ingraham, ed. *The Secret Eye: The Journal of Ella Gertrude Clanton Thomas, 1848–1889.* Chapel Hill: University of North Carolina Press, 1990.

Burton, L. W., et al., eds. *Annals of Henrico Parish.* Richmond: Williams Printing, 1904.

Clark, Mary Vida. "The Almshouse." *Proceedings of the National Conference on Charities and Corrections* (1900). Topeka: The Conference, 1900.

———. "Passing of the County Farm." *Survey* 42 (26 July 1919): 624–25.

Clark, S. E. "Almshouse Records." In *Proceedings of the National Conference on Charities and Corrections* (1912). Ft. Wayne, Ind.: Ft. Wayne Printing Company, 1912.

"Colored Social Workers." *Southern Workman* 49 (August 1920): 348.

"Commercial and Industrial Cities of the United States: Richmond, Virginia, 1859." *Hunt's Merchants' Magazine* 40 (1859): 54–66.

Cooley, Harris R. "Substitute for the Poorhouse." *Outlook* 97 (22 April 1911): 904–11.

Couch, W. T., ed. *These Are Our Lives.* Chapel Hill: University of North Carolina Press, 1939.

"County Superintendents of the Poor." *Charities* 10 (27 June 1903): 624–26.

Crumley, H. L. "Orphan Children of Georgia." *Charities* 10 (6 June 1903): 566–68.

Cushing, C. P. "Farm of Hope." *Collier's* 43 (14 August 1909): 19–20.

Cutchins, John A. *Memories of Old Richmond (1881–1944).* Verona, Va.: McClure Printing, 1973.

Daingerfield, Henderson. "Social Settlement and Education Work in the Kentucky Mountains." *Journal of the American Social Science Association* 39 (November 1901): 176–95.

De Forest, J. "Woodyard as a Labor Test." *Charities* 9 (1 November 1902): 443–46.

DeWitt, J. H. "Present Charitable Needs of the South." In *Proceedings of the National Conference on Charities and Corrections* (1914). Ft. Wayne, Ind.: Ft. Wayne Printing Company, 1914.

Dillingham, Pitt. "The Settlement Idea in the Cotton Belt." *Outlook* 70 (12 April 1902): 920–22.

Dinwiddie, E. W. "Virginia County Almshouse." *Charities* 7 (3 August 1901): 115–18.

Dix, Dorothea Lynde. *Memorial of Miss D. L. Dix, to the Honorable General Assembly in Behalf of the Insane of Maryland.* Annapolis: n.p., 1852.

———. *Memorial Soliciting Adequate Appropriations for the Construction of a State Hospital for the Insane in the State of Mississippi.* Jackson, Miss.: Fall and Marshall, state printers, 1850.

———. *Memorial Soliciting a State Hospital for the Insane.* Montgomery: Office of the Advertiser and Gazette, 1849.

———. *Memorial Soliciting a State Hospital for the Protection and Cure of the Insane: Submitted to the General Assembly of North Carolina, November 1848.* Raleigh: State Printer, 1848.

———. *Memorial Soliciting Enlarged and Improved Accommodations for the Insane of the State of Tennessee, by the Establishment of a New Hospital.* Nashville: B. R. M'Kennie, Printer, 1847.

———. *A Review of the Present Condition of the State Penitentiary of Kentucky, with Brief Notices and Remarks upon the Jails and Poor-houses in Some of the Most Populous Counties.* Frankfort, Ky.: A. G. Hodges, state printer, 1845.

"Does Poverty Kill Babies?" *Literary Digest* 56 (30 March 1918): 25–26.

Dosch, A. "Not Enough Babies to Go Around." *Cosmopolitan* 49 (September 1910): 431–39.

Drewry, W. F. *Care and Condition of the Insane in Virginia.* Richmond: n.p., 1908.

Edwards, Richard, comp. *Statistical Gazetteer of the State of Virginia.* Richmond: Richard Edwards, 1855.

Elliott and Nye's Virginia Directory and Business Register for 1852. Richmond: Elliott and Nye, 1852.

Ellis, L. B. "New Class of Labor in the South." *Forum* 31 (May 1901): 306–10.

Federal Emergency Relief Administration. *Final Statistical Report of the FERA.* Washington, D.C.: GPO, 1942.

———. *Unemployment Relief Census, October 1933.* Washington, D.C.: GPO, 1934.

Federal Works Agency. *Final Report on the WPA Program, 1935–43.* Washington, D.C.: GPO, 1946.

Fernandis, Sarah. "Social Settlement Work among Colored People." *Charities and the Commons* 21 (21 November 1908): 302.

Fleet, Betsy, and John D. P. Fuller, eds. *Green Mount: A Virginia Plantation Family during the Civil War: Being the Journal of Benjamin Robert Fleet and Letters of His Family.* Lexington: University of Kentucky Press, 1962.

Fleming, W. L. "Immigration to the Southern States." *Political Science Quarterly* 20 (June 1905): 276–97.

Fourth Annual Report of the Commissioner of Labor, 1888: Working Women in Large Cities. Washington, D.C.: GPO, 1889.

Fullerton, H. S. "Over the Hills to the Poorhouse: Who the Folks Are Who Land There." *American Magazine* 89 (April 1920): 42.

Gilman, Daniel. *The Organization of Charities.* Baltimore: Johns Hopkins University Press, 1894.

Glasgow, Ellen. *The Woman Within.* New York: Harcourt, Brace, 1954.

Guild, Jane Purcell. "Black Richmond." *Survey Graphic* 23 (June 1934): 276–78.

Hertz, Hilda, and Sue Warren Little. "Unmarried Negro Mothers in a Southern Urban Community." *Social Forces* 23 (October 1944): 73–79.

Hosen, Frederick E. *The Great Depression and the New Deal: Legislative Acts in Their Entirety (1932–1933) and Statistical and Economic Data (1926–1946).* Jefferson, N.C.: McFarland and Co., 1992.

"Hospital System on Trial." *Charities* 11 (26 September 1903): 267–68.

"How Atlanta Cleaned Up." *Literary Digest* 46 (3 May 1913): 1012–13.

"How Richmond Is Housed." *Survey* 32 (11 April 1914): 54.

Hummel, B. L., and C. G. Bennett. *Magnitude of the Emergency Relief Program in Rural Virginia.* Blacksburg: Virginia Polytechnic University, 1937.

Hunter, Robert F. "The Relation between Social Settlements and Charity Organization." *Journal of Political Economy* 11 (1902): 75–88.

Illegitimacy in Richmond, Va, 1910–1955. Richmond: Department of Public Welfare, 1957.

"Immigration and the South." *Nation* 82 (17 May 1906): 398–99.

"Imported Labor: Southern Working Conditions." *Charities* 17 (2 March 1907): 1026–27.

James, Arthur W. *The Juvenile and Public Welfare Laws of Virginia.* Richmond: State Department of Public Welfare, 1928.

———. "Local Welfare Development." *The Commonwealth* 3 (December 1936): 16–17.

Jaquette, Henrietta Stratton, ed. *South after Gettysburg: Letters of Cornelia Hancock, 1863–1868.* New York: Thomas Y. Crowell, 1956.

Johnson, A. "Back from over the Hill." *Survey* 62 (15 September 1929): 609–10.

Johnson, Alexander. *The Almshouse, Construction and Management.* New York: Charities Publication Committee, 1911.

Johnson, Kate Burr, and Nell Battle Lewis. "A Decade of Social Progress in North Carolina." *Journal of Social Forces* 1 (May 1923): 400–403.

Jones, J. B. *A Rebel War Clerk's Diary at the Confederate States Capital.* Edited by Howard Swiggett. New York: Old Hickory Bookshop, 1935.

Keiley, Anthony M. *Memoranda of the History of the Catholic Church in Richmond, Virginia, Since the Revolution: Reported to the Fourth Annual Convention of the*

Catholic Benevolent Union of Virginia. Norfolk: Virginian Book and Job Print, 1874. Reprint, Richmond: Catholic Historical Society, 1944.

Lay, Lucy. "Two Hospitals for an Almshouse, Vance County NC." *Survey* 64 (15 May 1930): 190–91.

Leucht, I. L. "Opportunities in the South for the Immigrant." *Charities* 16 (26 May 1906): 275–77.

Lowitt, Richard, and Maurine Beasley, eds. *One Third of a Nation: Lorena Hickok Reports on the Great Depression.* Urbana: University of Illinois Press, 1981.

MacDonell, Mrs. R. W. "Wesley Houses and the Social Work of the Woman's Home Mission Society." *Missionary Voice* 1 (March 1911): 46–49.

Manarin, Louis H., ed. *Richmond at War: The Minutes of the City Council, 1861–1865.* Chapel Hill: University of North Carolina Press, 1966.

Martin-Perdue, Nancy J., and Charles L. Perdue Jr., eds. *Talk about Trouble: A New Deal Portrait of Virginians in the Great Depression.* Chapel Hill: University of North Carolina Press, 1996.

Mason, J. D. "South and Immigration." *Harper's Weekly* 57 (12 July 1913): 5.

McCulloch, James E., ed. *Battling for Social Betterment: Southern Sociological Congress, Memphis Tennessee, May 6–10, 1914.* Nashville: The Congress, 1914.

McElvaine, Robert S., ed. *Down and Out in the Great Depression: Letters from the "Forgotten Man."* Chapel Hill: University of North Carolina Press, 1983.

McLean, Francis H., and Hilda K. Mills. *Survey of the Social Agencies of Richmond, Virginia.* [Richmond?]: American Association for Organizing Family Social Work, 1923.

McMain, Eleanor. "Kingsley House, New Orleans." *Charities* 11 (5 December 1903): 549.

Minor, Nannie J. "The Status of the Colored Public Health Nurse in Virginia." *Public Health Nurse* 16 (May 1924): 243–44.

————, and Sadie Cabiness. "The Nurses' Settlement in Richmond." *American Journal of Nursing* 3 (1903): 624–26.

Moore, J. Staunton, ed. *History of Henrico Parish and Old St. John's Church, Richmond, Virginia, 1611–1904.* 1904. Reprint, Bowie, Md.: Heritage Books, 1997.

Mordecai, Samuel. *Richmond in By-Gone Days.* 1860. Reprint, Richmond: Dietz Press, 1946.

"Move to Abolish the Poorhouse." *Literary Digest* 90 (4 September 1926): 10–11.

National Florence Crittenton Mission. *Fourteen Years Work with Street Girls.* Washington, D.C.: NFCM, 1897.

Negro Welfare Survey Committee. *The Negro in Richmond Virginia: The Report of the Negro Welfare Survey Committee.* Richmond: Richmond Council of Social Agencies, 1929.

Nuckols, Robert R. *A History of the Government of the City of Richmond, Virginia and a Sketch of Those Who Administer Its Affairs.* Richmond: William Printing, 1899.

"Nurses Settlement in Richmond." *Charities* 16 (7 April 1906): 47.

Odum, Howard W. "How New Is the South in Social Work?" *Survey* 60 (15 June 1928): 329.

"An Old Richmond Tavern as a Settlement House." *Charities* 14 (6 May 1905): 708.

Patterson, A. "Giving Babies Away." *Cosmopolitan* 39 (August 1905): 405–12.

Pember, Phoebe Yates. *A Southern Woman's Story: Life in Confederate Richmond.* Edited by Bell Irvin Wiley. Jackson, Tenn: McCowat-Mercer Press, 1959.

Perdue, Charles L., Thomas E. Barden, and Robert K. Phillips, eds. *Weevils in the Wheat: Interviews with Virginia Ex-Slaves.* Charlottesville: University Press of Virginia, 1976.

Potter, E. C. "Future Development of the Almshouse." In *Proceedings of the National Conference on Social Work* (1926). Chicago: University of Chicago Press, 1926.

Proceedings of the Annual Meetings, Virginia Conference of Charities and Correction. Richmond: privately printed, various years.

Puschner, Emma C. "Foundlings Are Keepings." *Survey* 51 (15 December 1923): 330–31.

Putnam, Sallie B. *In Richmond during the Confederacy.* 1867. Reprint, New York: Robert M. McBride Co., 1961.

Ramage, B. J. "Southern Poor Relief." *Nation* 70 (26 April 1900): 317.

Randall, E. B. "Admissions and Records in an Almshouse." In *Proceedings of the National Conference on Social Work* (1926). Chicago: University of Chicago Press, 1926.

Reid, Whitelaw. *After the War: A Tour of the Southern States, 1865–1866.* Edited by C. Vann Woodward. New York: Harper and Row, 1965.

"Removal of Children from Almshouses." *Charities Review* 9 (January 1900): 516–19.

Report of the Committee on Public Welfare, City of Richmond. Richmond: The Committee, 1948.

A Review of CWA Activities in Virginia. Richmond: Federal Civil Works Administration of Virginia, 1934.

Richmond, Mary E. *Friendly Visiting among the Poor: A Handbook for Charity Workers.* New York: MacMillan, 1914.

Richmond, Virginia, 1914: A Brief Sketch of Its History, Industrial Life, Government, and Educational Facilities. Richmond: n.p., 1914.

Rosenman, Samuel L., ed. *The Public Papers and Addresses of Franklin D. Roosevelt.* New York: Random House, 1938.

Rothman, David J., ed. *The Almshouse Experience: Collected Reports.* New York: Arno Press, 1971.

Rules and Regulations for the Government of the Officers and Employees of the Almshouse of Richmond, VA. Richmond: City Printer, 1888.

Sayles, Mary Buell. "Visiting Nurse and Nurses Settlement." *Outlook* 81 (21 October 1905): 419.

Sears, Amelia, and Florence Nesbitt. *The Charity Visitor: A Handbook for Beginners.* Chicago: Council of Social Agencies, 1913, 1923.

"Settlement at Hampton, VA." *Commons* 191 (September 1904): 438.

Shirer, H. H. "Problems in Common of the City Infirmary and the Small Almshouse." In *Proceedings of the Conference on Charities and Corrections* (1912). Ft. Wayne, Ind.: Ft. Wayne Printing Company, 1912.

Smith, William A. "VERA's Campaign for Re-employment." *The Commonwealth* 2 (June 1935): 28–29.

"Social Religion in the South." *Literary Digest* 45 (7 September 1912): 377–78.

Society for the Betterment of Housing and Living Conditions in Richmond. *Report on Housing and Living Conditions in the Neglected Sections of Richmond.* Richmond: Whittet and Shepperson, 1913.

"Sociology's Welcome in the New Southland." *Survey* 30 (10 May 1913): 212–13.

"Some Children Still in the Poorhouse." *Survey* 37 (11 November 1916): 147.

"South and Immigration." *Independent* 71 (6 August 1911): 385–86.

"South and the Immigrant." *Outlook* 84 (24 November 1906): 691.

"Southern Peonage and Immigration." *Nation* 85 (19 December 1907): 557.

Southern Women's Educational Alliance. *Social Work as a Profession in the South.* Richmond: The Alliance, 1921.

The State and Public Welfare in Nineteenth Century America: Five Investigations, 1833–1877. New York: Arno Press, 1976.

Stauffer, W. M. "Public Welfare in Virginia." *The Commonwealth* 6, no. 1 (January 1939): 15–18.

Stewart, E. M. *Cost of American Almshouses.* U.S. Bureau of Labor Bulletin 386 (Misc Series), 1925.

Studying Richmond's Hand in the "New Deal." Richmond: Chamber of Commerce, 1933.

Taylor, Graham. "The Southern Social Awakening." *Survey* 22 (14 September 1912): 744–45.

Terrill, Tom E., and Jerrold Hirsch, eds. *Such as Us: Southern Voices of the Thirties.* New York: W. W. Norton, 1979.

"To Send Immigrants South," *Literary Digest* 47 (11 October 1913): 617–18.

Tuttle, Emeth. *Mothers' Aid in North Carolina.* Raleigh: State Board of Charities and Public Welfare special bulletin no. 7, 1926.

"Typical Almshouses." *Charities Review* 10 (November 1900): 401–7.

Tyson, Helen Glenn. "The Poorhouse Persists." *Survey* 74 (March 1938): 76–77.

U.S. Congress. House. Committee on Invalid Pensions. *Claims of Confederate Soldiers Hearing,* 64th Cong., 1st sess. Washington, D.C.: GPO, 1916.

————. House. Committee on Military Affairs. *Homes for Confederate Soldiers Hearing,* 64th Cong., 1st sess. Washington, D.C.: GPO, 1916.

U.S. National Emergency Council. *Report on Economic Conditions of the South.* Washington, D.C.: GPO, 1938.

Virginia Department of Public Welfare. *Public Assistance Statistics.* Richmond: DPW, 1939.

Warner, Amos. *American Charities: A Study in Philanthropy and Economics.* New York: Thomas Y. Crowell, 1894. 3rd ed., 1919.

Warner, Amos, Stuart Alfred Queen, and Ernest Bouldin Harper. *American Charities and Social Work.* 4th ed. New York: Thomas Y. Crowell, 1930.

Waterfield, C. A. "Southern Sociological Congress." *Survey* 32 (May 1914): 244.

Waters, W. T. "Atlanta's Babies: A Subsidy Plan." *Collier's* 51 (12 July 1913): 32.

Waters, Yssabelle. *Visiting Nursing in the United States.* New York: Charities Publication Committee, 1909, 1912.

Watson, Frank Dekker. *The Charity Organization Movement in the United States.* New York: MacMillan, 1922.

Weller, Charles F. "Charity and Social Development in Two Southern Cities." *Charities* 13 (11 February 1905): 466–68.

Wines, Frederick. *Report on Crime, Pauperism, and Benevolence in the United States at the Eleventh Census, 1890.* Washington, D.C.: GPO, 1896.

———. *Report on the Defective, Dependent, and Delinquent Classes of the Population of the U.S. as Returned in the Tenth Census.* Washington, D.C.: GPO, 1888.

Woods, Robert, and Albert Kennedy, eds. *Handbook of Settlements.* New York: n.p., 1911.

Woodward, C. Vann, ed. *Mary Chesnut's Civil War.* New Haven: Yale University Press, 1981.

Work, Monroe. "Self Help among Negroes." *Survey* 22 (August 1909): 606–18.

Wright, A. O. "Employment in Poorhouses." In *Proceedings of the National Conference on Charities and Corrections* (1889). Boston: Press of George H. Ellis, 1889.

Young Men's Christian Association. *Through the Fourth Year of the Depression, 1933.* Richmond: YMCA, [1934?].

Younger, Edward, ed. *Inside the Confederate Government: The Diary of Robert Garlick Hill Kean.* New York: Oxford University Press, 1957.

Books, Articles, Dissertations, and Other Secondary Materials

Abbott, Grace. *From Relief to Social Security: The Development of the New Public Welfare Services and Their Administration.* New York: Russell and Russell, 1966.

Abel, Emily K. "Valuing Care: Turn-of-the-Century Conflicts between Charity Workers and Women Clients." *Journal of Women's History* 10 (autumn 1998): 32–52.

Abramovitz, Mimi. *Regulating the Lives of Women: Social Welfare Policy from Colonial Times to the Present.* Boston: South End Press, 1988.

Abrams, Douglas Carl. *Conservative Constraints: North Carolina and the New Deal.* Jackson: University Press of Mississippi, 1992.

Alabama Department of Pensions and Security. *A Brief History of Public Welfare in Alabama, from 1799 through 1968.* Montgomery: State Department of Pensions and Security, 1969. Pamphlet in Houston Cole Library, Jacksonville State University. Photocopy.

Albelda, Randy Pearl, and Ann Withorn, eds. *Lost Ground: Welfare Reform, Poverty, and Beyond.* Cambridge, Mass.: South End Press, 2002.

Alexander, Ruth. *The Girl Problem: Female Sexual Delinquency in New York, 1900–1930.* Ithaca: Cornell University Press, 1995.

Alston, Lee J., and Joseph P. Ferrie. *Southern Paternalism and the Rise of the American Welfare State: Economics, Politics, and Institutions in the South, 1865–1965.*

Cambridge: Cambridge University Press, 1998.

Amos, Harriet E. *Cotton City: Urban Development in Antebellum Mobile.* Tuscaloosa: University of Alabama Press, 1985.

Anderson, Eric, and Alfred A. Moss Jr. *Dangerous Donations: Northern Philanthropy and Southern Black Education, 1902–1930.* Columbia: University of Missouri Press, 1999.

Axinn, June, and Herman Levin. *Social Welfare: A History of the American Response to Need.* New York: Dodd, Mead, 1975.

Aydlett, A. Laurance. "History of the North Carolina State Board of Public Welfare, 1868–1947." *North Carolina Historical Review* 24 (January 1947): 1–33.

Ayers, Edward L. *Promise of the New South: Life after Reconstruction.* New York: Oxford University Press, 1992.

————. *Vengeance and Justice: Crime and Punishment in the Nineteenth Century American South.* New York: Oxford University Press, 1984.

Badger, Anthony J. *Prosperity Road: The New Deal, Tobacco, and North Carolina.* Chapel Hill: University of North Carolina Press, 1980.

Bailey, Hugh. *Liberalism in the New South: Southern Social Reformers and the Progressive Movement.* Coral Gables: University of Miami Press, 1969.

Barber, E. Susan. "Anxious Care and Constant Struggle: The Female Humane Association and Richmond's White Civil War Orphans." In *Before the New Deal: Social Welfare in the South, 1830–1930,* edited by Elna C. Green. Athens: University of Georgia Press, 1999.

————. "Cartridge Makers and Myrmidon Viragos: White Working-Class Women in Confederate Richmond." In *Negotiating Boundaries of Southern Womanhood: Dealing with the Powers That Be,* edited by Janet L. Coryell et al. Columbia: University of Missouri Press, 2000.

————. "The Quiet Battles of the Home Front War: Civil War Bread Riots and the Development of a Confederate Welfare System." Master's thesis, University of Maryland, 1986.

————. " 'Sisters of the Capital': White Women in Richmond, Virginia, 1860–1880." Ph.D. diss., University of Maryland at College Park, 1997.

Barr, Alwyn. "The Other Texas: Charities and Community in the Lone Star State." *Southwestern Historical Quarterly* 97 (July 1993): 1–10.

Bass, R. Aumon. *History of the Education of the Deaf in Virginia.* Staunton: Virginia School for the Deaf and the Blind, 1949.

Bauman, Mark K. "The Emergence of Jewish Social Service Agencies in Atlanta." *Georgia Historical Quarterly* 69 (1985): 488–508.

Bell, Michael Everette. "The German Immigrant Community of Richmond, Virginia: 1848–1852." Master's thesis, University of Richmond, 1990.

Bellows, Barbara. *Benevolence among Slaveholders: Assisting the Poor in Charleston, 1670–1860.* Baton Rouge: Louisiana State University Press, 1993.

Bender, Thomas. *Toward an Urban Vision: Ideas and Institutions in Nineteenth Century America.* Lexington: University Press of Kentucky, 1975.

Berkley, Kathleen. "Colored Ladies Also Contributed: Black Women's Activities from Benevolence to Social Welfare, 1866–1896." In *The Web of Southern Social Relations: Women, Family, and Education*, edited by Walter J. Fraser et al. Athens: University of Georgia Press, 1985.

Berkowitz, Edward. *America's Welfare State: From Roosevelt to Reagan*. Baltimore: Johns Hopkins University Press, 1991.

———. *Creating the Welfare State*. Lawrence: University Press of Kansas, 1992.

Berlin, Ira, and Leslie S. Rowland, eds. *Families and Freedom: A Documentary History of African-American Kinship in the Civil War Era*. New York: Free Press, 1979.

Berman, Myron. *Richmond's Jewry, 1769–1976: Shabbat in Shockoe*. Charlottesville: University Press of Virginia, 1979.

Bernhard, Virginia. "Poverty and the Social Order in Seventeenth Century Virginia." *Virginia Magazine of History and Biography* 85 (April 1977): 141–55.

Berry, Benjamin. "Plymouth Settlement House and the Development of Black Louisville, 1900–1930." Ph.D. diss., Case Western Reserve University, 1977.

Beven, Evelyn Campbell. *City Subsidies to Private Charitable Agencies in New Orleans: The History and Present Status, 1824–1933*. New Orleans: School of Social Work of Tulane University, 1934.

Bilderback, Elizabeth Pearce. "Women Welfare Workers in South Carolina Textile Mills, 1890–1935." Master's thesis, University of South Carolina, 1993.

Biles, Roger. *Memphis in the Great Depression*. Knoxville: University of Tennessee, 1986.

———. *The South and the New Deal*. Lexington: University Press of Kentucky, 1994.

Blair, William. *Virginia's Private War: Feeding Body and Soul in the Confederacy, 1861–1865*. New York: Oxford University Press, 1998.

Blassingame, John W. *Black New Orleans, 1860–1880*. Chicago: University of Chicago Press, 1973.

Bogger, Tommy L. *Free Blacks in Norfolk, Virginia, 1790–1860: The Darker Side of Freedom*. Charlottesville: University Press of Virginia, 1997.

Bongiorno, Angel Catherine. "White Women and Work in Richmond, Virginia, 1870–1880." Master's thesis, University of Virginia, 1978.

Bonnin, Patricia Dora. "The Problem of Relief for the Families of Confederate Soldiers in South Carolina." In *Proceedings of the South Carolina Historical Association* (1994). Columbia, S.C.: The Association, 1994.

Boyer, George R. *An Economic History of the English Poor Law, 1750–1850*. Cambridge: Cambridge University Press, 1990.

Braeman, John, Robert H. Bremner, and David Broday, eds. *The New Deal: The State and Local Levels*. Columbus: Ohio State University Press, 1975.

Bremner, Robert H. *The Public Good: Philanthropy and Welfare in the Civil War Era*. New York: Knopf, 1980.

Brewster, Ruby. "The Memorial Mercy Home-Hospital." Master's thesis, Tulane School of Social Work, 1942.

Bridenbaugh, Carl. *Vexed and Troubled Englishmen, 1590–1642.* New York: Oxford University Press, 1968.

Brilliant, Eleanor L. *The United Way: Dilemmas of Organized Charity.* New York: Columbia University Press, 1990.

Brinson, Elizabeth Stevens. "Helping Others to Help Themselves: Social Advocacy and Wage Earning Women in Richmond, Virginia, 1910–1932." Ph.D. diss., Union of Experimenting Colleges and Universities, 1984.

Brock, William R. *Welfare, Democracy, and the New Deal.* Cambridge: Cambridge University Press, 1988.

Brown, Dorothy M., and Elizabeth McKeown. *The Poor Belong to Us: Catholic Charities and American Welfare.* Cambridge: Harvard University Press, 1997.

Brown, Elsa Barkley. "Womanist Consciousness: Maggie Lena Walker and the Independent Order of Saint Luke." *Signs* 14 (spring 1989): 610–33.

Brown, Elsa Barkley, and Gregg D. Kimball. "Mapping the Terrain of Black Richmond." *Journal of Urban History* 21 (March 1995): 296–346.

Brown, Josephine Chapin. *Public Relief, 1929–1939.* New York: Henry Holt, 1940.

Brown, Roy M. *Public Poor Relief in North Carolina.* Chapel Hill: University of North Carolina Press, 1928.

Brumberg, Joan Jacobs. "Ruined Girls: Changing Community Responses to Illegitimacy in Upstate New York, 1890–1920." *Journal of Social History* (winter 1984): 247–72.

Bruno, Frank J. "Twenty-five Years of Schools of Social Work." *Social Service Review* 18 (1944): 152–64.

Bunzl, Rudolph H. "Immigrants in Richmond after the Civil War, 1865–1880." Master's thesis, University of Richmond, 1994.

Burwell, N. Yolanda. "Public Welfare Institutes for Negroes, 1926–1940." *Journal of Sociology and Social Welfare* 21 (1994): 55–65.

Cahn, Susan. "Spirited Youth or Fiends Incarnate: The Samarcand Arson Case and Female Adolescence in the American South." *Journal of Women's History* 9 (winter 1998): 152–80.

Callaway, Carla Sue. "Poor Relief in Mississippi, 1799–1935." Master's thesis, University of Mississippi, 1979.

Calo, Zachary Ryan. "From Poor Relief to the Poorhouse: The Response to Poverty in Prince George's County, Maryland, 1710–1770." *Maryland History Magazine* 93 (winter 1998): 393–427.

Campbell, Margaret M., ed. *Making a Difference: 1914–1989, Tulane School of Social Work.* New Orleans: Tulane University, 1990.

Cash, W. J. *The Mind of the South.* New York: Vintage Books, 1941.

Cassel, Elena Daly. "An Analysis of the Poor Relief System in Truro Parish, Virginia: 1732–1785." Master's thesis, George Mason University, 1977.

Cavan, Ruth Shonle, and Katherine Howland Ranck. *The Family and the Depression: A Study of One Hundred Chicago Families.* Chicago: University of Chicago Press, 1938.

Cei, Louis Bernard. "Law Enforcement in Richmond: A History of Police-Community Relations, 1737–1974." Ph.D. diss., Florida State University, 1974.

Cepuran, Joseph. *Public Assistance and Child Welfare: The Virginia Pattern, 1646 to 1964.* Charlottesville: n.p., 1968.

Chambers, Clarke A. "Toward a Redefinition of Welfare History." *Journal of American History* 73 (September 1986): 407–33.

———. " 'Uphill All the Way': Reflections on the Course and Study of Welfare History." *Social Service Review* 66 (December 1992): 492–505.

———. "Women in the Creation of the Profession of Social Work." *Social Service Review* 60 (March 1986): 1–33.

Chandler, Susan Kerr. "Almost a Partnership: African-Americans, Segregation, and the YMCA." *Journal of Sociology and Social Welfare* 21 (1994): 97–111.

Chapman, Bernadine Sharpe. "Northern Philanthropy and African-American Adult Education in the Rural South: Hegemony and Resistance in the Jeanes Movement." Ed.D. diss., Northern Illinois University, 1990.

Chappell, Mrs. Ralph R., and Mrs. J. W. S. Gilchrist. "A History of the YWCA of Richmond, Virginia, 1887–1937." *Fiftieth Annual Meeting of the Young Women's Christian Association.* Richmond: n.p., 1938.

Chatfield, Charles. "The Southern Sociological Congress: Organization of Uplift." *Tennessee Historical Quarterly* 19 (1960): 328–47.

———. "The Southern Sociological Congress: Rationale of Uplift." *Tennessee Historical Quarterly* 20 (1961): 51–64.

Chesson, Michael B. "Harlots or Heroines? A New Look at the Richmond Bread Riot." *Virginia Magazine of History and Biography* 92 (April 1984): 131–75.

———. *Richmond after the War, 1865–1890.* Richmond: Virginia State Library, 1981.

Clancy, Patrick. "Conserving the Youth: The Civilian Conservation Corps Experience in Shenandoah National Park." *Virginia Magazine of History and Biography* 105 (1996): 439–56.

Clement, Priscilla Ferguson. *Welfare and the Poor in the Nineteenth-Century City, Philadelphia, 1800–1854.* Rutherford, N.J.: Associated University Presses, 1985.

Click, Patricia Catherine. *The Spirit of the Times: Amusements in Nineteenth-Century Baltimore, Norfolk, and Richmond.* Charlottesville: University Press of Virginia, 1989.

Coddington, Edwin Broughton. "Soldiers' Relief in the Seaboard States of the Southern Confederacy." *Mississippi Valley Historical Review* 37 (June 1950): 17–38.

Colby, Ira C. "The Freedman's Bureau: From Social Welfare to Segregation." *Phylon* 46 (September 1985): 219–30.

Colcord, Joanna C. *Cash Relief.* New York: Russell Sage Foundation, 1936.

Cole, Jeffrey S. "The Impact of the Great Depression and New Deal on the Urban South: Lynchburg, Virginia as a Case Study, 1929–1941." Ph.D. diss., Bowling Green University, 1998.

Cole, Olen, Jr. *The African-American Experience in the Civilian Conservation Corps.* Gainesville: University Press of Florida, 1999.

Cole, William I. *Motives and Results of the Settlement Movement.* Cambridge: Harvard University Department of Social Ethics publication number 2, 1908.

Coleman, Maybelle. "Poverty and Poor Relief in the Plantation Society of South Carolina." Ph.D. diss., Duke University, 1943.

Cottrell, Debbie Mauldin. "The County Poor Farm System in Texas." *Southwestern Historical Quarterly* 93 (1989): 169–90.

Courtwright, David T. "The Hidden Epidemic: Opiate Addiction and Cocaine Use in the South, 1860–1920." *Journal of Southern History* 39 (February 1983): 57–72.

Cox, Kate Cabell. *Historical Sketch of Richmond's Oldest Chartered Charity, Memorial Home for Girls, 1805–1925.* Richmond: n.p., 1925.

Cray, Robert E., Jr. *Paupers and Poor Relief in New York City and Its Rural Environs, 1700–1830.* Philadelphia: Temple University Press, 1988.

Crenson, Matthew A. *Building the Invisible Orphanage: A Prehistory of the American Welfare System.* Cambridge: Harvard University Press, 1998.

Crocker, Ruth. *Social Work and Social Order: The Settlement Movement in Two Industrial Cities, 1889–1930.* Urbana: University of Illinois Press, 1992.

Cumbler, John T. "The Politics of Charity." *Journal of Social History* 14 (January 1980): 99–112.

Curtis, George Bartlett. "The Juvenile Court Movement in Virginia: The Child Savers, 1890–1973." Ph.D. diss., University of Virginia, 1973.

Dabney, Virginius. *Richmond: The Story of a City.* Charlottesville: University Press of Virginia, 1990.

Dailey, Jane. *Before Jim Crow: The Politics of Race in Postemancipation Virginia.* Chapel Hill: University of North Carolina Press, 2000.

Dain, Norman. *Disordered Minds: The First Century of Eastern State Hospital in Williamsburg, VA, 1766–1866.* Williamsburg: Colonial Williamsburg Foundation, 1971.

Davis, Allen F. *Spearheads for Reform: The Social Settlements and the Progressive Movement, 1890–1914.* New York: Oxford University Press, 1967.

Davis, Elizabeth Lindsay. *Lifting as They Climb.* Washington, D.C.: National Association of Colored Women, 1933.

Dew, Charles B. *Ironmaker to the Confederacy: Joseph R. Anderson and the Tredegar Iron Works.* New Haven: Harvard University Press, 1966.

Dorman, John Frederick, ed. *Virginia Revolutionary War State Pensions.* Richmond: Virginia Genealogical Society, 1980.

Dorr, Gregory Michael. "Segregation's Science: The American Eugenics Movement and Virginia, 1900–1980." Ph.D. diss., University of Virginia, 2000.

Dorr, Lisa Lindquist. "Arm in Arm: Gender, Eugenics, and Virginia's Racial Integrity Acts of the 1920s." *Journal of Women's History* 11 (spring 1999): 143–66.

Dowling, Harry F. *City Hospitals: The Undercare of the Underprivileged.* Cambridge: Harvard University Press, 1982.

Downs, Susan Whitelaw, and Michael W. Sherraden. "The Orphan Asylum in the Nineteenth Century." *Social Service Review* 57 (June 1983): 272–90.

Drake, Lurline. "A History of the Virginia Conference of Social Work, 1942–1953." Master's thesis, Virginia Commonwealth University, 1954.

Driver, Felix. *Power and Pauperism: The Workhouse System, 1834–84.* Cambridge: Cambridge University Press, 1993.

Du Bois, W. E. B. *Black Reconstruction.* New York: Harcourt, Brace and Co., 1935.

———. "The Freedmen's Bureau." *Atlantic Monthly* 87 (March 1901): 354–65.

———, ed. *Efforts for Social Betterment among Negro Americans.* Atlanta: Atlanta University Publications, 1909.

Dubroca, Isabelle. *Good Neighbor: Eleanor McMain of Kingsley House.* New Orleans: Pelican Publishing, 1955.

Dufour, Charles L. *Women Who Cared: One Hundred Years of the Christian Woman's Exchange.* New Orleans: Upton Printing, 1980.

Edwards, Laura F. *Gendered Strife and Confusion: The Political Culture of Reconstruction.* Urbana: University of Illinois Press, 1997.

"Effect of Social Security Program on Almshouses." *Monthly Labor Review* 47 (September 1938): 518–24.

Eggener, Keith L. "Old Folks, New South: Charleston's William Enston Home." *South Carolina Historical Magazine* 98 (1997): 251–80.

Ehrenreich, John. *The Altruistic Imagination: A History of Social Work and Social Policy in the U.S.* Ithaca: Cornell University Press, 1985.

Eisenberg, Ralph. *Virginia Votes, 1924–1968.* Charlottesville: University Press of Virginia, 1971.

Elia, Ricardo J. "Silent Stones in a Potter's Field: Grave Markers at the Almshouse Burial Ground in Uxbridge, Massachusetts." *Markers* 9 (1992): 132–57.

Elia, Ricardo J., and Al B. Wesolowsky, eds. *Archeaological Excavations at the Uxbridge Almshouse Burial Ground in Uxbridge Massachusetts.* New York: Oxford University Press, 1991.

Entrekin, William Frank. "Poor Relief in North Carolina in the Confederacy." Master's thesis, Duke University, 1947.

Ernst, William Joel. "Urban Leaders and Social Change: The Urbanization Process in Richmond, Virginia, 1840–1880." Ph.D. diss., University of Virginia, 1978.

Escott, Paul D. "The Cry of the Sufferers: The Problem of Welfare in the Confederacy." *Civil War History* 23 (1977): 228–40.

———. "Poverty and Governmental Aid for the Poor in Confederate North Carolina." *North Carolina Historical Review* 61 (1984): 462–80.

Ezekiel, Herbert T., and Gaston Lichtenstein. *The History of the Jews of Richmond from 1769 to 1917.* Richmond: H. T. Ezekiel, 1917.

Farmer, Marguerite Watson. "Analysis of Applications for Financial Assistance Made to the Family Service Society of Richmond, Virginia, January 1, 1948–December 31, 1948, with Special Consideration of Applications Referred at Intake to the Social Service Bureau of Richmond, Virginia." Master's thesis, College of William and Mary, RPI branch, 1950.

Farmer, Mary J. " 'Because They Are Women': Gender and the Virginia Freedmen's

Bureau's 'War on Dependency.' " In *The Freedmen's Bureau and Reconstruction: Reconsiderations*, edited by Paul A. Cimbala and Randall M. Miller. New York: Fordham University Press, 1999.

Faust, Drew Gilpin. "Altars of Sacrifice: Confederate Women and the Narratives of War." In *Divided Houses: Gender and the Civil War*, edited by Catherine Clinton and Nina Silber. New York: Oxford University Press, 1992.

Feder, Leah Hannah. *Unemployment Relief in Periods of Depression: A Study of Measures Adopted in Certain American Cities*. New York: Russell Sage Foundation, 1936.

Fisher, Jacob. *The Response of Social Work to the Depression*. Boston: G. K. Hall, 1980.

Flynt, J. Wayne. "Feeding the Hungry and Ministering to the Broken Hearted: The Presbyterian Church in the United States and the Social Gospel, 1900–1920." In *Religion in the South*, edited by Charles Reagan Wilson. Jackson: University Press of Mississippi, 1985.

———. *Poor but Proud: Alabama's Poor Whites*. Tuscaloosa: University of Alabama Press, 1989.

Foner, Eric. *Reconstruction: America's Unfinished Revolution*. New York: Harper and Row, 1988.

Foster, Gaines M. *Ghosts of the Confederacy: Defeat, the Lost Cause, and the Emergence of the New South, 1865 to 1913*. New York: Oxford University Press, 1987.

Franklin, John Hope. "Public Welfare in the South during Reconstruction, 1865–1880." *Social Service Review* 44 (December 1970): 379–92.

Franklin, John Hope, and Alfred A. Moss Jr. *From Slavery to Freedom: A History of African Americans*. 7th ed. New York: McGraw-Hill, 1994.

Fry, Joseph Andrew. "George Campbell Peery: Conservative Son of Old Virginia." Master's thesis, University of Virginia, 1970.

Fuchs, Rachel. *Abandoned Children: Foundlings and Child Welfare in Nineteenth-Century France*. Albany: State University of New York Press, 1984.

Furgurson, Ernest B. *Ashes of Glory: Richmond at War*. New York: Knopf, 1996.

Geddes, Anne E. *Trends in Relief Expenditures*. Washington, D.C.: GPO, 1937.

Gee, Wilson, and John J. Corson III. *A Statistical Study of Virginia*. Charlottesville: Institute for Research in the Social Sciences, 1927.

Gee, Wilson, and William Henry Stauffer. *Rural and Urban Living Standards in Virginia*. Charlottesville: Institute for Research in the Social Sciences, 1929.

Getis, Victoria. *The Juvenile Court and the Progressives*. Urbana: University of Illinois Press, 2000.

Giesberg, Judith Ann. *Civil War Sisterhood: The U.S. Sanitary Commission and Women's Politics in Transition*. Boston: Northeastern University Press, 2000.

Gilje, Paul. "Infant Abandonment in Early Nineteenth Century New York." *Signs* 8 (spring 1983): 580–90.

Gilman, Amy. "From Widowhood to Wickedness: The Politics of Class and Gender in New York City Private Charity, 1799–1860." *History of Education Quarterly* 24 (1984): 59–74.

Ginzberg, Lori D. *Women and the Work of Benevolence: Morality, Politics, and Class in the Nineteenth Century United States*. New Haven: Yale University Press, 1990.

Gittens, Joan. "Friendless Foundlings and Homeless Half-Orphans." *Chicago History* 24 (spring 1995): 40–72.

Glover, E. Elizabeth. "The Transient Situation in Richmond." Master's thesis, College of William and Mary, 1934.

Goldfield, David R. *Region, Race, and Cities: Interpreting the Urban South*. Baton Rouge: Louisiana State University Press, 1997.

———. *Urban Growth in the Age of Sectionalism: Virginia, 1847–1861*. Baton Rouge: Louisiana State University Press, 1977.

Gordon, Linda. "Black and White Visions of Welfare: Women's Welfare Activism, 1890–1945." *Journal of American History* 78 (1991): 559–90.

———. *The New Feminist Scholarship on the Welfare State*. Madison, Wis.: Institute for Research on Poverty, 1989.

———. *Pitied but Not Entitled: Single Mothers and the History of Welfare*. New York: Free Press, 1994.

Gorman, Kathleen. "Confederate Pensions as Southern Social Welfare." In *Before the New Deal: Social Welfare in the South, 1830–1930*, edited by Elna C. Green. Athens: University of Georgia Press, 1999.

Grantham, Dewey W. *Southern Progressivism: The Reconciliation of Progress and Tradition*. Knoxville: University of Tennessee Press, 1983.

Gray, Charles. "The Freedmen's Bureau: A Missing Chapter in Social Welfare History." D.S.W. diss., Yeshiva University, 1994.

Green, Elna C. "Infanticide and Infant Abandonment in the New South: Richmond, Virginia, 1865–1910." *Journal of Family History* 24 (April 1999): 187–211.

———. "National Trends, Regional Differences, Local Circumstances: Social Welfare in New Orleans, 1870s–1920s." In *Before the New Deal: Social Welfare in the South*. Athens: University of Georgia Press, 1999.

Guest, Geoffrey. "The Boarding of the Dependent Poor in Colonial America." *Social Service Review* 63 (1989): 92–112.

Haber, Carole. " 'And the Fear of the Poorhouse': Perceptions of Old Age Impoverishment in Early Twentieth-Century America." *Generations* 27 (summer 1993): 46.

Hacsi, Timothy A. *Second Home: Orphan Asylums and Poor Families in America*. Cambridge: Harvard University Press, 1998.

Hamburger, Susan. "We Take Care of Our Womenfolk: The Home for Needy Confederate Women in Richmond, Virginia, 1898–1990." In *Before the New Deal: Social Welfare in the South, 1830–1930*, edited by Elna C. Green. Athens: University of Georgia Press, 1999.

Hankins, Mary Coleman. "The Growth of Public Outdoor Relief in Richmond, Virginia." Master's thesis, College of William and Mary, RPI branch, 1935.

Hannon, Joan Underhill. "Poor Relief Policy in Antebellum New York State: The Rise and Decline of the Poorhouse." *Explorations in Economic History* 22 (1985): 233–56.

Hardesty, Katherine. "Eleanor McMain, Trail-Blazer of Southern Social Work." Master's thesis, Tulane School of Social Work, 1936.

Heinemann, Ronald L. *Depression and New Deal in Virginia: The Enduring Dominion.* Charlottesville: University Press of Virginia, 1983.

———. *Harry Byrd of Virginia.* Charlottesville: University Press of Virginia, 1996.

Hertz, Hilda, and Sue Warren Little. "Unmarried Negro Mothers in a Southern Urban Community." *Social Forces* 23 (October 1944): 73–79.

Hibbs, Henry H. *A History of the Richmond Professional Institute.* Richmond: RPI, 1973.

Higginbotham, Evelyn Brooks. *Righteous Discontent: The Women's Movement in the Black Baptist Church, 1880–1920.* Cambridge: Harvard University Press, 1993.

Hill, Louise B. *State Socialism in the Confederate States of America.* Charlottesville: Historical Publishing, 1936.

History of the Home for Needy Confederate Women, Richmond, Virginia, with Reports of Officers. Richmond: Hill Printing, 1904.

Hitchcock, Tim, Peter King, and Pamela Sharpe, eds. *Chronicling Poverty: The Voices and Strategies of the English Poor, 1640–1840.* New York: St. Martins Press, 1997.

Holloway, Pippa. "Tending to Deviance: Sexuality and Public Policy in Urban Virginia, Richmond and Norfolk, 1920–1950." Ph.D. diss., Ohio State University, 1999.

Hope, W. Martin, and Jason H. Silverman. *Relief and Recovery in Post–Civil War South Carolina: A Death by Inches.* Lewiston, N.Y.: Edwin Mellen Press, 1997.

Hudson, William E. *"The Least of These": The Beneficences of the Synod of Virginia.* Richmond: Presbyterian Committee of Publications, 1926.

Humbert, R. Lee, et al., eds. *Virginia: Economic and Civic.* Richmond: Whittet and Shepperson, 1933.

Humphreys, Margaret. *Yellow Fever and the South.* Baltimore: Johns Hopkins University Press, 1999.

Hunter, Robert F. "Virginia and the New Deal." In *The New Deal.* Vol. 2, *The State and Local Levels,* edited by John Braemen, Robert H. Bremner, and David Brody. Columbus: Ohio State University Press, 1975.

Hyde, Samuel C., Jr., ed. *Plain Folk of the South Revisited.* Baton Rouge: Louisiana State University Press, 1997.

Iacovetta, Franca, and Wendy Mitchinson, eds. *On the Case: Explorations in Social History.* Toronto: University of Toronto Press, 1998.

Ironmonger, Elizabeth Hogg, and Pauline Landrum Phillips. *History of the Woman's Christian Temperance Union of Virginia and a Glimpse of Seventy-five Years, 1883–1958.* Richmond: Cavalier Press, 1958.

Irons, Charles F. "And All These Things Shall Be Added unto You: The First African Baptist Church, Richmond, 1841–1865." *Virginia Cavalcade* 47 (winter 1998): 26–35.

Isaacson, Irma M. "A History of Jewish Philanthropy in New Orleans." Master's thesis, Tulane School of Social Work, 1937.

Jacobs, Claude F. "Benevolent Societies of New Orleans Blacks during the Late Nineteenth and Early Twentieth Centuries." *Louisiana History* 29 (winter 1988): 21–33.

James, Arthur Wilson. *Back from "Over the Hill": The Disappearance of the County Almshouse in Virginia*. Richmond: State Board of Public Welfare, 1926.

―――. *The Juvenile and Public Welfare Laws of Virginia*. Richmond: State Department of Public Welfare, 1928.

―――. "Local Welfare Development." *The Commonwealth* 3 (December 1936): 16–17.

―――. *The Public Welfare Function of Government in Virginia*. Richmond: n.p., 1934.

―――. *The State Becomes a Social Worker: An Administrative Interpretation*. Richmond: Garrett and Massie, 1942.

―――. *Virginia's Social Awakening: The Contribution of Dr. Mastin and the Board of Charities and Corrections*. Richmond: Garrett and Massie, 1939.

Jennings, Florence. "A Study of the W. E. and Frances Roberson Memorial Home (an Institution for Dependent Negro Children)." Master's thesis, Tulane School of Social Work, 1933.

Jennings, Knox G. "Almshouses in Alabama." Master's thesis, Florida State University, 1964.

Jernegan, Marcus Wilson. *Laboring and Dependent Classes in Colonial America, 1607–1783*. Chicago: University of Chicago Press, 1931.

Johnson, Christopher S. "Poor Relief in Antebellum Mississippi." *Journal of Mississippi History* 49 (1987): 1–21.

Johnson, Nessa Theresa Baskerville. *A Special Pilgrimage: A History of Black Catholics in Richmond*. Richmond: Diocese of Richmond, 1978.

Jordan, Ervin L., Jr. *Black Confederates and Afro-Yankees in Civil War Virginia*. Charlottesville: University Press of Virginia, 1995.

Jordan, Laylon Wayne. " 'The Method of Modern Charity': The Associated Charities Society of Charleston, 1880–1920." *South Carolina Historical Magazine* 88 (January 1987): 34–47.

Katz, Michael B. *In the Shadow of the Poorhouse: A Social History of Welfare in America*. New York: Basic Books, 1986, 1996.

―――. *Poverty and Policy in American History*. Philadelphia: Academic Press, 1983.

―――. *The Price of Citizenship: Redefining America's Welfare State*. New York: Metropolitan Books, 2001.

―――. *The Undeserving Poor: From the War on Poverty to the War on Welfare*. New York: Pantheon, 1989.

―――, ed. *The "Underclass" Debate: Views from History*. Princeton: Princeton University, 1993.

Kerr-Ritchie, Jeffrey R. *Freedpeople in the Tobacco South: Virginia, 1860–1900*. Chapel Hill: University of North Carolina Press, 1999.

Kerson, Toba Schwaber. "Almshouse to Municipal Hospital: The Baltimore Experience." *Bulletin of the History of Medicine* 55 (1981): 203–20.

Kevles, Daniel. *In the Name of Eugenics*. New York: Alfred Knopf, 1985.

Key, V. O., Jr. *Southern Politics in State and Nation*. New York: Alfred Knopf, 1949.

Kimball, Gregg D. *American City, Southern Place: A Cultural History of Antebellum Richmond*. Athens: University of Georgia Press, 2000.

King, Steven. *Poverty and Welfare in England, 1700–1850: A Regional Perspective.* Manchester, Eng.: Manchester University Press, 2000.

Kirby, Jack Temple. *Darkness at the Dawning: Race and Reform in the Progressive South.* Philadelphia: n.p., 1972.

———. *Westmoreland Davis, Virginia Planter-Politician, 1859–1942.* Charlottesville: University Press of Virginia, 1968.

Kirkwood, Robert. *"Fit Surroundings": District Homes Replace County Almshouses in Virginia.* Richmond: Department of Public Welfare, 1948.

Klebaner, Benjamin Joseph. *Public Poor Relief in America, 1790–1860.* New York: Arno Press, 1976.

———. "Some Aspects of North Carolina Public Poor Relief, 1700–1860." *North Carolina Historical Review* 31 (October 1954): 479–92.

Klein, Philip. *From Philanthropy to Social Welfare.* San Francisco: Jossey-Bass, 1971.

Klein, Randolph S. "Medical Expenses and the Poor in Virginia." *Journal of the History of Medicine* 30 (July 1975): 260–66.

Kneebone, John T., et al., eds. *Dictionary of Virginia Biography.* Richmond: Library of Virginia, 1998–.

Knupfer, Anne Meis. *Reform and Resistance: Gender, Delinquency, and America's First Juvenile Court.* New York: Routledge, 2001.

Koeniger, Alfred Cash. "The New Deal and the States: Roosevelt versus the Byrd Organization in Virginia." *Journal of American History* 68 (May 1982): 877–88.

———. " 'Unreconstructed Rebel': The Political Thought and Senate Career of Carter Glass, 1929–1936." Ph.D. diss., Vanderbilt University, 1980.

Kogut, Alvin. "The Negro and the Charity Organization Society in the Progressive Era." *Social Service Review* 44 (March 1970): 11–21.

Kousser, J. Morgan. *The Shaping of Southern Politics: Suffrage Restriction and the Establishment of the One-Party South, 1880–1910.* New Haven: Yale University Press, 1974.

Koven, Seth, and Sonya Michel. "Gender and the Origins of the Welfare State." *Radical History Review* 43 (winter 1989): 112–19.

———, eds. *Mothers of a New World: Maternalist Politics and the Origins of Welfare States.* New York: Routledge, 1993.

Krowl, Michelle A. " 'Her Just Dues': Civil War Pensions of African American Women in Virginia." In *Negotiating Boundaries of Southern Womanhood: Dealing with the Powers That Be,* edited by Janet L. Coryell et al. Columbia: University of Missouri Press, 2000.

Kuhn, Cliff. "Reminiscences: Interview with Atlanta New Deal Social Workers." *Atlanta Historical Journal* 30 (spring 1986): 107–16.

Kulikoff, Allan. *Tobacco and Slaves: The Development of Southern Cultures in the Chesapeake, 1680–1800.* Chapel Hill: University of North Carolina Press, 1986.

Kunzel, Regina. *Fallen Women, Problem Girls: Unmarried Mothers and the Professionalization of Social Work, 1890–1945.* New Haven: Yale University Press, 1993.

————. "The Professionalization of Benevolence: Evangelicals and Social Workers in Florence Crittenden Homes." *Journal of Social History* 22 (fall 1988): 21–43.

Ladd-Taylor, Molly. *Mother-Work: Women, Child Welfare, and the State, 1890–1930.* Urbana: University of Illinois Press, 1994.

LaMonte, Edward. *Politics and Welfare in Birmingham, 1900–1975.* Tuscaloosa: University of Alabama Press, 1995.

Larsen, William. *Montague of Virginia: The Making of a Southern Progressive.* Baton Rouge: Louisiana State University Press, 1965.

Lasch-Quinn, Elisabeth. *Black Neighbors, Race, and the Limits of Reform in the American Settlement House Movement, 1890–1945.* Chapel Hill: University of North Carolina Press, 1993.

Lebsock, Suzanne. *The Free Women of Petersburg: Status and Culture in a Southern Town, 1784–1860.* New York: W. W. Norton, 1984.

Lees, Lynn Hollen. *The Solidarities of Strangers: The English Poor Laws and the People, 1700–1948.* Cambridge: Cambridge University Press, 1998.

Leff, Mark H. "A Consensus for Reform: The Mothers' Pension Movement in the Progressive Era." *Social Service Review* 47 (1973): 397–429.

Leiby, James. "Charity Organization Reconsidered." *Social Service Review* 58 (December 1984): 523–38.

————. *History of Social Welfare and Social Work in the U.S.* New York: Columbia University, 1978.

Leighninger, Leslie. *Social Work: Search for Identity.* New York: Greenwood Press, 1987.

Leuchtenburg, William E. *The Perils of Prosperity, 1914–32.* Chicago: University of Chicago Press, 1958.

Levine, Daniel. "A Single Standard of Civilization: Black Private Social Welfare Institutions in the South, 1880s–1920s." *Georgia Historical Quarterly* 81 (spring 1997): 52–77.

Levine-Clark, Marjorie. "Engendering Relief: Women, Ablebodiedness, and the New Poor Law in Early Victorian England." *Journal of Women's History* 11, no. 4 (2000): 107–30.

Lewis, Earl. *In Their Own Interests: Race, Class, and Power in Twentieth-Century Norfolk, Virginia.* Berkeley: University of California Press, 1991.

Lieberman, Robert C. "Race and the Development of the American Welfare State from the New Deal to the Great Society." Ph.D. diss., Harvard University, 1994.

Link, Arthur S. "The Progressive Movement in the South, 1870–1914." *North Carolina Historical Review* 23 (April 1946): 172–95.

Link, William A. *The Paradox of Southern Progressivism, 1880–1930.* Chapel Hill: University of North Carolina Press, 1993.

Lisenby, William Foy. "An Administrative History of Public Programs for Dependent Children in North Carolina, Virginia, Tennessee, and Kentucky, 1900–1942." Ph.D. diss., Vanderbilt University, 1962.

Lissak, Rivka. *Pluralism and Progressives: Hull House and the New Immigrants.* Chicago: University of Chicago Press, 1989.

Lloyd, Gary A. *Charities, Settlements, and Social Work: An Inquiry into Philosophy and Method, 1890–1915.* New Orleans: Tulane University Studies in Social Welfare, 1971.

Lombardo, Paul A. "Eugenic Sterilization in Virginia: Aubrey Strode and the Case of Buck v. Bell." Ph.D. diss., University of Virginia, 1982.

Lowe, Richard. *Republicans and Reconstruction in Virginia, 1856–70.* Charlottesville: University Press of Virginia, 1991.

Lubove, Roy. *The Professional Altruist: The Emergence of Social Work as a Career, 1880–1930.* Cambridge: Harvard University Press, 1965.

Luker, Ralph. *The Social Gospel in Black and White: American Racial Reform.* Chapel Hill: University of North Carolina Press, 1991.

Lundberg, Emma O. *Social Welfare in Florida.* Tallahassee: State Board of Public Welfare publication no. 4, 1934.

Lynn, Robert DeWese. "The Social Functions of the Salvation Army in Richmond, Virginia." Master's thesis, College of William and Mary, RPI branch, 1935.

Mackey, Howard. "The Operation of the English Old Poor Law in Colonial Virginia." *Virginia Magazine of History and Biography* 73 (January 1965): 29–40.

MacLeod, Margaret E. "A Case Study of Poor Relief in Christ Church Parish, Virginia, 1666–1730." Master's thesis, University of Wisconsin–Milwaukee, 1980.

Mandler, Peter, ed. *The Uses of Charity: The Poor on Relief in the Nineteenth-Century Metropolis.* Philadelphia: University of Pennsylvania Press, 1990.

Maney, Patrick J. *The Roosevelt Presence: A Biography of Franklin Delano Roosevelt.* New York: Twayne Publishers, 1992.

Marcello, Ronald E. "The Politics of Relief: The North Carolina WPA and the Tar Heel Elections of 1936." *North Carolina Historical Review* 68 (January 1991): 17–37.

Massey, Mary Elizabeth. "The Free Market of New Orleans, 1861–1862." *Louisiana History* 3 (1962): 202–20.

————. *Refugee Life in the Confederacy.* Baton Rouge: Louisiana State University Press, 1964.

McCandless, Peter. *Moonlight, Magnolias, and Madness: Insanity in South Carolina from the Colonial Period to the Progressive Era.* Chapel Hill: University of North Carolina Press, 1996.

McClintock, Megan J. "Civil War Pensions and the Reconstruction of Union Families." *Journal of American History* 83 (September 1996): 456–80.

McDaid, Jennifer Davis. "With Lame Legs and No Money: Virginia's Disabled Confederate Veterans." *Virginia Cavalcade* 47 (winter 1998): 14–25.

McDowell, John P. *The Social Gospel Movement in the South: The Women's Home Mission Movement in the Methodist Episcopal Church, South 1886–1939.* Baton Rouge: Louisiana State University Press, 1982.

McFeely, William S. *Yankee Stepfather: General O. O. Howard and the Freedmen.* New Haven: Yale University Press, 1968.

McJimsey, George. *Harry Hopkins: Ally of the Poor and Defender of Democracy.* Cambridge: Harvard University Press, 1987.

McKinley, Charles, and Robert W. Frase. *Launching Social Security: A Capture-and-Record Account, 1935–1937*. Madison: University of Wisconsin Press, 1970.

McKinley, Edward H. *Marching to Glory: The History of the Salvation Army in the United States of America, 1880–1980*. San Francisco: Harper and Row, 1980.

McLeod, Norman C. "Free Labor in a Slave Society: Richmond, Virginia, 1820–1860." Ph.D. diss., Howard University, 1991.

———. "Not Forgetting the Land We Left: The Irish in Antebellum Richmond." *Virginia Cavalcade* 47 (winter 1998): 36–47.

Mettler, Suzanne. *Dividing Citizens: Gender and Federalism in New Deal Public Policy.* Ithaca: Cornell University Press, 1998.

Miller, Thomas L. "Texas Land Grants to Confederate Veterans and Widows." *Southwestern Historical Quarterly* 69 (1965): 59–65.

Miller, Zane L. "Urban Blacks in the South, 1865–1920: The Richmond, Savannah, New Orleans, Louisville, and Birmingham Experience." In *The New Urban History: Quantitative Explorations by American Historians*, edited by Leo F. Schnore. Princeton: Princeton University Press, 1975.

Moger, Allen W. *Virginia: Bourbonism to Byrd, 1870–1925*. Charlottesville: University Press of Virginia, 1968.

Mohl, Raymond A. *Poverty in New York, 1783–1825*. New York: Oxford University Press, 1971.

Montgomery, Rebecca. "Lost Cause Mythology in New South Reform: Gender, Class, Race, and the Politics of Patriotic Citizenship in Georgia, 1890–1945." In *Negotiating Boundaries of Southern Womanhood: Dealing with the Powers That Be*, edited by Janet L. Coryell et al. Columbia: University of Missouri Press, 2000.

Moore, John S. *The History of Second Baptist Church, Richmond, Virginia: 1820–1995*. Richmond: Second Baptist Church, The American Book Co., 1998.

Moran, Robert. "The Negro Dependent Child in Louisiana, 1800–1935." *Social Service Review* 45 (March 1971): 53–61.

Morgan, Edmund S. *American Slavery, American Freedom: The Ordeal of Colonial Virginia*. New York: Norton, 1975.

Morgan, Lynda J. *Emancipation in Virginia's Tobacco Belt, 1850–1870*. Athens: University of Georgia Press, 1992.

Morgan, Thomas S., Jr. "A Step toward Altruism: Relief and Welfare in North Carolina, 1930–1938." Ph.D. diss., University of North Carolina, 1969.

Morton, Marian J. *And Sin No More: Social Policy and Unwed Mothers in Cleveland, 1855–1990*. Columbus: Ohio State University Press, 1993.

Muncy, Robyn. *Creating a Female Dominion in American Reform, 1890–1935*. New York: Oxford University Press, 1994.

Nadler, Samuel. "A History of the Instructive Visiting Nurses Association of Richmond, Virginia, 1900–1950." Master's thesis, School of Social Work, Richmond Professional Institute of William and Mary, 1951.

Neary, Margaret R. "Some Aspects of Negro Social Life in Richmond, VA, 1865–1880." *Maryland Historian* 1 (1970): 105–19.

Newby, I. A. *Plain Folk in the New South: Social Change and Cultural Persistence, 1880–1915.* Baton Rouge: Louisiana State University Press, 1989.

Noble, Charles. *Welfare as We Knew It: A Political History of the American Welfare State.* Ithaca: Cornell University Press, 1997.

Noll, Steven. *Feeble-Minded in Our Midst: Institutions for the Mentally Retarded in the South, 1900–1940.* Chapel Hill: University of North Carolina Press, 1995.

Nuckols, Robert R. *A History of the Government of the City of Richmond, Virginia and a Sketch of Those Who Administer Its Affairs.* Richmond: William Printing, 1899.

O'Brien, John T. "Factory, Church, and Community: Blacks in Antebellum Richmond." *Journal of Southern History* 44 (November 1978): 509–36.

———. *From Bondage to Citizenship: The Richmond Black, 1865–1867.* New York: Garland, 1990.

———. "Reconstruction in Richmond: White Restoration and Black Protest." *Virginia Magazine of History and Biography* 89 (July 1981): 259–81.

Odem, Mary E. *Delinquent Daughters: Protecting and Policing Adolescent Female Sexuality in the United States, 1885–1920.* Chapel Hill: University of North Carolina Press, 1995.

O'Donnell, Sandra M. "The Care of Dependent African-American Children in Chicago: The Struggle between Black Self-Help and Professionalism." *Journal of Social History* 27 (summer 1994): 763–76.

Opdycke, Sandra. *No One Was Turned Away: The Role of Public Hospitals in New York City Since 1900.* New York: Oxford University Press, 1998.

Osthaus, Carl R. *Freedmen, Philanthropy, and Fraud: A History of the Freedman's Savings Bank.* Urbana: University of Illinois Press, 1976.

Parrott, Angie. " 'Love Makes Memory Eternal': The United Daughters of the Confederacy in Richmond, Virginia, 1897–1920." In *The Edge of the South: Life in Nineteenth-Century Virginia,* edited by Edward L. Ayers and John C. Willis. Charlottesville: University Press of Virginia, 1991.

Paul, Aaron. "The Rural Almshouse of Virginia." Master's thesis, College of William and Mary, RPI branch, 1936.

Piven, Frances Fox, and Richard A. Cloward. "The New Deal and Relief." In *Poverty and Public Policy in Modern America,* edited by Donald T. Critchlow and Ellis W. Hawley. Chicago: Dorsey Press, 1989.

———. *Regulating the Poor: The Functions of Public Welfare.* New York: Random House, 1971.

Plater, Michael A. *African American Entrepreneurship in Richmond, 1890–1940: The Story of R. C. Scott.* New York: Garland Publishing, 1996.

Pollard, Leslie J. "Black Beneficial Societies and the Home for the Aged and Infirm Colored Persons." *Phylon* 41 (summer 1980): 230–34.

Poole, Herbert. "Final Encampment: The North Carolina Soldiers' Home." *Confederate Veteran* (July–August 1987): 10–17.

Porter, Albert Ogden. *County Government in Virginia: A Legislative History, 1607–1904.* New York: Columbia University Press, 1947.

Pulley, Raymond H. *Old Virginia Restored: An Interpretation of the Progressive Impulse, 1870–1930*. Charlottesville: University Press of Virginia, 1968.

Quadagno, Jill. *The Color of Welfare: How Racism Undermined the War on Poverty*. New York: Oxford University Press, 1994.

———. "From Old-Age Assistance to Supplemental Security Income: The Political Economy of Relief in the South, 1935–1972." In *The Politics of Social Policy in the United States*, edited by Margaret Weir, Ann Shola Orloff, and Theda Skocpol. Princeton: Princeton University Press, 1988.

———. *The Transformation of Old Age Security: Class and Politics in the American Welfare State*. Chicago: University of Chicago Press, 1988.

Quiroga, Virginia A. Metaxas. *Poor Mothers and Babies: A Social History of Childbirth and Child Care Hospitals in Nineteenth Century New York City*. New York: Garland Publishing, 1989.

Rabinowitz, Howard N. "From Exclusion to Segregation: Health and Welfare Services for Southern Blacks, 1865–1890." *Social Service Review* 48 (September 1974): 565–94.

———. *Race Relations in the Urban South: 1865–1890*. New York: Oxford University Press, 1978.

Rable, George C. *Civil Wars: Women and the Crisis of Southern Nationalism*. Urbana: University of Illinois Press, 1989.

Rachleff, Peter J. *Black Labor in the South: Richmond, Virginia, 1865–1890*. Philadelphia: Temple University Press, 1984.

Ransel, David L. *Mothers of Misery: Child Abandonment in Russia*. Princeton: Princeton University Press, 1988.

Reed, Adolph L., ed. *Without Justice for All: The New Liberalism and Our Retreat from Racial Equality*. Boulder, Colo.: Westview Press, 1999.

Reed, Mark Alan. "Thieving Times: Criminals, Victims, and the Judicial System in Richmond, Virginia, 1869–1872." Master's thesis, University of Virginia, 1985.

Resch, John Phillips. *Suffering Soldiers: Revolutionary War Veterans, Moral Sentiment, and Political Culture in the Early Republic*. Amherst: University of Massachusetts Press, 1999.

Richardson, E. Allen. "Architects of a Benevolent Empire: The Relationship between the American Missionary Association and the Freedmen's Bureau in Virginia, 1865–1872." In *The Freedmen's Bureau and Reconstruction: Reconsiderations*, edited by Paul A. Cimbala and Randall M. Miller. New York: Fordham University Press, 1999.

Richardson, Joe M. *Christian Reconstruction: The American Missionary Association and Southern Blacks, 1861–1890*. Athens: University of Georgia Press, 1986.

Robinson, John L. *Living Hard: Southern Americans in the Great Depression*. Washington, D.C.: University Press of America, 1977.

Rodgers, Mark E. *Tracing the Civil War Veteran Pensions System in the State of Virginia: Entitlement or Privilege*. Lewiston, N.Y.: Edwin Mellen Press, 1999.

Rosenberg, Charles E. "From Almshouse to Hospital: The Shaping of Philadelphia General Hospital." *Health and Society* 60 (1982): 108–54.

Rosenburg, R. B. *Living Monuments: Confederate Soldiers' Homes in the New South.* Chapel Hill: University of North Carolina Press, 1993.

Ross, Edith L. "Black Heritage in Social Welfare: A Case Study of Atlanta." *Phylon* 37 (winter 1976): 297–307.

Rothman, David J. *Conscience and Convenience: The Asylum and Its Alternatives in Progressive America.* Boston: Little Brown, 1980.

———. *The Discovery of the Asylum: Social Order and Disorder in the New Republic.* Boston: Little Brown, 1971.

Rouse, Jacquelyn Anne. *Lugenia Burns Hope, Black Southern Reformer.* Athens: University of Georgia Press, 1992.

Rousey, Dennis C. "Friends and Foes of Slavery: Foreigners and Northerners in the Old South." *Journal of Social History* 35 (winter 2001): 373–96.

Rowe, Elizabeth. "Alabama's Disappearing Almshouses." Master's thesis, Tulane University, 1946.

Salem, Dorothy. *To Better Our World: Black Women in Organized Reform.* Brooklyn: Carlson Publishing, 1990.

Salmond, John. *A Southern Rebel: The Life and Times of Aubrey Willis Williams, 1890–1965.* Chapel Hill: University of North Carolina Press, 1983.

Sander, Kathleen Waters. *The Business of Charity: The Woman's Exchange Movement, 1832–1900.* Urbana: University of Illinois Press, 1998.

Sargent, James E. "Clifton A. Woodrum of Virginia: A Southern Progressive in Congress, 1923–1945." *Virginia Magazine of History and Biography* 89 (1981): 341–64.

Sarson, Steven. " 'Objects of Distress': Inequality and Poverty in Early Nineteenth-Century Prince George's County." *Maryland Historical Magazine* 96 (summer 2001): 140–62.

Sato, Chitose. "Senator Harry F. Byrd and the New Deal Reform Policy in Virginia, 1933–1938." Master's thesis, College of William and Mary, 1991.

Sayles, Mary Buell. "Visiting Nurses and Nurses Settlement." *Outlook* 81 (21 October 1905): 419.

Schell, Ellen. "The Origins of Geriatric Nursing: The Chronically Ill Elderly in Almshouses and Nursing Homes, 1900–1950." *Nursing History Review* 1 (1993): 203–16.

Schoen, Johanna. " 'A Great Thing for Poor Folks': Birth Control, Sterilization, and Abortion in Public Health and Welfare in the Twentieth Century." Ph.D. diss., University of North Carolina at Chapel Hill, 1996.

School of Social Work, Virginia Commonwealth University. *Past, Present, and Future, 1917–1987.* Richmond: Virginia Commonwealth University, 1987.

Schulman, Bruce J. *From Cotton Belt to Sunbelt: Federal Policy, Economic Development, and the Transformation of the South, 1938–1980.* New York: Oxford University Press, 1991.

Schuricht, Hermann. *History of the German Element in Virginia.* Vol. 2. Baltimore: Kroh, 1900.

Scott, Anne Firor. *The Southern Lady: From Pedestal to Politics, 1830–1930.*
Charlottesville: University Press of Virginia, 1970, 1995.

Scott, Mary Wingfield. *Houses of Old Richmond.* Richmond: Valentine Museum, 1941.

————. *Old Richmond Neighborhoods.* Richmond: Whittet and Shepperson, 1950.

Sealander, Judith. *Private Wealth and Public Life: Foundation Philanthropy and the Reshaping of American Social Policy from the Progressive Era to the New Deal.* Baltimore: Johns Hopkins University Press, 1997.

Shelburne, Mary Frances. "A Brief History of the Family Service Society of Richmond, Virginia." Master's thesis, College of William and Mary, 1932.

Sheldon, Marianne Patricia Buroff. "Richmond, Virginia: The Town and Henrico County to 1820." Ph.D. diss., University of Michigan, 1975.

Shepherd, Samuel. "Churches at Work: Richmond, Virginia, White Protestant Leaders and Social Change in a Southern City, 1900–1929." Ph.D. diss., University of Wisconsin–Madison, 1980.

Shield, Bernice. *History of the Virginia Conference of Social Work from 1900–1942.* Richmond: C. W. Saunders, 1942.

Shifflett, Crandall A. *Patronage and Poverty in the Tobacco South: Louisa County, Virginia, 1860–1900.* Knoxville: University of Tennessee Press, 1982.

Shivers, Lyda. "Social Welfare Movement in the South: A Study in Regional Culture and Social Organization." Ph.D. diss., University of North Carolina, 1935.

Shivery, Louie D. "The History of Organized Social Work among Atlanta Negroes, 1890–1935." Master's thesis, Atlanta University, 1936.

————. "The Neighborhood Union: A Survey of the Beginnings of Social Welfare Movements among Negroes in Atlanta." *Phylon* 3 (spring 1942): 149–62.

Sibert, Drusilla Evangeline. "The Development of the Community Houses in Richmond, Virginia." Master's thesis, Virginia Commonwealth University, 1932.

Sidbury, James. *Ploughshares into Swords: Race, Rebellion, and Identity in Gabriel's Virginia, 1730–1810.* Cambridge: Cambridge University Press, 1997.

Silver, Christopher. *Twentieth Century Richmond: Planning, Politics, and Race.* Knoxville: University of Tennessee Press, 1984.

Simpson, Eileen. *Orphans, Real and Imaginary.* New York: Weidenfeld and Nicholson, 1987.

Singleton, Jeff. *The American Dole: Unemployment Relief and the Welfare State in the Great Depression.* Westport, Conn.: Greenwood Press, 2000.

Sitkoff, Harvard. *Fifty Years Later: The New Deal Evaluated.* New York: Knopf, 1985.

————. *A New Deal for Blacks: The Emergence of Civil Rights as a National Issue.* New York: Oxford University Press, 1978.

Sitton, Sarah C. *Life at the Texas State Lunatic Asylum, 1857–1997.* College Station: Texas A and M University Press, 1999.

Skocpol, Theda. *Protecting Soldiers and Mothers: The Political Origins of Social Policy in the United States.* Cambridge: Belknap Press of Harvard University Press, 1992.

Smith, Bradford, et al. *Philanthropy in Communities of Color.* Bloomington: Indiana University Press, 1999.

Smith, Daniel Scott. "Premarital Pregnancy in America, 1640–1971." *Journal of Interdisciplinary History* 5 (spring 1975): 537–70.

Smith, Douglas L. *The New Deal in the Urban South*. Baton Rouge: Louisiana State University Press, 1988.

Smith, John Douglas. "Managing White Supremacy: Politics and Culture in Virginia, 1919–1939." Ph.D. diss., University of Virginia, 1998.

Smith, Susan Lynn. *Sick and Tired of Being Sick and Tired: Black Women's Health Activism in America, 1890–1950*. Philadelphia: University of Pennsylvania Press, 1995.

―――. "Welfare for Black Mothers and Children: Health and Home in the American South." *Social Politics* 4 (spring 1997): 49–64.

Soule, Gladys Geraldine. "A History of the Family Service Society." Vol. 1, "The Charity Organization Society, 1883–1925." Master's thesis, Tulane School of Social Work, 1947.

Speizman, Milton. "The Movement of the Settlement House Idea into the South." *Southwestern Social Science Quarterly* 44 (December 1963): 237–46.

Spruill, Julia Cherry. *Women's Life and Work in the Southern Colonies*. Chapel Hill: University of North Carolina Press, 1938.

Stacey, Christopher L. "Pillars of Philanthropy: Social Welfare in the South, 1800–1865." Master's thesis, University of Southern Mississippi, 2000.

―――. "The Political Culture of Slavery and Public Poor Relief in the Antebellum South." *Journal of Mississippi History* 63 (summer 2001): 129–45.

Stampp, Kenneth M. *The Era of Reconstruction, 1865–1877*. New York: Vintage Books, 1967.

Stanard, Mary N. *Richmond: Its People and Its History*. Philadelphia: n.p., 1923.

Steger, Werner H. " 'United to Support, but Not Combined to Injure': Free Workers and Immigrants in Richmond, Virginia, During the Era of Sectionalism, 1847–1865." Ph.D. diss., George Washington University, 1999.

Storrs, Landon R. Y. "Gender and the Development of the Regulatory State: The Controversy over Restricting Women's Night Work in the Depression-Era South." *Journal of Policy History* 10 (1998): 179–206.

St. Paul's Episcopal Church (Richmond, Va.). *St. Paul's Episcopal Church: 150 Years, 1845–1995*. Richmond: The Church, 1995.

Stuart, Paul H. "The Kingsley House Extension Program: Racial Segregation in a 1940s Settlement Program." *Social Service Review* 66 (March 1992): 112–20.

A Study of Welfare Activities in a Group of Virginia Communities. Richmond: Bureau of County and City Organizations, 1932.

Sullivan, Patricia. *Days of Hope: Race and Democracy in the New Deal Era*. Chapel Hill: University of North Carolina Press, 1996.

Swain, Martha H. *Ellen S. Woodward: New Deal Advocate for Women*. Jackson: University Press of Mississippi, 1995.

Takagi, Midori. *"Rearing Wolves to Our Own Destruction": Slavery in Richmond, Virginia, 1782–1865*. Charlottesville: University Press of Virginia, 1999.

Taliaferro, Grace E. S. *A Story of St. John's Church, 1607–1964*. Richmond: n.p., 1968.

Taylor, Alrutheus Ambush. *The Negro in the Reconstruction of Virginia*. Washington, D.C.: The Association for the Study of Negro Life and History, 1926.

Taylor, Brenda Jeanette. "The New Deal and Health: Meeting Farmers' Needs in Ropesville, Texas, 1933–1943." *Journal of the West* 36 (January 1997): 38–46.

Taylor, Lloyd C. "Lila Meade Valentine: The FFV as Reformer." *Virginia Magazine of History and Biography* 70 (October 1962): 471–87.

Teipe, Emily J. *America's First Veterans and the Revolutionary War Pensions*. Lewiston, N.Y.: E. Mellen Press, 2002.

Thomas, Emory M. *The Confederate State of Richmond: A Biography of the Capital*. Austin: University of Texas Press, 1971.

———. "To Feed the Citizens: Welfare in Wartime Richmond, 1861–1865." *Virginia Cavalcade* 22 (1972): 22–29.

Thomas, Jerry Bruce. *An Appalachian New Deal: West Virginia in the Great Depression*. Lexington: University Press of Kentucky, 1998.

Tindall, George B. *The Emergence of the New South, 1913–1945*. Baton Rouge: Louisiana State University Press, 1967.

Trattner, Walter. *From Poor Law to Welfare State: A History of Social Welfare in America*. New York: Free Press, 1979, 1994.

Treadway, Sandra Gioia. *Women of Mark: A History of the Woman's Club of Richmond, Virginia, 1894–1994*. Richmond: Library of Virginia, 1995.

Trolander, Judith. *Professionalism and Social Change: From the Settlement House Movement to Neighborhood Centers, 1886 to the Present*. New York: Columbia University Press, 1987.

———. *Settlement Houses and the Great Depression*. Detroit: Wayne State University Press, 1975.

Trost, Jennifer Ann. "Gateway to Justice: A Social History of the Juvenile Court and Child Welfare in Memphis, Tennessee, 1910–1929." Ph.D. diss., Carnegie Mellon University, 1996.

Trotti, Michael. "Charting Richmond's Fun: The Changing Shape of Commercial Amusement in Richmond, Virginia, 1880–1920." Master's thesis, University of North Carolina at Chapel Hill, 1993.

Trout, Charles H. "Welfare in the New Deal Era." *Current History* 65 (July 1973): 11–14.

Tulane University School of Social Work. *Current Phases of Georgia Welfare*. New Orleans: Tulane University, 1935.

———. *Public Welfare Administration: Arkansas*. New Orleans: Tulane University, 1935.

———. *Public Welfare Administration in Mississippi*. New Orleans: Tulane University, 1935.

———. *Public Welfare Administration in Texas*. New Orleans: Tulane University, 1935.

———. *Public Welfare in Alabama*. New Orleans: Tulane University, 1935.

———. *State Department of Public Welfare for Mississippi*. New Orleans: Tulane University, 1935.

————. *Study of Public Welfare Administration in Texas.* New Orleans: Tulane University, 1935.

Tyler-McGraw, Marie. *At the Falls: Richmond, Virginia, and Its People.* Chapel Hill: University of North Carolina Press, 1994.

Tynes, Harriet L. "History of Poor Relief Legislation in Virginia." Master's thesis, School of Social Service Administration, University of Chicago, 1932.

Vandal, Gilles. "The Nineteenth-Century Municipal Responses to the Problem of Poverty: New Orleans' Free Lodgers, 1850–1880." *Journal of Urban History* 19 (November 1992): 30–59.

Van Zelm, Antoinette G. "Virginia Women as Public Citizens: Emancipation Day Celebrations and Lost Cause Commemorations, 1863–1890." In *Negotiating Boundaries of Southern Womanhood: Dealing with the Powers That Be,* edited by Janet L. Coryell et al. Columbia: University of Missouri Press, 2000.

Varon, Elizabeth R. " 'We Mean to Be Counted': White Women and Politics in Antebellum Virginia." Ph.D. diss., Yale University, 1993.

Virginia Department of Public Welfare. *Public Assistance Statistics.* Richmond: DPW, 1939.

Vogt, Daniel C. "Poor Relief in Frontier Mississippi, 1798–1832." *Journal of Mississippi History* 51 (1989): 181–99.

Vouga, Anne F. "Presbyterian Missions and Louisville Blacks: The Early Years, 1898–1910." *Filson Club Historical Quarterly* 58 (July 1984): 310–35.

Walker, Harry Joseph. "Negro Benevolent Societies in New Orleans." Master's thesis, Fisk University, 1937.

Walkowitz, Daniel J. "The Making of a Feminine Professional Identity: Social Workers in the 1920s." *American Historical Review* 95 (October 1990): 1051–75.

————. *Working with Class: Social Workers and the Politics of Middle-Class Identity.* Chapel Hill: University of North Carolina Press, 1999.

Wallenstein, Peter. *From Slave South to New South: Public Policy in Nineteenth-Century Georgia.* Chapel Hill: University of North Carolina Press, 1987.

Ward, Harry M., and Harold E. Greer Jr. *Richmond during the Revolution, 1775–83.* Charlottesville: University Press of Virginia, 1977.

Watkinson, James D. " 'Fit Objects of Charity': Community, Race, Faith, and Welfare in Antebellum Lancaster County, Virginia, 1817–1860." *Journal of the Early Republic* 21 (spring 2001): 41–70.

————. "Rogues, Vagabonds, and Fit Objects: The Treatment of the Poor in Antebellum Virginia." *Virginia Cavalcade* 49 (winter 2000): 16–29.

Watson, Alan D. "Public Poor Relief in Colonial North Carolina." *North Carolina Historical Review* 54 (1977): 347–66.

Weaver, H. N. "African Americans and Social Work: An Overview of the Antebellum through Progressive Eras." *Journal of Multicultural Social Work* 2 (1992): 91–102.

Weldon, Robert Houston. "A Study of the Structural Organization of the William Byrd Community House." Master's thesis, School of Social Work, Richmond Professional Institute of College of William and Mary, 1948.

Wenocur, Stanley. *From Charity to Enterprise: The Development of American Social Work in a Market Economy*. Urbana: University of Illinois Press, 1989.

Whites, LeeAnn. "The Charitable and the Poor: The Emergence of Domestic Politics in Augusta, Georgia, 1860–1880." *Journal of Social History* 17 (summer 1984): 601–15.

Williams, Edward A. *Federal Aid for Relief*. New York: Columbia University Press, 1939.

Williams, Emily J. "A Home . . . for the Old Boys: The Robert E. Lee Camp Confederate Soldiers Home." *Virginia Cavalcade* 28 (1979): 40–47.

Windle, Charles. "Factors in the Passage of Sterilization Legislation: The Case of Virginia." *Public Opinion Quarterly* 29 (summer 1965): 306–14.

Winslow, Emma A. *Trends in Different Types of Public and Private Relief in Urban Areas, 1929–1935*. Washington, D.C.: U.S. Department of Labor, 1937.

Wisner, Elizabeth. "The Howard Association of New Orleans." *Social Service Review* 41 (1967): 411–18.

———. *Public Welfare Administration in Louisiana*. Chicago: University of Chicago, 1930.

———. *Social Welfare in the South from Colonial Times to World War I*. Baton Rouge: Louisiana State University Press, 1970.

Woodward, C. Vann. *Origins of the New South, 1877–1913*. Baton Rouge: Louisiana State University Press, 1951.

Wright, Charles Scott. "Creating a New Deal: The Importance of Black Self-Help Organizations in Lynchburg, Virginia, 1930–1940." Master's thesis, University of North Carolina at Charlotte, 1998.

Young, James R. "Confederate Pensions in Georgia, 1886–1929." *Georgia Historical Quarterly* 66 (spring 1982): 47–52.

Zornow, William Frank. "Aid for Indigent Families of Soldiers in Virginia, 1861–1865." *Virginia Magazine of History and Biography* 66 (1958): 454–58.

INDEX

www.ingramcontent.com/pod-product-compliance
Lightning Source LLC
Chambersburg PA
CBHW010114270326
41929CB00023B/3346